SHORT GUIDE
to
PARIS

THE BLUE GUIDES

Some of these Titles are temporarily out of print

LONDON AND ITS ENVIRONS : Atlas and 33 Maps and Plans (1935)

SHORT GUIDE TO LONDON : 32 Maps and Plans (1951)

70 MILES AROUND LONDON (A Guide to the Road) : 59 Maps and Plans (1930)

ENGLAND : 72 Maps and Plans (1950)

WALES : 23 Maps and Plans (1936)

SCOTLAND : Atlas and 34 Maps and Plans (1949)

IRELAND : Atlas and 15 Maps and Plans (1949)

GREAT BRITAIN : 90 Maps and Plans (1930)

PARIS AND ITS ENVIRONS : 64 Maps and Plans (1927)

SHORT GUIDE TO PARIS : 40 Maps and Plans (1951)

SOUTHERN FRANCE : Atlas and 72 Maps and Plans (*New edition in preparation*)

THE FRENCH ALPS : 25 Maps and Plans (1926)

NORMANDY : 13 Maps and Plans (1928)

BRITTANY : 15 Maps and Plans (1928)

NORTH-WESTERN FRANCE : Atlas and 33 Maps and Plans (1932)

NORTH-EASTERN FRANCE : Atlas and 54 Maps and Plans (1930)

BELGIUM : 33 Maps and Plans (1929)

HOLLAND AND THE RHINE : Atlas and 48 Maps and Plans (1933)

SWITZERLAND : 76 Maps and Plans (1948)

NORTHERN ITALY : Atlas and 45 Maps and Plans (*New edition in preparation*)

ROME AND CENTRAL ITALY (*In preparation*)

SOUTHERN ITALY (with Sicily and Sardinia) : 76 Maps and Plans (1929)

SOUTHERN SPAIN AND PORTUGAL : Atlas and 38 Maps and Plans (1929)

NORTHERN SPAIN (with the Balearic Islands) : Atlas and 40 Maps and Plans (1930)

SWEDEN : Atlas and 25 Maps and Plans (1951)

THE BLUE GUIDES

SHORT GUIDE to PARIS

Edited by

L. RUSSELL MUIRHEAD

With 40 Maps and Plans

LONDON
ERNEST BENN LIMITED
1951

DISTRIBUTED IN THE U.S.A. BY
RAND McNALLY & COMPANY, CHICAGO

PRINTED IN GREAT BRITAIN

PREFACE

THE present SHORT GUIDE TO PARIS, like the companion volume on London, is intended for those who have but little time to devote to the most charming of the capitals of Europe, but who wish to be guided quickly and clearly to the chief points of interest, to be enabled to plan their time to the best advantage, and to be assisted to an intelligent appreciation of what they see. An attempt has been made to interest the traveller in Paris as a city with a great tradition of history and art and a lively appreciation of all kinds of present-day activities; while, in consideration of the restricted purses of many visitors, perhaps rather less attention than usual has been paid to Paris as a centre of gastronomy and fashion. Though Paris in 1939–45 suffered only lightly from war damage in the physical sense, the life of the city was completely disorganised, and recovery is not yet quite complete. Many of the important collections in the great museums (for example) have not yet been restored to their normal condition; so that the descriptions in the present volume must needs be provisional in many instances. The salient attractions of Paris, however, both major and minor, are here described succinctly but not curtly, while the section on Practical Information is intended to smooth the way of the stranger in Paris and to familiarise him with some of its ways and customs. The Table of Chief Sights will remind him at a glance of what there is to see, and the Summary of the Motor-Buses and of the Métro will enable him to find his way to any point without difficulty. A specially simplified plan of the Métro system has been placed at the beginning of the book for handy reference, while a plan of the motor-bus routes is incorporated with the summary. Small and simplified street plans, specially prepared for this edition, illustrate the main centres of tourist interest; their limits are indicated on the Index Map at the end of the book. A brief section is devoted to the principal excursions around Paris (Versailles, Chantilly, Fontainebleau, etc.), but these are more fully described and largely supplemented in the larger guide (see below). The full and detailed Index will, it is hoped, add materially to the usefulness of the volume.

This short guide is planned on the lines of the larger BLUE GUIDE TO PARIS, long recognised as the standard guide in English to the capital of France. In that volume, which at the moment is still unhappily out of print, more space is devoted to the innumerable fascinations of Paris than can be attempted in a shorter volume, and greater justice is done to the wealth of suggestive associations that contribute so much to the true 'atmosphere' of a historic city. It is hoped that many, who may find this short guide of use, will be tempted to increase their knowledge of this most fascinating of cities by acquiring also the larger guide when a new edition of it is published.

Special acknowledgements for assistance are due to Mr. Richard H. Butcher, who made a prolonged stay in Paris for the purpose of this guide and whose intimate knowledge of the city was invaluable in arranging the abridgement and in bringing the work up-to-date ; to Miss Elizabeth Jackson, for her generous co-operation in this work ; to Miss Louie B. Russ for her selective knowledge in compiling the bibliography ; to Monsieur C. Metman, Conservateur du Musée des Arts Décoratifs, for his expert and untiring aid ; and to many other authorities in museums and public institutions who assisted with advice and information.

No one is better aware than the Editor and his Staff of the difficulty of avoiding errors, whether of omission or commission, and suggestions for the correction or improvement of the Guide will be most gratefully welcomed. Advertisements of every kind are rigorously excluded from this and every other volume of the Blue Guide Series. L. R. M.

CONTENTS

Page

PREFACE v

PRACTICAL INFORMATION

I. ON THE WAY TO PARIS . . . xv
Railway and Steamer Services, Air Services xv. Passports, Customs, and Currency Regulations xvii. Railway Termini xviii. Arrival in Paris xix.

II. GENERAL HINTS xix
Season, Language, Money and Expenses xix. Police xx. Some French Usages xx.

III. HOTELS xxi

IV. RESTAURANTS. CAFÉS AND TEA ROOMS xxiii

V. CONVEYANCES xxvi
Taxis xxvi. Motor-Buses, Underground Railways xxvii.

VI. POSTAL INFORMATION . . xxviii
Information Bureaux, Tourist Agents xxx.

VII. AMUSEMENTS xxx
Theatres xxx. Music Halls xxxi. Cinemas, Art Exhibitions xxxii. Music xxxiii. Sports and Games, xxxiii.

VIII. USEFUL ADDRESSES . . . xxxiv
Embassies and Consulates xxxv. English Churches xxxv. Banks xxxvi.

IX. THE SIGHTS OF PARIS . . xxxvii

X. CALENDAR OF EVENTS . . xxxix

XI. SOME BOOKS ABOUT PARIS . . . xl

PARIS

I. THE RIGHT BANK

ROUTE Page

1. FROM THE PLACE DE L'OPÉRA TO THE TUILERIES 1
Opéra 1. Rue de la Paix 3. Vendôme Column 3. St-Roch 3. Théâtre-Français 4. Rue de Rivoli 5. Tuileries 5. Place de la Concorde 7.

2. FROM THE PLACE DE LA CONCORDE TO THE ARC DE TRIOMPHE 8
Champs-Elysées 8. Petit Palais 10. Grand Palais 10. Place de l'Etoile 10.

3. THE GRANDS BOULEVARDS 11
A. The Western Boulevards: from the Rue Royale to the Porte St-Martin 11
Madeleine 11. Sewers 12. Musée Cognacq-Jay 14. Opéra-Comique 14. Porte St-Denis 15. Porte St-Martin 15.
B. The Eastern Boulevards: from the Porte St-Martin to the Bastille 16
Place de la République 16. Place de la Bastille 17. July Column 17.

4. THE CENTRAL QUARTERS BETWEEN THE BOULEVARDS AND THE LOUVRE 17
A. West Section: between the Avenue de l'Opéra and the Rues Montmartre and du Louvre . . 18
Bourse 18. Rue de Richelieu 18. Palais-Royal 19. Banque de France 20.
B. East Section: between the Rues Montmartre and du Louvre and the Boulevard de Sébastopol . 21
General Post Office 21. St-Germain-l'Auxerrois 21. Halles Centrales 22. St-Eustache 23. St-Leu-St-Gilles, 24.

5. FROM THE PLACE DU CHÂTELET TO THE BASTILLE 25
Tour St-Jacques 25. Hôtel de Ville 26. St-Gervais-St-Protais 27. Hôtel de Sens 28. Quartier de l'Arsenal 29. Rue St-Antoine 29.

6. THE DISTRICTS TO THE NORTH OF THE RUE DE RIVOLI AND RUE ST-ANTOINE 30
Marais 30. Place des Vosges 30. Musée Victor-Hugo 31. Rue des Francs-Bourgeois 32. Rue Vieille-du-Temple 32. Hôtel de Rohan 33. Archives Nationales 33. Quartier du Temple 34. St-Merri 36.

ROUTE Page

7. THE DISTRICTS TO THE NORTH OF THE GRANDS BOULEVARDS 37
A. Between the Canal St-Martin and the Rue de la Chaussée-d'Antin 37
St-Laurent 37. Rue de La Fayette 38. St-Vincent-de-Paul 38. Rue de la Chaussée-d'Antin 39.
B. Montmartre 40
Place de Clichy 40. Place Pigalle 42. Sacré-Cœur 43. St-Pierre-de-Montmartre 43.
C. Quartier de l'Opéra, Quartier de l'Europe, and Batignolles 44
Boulevard Haussmann 44. Chapelle Expiatoire 45. St-Augustin 45. Conservatoire de Musique 46.

8. THE WESTERN DISTRICTS 47
A. To the North of the Champs-Elysées . . 47
Parc Monceau 47. Musée Cernuschi 47. Rue du Faubourg-St-Honoré 48. Neuilly 50. Chapelle St-Ferdinand 50.
B. To the South of the Champs-Elysées . . 50
Cours-la-Reine 51. Place de l'Alma 51. Musée National d'Art Moderne 52. Palais de Chaillot 54. Passy 55. Auteuil 56.

9. THE BOIS DE BOULOGNE 56
Musée D'Ennery 56. Longchamp 57. Bagatelle 58.

10. THE EASTERN DISTRICTS 58
La Villette 59. Buttes-Chaumont 59. Père-Lachaise 60. Faubourg St-Antoine 61. Place de la Nation 62. Cimetière de Picpus 62.

II. THE SEINE, THE CITÉ, AND THE LEFT BANK

11. THE SEINE 65
A. From the Louvre to the Pont National . . 66
Pont-Neuf 66. Pont au Change 67. Pont Sully 67. Pont d'Austerlitz 68.
B. From the Louvre to Auteuil 68
Pont des Arts 68. Pont de la Concorde 69. Pont Alexandre-III 69. Pont d'Iéna 69. Pont-Viaduc d'Auteuil 70.

12. THE CITÉ AND THE ILE ST-LOUIS 70
Palais de Justice 70. Sainte-Chapelle 72. Conciergerie 74. Notre-Dame 75.

ROUTE Page
13. THE LATIN QUARTER 79
St-Séverin 80. St-Julien-le-Pauvre 81. Boulevard St-Michel 81. Ecole de Médecine 81. St-Nicolas-du-Chardonnet 82. St-Médard 83. St-Etienne-du-Mont 84. Panthéon 85. Bibliothèque Ste-Geneviève 86. Sorbonne 87.

14. THE JARDIN DES PLANTES AND FAUBOURG ST-MARCEL 89
Halle aux Vins 89. Salpêtrière 91.

15. THE FAUBOURG ST-GERMAIN 91
A. East Part of the Faubourg St-Germain . . 91
Palais de l'Institut 91. Hôtel des Monnaies 93. Ecole des Beaux-Arts 94. Place de l'Odéon 96. Palais du Luxembourg 97. St-Sulpice 100.
B. West Part of the Faubourg St-Germain . 101
Quai d'Orsay 101. Palais-Bourbon 102. St-Germain-des-Prés 105. Rue de Grenelle 108. Rue de Varenne 108.

16. THE INVALIDES, CHAMPS-DE-MARS, AND S.W. DISTRICTS 109
Hôtel des Invalides 109. Ecole Militaire 113. Champ-de-Mars 113. Eiffel Tower 114.

17. THE SOUTHERN QUARTERS 114
Val-de-Grâce 116. Gobelins 116. Place d'Italie 117. Observatoire 118. Institut Pasteur 118. Catacombs 119. Montsouris 120. Cité Universitaire 120.

III. THE LOUVRE AND OTHER GREAT COLLECTIONS

18. THE LOUVRE 121

19. MUSÉE DE L'ARMÉE 152

20. MUSÉE DES ARTS DÉCORATIFS . . . 153

21. CONSERVATOIRE DES ARTS ET MÉTIERS . . 157

22. BIBLIOTHÈQUE NATIONALE 160

23. MUSÉE CARNAVALET 162

24. PALAIS DE CHAILLOT 169
Musée des Monuments Français 169. Musée de l'Homme 170. Musée de la Marine 172.

25. MUSÉE DE CLUNY 172

ROUTE Page
26. Musée Guimet 175
27. Musée Jacquemart André 178
28. Musée du Jeu de Paume 180
29. Musée Nissim de Camondo 181
30. Musée Rodin 183

IV. EXCURSIONS FROM PARIS

31. Versailles 186
The Palace of Versailles 188. The Trianons 197.
32. Vincennes 200
33. La Malmaison 202
34. Saint-Denis and Chantilly 204
Musée Condé 208.
35. Fontainebleau 217
Summary of Motor-Buses and Underground Railways of Paris 225
INDEX 232

MAPS AND PLANS

MÉTROPOLITAIN . . *At the beginning of the book*
ENVIRONS OF PARIS . . *Before the title-page*
MOTOR-BUS ROUTE MAP . . . 226, 227
INDEX MAP . . . *At the end of the book*
STREET PLANS:
I. CHAMPS-ELYSÉES–INVALIDES . . 9
II. GRANDS BOULEVARDS WEST . . 13
III. GARE DU NORD–TEMPLE . . 35
IV. MONTMARTRE 41
V. PARC MONCEAU 49
VI. ETOILE-PASSY 53
VII. BASTILLE–GARE DE LYON . . 63
VIII. CITÉ–QUARTIER LATIN . . . 71
IX. ST-GERMAIN–MONTPARNASSE . . 99
ARTS DÉCORATIFS, MUSÉE DES . 154, 155, 156
ARTS ET MÉTIERS, CONSERVATOIRE DES 158, 160
CARNAVALET, MUSÉE 164, 168
CHANTILLY, MUSÉE CONDÉ 210
CHANTILLY, PARK 216
CLUNY, MUSÉE DE 173, 174
FONTAINEBLEAU PALACE . . . 220, 221
GUIMET, MUSÉE 176
INVALIDES, HÔTEL DES 111
LOUVRE, HISTORICAL PLAN . . . 121
LOUVRE, GROUND FLOOR . . 126, 127, 149
LOUVRE, FIRST FLOOR . . . 140, 141
NOTRE-DAME 77
ST-GERMAIN-DES-PRÉS 106
VERSAILLES PALACE 193
VERSAILLES, TOWN 192

PARIS

PARIS, the capital of France, is situated on the *Seine*, near the middle of the so-called Paris basin, at a height above sea-level varying from 85 ft. to 419 ft., and at a distance from the sea of 92 m., or over 200 m. by the windings of the river. Until 1919, Paris, unlike London or New York, was bounded by a definite line of ramparts, which have since been demolished and the sites built upon. The city, c. 38 sq. m. in area, is 8 m. long from W. to E. and 6 m. broad from N. to S. Its population, denser than any other city in Europe, was 2,725,347 in 1946; including the suburbs beyond the line of the old walls it exceeded 4 millions. The chief magistrate of Paris is the *Préfet de la Seine*, appointed by Government, who is assisted by an elected *Conseil Municipal*. For administrative purposes the city is divided into twenty *Arrondissements*, or municipal boroughs, each with its *Maire* and *Mairie*, or town-hall.

Paris is physically divided into two unequal parts by the Seine, which enters from the S.E., forms the Ile St-Louis and the Ile de la Cité, near the centre of the city, and describes a curve to the S.W. where it leaves the walls. The N. bank (Rive Droite) is of principal interest for the tourist, but the S. bank (Rive Gauche) figures much more prominently in the life of the city than does the S. side of the Thames in London. The key to the topography of Paris is the straight line drawn roughly N.W. to S.E., just N. of the river, following the Avenue des Champs-Elysées, Rue de Rivoli, and Rue St-Antoine, cutting Paris into two approximately equal parts. To the N. of this line the Grands Boulevards form an irregular semi-circle, from the Place de la Concorde to the Place de la Bastille, while to the S. a smaller arc is described by the Boul. Henri-IV (crossing the river) and the Boul. St-Germain. The heart of Paris lies within the oval thus defined. Outside lies a ring of old suburbs (faubourgs), bounded by the Outer Boulevards, or Boulevards Extérieurs, the official city limits until 1860, and still farther out are the Boulevards d'Enceinte, skirting the circle of the 19th cent. fortifications. The main N. to S. artery of traffic is formed by the Boulevards de Strasbourg, de Sébastopol, du Palais, and St-Michel.

As in London, various quarters of the city are often more familiarly known by unofficial titles. Within the curve of the Grands Boulevards, to the W. of the Boul. de Sébastopol, is the chief region of business and pleasure, centring in the Avenue de l'Opéra, the Rue de la Paix, the Rue St-Honoré, and the Rue de Rivoli. Eastward lies the commercial and industrial quarter of the *Marais*, and beyond the Bastille is the *Faubourg St-Antoine*, the centre of Revolutionary Paris. To the N. of the Marais are the *Temple* and *St-Martin*, also primarily commercial. Many of the old houses in these quarters have been demolished and replaced in recent years. Between the Place de la Concorde and the Bois de Boulogne are the *Faubourg St-Honoré* and the *Champs-Elysées*, while beyond these lie the elegant residential quarters of *Etoile* and *Chaillot*. In the extreme W., pleasantly situated between the Seine and the Bois, are the districts of *Passy* and *Auteuil*, comfortable rather than fashionable. The wealthy quarters of *Courcelles* and *Monceau*, the N. of the Arc de Triomphe, are continued by the less fashionable *Batignolles*, which is adjoined on the E. by *Montmartre*, with its famous hill. Thence a series of industrial suburbs (*La Villette, Belleville, Ménilmontant, Charonne*) curves round the N.E. of Paris to join the Faubourg St-Antoine.—On an island in the Seine is the *Cité*, the ancient heart of Paris ; and south of the river the Boul. St-Germain traverses part of the *Latin Quarter*, which is continued on the W. by the aristocratic *Faubourg St-Germain*, with the hotels of the 'vieille noblesse,' and that again by the quarter of the *Gros-Caillou*, with its broad avenues. The more southerly district of *Montparnasse* has in recent years become frequented by large colonies of artists and foreigners.

The open spaces within the walls of Paris are inadequate, some of the largest being cemeteries ; but the formal beauties of the *Tuileries Gardens* and the *Champs-Elysées* are balanced by the natural attractions of the *Bois de Boulogne* to the W., and the *Bois de Vincennes*, to the S.E., outside the old fortifications.

PRACTICAL INFORMATION

I. ON THE WAY TO PARIS

Railway and Steamer Services. Full information about seat reservations, times of departure, etc., may be obtained at the Continental Enquiry Office, British Railways (Southern Region), Victoria Station, London, S.W.1 ; from the British Railway's West End Office, 71 Regent Street, London, W.1 ; or from the principal travel agencies. In Paris similar facilities are provided at the British Railways Office, 12 Boul. de la Madeleine (Tel. OPEra 56–70) and at travel agencies.

The following are the five main routes from London at present in service ; the fares quoted here applied to summer, 1951. Return tickets are valid for 2 months.

(i) Viâ Dover and Calais, 288 m. Daily service by 'Golden Arrow' in c. 7 hrs. Return fares, 1st cl. £13 6/6, 2nd cl. £10 18/2, with extra pullman charge (23/, 15/10) ; ½ hr. longer by ordinary train.

(ii) Viâ Dover and Dunkerque, 319 m. Nightly service by the 'Night Ferry' in c. 11½ hrs. Return fares £12 13/6, £10 14/10. Sleeping-car reservations £3 6/6, £2 8/2 extra.

(iii) Viâ Folkestone and Calais, 288 m. Daily service in c. 8 hrs. Fares as for (i). Twice daily service also in June to Sept. viâ Folkestone and Boulogne, 262 m. in 7–8 hrs. (fares are slightly lower than viâ Calais).

(iv) Viâ Newhaven and Dieppe, 235 m. Daily service in c. 9 hrs. (extra Sat. service June–Sept.). Return fares £11 5/8, £10 1/8, £6 17/. Night service also in summer: Tues., Thurs., Sat. c. June 30th–Sept. 30th, nightly c. July 28th–Sept. 4th.

(v) Viâ Southampton and Havre, 341 m. Night service on Mon. and Fri. (also Wed. June 6th–Sept. 26th) in c. 14¾ hrs. Return fares £11 5/8, £10 1/8, £8 5/.

There are reduced fares for children (4 to 10 years) by all routes ; 66 lb. of baggage are conveyed free to Paris ; 44 lb. may be taken free on a child's ticket.

Air Services. Regular air services between Paris and *London* (Northolt or Heathrow), *Birmingham* (Elmdon), *Manchester* (Ringway), and (in summer) *Glasgow* (Renfrew or Prestwick) are maintained by British European Airways and Air France. B.E.A. planes use Northolt (usually) and Renfrew, A.F. planes use Heathrow and Prestwick. Full particulars from the offices of the companies: B.E.A., 14 Regent St., London, S.W.1.; 38 Av. de l'Opéra, Paris 2e (TAItbout 60–50), etc. ; Air France, 52 Haymarket, London, S.W.1 ; 119 Av. des Champs-Elysées, Paris 8e (BALzac 50–29), etc.

Flying times: from London c. 1½ hr.; Birmingham c. 2 hrs. 20 min.; Manchester c. 3 hrs. 20 min. ; Glasgow c. 5 hrs. 40 min.—Return fares (valid 6 months), from London, £14 8/ (excursion, £12 4/ or £10) ; from Birmingham, £18 (£15 10/) from Manchester, £19 16/ (£17 10/) ; from Glasgow, £28 16/ (£25 8/).

Motor Cars, Motor Cycles, and Bicycles. Motorists and motor-cyclists proposing to tour in France will save trouble by joining the Automobile Association, the Royal Automobile Club, the Royal Scottish Automobile Club, or other club recognised by the Automobile Club de France. In exchange for a deposit or a guarantee of the amount of the customs dues on the car, these societies issue to their members the requisite customs documents. These include (i) a specification form in duplicate, the original of which is retained by the British customs authorities at the port of embarkation, so that when (on the return of the vehicle to Britain) the duplicate is produced, the car may be admitted duty-free ; and (ii) a 'triptyque' or entry-permit (acquit-à-caution for France only ; 'carnet de passages' for more than one country), which reduces frontier formalities to a minimum. These clubs also supply the oval 'G.B.' plate which must be affixed to the rear of the vehicle ; and they maintain officers at all ports to give assistance to their members. It may be noted that in France there are small dues to be paid at the ports on landing and embarkation. If visiting France, Belgium, Luxembourg, Switzerland, and Italy, British owners may use their national driving licence and registration book ; for most other countries an international driving permit and an international certificate for motor vehicles is required.

Lighting. Although foreign-registered cars which have a forward lighting system approved in their countries of origin are legally entitled to use the same system in France, in practice the difference between the British and the French rule of the road makes it undesirable to use a British dipping or dimming system for headlights without some modification. It is now obligatory for French-registered vehicles to use amber-coloured headlights. As a matter of courtesy, British motorists will probably wish to follow this practice. They should also have their dipping or dimming system modified so that the off-side headlight may be dipped or dimmed when driving on the right, so as to avoid approaching motorists. Where a single rear and stop light is fitted, suitable for driving on the left, a second one should be installed so that it can readily be seen by traffic keeping to the right of the road. The G.B. plate should be so arranged that it is illuminated by the tail lamp.

Petrol is not now rationed in France. The price varies from district to district. Ordinary petrol costs from 45 fr. 50 to 49 fr. 50 per litre (c. 4/2 to 4/6½ per gall.); high-octane fuel ('super-carburant') from 50 fr. 80 to 54 fr. 50 per litre (c. 4/8½ to 5/0½ per gall.). These prices are likely to increase.

Car Ferries. Motor vehicles can be shipped to France on all the regular passenger cross-channel passenger services listed above, and four special carrier services are likewise available, all of which (except Newhaven–Dieppe) carry passengers accompanying their cars. On all services vehicles may be shipped with the main petrol tank full. Petrol in separate containers is not allowed.

In most cases cars should be ready on the quayside for shipment c. 2½ hrs. before departure (exceptionally at Southampton 3½ hrs. before departure, at Cherbourg 3¾ hrs.). The fares (for 1950) quoted below are for the shipment of cars at owner's risk (company's risk c. one-third more). Berths for cars, especially in the summer season, should be reserved well in advance, preferably through the A.A., R.A.C., or R.S.A.C.

On the following PASSENGER SERVICES the freight charge on a car to France is from £8 5/ to £17, according to wheelbase: *Dover or Folkestone to Calais* (passenger fare, 1st cl. 47/6, 3rd cl. 33/6); *Newhaven to Dieppe* (66/; 40/); *Southampton to Havre* (90/9; 67/7).

On the *Southampton–Cherbourg* passenger service (mid-May to c. Oct. 7th only) the car freight is from £6 10/ to £16; passenger fare 85/ or 64/.

On the CAR-FERRY SERVICES the freight charge varies from £5 to £12 10/; the ordinary fare for passengers accompanying the car (up to 4) is 30/: *Dover–Calais* (Townsend Bros., Ltd.; week before Easter to mid-Oct. only); *Dover–Dunkerque*; *Dover–Boulogne*; *Folkestone–Calais*. The *Newhaven–Dieppe* car-ferry service does not carry passengers.

Air Ferry (Silver City Airways, Ltd.) for cars from *Lympne Airport*, near Folkestone, to *Le Touquet Airport*, S. of Boulogne, in 20 min., every ½ hr. in the summer season, every hour or 2 hrs. at other times.

Charges: £27 (up to 14 ft. wheelbase) or £32. Special winter rates (mid-Sept.–Easter), £19 and £25. These prices include the transport of 4 persons per car. The aircraft carry two cars at a time. Petrol tanks should be not more than three-quarters full.

Motor Cycles cost 25/ on the ferry services, 36/3 on the passenger services (34/ viâ Cherbourg), including 1/ registration fee.

Bicycles may now be taken into France without any need to produce a customs document. The machine should be declared to the British Customs before leaving Great Britain to ensure duty-free re-entry. Bicycles must be equipped with adequate brakes, a bell that works, a forward lighting system and a red rear *lamp* (a reflector is NOT sufficient). The cost of taking a bicycle from London to one of the French Channel ports is 11/9, plus 1/ registration fee. Cross-channel fare, 8/6, plus 1/.

In France a bicycle travels on the railways as ordinary registered luggage. The great majority of country bus services will accept bicycles as luggage (they travel on the roof).

Passports are necessary for all foreign travellers entering France and must bear the photograph of the holder. Every foreign traveller must report to the Police within 48 hrs. of arrival in Paris. The usual procedure is to fill in a form provided by the hotel, but foreigners staying with friends, etc., should not fail to report to the authorities. Any traveller wishing to remain in France for more than three months should apply (in advance) at the Ministère de l'Intérieur, Bureau des Etrangers (2e Bureau), 11 Rue des Saussaies, for a 'certificat de domicile', a visa (5 photographs, profile), and a 'carte d'identité' (3 photographs, profile).

British, American, Irish, Canadian, and New Zealand passports do not require visas, but travellers from other British Dominions must obtain a French consular visa.

Customs and Currency Regulations. Hand luggage is examined in France at the port of entry and departure; luggage registered to Paris is examined there. Provided that dutiable articles are declared, bonâ-fide travellers will find the French customs authorities courteous and reasonable.

Tobacco is dutiable, but 500 cigarettes or 2 lb. of tobacco are usually passed free. One camera or cine-camera with 10 rolls of film, if declared, will be admitted free, and not more than two *used* packs of cards. Travellers returning to England should remember that practically every article imported from abroad is liable to Customs duty, and are strongly advised to declare all their purchases, gifts, etc.

The British Treasury allowance for pleasure travel for the year ending April 30th, 1952, is £100 for adults and £75 for children under the age of 15. Residents in Great Britain taking their own car to France are entitled to an additional allotment of exchange of £20. British visitors are reminded that they are not allowed to take out of England or bring in more than £10 in sterling notes, at the present time, and before starting out, the traveller is well advised to leave his surplus cash at home, as this cannot be left with the Customs or Immigration Officers. Not more than 50,000 fr. in French notes may be taken out of France.

Railways. The principal railways radiating from Paris correspond to five regions of the Société Nationale des Chemins de Fer Français (the French equivalent of British Railways). On the main routes corridor trains are the rule, and boat-trains and international expresses have restaurant and sleeping cars. Not all trains have first-class carriages, but the second class is at least as comfortable as the English third class. Third-class carriages should be avoided by travellers wishing to make a lengthy journey. Sunday train services run nearly as frequently as those on weekdays.

Smoking compartments are labelled 'fumeurs', and ladies' compartments are marked 'dames seules.' The guard is called 'chef de train'; a porter is 'porteur.'

Railway fares in France are rising continually, but mile for mile, they are still considerably cheaper than the English equivalent (c. 20–25 per cent. less). There is no reduction for a return ticket.

The traveller who restricts his luggage to what he himself can carry avoids much trouble and saves time; but, if necessary, all the main line stations deal with registered luggage.

The chief Time-Tables in France are the *Indicateur Chaix*, for all the railways, and various *Livrets Chaix* for the various regions. Travellers should remember that France enjoys summer time throughout the whole year, and watches should be adjusted accordingly.

Information can be obtained at the S.N.C.F. information and booking offices, 127 Av. des Champs-Elysées, 16 Boul. des Capucines, and 88 Rue St-Lazare. Telephone information can be obtained by ringing LABorde 92–00.

Railway Termini. Below is an alphabetical list of the chief Paris termini. All of them are connected by underground (Métro) and motor-bus routes and are provided with restaurants (not cheap), telegraph offices, and left-luggage offices (consigne). It may be noted here that payment for articles left at the consigne (at present 16 fr. per day per suitcase) is made on withdrawal.

Gare d'Austerlitz (or Gare d'Orléans ; Pl. IV), for the Région Sud-Ouest of the S.N.C.F. (Tours, Bordeaux, Toulouse, the Pyrenees, Madrid, etc.).

Gare de l'Est (Pl. III), for the Région Est (Reims, Metz, Strasbourg, Germany, etc.).

Gare des Invalides (Pl. I), for some electric trains to Versailles, but more important as the town terminal of all air services.

Gare de Lyon (Pl. IV), for the Région Sud-Est (Lyons, Geneva, Provence, the Riviera, Barcelona, etc.).

Gare Montparnasse (Pl. IX), a terminus of the Région Ouest (lines to Brittany, La Rochelle, etc.).

Gare du Nord (Pl. III), for the Région Nord (Lille, Laon, Brussels, etc.) and for boat-trains to Boulogne, Calais, and Dunkerque.

Gare St-Lazare (Pl. II), another terminus of the Région Ouest (Normandy lines), and for boat-trains to Dieppe, Le Havre, and Cherbourg.

Other termini of minor importance are the *Gare du Quai d'Orsay* (Pl. IX), for suburban trains to Orly, Juvisy, Etampes, and Dourdan ; the *Gare du Luxembourg*, Rue Gay-Lussac (Pl. IX and Métro Plan), for suburban trains to Sceaux, St-Rémy-lès-Chevreuse, and other S. suburbs ; and the *Gare de Vincennes* or *de la Bastille*, for trains to Vincennes, Joinville-le-Pont, Boissy-St-Léger, and other E. suburbs.

Arrival in Paris. (*a*) BY TRAIN. A porter should at once be engaged and a taxi secured. The porter is then sent, with the luggage-ticket (bulletin de bagages), to fetch the registered luggage which can only be recovered by producing the luggage-ticket), and if this has not been examined at the frontier the traveller must appear in person in the ' salle des bagages ' or ' douane ' to clear it. Railway porters are entitled to a fee of (roughly) 35 fr. per article of luggage (maximum 4 articles), and expect a small tip in addition.

(*b*) BY AIR. The principal termini of the planes serving Paris are *Orly*, 11½ m. S., and *Le Bourget*, 10 m. N.E., of the centre of the town. Free transport is provided by the flying companies between the airports and the air-terminal at the Gare des Invalides (see above). Most of the services from England, apart from two Air France evening services from London, arrive at Le Bourget. Long-distance services mostly arrive at Orly, but in all cases a time-table, or the companies concerned, should be consulted.

The *A.B.C. World Airways Guide* (monthly ; 5/) is the most comprehensive air travel guide published in England.

II. GENERAL HINTS

Season. The fashionable season in Paris extends from Nov. to the ' Grand-Prix ' in June. Summer (June–August), sometimes very warm, is the tourist season, though the city is almost deserted by its regular inhabitants and many of the theatres and libraries, etc., are closed. In spring and autumn, though the days are shorter, the weather is better adapted for the active sightseer.

Language. The traveller who knows no language but English can get along quite comfortably in Paris, though he will probably pay in cash for his ignorance. Even a slight knowledge of French makes the visit not only cheaper but also much more interesting and more intellectually profitable.

Money and Expenses. The unit is the franc, theoretically subdivided into centimes. However, since the war the currency has been so depreciated in value that the centime is no longer used. Banknotes for 5, 10, 20, 50, 100, 300, 500, 1000, 5000, and 10,000 fr. are in circulation, and there are also coins of 1, 2, 5, 10, and 20 fr. Travellers' cheques are best exchanged at English or American banks (passports must be shown to the cashier) ; many of the larger hotels display a notice to the effect that they are officially entitled to change such cheques, affording a convenient service outside banking hours. The abnormal state of the exchange precludes any accurate attempt to value the franc in British or American money, but the rate of exchange of the pound sterling is at present (1951) c. 980 fr., of the dollar c. 350 fr. Expenses have grown much heavier since before the War. Though for the American traveller, favoured by the exchange, the cost of living is extremely light, the English visitor must keep a wary eye on unnecessary expenditure. For the ordinary tourist in Paris, living in average comfort and visiting the usual sights, the minimum daily expense cannot be less than 1500 fr. (i.e. c. 30/).

Police. The chief Préfecture de Police is situated in the Boul. du Palais (No. 7). In cases of disputes with cabmen, or when in need of information, visitors should apply to the nearest policeman (sergent de ville) to whom no gratuity should ever be offered. Complaints against proprietors of hotels, restaurants, etc., should be addressed in writing to M. le Préfet de Police. In serious cases, such as theft or violence, it is advisable to have a personal interview with a 'commissaire de police.'

Lost Property. Articles lost in the streets, in the Métro or in motor-buses, should be enquired for at the Préfecture de Police at 36 Rue des Morillons (Métro station: Convention, line 12: motor-bus 62. Open weekdays 8.30–12, 2–6.15; 8.30–12.30 only on Sat.).

Courses for Foreign Students. The 'Livret de l'Etudiant,' published at the beginning of each academic year, gives a complete list of lectures, courses, etc., at the Sorbonne and every other centre of learning in Paris. Students anxious to acclimatise themselves to student life in Paris, are advised to take their problems to the Comité d'Accueil aux Etudiants Etrangers, 96 Boulevard Raspail (6e).

Some French Usages. Forms of politeness are more ceremonious in France than in Great Britain or America. Men doff their hats in restaurants and cafés, and frequently also in shops, picture-galleries, and the like. Gentlemen are expected to salute a lady before she bows to them, and, in speaking to her, to remain uncovered until requested to resume their hats. Hats are also raised to any lady passed on the stair of a flat and when a funeral is passed in the streets. The afternoon (after 3.30) is the proper time for formal calls and for the presentation of letters of introduction, which should never be sent by post. The usual lunch hour is about 12.30 p.m., the dinner hour about 7.45 p.m.

Business begins earlier in Paris than it does in London; principals may be found at their offices even before 9 a.m. Banks are open 9–12 and 2–4 from Mon. to Fri. (closed Sat. and Sun.). The Saturday half-holiday is not universal, but most shops are closed all day on Monday. All food shops are open on Sunday morning until 10 or 11.

Public Holidays. The chief public holidays are New Year's Day, Easter Monday, Ascension Day, Whit Monday, July 14th (Fête Nationale), Assumption Day (Aug. 15th), All Saints' Day (Nov. 1st), Armistice Day (Nov. 11th), and Christmas Day. Business is generally suspended on most of these days and banks are closed.

Tobacconists always have postage stamps, post-cards, and carte-lettres on sale.

House Numbering. In streets parallel with the Seine the houses are numbered from E. to W.; in those at right angles with the Seine, from the nearest end to the river.

Minuterie. The notice 'minuterie' in apartment houses, etc., indicates a push-button, pressure on which will illuminate the staircase for about three minutes.

III. HOTELS

Hotels of every class and size abound in Paris, but during the tourist season they are often full, and it is prudent to engage rooms in advance, especially if the traveller arrives late in the evening. The most expensive hotels, the clientèle at which is international (largely American), are mostly situated in the neighbourhood of the Place Vendôme, the Place de la Concorde, and the Champs-Elysées. For the average visitor the most convenient quarters are near the Boulevards, from the Madeleine to the Faubourg Poissonnière and the adjoining regions, the Avenue de l'Opéra, the Rue de Rivoli between the Palais-Royal and the Place de la Concorde, the Faubourg St-Honoré, and the Champs-Elysées neighbourhood. But there are many good hotels outside these limits.

Before taking possession of his rooms at a hotel the traveller should have a precise understanding as to the charge. Bills should be paid at reasonably short intervals, as mistakes are then more easily checked. Notice of departure should be given before noon. Valuables or money should not be kept in the traveller's trunk, but should be deposited with the manager of the hotel, in exchange for a receipt, or at a bank.

CHARGES. The charges formerly quoted in our list of hotels and based upon tariffs issued by the hotel-keepers and upon the bills of travellers are not included in the present edition, as the instability of prices prohibits any but the roughest approximation. Generally speaking, the more expensive houses in each section are mentioned first. The charge for rooms generally covers also the use of the public bathrooms, but otherwise baths are extra (c. 60 fr.). The charges for better rooms, e.g. with bathroom or dressing-room attached, and for meals served in private rooms, are, of course, higher. A tax of 10 per cent. is added to the charges for lodging, food, and drink at all hotels, restaurants, or cafés that are classed as 'établissements de luxe'; in second- and third-class hotels the tax is proportionately less.

GRATUITIES. The maître d'hôtel (head-waiter, through whom the bill is generally paid), the waiter who has attended the visitor at meals, the chambermaid, the valet de chambre, and the hall-porter all expect to be 'tipped'. To get full value for one's tips, they should be distributed at least once a week. At a hotel of moderate class not less than 10 per cent. of the bill (not including the luxury-tax) should be given in gratuities; a one-night visitor gives more. The head-waiter receives rather more than the other servants. An occasional 20 fr. is enough for the page or lift-boy. In most hotels 10–15 per cent. is added to the bill for 'service'; at these no gratuities need be given.

The following list, making no claim to be an exhaustive catalogue of the hotels of Paris, is intended to offer the visitor a comprehensive choice of accommodation. The omission of a name from our lists implies no derogatory judgment. Some of the larger and more expensive hotels, and the hotels near the chief railway stations, have been grouped together, but otherwise the hotels are arranged according to districts.

i. Hôtels de luxe and large First-class Hotels

The following are hôtels de luxe, sumptuously fitted up with palatial suites of rooms, restaurants, grill-rooms, etc., and with corresponding charges.

George V, 31 Av. George V; **Crillon,** 10 Place de la Concorde; **Meurice,** 228 Rue de Rivoli; **Raphael,** 17 Av. Kléber; **Ritz,** 15 Place Vendôme; **Plaza-Athénée,** 23 Av. Montaigne; **Astoria,** 131 Av. des Champs-Elysées; **Lancaster,** 7 Rue de Berri; **Prince de Galles,** 33 Av. George V; **Royal-Monceau,** 35 Av. Hoche; **Princess,** 10 Rue de Presbourg; **Continental,** 3 Rue de Castiglione; **Chatham,** 18 Rue Volney; **Westminster,** 13 Rue de la Paix; **Lotti,** 7 Rue de Castiglione; **Paris,** 8 Boul. de la Madeleine; **Grand-Hôtel,** 12 Rue Scribe; **Scribe,** 1 Rue Scribe; **Vendôme,** 1 Place Vendôme.

ii. Hotels at the Chief Railway Stations

Gare St-Lazare: **Chicago,** 99bis Rue de Rome; **Dieppe,** 22 Rue d'Amsterdam. Gare de l'Est and Gare du Nord: **Terminus-Est,** 5 Rue de Strasbourg; **Terminus-Nord,** 87 Rue de Dunkerque; **Francia,** 100 Rue La Fayette. Gare de Lyon: **Paris-Lyon-Palace,** 11 Rue de Lyon; **Terminus-Lyon,** 19 Boul. Diderot. Gare Montparnasse: **Victoria-Palace,** 6 Rue Blaise-Desgoffe. Gare d'Austerlitz: **Terminus-Austerlitz,** 12 Boul. de l'Hôpital.

iii. Other Hotels arranged topographically

The following groups include both first-class hotels and those of a simpler character, the less expensive hotels being mentioned towards the end of each group.

(*a*) Between the Av. de l'Opéra, the Madeleine, Place de la Concorde, and the Louvre: **Du Louvre,** Place du Théâtre-Français ; **Normandy,** 7 Rue de l'Echelle ; **Régina,** 2 Place des Pyramides ; **Deux-Mondes,** 22 Av. de l'Opéra ; **France et Choiseul,** 239 Rue St-Honoré ; **Saint-James et d'Albany,** 211 Rue St-Honoré; **Calais,** 5 Rue des Capucines ; **Cambon,** 3 Rue Cambon ; **Duminy,** 3/5 Rue de Mont-Thabor.

(*b*) Near the Rond-Point des Champs-Elysées and the Place de l'Etoile: **Astoria,** 131 Av. des Champs-Elysées ; **California,** 16 Rue de Berri ; **Claridge,** 74 Av. des Champs-Elysées ; **Elysées-Park,** 2 Rond-Point des Champs-Elysées ; **Stockholm,** 125 Av. des Champs-Elysées ; **Celtic,** 6 Rue Balzac ; **Matignon,** 6 Av. Matignon ; **du Rond-Point des Champs-Elysées,** 10 Rue de Ponthieu ; **des Théâtres des Champs-Elysées** (no restaurant), 6 Av. Montaigne ; **Elysées Palace,** 12 Rue de Marignan ; **de l'Elysée** (no restaurant), 12 Rue des Saussaies.

(*c*) Between the Av. de l'Opéra, the Boul. des Italiens, and the Rue de Richelieu: **Louvois,** 1 Rue de Lulli ; **des Etats-Unis,** 16 Rue d'Antin ; **de Malte,** 63 Rue de Richelieu ; **d'Antin,** 18 Rue d'Antin ; **Cusset,** 95 Rue de Richelieu ; **de France,** 22 Rue d'Antin ; **de Noailles,** 9 Rue de la Michodière.

(*d*) Near the Palais Royal, the Bourse de Commerce, and the Louvre: **du Palais-Royal,** 4 Rue de Valois ; **du Rhône,** 5 Rue J.-J. Rousseau ; **des Empereurs,** 20 Rue J.-J. Rousseau ; **du Globe,** 4 Rue Croix-des-Petits-Champs.

(*e*) In the Latin Quarter and near the Odéon and Luxembourg: **Claude-Bernard,** 43 Rue des Ecoles ; **Dagmar,** 225 Rue St-Jacques ; **Excelsior,** 20 Rue Cujas; **d'Angleterre,** 44 Rue Jacob ; **Royal-Condé,** 10 Rue de Condé ; **des Saints-Pères,** 65 Rue des Saints-Pères ; **Trianon-Palace,** 3 Rue de Vaugirard; **Malherbe,** 11 Rue de Vaugirard ; **d'Isly,** 29 Rue Jacob ; **Récamier,** 3bis Place St-Sulpice ; **des Etrangers,** 2 Rue Racine.

(*f*) In the Faubourg St-Germain: **Montalembert,** 3 Rue Montalembert; **Bourgogne et Montana,** 7 Rue de Bourgogne ; **Cayre,** 4 Boul. Raspail.

Pensions or Boarding Houses. The 'pensions de famille' are adapted for visitors making a stay of some length, but owing to the increase in the student population and the growing number of tourists visiting Paris, vacancies are hard to find. As a rule pensions have table d'hôte meals at fixed hours, reading rooms, etc., and tend to be less noisy than hotels, while their charges are distinctly lower. The best method of choosing satisfactory quarters is through someone who knows both the traveller and the house. The servants in boarding-houses expect to be periodically 'tipped'.

IV. RESTAURANTS

Good **Restaurants** of every class abound in Paris, and it may be noted that meals at nearly all the hotels are open also to non-residents. Prices are very much higher than before the War, and except in the less pretentious establishments the convenient table d'hôte at fixed prices ('à prix fixe') is very much less frequent. At most restaurants the day's menu, with prices, is affixed outside the establishment. The head-waiter ('maître d'hôtel') should not be addressed as 'garçon', a term reserved for his subordinates.

The famous French cookery reaches its perfection in the sumptuous à la carte restaurants of the highest class, where 1500 fr. is a conservative estimate for the price of a reasonable dinner. The diner will note that such items as hors d'œuvre, fruit, etc., will swell the bill very considerably, and he should not allow the suggestions of the waiter to add more dishes to the menu than he really wishes. It is, moreover, uneconomical to dine alone at these restaurants, as a 'portion' is often sufficient for two. The bill is subject to the luxury-tax of 10 per cent.

Excellent meals at considerably lower charges (600 or 700 fr. upwards) may be enjoyed in other good à la carte restaurants in the Grands Boulevards and other main thoroughfares; and various restaurants, brasseries, and café-restaurants offer meals at fixed prices ranging from c. 300 fr. upwards. Even at the cheaper establishments the standard of cooking will be found remarkably good. In restaurants à la carte there is a liberal choice of wines at relatively high prices. The red, white, and 'rosé' table-wines in carafes or 'pichets' (jugs) are usually very fair at any restaurant, and the beer of Paris is reasonably good.

The bill (l'addition) should be in writing, and the prudent traveller will check the items charged. In the larger restaurants 12 per cent. of the bill (before the addition of the luxury tax) is an adequate gratuity to the waiter.

The following list of restaurants, without claiming to be exhaustive, aims at providing the traveller with a reasonable choice of such establishments. The omission of a name from the list does not imply any derogatory judgment. In each section the restaurants are roughly arranged in the order of their charges, the cheaper restaurants being named last (except for the restaurants de luxe).

Restaurants de Luxe

Angelina, 226 Rue de Rivoli; **Le Coucou de l'Opéra,** 3 Rue Danielle-Casanova; **L'Escargot,** 38 Rue Montorgueil; **Le Grand Véfour,** 17 Rue de Beaujolais; **Hôtel Meurice,** 228 Rue de Rivoli; **Prunier,** 9 Rue Duphot; **Le Relais de la Belle Aurore,** 6 Rue Gomboust; **Hôtel Ritz,** 15 Place Vendôme; **Le Vert Galant,** 42 Quai des Orfèvres; **Café de Paris,** 41 Av. de l'Opéra; **Le Chatham,** 17 Rue Daunou; **Drouant,** 18 Rue Gaillon; **Griffon,** 6 Rue d'Antin; **La Tour d'Argent,** 15 Quai de la Tournelle; **Rôtisserie Périgourdine,** 2 Place St-Michel; **Auberge du Père Jean,** 27 Rue du Colisée; **Berkeley Hôtel,** 7 Av. Matignon; **La Bourride,** 5 Rue Paul-Cézanne; **Chez Francis,** 7 Place de l'Alma; **Hôtel Claridge,** 74 Av. des Champs-Elysées; **La Crémaillère,** 92 Rue du Fg. St-Honoré; **Hôtel de Crillon,** 10 Place de la Concorde; **Fouquet's,** 99 Av. des Champs-Elysées; **Lasserre,** 17 Av. Franklin-Roosevelt; **Lucas,** 9 Place de la Madeleine; **La Marée,** 1 Rue Daru; **Maxim's,** 3 Rue Royale; **Pavillon de l'Elysée,** Av. des Champs-Elysées; **Le Périgord,** 5 Av. Matignon; **Rôtisserie de la Reine Pédauque,** 6 Rue de la Pépinière; **Yvonne et André,** 25 Rue Boissy-d'Anglas; **Hôtel Scribe,** 1 Rue Scribe; **Cassagne,** 129 Boul. de Grenelle; **Les Mousquetaires,** 141 Av. Malakoff; **Pré Catelan,** Bois de Boulogne; **Auberge d'Armaillé,** 6 Rue d'Armaillé.

Restaurants in and near the Grands Boulevards

L'Escargot d'Or, 250 Rue St-Denis; **Le Delmonico,** 39 Av. de l'Opéra; **Le Caneton,** 3 Rue de la Bourse; **Gourdeau,** 13 Rue Monsigny; **Paris-Bourse,** 10 Rue St-Marc; **Zimmer-Blondel,** Rue Blondel; **Juillet,** 237 Rue St-Denis; **Auberge Chanteclair,** 6 Rue du Helder; **Auberge Drouot,** 8 Rue Drouot; **L'Ange Rouge,** 28 Av. Trudaine; **Café de Madrid,** 8 Boul. Montmartre; **Café de la Paix,** 12 Boul. des Capucines; **Gentilhomme,** 4 Boul. des Capucines; **Aux Armes de France,** 14 Boul. des Italiens; **Pam-Pam,** 1 Rue Auber; **Royal Vendôme,** 26 Rue Danielle-Casanova.

RESTAURANTS NEAR THE TUILERIES, THE PALAIS-ROYAL, AND THE LOUVRE

Le Cambridge, 20 Av. de l'Opéra ; **Hôtel du Louvre,** Place du Théâtre-Français ; **L'Embassy,** 280 Rue St-Honoré ; **A la Cigogne,** 17 Rue Duphot ; **Colombine,** 4 Rue Cambon ; **Normandie,** 7 Rue l'Echelle ; **Les Deux Pigeons,** 12 Rue d'Argenteuil ; **Pharamond,** 24 Rue de la Grande-Truanderie ; **Zimmer-Châtelet,** Place du Châtelet ; **Brasserie Universelle,** 31 Av. de l'Opéra ; **Au Caveau Montpensier,** 15 Rue de Montpensier.

RESTAURANTS IN AND NEAR THE CHAMPS-ELYSÉES, THE PLACE DE L'ETOILE, AND THE BOIS DE BOULOGNE

Le Rond-Point des Champs-Elysées, 1 Av. Matignon ; **Le Nouveau Marignan,** 27 Av. des Champs-Elysées ; **Larue,** 27 Rue Royale ; **Hostaria,** 32 Av. Matignon ; **Le Jour et la Nuit,** 2 Rue de Berri ; **Club des Champs-Elysées,** 3 Av. Matignon ; **Chez Louis,** 14 Rue Lincoln ; **Auberge de la Truite,** 30 Fg. St-Honoré ; **Pagès,** 124 Rue La Boétie ; **L'Alpe d'Huez,** 1 Rue Lincoln ; **Le Cabaret,** 4 Av. Franklin-Roosevelt ; **Louis Cherry,** 6 Rond-Point des Champs-Elysées ; **Le Berlioz,** 136 Av. Malakoff ; **Chantago,** 174 Rue de la Pompe ; **Relais St-James,** 88bis Av. Kléber ; **L'Escargot, Le Petit Matelot, Le Cottage,** 109, 122 and 115 Av. de Villiers (near Porte Champerret).—**Pavillon d'Armenonville, *Pavillon Royal, Croix Catelan,** these three in the Bois de Boulogne.

RESTAURANTS TO THE E. AND N.E. OF THE LOUVRE AS FAR AS THE BASTILLE AND THE PLACE DE LA RÉPUBLIQUE

Le Coq en Plat, 9 Rue Ste-Apolline ; **Chez l'Ami Louis,** 32 Rue de Vertbois ; **Taverne de Paris,** 23 Place de la République ; **Brasserie Tourtel,** 21 Place de la République ; **Le Bossu,** 27 Quai de Bourbon ; **Mustapha,** 16 Rue de Jouy ; **Bofinger,** 5 Rue de la Bastille ; **L'Escargot,** 9 Rue de la Bastille ; **Chez Benoît,** 20 Rue St-Martin ; **Au Vrai Béarnais,** 36 Boul. Henri IV.

RESTAURANTS IN MONTMARTRE

Auberge du Sanglier Bleu, 102 Boul. de Clichy ; **Chez Graff,** 92 Boul. de Clichy ; **Dupeux,** 78 Boul. de Clichy ; **Pierrot de la Butte,** 41 Rue Caulaincourt ; **Gafner,** 39 Rue Lepic ; **Chez Tournaud,** 25 Rue Durantin ; **Curtis,** 3 Rue Houdon ; **A la Mère Catherine,** Place du Tertre.

RESTAURANTS ON THE LEFT BANK

Chez Magdelaine, 61 Quai de la Tournelle ; **El Koutoubia,** 30 Rue des Ecoles ; **Casenave,** 7 Place de l'Odéon ; **La Pérouse,** 51 Quai des Grands-Augustins ; **Le Cochon de Lait,** 7 Rue Corneille ; **Chez Allard,** 41 Rue St-André-des-Arts ; **Hôtel Lutétia,** 43 Boul. Raspail ; **Le Catalan,** 16 Rue des Grands-Augustins ; **Le Radar,** 159 Rue de Rennes ; **La Rotonde en Montparnasse,** 105 Boul. Montparnasse ; **Porquerolles,** 12 Rue de l'Eperon ; **Chope Danton, Potée Champenoise,** Carrefour de l'Odéon ; **La Méditerranée,** 2 Place de l'Odéon ; **L'Alsacienne,** 54 Boul. St-Michel ; **Saint-Germain,** 165 Boul. St-Germain ; **Brasserie de la Sorbonne,** 45 Boul. St-Michel ; **Chez George,** 34 Rue Mazarine ; **Chataigner,** 75 Rue du Cherche-Midi ; **Le Minaret,** 8 Rue Vaugirard ; **Hoggar,** Rue Monsieur-le-Prince ; **Aux Gourmets,** 19 Rue des Canettes ; **Palais d'Orsay,** 9 Quai Anatole-France ; **Albert,** 124 Rue de Grenelle ; **Chez Marius,** 9 Rue de Bourgogne ; **David,** 36 Av. de La Motte-Picquet ; **Le Rapide,** 5 Rue de Bellechasse ; **La Toque Blanche,** 66 Av. Bosquet ; **Gardes,** 30 Rue du Bac ; **Plat d'Argent,** 10 Rue des Saints-Pères ; **Taverne du Palais,** 5 Place St-Michel.

FOREIGN RESTAURANTS

Arabian: **Mosquée,** 39 Rue Geoffroy St-Hilaire.—Greek: **Acropole,** 3 Rue de l'Ecole-de-Médecine.—Algerian : **Cous-Cous,** 10 Rue Montyon.—Chinese ; **Chou-Chen,** 3 Rue de Cluny.—Russian : **Gil,** 8 Rue des Martyrs.

Cafés. The thousand cafés of Paris are distributed all over the city, but are most numerous on the Boulevards, near the railway stations, and in the larger streets. Many of them provide music in the afternoon and evening, and in most cases tables and chairs are set out on the pavement in front (the ' terrasse '), where the customer may spend a pleasant hour in watching the passers-by. The coffee, beer, liqueurs, and other beverages supplied are generally of good quality. Café nature or café crème is served both in cups and in glasses. Café filtre served in a glass or cup with a percolator is of better quality. A mazagran is a glass of iced coffee. The usual order for beer is for a bock or a demi. Customers should not pay the waiter after each drink, but wait until they wish to leave.

In all cafés ' petit déjeuner ' may be obtained in the morning, consisting of coffee or chocolate, rolls or ' croissants', and butter. French tea-making leaves much to be desired, and travellers are advised to limit themselves to the coffee and chocolate, both of which are excellent. Given below are the names of a few of the better-known cafés.

NEAR THE OPÉRA AND GRANDS BOULEVARDS

Baltazard, 2bis Boul. St-Martin ; ***Café de la Paix,** 12 Boul. des Capucines ; **Cardinal,** 1 Boul. des Italiens ; **Napolitain,** 1 Boul. des Capucines ; **Royal Capucines,** 24 Boul. des Capucines ; **Viel,** 8 Boul. de la Madeleine.

NEAR THE CHAMPS-ELYSÉES AND ETOILE

Le Colisée, 44 Av. des Champs-Elysées ; **Grande Taverne,** 21 Av. des Champs-Elysées ; **Le Select,** 100 Av. des Champs-Elysées ; **Monte Carlo,** 9 Av. de Wagram.

IN MONTPARNASSE

Closerie des Lilas, 20 Av. de l'Observatoire ; **Le Dôme,** 108 Boul. Montparnasse ; **La Rotonde,** 103 Boul. Montparnasse.

IN MONTMARTRE

Graff, 92 Boul. de Clichy ; **Wepler,** 14 Place Clichy.

IN THE LATIN QUARTER

Capoulade, 63 Boul. St-Michel ; **Café de Flore,** 172 Boul. St-Germain ; **Deux Magots,** 170 Boul. St-Germain ; **Harcourt,** 47 Boul. St-Michel.

NEAR THE GARES DU NORD AND DE L'EST

Taverne des Flandres, 8 Boul. de Denain ; **Ducastaing,** 4 Boul. de Denain.

NEAR THE GARE ST-LAZARE

Diamente, 12 Boul. St-Augustin ; **Mollard,** 115 Rue St-Lazare ; **Garnier,** 111 Rue St-Lazare.

Among the many ' bars-Américains ' which have sprung up recently, the *King Charles,* 8 Rue Cambon, and *Harry's Bar,* 5 Rue Daunou, are noteworthy.

Tea Rooms. Afternoon tea in the English style is highly popular, the usual hour being between 5 and 6. *A la Marquise de Sévigné,* 11 Boul. de la Madeleine ; *Closerie des Lilas* 20 Av. de l'Observatoire ; *Ixe Opéra,* 6 Rue Halévy ; *Ixe Royale,* 24 Rue Royale ; **Royalty,* Av. des Champs-Elysées (Rue Marignan) ; *Rumpelmayer,* 9 Rue du Fg. St-Honoré ; *Sherry,* 6 Rond-Point des Champs-Elysées.

V. CONVEYANCES

Taxis. Present charge, 25 fr. on hiring, then 24 fr. per km. (day rates) or 40 fr. per km. (night rates ; 11 p.m.–6.30 a.m.), plus 10 fr. for each small suitcase, 20 fr. for a large case or trunk or a bicycle. Drivers expect a tip of 15–20 per cent.

PRIVATE MOTOR CARS can be hired through any of the larger tourist agencies.

Motor-Buses (list, see pp. 225–228). All the motor-buses and the underground railway (Métro) in Paris are controlled by the R.A.T.P., 53ter Quai des Grands-Augustins.

Bus services are arranged in a system of numbered routes. The numbers displayed on the buses correspond with those on the list and route-map. Tickets are bought by the 'carnet' of 20 tickets (150 fr.), and the number of tickets required from fare-stage to fare-stage is indicated on a little map in the interior of the bus, but strangers should state their destination to the conductor in order to avoid any misunderstanding. Smoking is allowed on the standing platform at the back of the bus only, which is also reserved for standing passengers. Ordinary bus-stops are indicated by red placards and request stops by green placards. During the 'rush hours' (8–9 a.m., 12–2 p.m., and 6.30–7.30) it is advisable to take a 'numéro d'ordre' (a numbered queue ticket) from the apparatus at the bus-stop, in order to establish one's position in the queue. A notice with the word 'complet' means that a bus is full. The normal service runs between 6 a.m. and 9 p.m.

Underground Railways (list, see pp. 229–231). The elaborate and convenient system of electric railways in Paris (the 'Métro' or Métropolitain) provides a cheap and fairly rapid method of transit. The stations, almost uniformly 500 metres (⅓ m.) apart, are reached by staircases, in some cases by lifts and moving staircases. Trains run at intervals of 2–8 min. from 5.30 to 1.15 a.m. The halts are very brief and there is frequent overcrowding. The fares (1st cl. 35 fr., 2nd cl. 22 fr.) are the same for any distance, including all necessary changes. 'Carnets' of five tickets (10 journeys) are on sale at all booking offices (1st cl. 225 fr., 2nd cl. 150 fr.), and it is cheaper and more convenient to buy a carnet rather than a 'billet simple.' A 'carte hebdomadaire,' valid from Monday to Monday (available from the previous Friday) is issued at a specially reduced price for two journeys a day, provided that the traveller both starts his first journey and finishes his second journey at the same Métro station.

Fares on the *Ligne de Sceaux* (connecting with the Métro at Denfert–Rochereau) are not covered by one price, and visitors should state their destination at the ticket office. Smoking is not forbidden on this line, as it is in the Métro.

The various lines of the Métro are called by the names of their terminal stations (e.g. Ligne 1, Vincennes-Neuilly) and the direction of the trains (which keep to the right) is indicated by a placard with the name of the terminus. The connecting passages at exchange stations are indicated by an orange-lighted sign 'Correspondance,' followed by the terminal station of the connecting line (e.g. Correspondance Clignancourt).

Motor Coaches. During the season, the *Régie Autonome des Transports Parisiens* (R.A.T.P.) organises drives (Sun. and holidays) to Malmaison, Fontainebleau, Versailles, etc. Full particulars may be obtained from the Bureau des Excursions in the Place de la Madeleine (opp. Nos. 18–20 ; tel. ANJou 31–18). It is advisable to book seats in advance. Many of the tourist agencies run daily trips to the numerous historic and picturesque spots around Paris, and visitors who wish to strike out on their own should take full advantage of the services (from 100 km. to 200 km. outside Paris) run by the following firms :

Cars Citroën (34 Boul. Haussmann) : coaches to Meaux, Beauvais, Compiègne, Chantilly, etc. ;

Cars Briards (37 Boul. Bourdon) : coaches to Sucy-en-Brie, Chaumes, Brie-Comte-Robert, etc. ;

Phocéens-Cars (19 Rue de l'Arcade) : coaches to Arpajon, Fontainebleau, Sens, etc. ;

Cars Renault (92 Rue de Sèvres) : coaches to Compiègne, Chantilly, Senlis, Fontainebleau, Orléans, etc.

River Steamers. The regular passenger services on the Seine have not been revived since the war, but ' Les Bateaux Mouches ' run pleasure trips for visitors during the summer months. The embarkation point is on the left bank between the Pont de la Concorde and the Pont de Solférino. Full particulars can be obtained from the offices at 17 Rue d'Astorg.

VI. POSTAL AND OTHER SERVICES

Postal Information

The postal rates given below are for Oct. 1950, and travellers should expect certain modifications according to the fluctuating value of the franc.

	In France.	Abroad.
Letters . .	15 fr. for 20 gr. ; 20 fr. for 50 gr. ; 30 fr. for 100 gr. et seq.	30 fr. for 20 gr., then 18 fr. per 20 gr.
Post Cards .	8 fr. (not more than 5 words). 12 fr. (more than 5 words).	6 fr. (not more than 5 words). 18 fr. (more than 5 words).
Newspapers .	10 fr. for 50 gr. ; 15 fr. for 100 gr. ; 30 fr. for 300 gr.	6 fr. for 50 gr., maximum 3 kg.
Telegrams .	12 fr. per word, minimum 10 words.	To Great Britain, 26½ fr. per word. To New York, 128 fr. 80 c. per word.

The General Post Office in Paris is the *Hôtel des Postes* at 48–52 Rue du Louvre. Post offices are open on weekdays from 8 a.m. to 7 p.m.; but are closed on Sundays, except for one office in each arrondissement which remains open until 11 a.m. The offices at the Bourse and at 103 Rue de Grenelle are open permanently (day and night) for telegrams, etc. Letter boxes in Paris are painted blue.

Letters, etc., for Paris should have the surname of the addressee very legibly written, and the number of the arrondissement added.

REGISTRATION. Letters may be registered for a fee of 35 fr.—POSTE RESTANTE letters are subject to a delivery-tax of 10 fr. each (passport must be presented as proof of identity).

AIR MAIL. Letters may be sent by air to Great Britain and the U.S.A. at the following rates: Great Britain—38 fr. for 20 gr., then 26 fr. per 20 gr.; U.S.A.—53 fr. for 5 gr., 76 fr. for 10 gr., 99 fr. for 15 gr., 112 fr. for 20 gr., and 163 fr. for 25 gr.

Telegrams. Full information about telegrams to foreign countries can be obtained in any post office, or from the following private companies:

Western Union, 2 Rue des Italiens; *Commercial Cable*, 24 Boul. des Capucines; *Eastern Telegraph*, 73 Rue de Richelieu; *Radio-France*, 166 Rue Montmartre.

TÉLÉGRAMMES PNEUMATIQUES. For messages within Paris and certain suburbs 'cartes télégrammes,' transmitted by pneumatic tubes, are much cheaper than telegrams and almost as quick. They should be posted in the special letter-boxes marked 'cartes pneumatiques' (last collection c. 7.30 p.m.).

Telephones. Public call offices are found at nearly all post offices, Métro stations, restaurants, etc. The dialling system in Paris is exactly the same as that in London. However, a 'jeton' (22 fr. at the Métro booking office, etc.) is inserted in the box instead of coins. There is no 'button B' in a Paris call box, but the 'jeton' may be recovered by replacing the receiver should the number be engaged. Callers should remember to press the equivalent of 'button A' when the number answers the call. At the post offices the number required should be given (preferably in writing) to an employee who will establish the connection. Calls outside Paris vary according to the distance and number of minutes the caller is on the line. Paris has telephonic communication with all parts of the British Isles.

Parcels, though called Colis Postaux, are not carried by the French post office. In Paris they are handled by a private firm (head office, 96 Rue Amelot), with numerous receiving offices throughout the city; and for the rest of France and abroad by the railways. It is forbidden to enclose letters, money or valuables, in any parcel. Parcels for abroad are generally examined before acceptance by the officials. Full information about tariffs (which are variable and high) can be obtained from any post office.

Information Bureaux

The *Bureau National de Tourisme,* 127 Av. des Champs-Elysées (daily 9–12, 1.30–6.30 ; closed on Sat., Sun., and holidays at 6), is the headquarters of the 'tourist industry' in France, and supplies the fullest and most authoritative answers to visitors' problems. A railway booking and information office is located in the same hall (r. of the entrance). There are other offices of the French Railways at 16 Boul. des Capucines and 88 Rue St-Lazare.

The Commissariat Général au Tourisme have a *Bureau d'Accueil et d'Information* (with a most helpful staff who speak English ; tel. OPEra 17–71) at No. 8 Av. de l'Opéra (daily 9–7 ; 9–6.30 on Sat. ; 9–6 on Sun.). The hotel information service (1st floor) is open daily 9–12, 2–6 ; 9–12 only on Sat., and closed on Sun.

Tourist Agents. *Wagons-Lits/Cook,* 2 Place de la Madeleine, 62 Rue du Bac, 14 Boul. des Capucines ; *American Express,* 11 Rue Scribe ; *Polytechnic,* 26 Rue de la Pépinière ; *Bennett's,* 4 Rue Scribe ; *Le Tourisme Français,* 3 Rue Faidherbe, and 96 Rue de la Victoire ; *Cie. Française de Tourisme,* 14 Boul. de la Madeleine.

British Railways, 12 Boul. de la Madeleine ; *British Travel Centre,* 6 Place Vendôme.

VII. AMUSEMENTS

Useful and topical information about theatres, cinemas, cabarets, restaurants, night clubs, and sport, are given in the 'Semaine de Paris' (in French) and the 'Parisian Weekly Information' (in English), published every Wednesday, at 25 fr. and 30 fr. respectively (at all bookstalls).

Theatres. In most of the Paris theatres performances are given nightly, starting about 8.30 to 9 and finishing about 11.45. Except at the height of summer, matinée performances are given on Sundays, and sometimes on Thursdays, starting at 2.30 to 3, and finishing about 5.30. Nearly all the big theatres close for some weeks in the summer and most theatres are closed on one evening every week (usually Mon. or Tues.). The best seats are the 'fauteuils d'orchestre' or stalls, and next come the 'fauteuils de balcon' (dress circle) and the 'loges de face.' The side seats should be avoided. Seats may be booked in advance either at the theatre box-office (generally open for booking 10–7) or through theatrical agencies (6 Place de l'Opéra ; 14 Boul. Madeleine ; 26 Av. de l'Opéra ; 2 Place Vendôme). Tickets bought at an agency or in advance are more expensive than those bought on the night. Official programme sellers and usherettes expect to be tipped. Smoking is forbidden in theatres.

Over and above the two national 'lyric' theatres (the Opéra and Opéra Comique), there are two "théâtres nationaux," i.e., state-subsidised theatres in Paris. By far the most famous is the COMÉDIE FRANÇAISE or THÉÂTRE

Français, which stages performances (nightly; matinées on Thurs. and Sun.) at two 'Salles': the Salle Richelieu, in the Place du Théâtre-Français, devoted to French classics, and the Salle du Luxembourg (the former Théâtre de l'Odéon), in the Place de l'Odéon, for the works of modern playwrights. The other national theatre is the Théâtre National Populaire, in the Palais de Chaillot (Place du Trocadéro), which is used for every sort of performance, including concerts, ballet, and opera.

The Opéra (p. 1), the most famous house of entertainment in Paris, stages performances of opera and ballet on Sun., Mon., Wed., Fri., and Sat. (matinée on Sun. during the season). The box-office is open 11–5.30. At the Opéra-Comique (p. 14), Place Boïeldieu, similar performances are given on Sun., Tues., Wed., Fri., and Sat. (matinée on Sun.), the distinction between the repertoires of the two being quite conventional and arbitrary. For some weeks in summer the Opéra-Comique company performs at the Palais de Chaillot. Box-office open 11–5.

The following is an alphabetical list of the other principal theatres:

Ambassadeurs, 1 Av. Gabriel; Ambigu, 2ter Boul. St-Martin; Antoine, 14 Boul. de Strasbourg; Arsenal, Rue du Petit-Musc; Atelier, Place Dancourt; Athénée, 24 Rue Caumartin; Bobino, 20 Rue de la Gaîté; Bouffes-Parisiens, 4 Rue Monsigny; Capucines, 39 Boul. des Capucines; Champs-Elysées, 15 Av. Montaigne; Chapiteau, 1 Place Pigalle; Charles de Rochefort, 64 Rue du Rochers; Châtelet, Place du Châtelet; Comédie des Champs-Elysées, 15 Av. Montaigne; Edouard VII, 10 Place Edouard-VII; Etoile, 35 Av. de Wagram; Européen, 6 Rue Biot; Gaîté-Lyrique, Square des Arts-et-Métiers; Gaîté-Montparnasse, 24 Rue de la Gaîté; Gramont, 30 Rue Gramont; Grand-Guignol, 25bis Rue Chaptal; Gymnase, 38 Boul. Bonne Nouvelle; Hébertot, 78bis Boul. des Batignolles; Huchette, 23 Rue de la Huchette; Humour (American Theatre Club), 42 Rue Fontaine; La Bruyère, 5 Rue La Bruyère; Madeleine, 19 Rue de Surène; Marigny, Av. de Marigny; Mathurins, 36 Rue des Mathurins; Michel, 38 Rue des Mathurins; Michodière, 4bis Rue de la Michodière; Mogador, 25 Rue de Mogador; Monceau, 16 Rue de Monceau; Montparnasse, 31 Rue de la Gaîté; Noctambules, 7 Rue Champollion; Nouveautés, 24 Boul. Poissonnière; Œuvre, 55 Rue de Clichy; Palais-Royal, 38 Rue Montpensier; de Paris, 15 Rue Blanche; Pigalle, 10 Rue Pigalle; de Poche, 75 Boul. Montparnasse; Porte-St-Martin, 16 Boul. St-Martin; Potinière, 7 Rue Louis-le-Grand; Renaissance, 20 Boul. St-Martin; Rire, 5 Rue de la Gaîté; Sarah-Bernhardt, Place du Châtelet; St-Georges, 51 Rue St-Georges; Studio des Champs-Elysées, 13 Av. Montaigne; Variétés, 7 Boul. Montmartre; Verlaine, 66 Rue Rochechouart; Vieux-Colombier, 21 Rue du Vieux-Colombier.

Open-air performances are given on Sun. afternoon in summer at the Théâtre de Verdure in the Jardin des Tuileries.

Music Halls and chansonniers are numerous and vary, of course, in character. Clever variety turns may be seen at the former, but many of them are devoted to revues of no very refined nature. The latter have an amusing enough atmosphere, but the visitor should have a very sound knowledge of French in order to appreciate them fully. Smoking is permitted.

Music Halls. A.B.C., 11 Boul. Poissonnière; AGNÈS CAPRI, 26 Rue de la Gaîté; ALHAMBRA, 50 Rue de Malte; CASINO MONTPARNASSE, 35 Rue de la Gaîté; CASINO DE PARIS, 16 Rue de Clichy; CENTRAL DE LA CHANSON, 13 Rue du Fg. Montmartre; FOLIES-BERGÈRE, 32 Rue Richer; MAYOL, 10 Rue de l'Echiquier; PETIT CASINO, 12 Boul. Montmartre; TABARIN, 36 Rue Victor-Massé.

Chansonniers. The charge for refreshments at these is apt to increase with the price of the seat. The announcement of 'free admission' (entrée libre) at some simply means that the price of admission is added to the charge for 'consommations' which the visitor is expected to order.

A LA LUNE ROUSSE, 58 Rue Pigalle; AU CAVEAU DE LA RÉPUBLIQUE, AU COUCOU, 1 and 33 Boul. St-Martin; AUX DEUX ANES, 100 Boul. de Clichy; AU DIX HEURES, 36 Boul. de Clichy; ŒIL DE PARIS, 4bis Rue de l'Etoile; CAVEAU DU CHAT NOIR, 68 Boul. de Clichy; TROIS BAUDETS, 2 Rue Couston.

Cabarets-Dancings. Among the numerous establishments which provide dancing and cabaret shows, we list a few of the most fashionable below.

L'AIGLON, 11 Rue de Berri; LE BŒUF SUR LE TOIT, 34 Rue du Colisée; BADINAGE, 1 Rue Balzac; BIG BEN, 70 Rue Ponthieu; LE CORSAIRE, 14 Rue Marignan; LA PUERTA DEL SOL, 52 Rue Pierre-Charron; MAXIM'S, 3 Rue Royale; OLYMPIA, 28 Boul. des Capucines; GIPSY'S, 20 Rue Cujas; VÉNUS, 124 Boul. du Montparnasse; CIRO'S, 6 Rue Daunou.

Cinemas are numerous in all parts of Paris, and performances (often in English) run continuously from about 2 p.m. Smoking is not allowed, and visitors should tip the usherette who shows them to their seats. Full particulars (with convenient Métro stations) of the various shows are given in the 'Semaine de Paris.'

Other Entertainments. The following varied places of entertainment are generally open to visitors to Paris.

The MUSÉE GRÉVIN, 10 Boul. Montmartre, the Paris Madame Tussaud's, has admirable waxwork groups and portraits.—LUNA PARK, at the Porte Maillot, has a dance hall, skating rink, and other attractions.—The PALAIS DE GLACE, Champs-Elysées (winter only) has a skating rink, buffet bar, etc.—The CIRQUE MÉDRANO (63 Boul. Rochechouart) and the CIRQUE D'HIVER (110 Rue Amelot) both give excellent circus performances.

Art Exhibitions. The chief annual art exhibitions in Paris are the *Salon de la Société Nationale des Beaux Arts et des Artistes Français* (*the* 'Salon' par excellence), and the *Salon de l'Automne*, held in the Grand Palais (Champs-Elysées) in April–July; the *Salon des Indépendants*, held in the Palais de la Ville (Musée d'Art Moderne, Quai de New-York), in April–May; and the *Salon des Humoristes*, at 11 Rue Royale, in April. Other exhibitions of a very varied nature are held at the *Maison de la Pensée Française*, 2 Rue de l'Elysée.

Smaller art shows are held at various galleries and picture-dealers' shops, mostly in and near the Faubourg St-Honoré, and on the left bank near St-Germain-des-Prés.

Foreign artists in Paris should take full advantage of the *Maison des Artistes*, 11 Rue Berryer, which is run by a group of French artists willing to help and co-operate with newcomers to Parisian artistic circles.

Music. Particulars of concerts, etc., will be found in the weekly publications 'Opéra' and 'Le Guide du Concert,' as well as in the 'Semaine de Paris.' The following societies give regular weekly concerts of classical music, all starting at 5.45 p.m.

Société des Concerts du Conservatoire, at the Théâtre des Champs-Elysées on Sun.

Concerts Colonne, at the Théâtre du Châtelet on Sat. and Sun.

Concerts Pasdeloup, at various concert halls (Salle Pleyel, 22 Rue Rochechouart; Palais de Chaillot, etc.) on Sat. and Sun.

Concerts Lamoureux, at the Salle Gaveau, 45 Rue La Boétie, on Sat. and Sun.

Excellent Church Music can be heard at the Madeleine, St-Eustache, St-François-Xavier, St-Merry, St-Sulpice, and Notre-Dame.

Sports and Games. The visitor to Paris at the proper season has many opportunities of seeing interesting sporting events and competitions, a few particulars of which are given below. All the various sporting clubs in France are grouped under one *Comité National des Sports* (headquarters, 55 Boul. Haussmann).

Athletics are governed by the *Fédération Française d'Athlétisme,* 32 Boul. Haussmann. The *Paris University Club* ('Puc'), 11 Rue Soufflot, the *Racing Club de France,* 81 Rue Ampère, and the *Club Athlétique des Sports Généraux,* 29 Boul. Haussmann, all have their own football and 'rugger' grounds, tennis courts, etc.

Billiards. Good tables are to be found at the *Académie de Billard,* 47 Av. de Wagram, the *Académie de Billard de la Place Clichy,* 84 Rue de Clichy, and the *Billard-Palace,* 3 Boul. des Capucines.

Boxing. Information from the *Central Sporting Club,* 57 Faubourg St-Denis; matches take place at the *Palais de Glace* in the Champs-Elysées, and also at the *Salle Wagram,* 39 Av. de Wagram.

Cricket. Matches are arranged by the *Standard Athletic Club,* which has sports grounds near the Bois de Meudon. Full information can be obtained from Mr. C. H. Voss, Hon. Sec. of the Club, 14 Rue las Cases (7e), or from the club headquarters at the Hotel Pétrograd, 33 Rue Caumartin.

Cycling is governed by the *Fédération Française de Cyclisme,* and the *Fédération Française de Cyclo-Tourisme,* 10 Rue Lancry. The chief cycling tracks in Paris are: *Vélodrome Municipal* (Bois de Vincennes), *Vélodrome du Parc des Princes* (Pte. d'Auteuil), *Vélodrome d'Hiver* (1 Rue Nélaton), and *Vélodrome de St-Denis* (43 Route de Gonesse). The cycling 'centre' of Paris is between the Porte Maillot and the Av. de la Grande Armée.

Fencing. Public exhibitions are organised by the *Fédération Française d'Escrime,* 13 Rue de Londres, and the *Cercle Hoche,* 22 Rue Daru.

Football. Rugby and Association matches are played in winter in the *Parc des Princes* in the Bois de Boulogne, at *Colombes* (Rue François Faber), at the *Faisanderie* in the Park of St-Cloud, etc. Students at the Sorbonne who wish to play Rugby should apply to the office of the *Paris University Club,* 11 Rue Soufflot (3rd floor, right hand door).

Golf. An introduction is necessary in order to play on any of the courses mentioned below. The *Golf Club de Paris* has an excellent course (18 holes) at La Boulie, near Versailles. There is a course at the American Country Club at the Château des Agneux, Ozoir-la-Ferrière (S.-et-M.), and others at St-Cloud, Chantilly, Fontainebleau, and St-Germain-en-Laye. The *Golfers' Club* (5 Av. Gabriel) has courses at Port-Marly and Morfontaine.

Horse-Racing in France is governed by the *Fédération Française des Sports Equestres* (6 Rue Lauriston). The racing season lasts from February to December. The chief attractions are held in the spring at Longchamp and Auteuil, and attract large numbers of fashionable spectators. Bookmaking in France is prohibited by law, and betting can be conducted only through the official 'Pari-Mutuel' or totalisator, which deducts a percentage of its gross receipts for the Société d'Encouragement (see below) and for the poor. The following are the recognised societies, with the race-meetings they control. The *Fédération Internationale Equestre et Société Hippique Française*, 26 Rue Brunel; *Société d'Encouragement*, 7 Rue Astorg (Vincennes); *Société des Steeple-Chases*, 137 Fg. St-Honoré (Auteuil); *Société du Sport de France*, 7 Rue Louis Murat (Le Tremblay); *Société Sportive d'Encouragement*, 133 Fg. St-Honoré (Enghien, Maisons-Laffitte).

The following is a list of the principal racecourses with the chief meetings.

LONGCHAMP (flat-races). Meetings in spring, from the 1st Sun. in April; in June, with the Grand Prix de Paris on the last Sunday; in October, with the Prix du Conseil Municipal and the Prix de l'Arc de Triomphe. The course may be reached by railway from the Gare St-Lazare; by motor-bus from the Place de la République, Boul. St-Michel, etc.; or by motor-coach.

AUTEUIL (steeplechases). Meetings in spring, April, including the Prix du Président de la République (2nd Sun.); in summer, including the Grand Steeple-Chase d'Auteuil, on the Sun. before the Grand Prix; and in Oct.–Dec. Auteuil station may be reached from the Gare St-Lazare, or by motor-coach.

CHANTILLY (flat-races). Meetings on the first two Sun. in June, with the Prix de Diane and the Prix du Jockey-Club (the French 'Derby'); in July; and in September.

Other race-meetings are held at *St-Cloud* (Prix du Président de la République, on the 2nd Sun. in April), *Vincennes*, *Maisons-Laffitte* (international meetings at the end of Sept.), *Enghien*, and *Le Tremblay* (near Joinville-le-Pont, beyond Vincennes).

Lawn Tennis. The organising society of tennis clubs is the *Fédération Française du Lawn-Tennis*, 22 Rue de Londres. The *Racing Club de Paris* (see above) runs a tennis club with its own courts, etc. Other clubs and courts are the *Tennis-Club de France*, 13 Rue de Châtillon; *Tennis-Club de St-Cloud*, 48bis Rue des Tennecolles, St-Cloud; *Tennis de la Comète*, 14 Rue de la Comète; *Tennis Couverts*, 5 Rue Eblé (7e).—Davis Cup and other important matches are played at the Stade Roland-Garros, just beyond the Porte d'Auteuil.

Motor Racing. The principal motor-racing track is at Linas near Montlhéry (Paris office, 26 Rue de la Pépinière). A motor show is held annually at the Grand Palais, starting on the first Thurs. in October.

Polo. The *Société de Polo* (84 Rue Lauriston) has a ground at Bagatelle in the Bois de Boulogne. The season opens in the first week of May.

Riding. Horses may be hired from the following riding schools: *Ecole d'Equitation Manège Pellier*, Jardin d'Acclimatation, Bois de Boulogne; *St-James Equitation*, 27 Rue du Bois-de-Boulogne (Neuilly); *Manège Dassonville*, 5 Rue Leroux; *Manège Howlett*, 37 Rue de la Ferme (Neuilly); *Manège du Tattersall Français*, 26 Rue Jacques-Dulud (Neuilly).—Horse show in spring at the Cercle de l'Etrier, Bois de Boulogne.

Rowing and Sailing. Rowing boats may be hired at most of the riverside resorts near Paris on the Seine and the Marne, the principal centres being Asnières, Argenteuil, Chatou (on the Seine below Paris), Joinville-le-Pont, and Nogent (on the Marne). The leading rowing and yachting societies are the *Yacht Club de France* (82 Boul. Haussmann); *Fédération Française des Sociétés d'Aviron* (93 Rue St-Lazare); *Société Nautique de la Basse Seine* (87 Quai du Maréchal-Joffre); *Fédération Française de la Voile* (82 Boul. Haussmann).

Swimming. The *Fédération Française de Natation* (20 Rue de la Chaussée d'Antin) is the controlling body of this sport. The principal swimming baths are *La Jonquière*, 79 Rue de la Jonquière; *Centre Social de la Jeunesse*, 44 Rue de Trévise; *Château-Landon*, 31 Rue de Château-Landon; *Neptuna*, 28 Boul. de Bonne-Nouvelle; *Sporting Club de Paris*, 53 Rue François 1er; *Hôtel Claridge*, 74 Av. des Champs-Elysées. Championships are decided at the *Stade des Tourelles*, near the Porte des Lilas (Métro 3 or 11).

VIII. USEFUL ADDRESSES

Directories. Any required address may be turned up in the *Annuaire du Commerce Didot-Bottin* (' *Le Bottin* '), a large work in five volumes of which the first two deal with

Paris. This may be consulted at post offices, hotels, restaurants, cafés, shops, etc. (notices are usually displayed : 'Ici on consulte le Bottin'). Residential and official addresses may be found also in the *Bottin Mondain*, which gives in addition particulars about theatres (plans and prices), and other amusements, motor-buses, etc.

Embassies, Legations, and Consulates

GREAT BRITAIN. Embassy, 35 Rue du Faubourg St-Honoré.—Consulate, 24 Av. Gabriel (visa office, 3 Rue d'Aguesseau).

AMERICA (United States). Embassy and Consulate, 2 Av. Gabriel.

AUSTRALIA. Embassy and Consulate, 14 Rue Las Cases.

CANADA. Embassy, 72 Av. Foch.—Consulate, 3 Rue Scribe.

INDIA. Embassy and Consulate, 7 Av. Kléber.

PAKISTAN. Embassy and Consulate, 107 Boul. Pereire.

SOUTH AFRICA. Embassy and Consulate, 51 Av. Hoche.

IRELAND, Republic of. Legation and Consulate, 37bis Rue Paul-Valéry.

Argentina. Embassy, 33 Rue Galilée. Consulate, 11 Rue de Madrid.—*Belgium.* Embassy and Consulate, 17 Rue d'Aguesseau.—*Bolivia.* Legation and Consulate, 27 Av. Kléber.—*Brazil.* Embassy, 45 Av. Montaigne. Consulate 122 Av. des Champs-Elysées.—*Chile.* Embassy, 2 Av. La Motte-Picquet. Consulate, 64 Boul. de La Tour-Maubourg.—*China.* Embassy, 11 Av. George-V. Consulate, 47 Rue Pergolèse.—*Colombia.* Embassy and Consulate, 22 Rue de l'Elysée.—*Czecho-Slovakia.* Embassy, 15 Av. Charles-Floquet. Consulate, 24 Rue Hamelin.—*Denmark.* Embassy and Consulate, 77 Av. Marceau.—*Egypt.* Embassy and Consulate, 56 Av. d'Iéna.—*Finland.* Legation, 30 Cours Albert 1er. Consulate, 11 Rue de la Pépinière.—*Greece.* Embassy, 17 Rue Auguste Vacquerie. Consulate, 24 Rue de Longchamp.—*Iran.* Embassy and Consulate 5 Rue Fortuny.—*Iraq.* Legation and Consulate, 10 Place des Etats-Unis.—*Israel.* Legation, 143 Av. de Wagram.—*Italy.* Embassy, 47 Rue de Varenne. Consulate, 50 Rue de Varenne.—*Mexico.* Embassy and Consulate, 9 Rue de Longchamp.—*Netherlands.* Embassy, 85 Rue de Grenelle. Consulate, 11 Rue de Constantine.—*Norway.* Embassy and Consulate, 10 Rue Treilhard.—*Peru.* Embassy, 37 Rue Pierre 1er de Serbie. Consulate, 50 Av. Kléber.—*Poland.* Embassy, 1 Rue de Talleyrand. Consulate, 31 Rue Jean-Goujon.—*Portugal.* Embassy, 3 Rue de Noisiel. Consulate, 18 Av. Kléber.—*Spain.* Embassy, 15 Av. George-V. Consulate, 165 Boul. Malesherbes.—*Sweden.* Embassy, 58 Av. Marceau. Consulate, 125 Av. des Champs-Elysées.—*Switzerland.* Legation and Consulate, 142 Rue de Grenelle.—*Turkey.* Embassy, 17 Rue Berton. Consulate, 170 Boul. Haussmann.—*U.S.S.R.* Embassy, 79 Rue de Grenelle. Consulate, 14 Place Malesherbes.—*Uruguay.* Legation, 29 Av. d'Eylau. Consulate, 129 Av. Malakoff.—*Venezuela.* Embassy and Consulate, 11 Rue Copernic.—*Yugoslavia.* Embassy and Consulate, 3 Rue Spontini.

English Churches. EPISCOPAL. *British Embassy Church,* 5 Rue d'Aguesseau.—*St. George's,* 7 Rue Auguste-Vacquerie.—*Christ Church,* 33 Boul. Victor-Hugo and 49 Boul. Bineau, Neuilly.—*Holy Trinity* (American), 23 Av. George-V.—*American Church in Paris,* Quai d'Orsay (corner of the Rue Jean-Nicot).—*St. Luke's Chapel* (American), 161 Boul. Raspail. *Church of Scotland,* 17 Rue Bayard.—*Congregational*

Chapel, 48 Rue de Lille.—*Methodist Chapel*, 4 Rue Roquépine.—*Society of Friends*, 50 Av. Victoria.—*First Church of Christ Scientist*, 10 Av. d'Iéna.—*Second Church of Christ Scientist*, 58 Boul. Flandrin.—*Third Church of Christ Scientist*, 45 Rue de La Boétie.—*Salvation Army* (Armée du Salut), 76 Rue de Rome.—*St. Joseph's* (R.C.) *Church*, 50 Av. Hoche.

Banks. Most of the French banks have numerous branches throughout the city. All banks are open 9–12 and 2–4, and 9–12 on Sat.

British Banks. *Barclays*, 33 Rue du Quatre-Septembre ; *Lloyds*, 43 Boul. des Capucines ; *Westminster*, 18 Place Vendôme ; *Royal Bank of Canada*, 3 Rue Scribe.

American Banks. *Chase Bank*, 11 Boul. de la Madeleine ; *Equitable Trust*, 23 Rue de la Paix ; *Guaranty Trust*, 4 Place de la Concorde ; *Morgan's*, 37 Rue Caumartin.

Chambers of Commerce. *British*, 6 Rue Halévy.—*American*, 4 Place de l'Opéra.

Clubs. Admission to the social clubs of Paris is, as might be expected, obtained only on the introduction of a member. The following are the addresses of some larger French institutions of which foreigners may become members without undue formality.

Automobile Club de France, 6 Place de la Concorde ; *Club Alpin Français*, 7 Rue de La Boétie ; *Touring Club de France*, 65 Av. de la Grande-Armée.

British clubs have ceased to exist in Paris since the war, but the *British Colony Committee* (at the offices of the British Chamber of Commerce, see above) gives evening 'socials' from time to time (particulars in the British Colony News Bulletin).—The *Y.M.C.A.* has a club-house at 14 Rue de Trévise (9e ; Métro station Cadet). The *Y.W.C.A.* has houses at 22 Rue de Naples (8e), 26 Rue d'Anjou (8e), both near the Gare St-Lazare, at 40 Rue Boulard (14e ; Métro station Denfert) and at 65 Rue Orfila (20e ; Métro station Martin-Nadaud).

American Clubs. *American Officers' Club*, 131 Av. des Champs-Elysées ; *American Legion*, 49 Rue Pierre-Charron ; *American Club of Paris*, 7 Place Vendôme ; *American University Union in Europe*, 173 Boul. St-Germain (excellent lectures, library, etc.). *American Library*, 9 Rue Téhéran.

The British Council has premises at No. 9 Rue de Chanaleilles (7e), with reading rooms, a library of c. 15,000 vols. (all English), and an intake of 200 periodicals. Books may be borrowed from the library on a deposit of 500 fr., with a maximum of three books withdrawn at one time. Students of the University of Paris may have the loan of books free. Books must be returned within 14 days. The library is open Mon.–Fri. 9.30–12.30 and 2–6, on Sat. 9.30–12.30.

Shops. The best-known shopping streets are the Rue du

Faubourg St-Honoré, Rue de la Paix, Boulevard de la Madeleine, Boulevard des Capucines, Boulevard des Italiens, and Avenue de l'Opéra, the first two of which may, perhaps, claim to be par excellence the street of the fashionable shop proper. Other very good shops are found in all the streets between the Opéra, the Tuileries, and the Palais-Royal; while several of the excellent large departmental stores lie outside these limits.

Among the best known of the departmental stores, where every ordinary want of the traveller may be met on the premises, are the *Bazar de l'Hôtel de Ville*, 52/64 Rue de Rivoli; *Belle Jardinière*, 2 Rue du Pont-Neuf; *Bon Marché*, Rues du Bac and de Sèvres; *Galeries Lafayette*, 38/46 Boul. Haussmann; *Magasins Réunis*, 30 Av. des Ternes, 136 Rue de Rennes, and Place de la République; *Au Printemps*, 64 Boul. Haussmann; *Samaritaine*, 67/81 Rue de Rivoli; *Samaritaine de Luxe*, 27 Boul. des Capucines; *Trois-Quartiers*, 17/25 Boul. de la Madeleine.

IX. THE SIGHTS OF PARIS

A good deal of Paris may be seen in a week in summer by the tireless traveller who makes a free use of taxicabs and is satisfied with the most superficial glance at the treasures of the galleries and museums. But not less than three weeks should be devoted to Paris, and even in that case a careful plan should be made beforehand so as to utilise every hour of every day.

The **Table of the Principal Sights** overleaf, with the information given below, will enable the visitor to arrange his plan of campaign. When alternative hours of closing are indicated, the earlier hours refer to winter (usually Oct.–April), the later to summer. Most collections are closed on public holidays and Tuesdays. Some collections are free on Sundays and others half-price. Special note should be taken of the days and hours at which particular collections are open; and applications for special permits should be made in good time.

Although the table at the beginning of the book includes some of the principal attractions of Paris and its environs, it by no means exhausts the lists of things to see. The traveller is reminded, therefore, of the following additional points of interest, details of which will be found in the text.

Public and other Institutions. *Arc de Triomphe.—Arènes de Lutèce.—Banque de France.—Chapelle Expiatoire.—Chapelle St-Ferdinand.—Collège de France.—Eiffel Tower.—Halles Centrales.—July Column.—Opera House.—Opéra-Comique.—Palais Royal.—Scots College.—Théâtre Français.*

Churches.—Besides *Notre-Dame* perhaps the most interesting churches are the *Madeleine.—Sacré-Cœur.—St-Eustache.—St-Etienne-du-Mont.—St-Germain-l'Auxerrois.—St-Germain-des-Prés.—St-Séverin.—St-Sulpice.*—Church of the *Sorbonne.*

Parks and Gardens. The *Bois de Boulogne*, the *Tuileries Gardens*, the *Champs-Elysées*, the *Luxembourg Gardens*, etc., are not likely to be overlooked by the visitor to Paris; but some of the less central parks, such as the *Parc Monceau*, the *Parc de Montsouris*, and the *Parc des Buttes-Chaumont*, likewise repay a visit.—Cemeteries are open 7–6.30 in summer, 8–4.30 in winter. The chief are *Père-Lachaise* and the cemeteries of *Montmartre* and *Montparnasse*; and many will be interested in the little *Cimetière de Picpus*.

HOURS AND CHARGES OF ADMISSION TO THE CHIEF SIGHTS

†Archives	2–5	50 fr.
†Balzac's House	1.30–5	20 fr.
†Beaux-Arts, Ecole des	Thurs. 2–4	closed July 1st–Oct. 15th.
Bibliothèque Nationale	9–6	free; closed Sun.
Musée des Médailles	9.30–12, 2–4.45	10 fr., closed Sun.
†**Chantilly,** Château de	1.30–4.30 or 5.30	50 fr., closed Fri., and Nov.–Feb.
†Conciergerie	10–12, 1.30–4 or 5	30 fr., Sun. 15 fr.
Eiffel Tower	10.45–5	70–150 fr.
Fontainebleau, Palais de	10 or 11–12, 2–5	30 fr.
†Gobelins	Thurs. 2–4	free.
†Institut de France	Sat. 10–12, 1.30–4.30, Sun. 10–12	free.
Invalides:		
Tomb of Napoleon	9.30–5	30 fr.
†Musée de l'Armée	10–12.45, 1.30–5 or 5.30	10 fr. per section; closed Sun. morning.
Jardin des Plantes:		
Menagerie	9–5 or 6	20 fr.
†Galleries	1.30–5	15 fr.
†**Louvre**	10–4 or 5	30 fr., Sun. free.
†Maisons-Laffitte, Château	10–12, 2–4 or 5	30 fr.; closed Fri. morning.
†Malmaison, La	10 or 11–12, 1.30–4 or 5	30 fr., Sun. 15 fr.
Mint	2–5	free; closed Wed.
†Musée d'Antiquités Nationales (St-Germain)	10–12, 1.30–5	30 fr., Sun. 15 fr.
† „ **des Arts Décoratifs**	10–12, 2–5	30 fr., Sun. free
„ **des Arts et Métiers**	1.30–5.30, Sun. 10–5	16 fr., Sun. free; closed Mon.
† „ d'Art Moderne	10–5	30 fr., Sun. free.
† „ **Carnavalet**	10–12, 2–5 or 6	30 fr., Sun. free.
† „ Cognacq-Jay	10–12, 2–5	20 fr.
† „ **de Cluny**	10–12.45, 2–5	30 fr., Sun. 15 fr.
† „ Guimet	10–5	30 fr., Sun. 15 fr.
„ **Jacquemart-André**	1–4 or 5	20 fr., Tues. & Sun. 10 fr., closed Fri.
† „ **du Jeu-de-Paume**	10–12.45, 2–5	30 fr., Sun. 15 fr.
† „ Marmottan	Sun. & Thurs. 2–5	30 fr.
„ **Nissim de Camondo**	Sun. 10–12.30, 2–5, Tues., Thurs. & Sat. 1–5	30 fr., closed July 14th–Sept. 15th.
„ de l'Opéra	10–5	10 fr., closed Sun.
† „ Rodin	1–4 or 6	30 fr., Sun. 15 fr.
† „ Victor-Hugo	10–12.30, 2–5	25 fr., Sun. free.
†**Notre-Dame,** Towers	10–5	30 fr., Sun. 15 fr.
Palais de Chaillot:		
†Musée de l'Homme	10–4	30 fr.
† „ de la Marine	10–6	30 fr.
† „ des Monuments Français	10–5	30 fr.
Palais de Justice	11–6	free, closed Sun.
†Pantheon	10–4 or 5	30 fr.
†**St-Denis,** Tombs	10–12, 2–4 or 5	30 fr., closed Sun. morning.
†**Sainte-Chapelle**	10–12, 1.30–4 or 5	30 fr., Sun. 15 fr.
†Sèvres Museum	10–4 or 5	30 fr., Sun. 15 fr.
†Trianons, The	2–5 or 6	30 fr.
†**Versailles,** Palais de	10–5	30 fr.
Vincennes, Château	10–4.30 or 5.30	20 fr., closed Fri.
Parc Zoölogique	9–4	30 fr.

† All museums, etc., thus marked are closed all day on Tuesday

X. CALENDAR OF EVENTS

The following is a list of some annual events of interest taking place in and near Paris on fixed or approximately fixed dates.

JAN. 1ST	Jour de l'An; the chief day for exchanging gifts (étrennes).
JAN. 3RD	Pilgrimage to the tomb of St. Geneviève at St-Etienne-du-Mont.
JAN. 6TH	Journée des Rois (Epiphany); boxing-day for bakers, who provide a special cake (galette) for the occasion.
FEB. 2ND	La Chandeleur (Candlemas); tossing the pancake in French households.
SHROVE TUESDAY	Mardi Gras; crowds on the Boulevards.
MID-LENT (4th Thurs.)	Mi-Carême; procession in the Champs-Elysées.
PALM SUNDAY	Sprigs of box ('buis bénit') carried by the faithful.
MARCH (end)	Concours Hippique (Horse Show) at the Cercle de l'Etrier, Bois de Boulogne (or in June).
APRIL (first half)	Concours Lépine, for inventions of the past year, Quai de New York.
GOOD FRIDAY	Holy Sepulchres decorated in the churches. Butchers' shops closed.
APRIL 15TH	Opening of Salon des Indépendants, Musée d'Art Moderne; Salon des Humoristes, 11 Rue Royale.
APRIL (last week)	Azalea show at the Jardin Fleuriste, Porte d'Auteuil.
APRIL (last Sun.)	Grand Prix de Paris (motor race at Montlhéry).
APRIL 30TH	'Vernissage' (varnishing day) at the Salon.
MAY 1ST	Salon opens. Lily of the valley sold in the streets.
MAY 6TH	Feast of St. Joan of Arc; decoration of her statues.—Lily of the valley fête at Rambouillet.
MAY 8TH	Victory celebrations commemorating the capitulation of 1945.
MAY 10TH	Exhibition of the Femmes Peintres et Sculpteurs in the Musée d'Art Moderne opens.
MAY (2nd Sun.)	French football cup final at Colombes.
MAY (second half)	Foire de Paris at the Porte de Versailles.
MAY 28TH	Decoration of the Mur de Fédérés.
MAY 30TH	American Memorial Day; services at Holy Trinity, Av. George-V, and Mont-Valérien Cemetery.
JUNE (1st Sun.)	Prix de Diane at Chantilly.
JUNE 3RD	Fête-Dieu (Corpus Christi). Processions of 'First Communion' children.
JUNE (2nd Sun.)	Prix du Jockey-Club (the 'French Derby') at Chantilly.
JUNE (2nd Mon.)	Prix du Président at Vincennes.
JUNE 13TH–27TH	Fête de Neuilly.
JUNE 16TH	Pilgrimage to the Sacré-Cœur.
JUNE 16TH–19TH	Dog show at the Porte de Versailles.
MID-JUNE	Roses in bloom at Bagatelle.
JUNE (second half)	Special display in shops in the Faubourg St-Honoré.
JUNE (3rd Sun.)	Grand Steeplechase at Auteuil.
JUNE (4th Fri.)	Journée des Drags at Auteuil.
JUNE (4th Sun.)	Grand Prix at Longchamp.
JUNE (last week)	Versailles Week. Indoor and open-air concerts and ballet.
JUNE–JULY	Sailing regattas at Asnières and Courbevoie.
JULY 9TH	Fête de l'eau at Rambouillet.
JULY 13TH	Start of the 'Tour de France' bicycle race.
JULY 14TH	Fête Nationale; review of soldiers in the Champs-Elysées; firework display at the Pont-Neuf.

AUG. 7TH . . .	Finish of the 'Tour de France' bicycle race in the Parc des Princes.
AUG. (end) . . .	'Coupe de Paris' (rowing championship of France) decided at Bry-sur-Marne.
SEPT. 5TH . . .	Victory of the Marne; commemoration at Meaux.
SEPT. (1st Sun.) . .	Bicycling championship at Longchamp.
OCT. (beginning) . .	Salon de l'Automobile in the Grand Palais.
OCT. (1st Sun.) . .	Journée du Souvenir. Athletic meeting commemorating the Liberation.
OCT. (2nd Sun.) . .	Prix de l'Arc de Triomphe at Longchamp.—Harvest festival in Montmartre.
OCT. 9TH . . .	Feast of St. Denis.—Pilgrimage to the Basilica.
OCT. (second half) .	Chrysanthemum show at the Jardin Fleuriste, Porte d'Auteuil.
OCT. (4th Sun.) . .	Prix du Conseil Municipal at Longchamp.
OCT. 25TH . . .	Annual General Meeting of the Academies of the Institut.
NOV. 1ST . . .	Toussaint } Decoration of graves in the principal cemeteries.
NOV. 2ND . . .	Jour des Morts }
NOV. 11TH . . .	Armistice Day.
NOV. 22ND . . .	Sainte-Cécile; choral mass in St-Eustache.
NOV. 25TH . . .	Sainte-Catherine; procession in the Boulevards of unmarried work-girls who have reached the age of 25; Mass at N.D. de Bonne-Nouvelle; decoration of the saint's statue, Rue de Cléry.
DEC. 24TH . . .	Midnight masses. Children put their shoes out for presents.
DEC. 25TH . . .	Noël. Crèches decorated in the churches.

XI. SOME BOOKS ABOUT PARIS

In the following brief list are the names of sixteen books in English which touch upon a variety of aspects. It may be found useful as a suggestive basic bibliography from which the average traveller will be able to pursue his study of Paris.

The standard work on Paris may be taken to be *Okey (Thomas)*: The Story of Paris (1906; reprinted 1919).

Bidou (H.): Paris (1939). *Escholier (Raymond)*: Paris (1930). *Harrison (Wilmot)*: Memorable Paris Houses (1893). *Hiatt (Charles)*: Notre Dame de Paris (1902; Bell's Cathedral Handbooks). *Lonergan (Walter F.)*: Historic Churches of Paris (1896). *Lucas (E. V.)*: A Wanderer in Paris (1909); Introducing Paris (1928). *Martin (B. E. and C. M.)*: The Stones of Paris in History and Letters (1899; reprinted 1912). *Maurois (André)*: A History of France (1949). *Maxwell (Constantia)*: The English Traveller in France 1698–1815 (1932). *Studio Zenith*: Paris—charm of two Cities (1949; photographs of Paris and London). *Potter (Mary Knight)*: The Art of the Louvre, with a short History of the Building and Gallery (1904). *Robinson (W.)*: The Parks, Promenades and Gardens of Paris (1869). *Whelpton (E.)*: Paris To-day (1948). *Wolff (Jetta Sophia)*: Historic Paris (1921).

I. THE RIGHT BANK

On the RIGHT BANK (Rive Droite) of the Seine lies the most important part of Paris. On 'this side of the water' are most of the leading hotels, restaurants and theatres, the handsomest and most expensive shops, the busiest streets, and the most fashionable residential quarters. Here also are the Louvre, and most of the other great public collections, the Hôtel de Ville, the Palais-Royal, the Bibliothèque Nationale, and the Palais de Chaillot.

---

1. FROM THE PLACE DE L'OPÉRA TO THE TUILERIES.
Rue de la Paix, Rue St-Honoré, Rue de Rivoli.

MÉTRO stations: *Opéra* (lines 3, 7, 8); *Palais-Royal* (lines 1 and 7); *Concorde* (lines 1, 8, 12).—MOTOR-BUSES: Opéra (routes 20, 21, 27, 52, 66, 68, 95); Palais-Royal (routes 21, 27, 48, 67, 69, 72, 73, 74, 85, 95); Concorde (routes 52, 72, 73, 84, 94).

The **Place de l'Opéra,** with the imposing façade of the opera-house as its architectural background on the N., is, like the Place du Palais-Royal at the other end of the Av. de l'Opéra, one of the busiest centres of traffic in Paris. Seven important streets meet here. The Boul. des Capucines crosses it from W. to E. The Rue Auber and the Rue Halévy, to the left and right of the opera-house, lead to the Boul. Haussmann, the former serving as an approach to the Gare St-Lazare. On the S. side of the square radiate the Rue du Quatre-Septembre (leading to the Bourse); the AVENUE DE L'OPÉRA, an important thoroughfare of handsome shops leading to (nearly ½ m.) the Place du Théâtre-Français; and the Rue de la Paix. In the angle between the Boul. des Capucines and the Rue Auber are the Grand-Hôtel and the Café de la Paix.

Mme de Montespan and the painter Rigaud had houses in the Rue Louis-le-Grand; while Napoleon and Josephine Beauharnais were married in 1796 at No. 3 Rue d'Antin, then the Mairie of the 2nd Arrondissement. The *Fontaine Gaillon,* in the Rue St-Augustin, is by Visconti and Jacquot (1823).

The magnificent ***Opéra** or *Opera House* was built in 1861–75 from the designs of *Charles Garnier*. In superficial area (3 acres) it is the largest theatre in the world, but it contains only 2158 seats as compared with the 3600 of the Châtelet and the 2800 of the Scala at Milan. The director (or directors) is appointed by government.

The first opera-house in Paris was established in 1669 by the Abbé Perrin, Champeron, and the Marquis de Sourdéac on the left bank, between the Rue de Seine and the Rue Mazarine. The first director was the celebrated Lulli, under whom it acquired its secondary title of *Académie Royale de Musique*.

The façade, approached by a broad flight of steps, is lavishly decorated with coloured marble and sculptures. The outermost arches on each side of the arcade opening into the vestibule are flanked with sculptured groups, including (l.) the Celebrated Dance, by *Carpeaux*; above these are medallions of musical composers. Between the monolithic Corinthian columns of the loggia on the first story are bronze-gilt busts of other composers, and on the attic story is a row of bronze-gilt masks, with figures at the ends. Behind the low dome of the auditorium is a huge triangular pediment (indicating the front of the stage), crowned with a statue of Apollo of the Golden Lyre.

The side façades of the opera-house are adorned with busts of musicians and the coats-of-arms of their native towns. The E. pavilion in the Rue Halévy is the subscribers' entrance, and here and in the Rue Gluck are fine bronze candelabra by *Carrier-Belleuse*. The 'Pavilion d'Honneur' on the W., in the Rue Auber, is the entrance to the Library and Museum, and here stands the monument to Charles Garnier, by *Pascal*, with bust by *Carpeaux*.

In the first vestibule are statues of composers; the second vestibule contains the box-office. Visitors entering by the subscribers' entrance pass through a large circular vestibule, on the ceiling of which is a 'Mauresque' inscription in which Garnier, the architect, has signed and dated his work, and reach the second vestibule through a corridor with a bronze fountain-figure. The *GRAND STAIRCASE, with its white marble steps 33 ft. wide and its onyx balustrade on a base of rosso antico, is one of the most striking features of the building. On the first floor, where it divides into two branches, is the entrance to the stalls and the amphitheatre, flanked with caryatids representing Tragedy and Comedy. Monolithic marble columns rise hence to the third floor, and support a vaulted ceiling. On each floor are balconies commanding a view of the staircase below. The Avant-Foyer leads into the spacious and elaborate *GRAND FOYER, with its noteworthy allegorical paintings by *Paul Baudry*, representing the Progress of the Arts. Seven glass doors communicate with the LOGGIA overlooking the Place de l'Opéra; by the middle door is a bust of Garnier by *Carpeaux*. The *AUDITORIUM, decorated in red and gold, has four tiers of boxes. The ceiling, resting on eight great pillars of polished marble, has paintings on copper of the Hours of the Day and Night, by *Lenepveu*. The STAGE (46 ft. high, 50 ft. wide, 82 ft. deep) is said to be the loftiest and widest in existence. Behind the scenes is the Foyer de la Danse, the scene of many paintings by Degas, with a mirror measuring 23 by 33 ft.

The **Musée de l'Opéra** (open daily 10–5, except Sun. and holidays, and the fortnight following the Sun. after Easter; adm 10 fr.), on the first floor of the Pavillon d'Honneur in the Rue Auber (l.), is an admirably arranged little theatrical museum. The library consists of a complete collection of operas and ballets performed at the Paris Opéra since its foundation.

The Rue de la Paix, which leads from the S.W. corner of the Place de l'Opéra to the Place Vendôme, is the 'Bond Street' of Paris, famous for its luxurious shops. Near the end of the street the Rue des Petits-Champs leads to the left to the Av. de l'Opéra.

The octagonal *Place Vendôme is surrounded with houses of uniform design by Hardouin-Mansart (d. 1708). Originally called the Place des Conquêtes, it owes its present name to a mansion built here in 1603 by César, Duc de Vendôme, son of Henri IV and Gabrielle d'Estrées. The Hôtel du Rhin was the residence of Louis Napoleon as deputy in 1848. At Nos. 11 and 13 is the *Ministère de la Justice.* Chopin died in 1849 at No. 12; and Law (p. 37) lived at No. 21 as controller general of finance. In the centre of the Place is the **Vendôme Column,** constructed by *Denon* in 1806–10 in the style of Trajan's Column at Rome. The statue of Napoleon on the top is a copy (1863) of the original statue by Chaudet.

Encircling the column, which is 143 ft. high and c. 12 ft. in diameter, is a spiral band of bronze bas-reliefs, designed by *Bergeret* and made of the metal of Russian and Austrian cannon, in which the principal feats of arms in the campaigns of 1805–7 are glorified.

The Rue de Castiglione continues the line of the Rue de la Paix from the S. side of the square to the Rue de Rivoli.

The long Rue St-Honoré, which crosses it, was the fashionable street in the 17–18th centuries. To the W. (r.), near the corner of the Rue Cambon, is the church of the *Assumption,* built in 1670 as the chapel of the convent of the Haudriettes. No. 265 was the birthplace of Sarah Bernhardt (1844–1923), and at No. 398 once stood the house where Robespierre lodged with the cabinet-maker Duplay.

In the Rue Cambon, behind the church, is the *Cour des Comptes,* a court dealing with official finance. Alfred de Musset died in 1857 at No. 6 Rue du Mont-Thabor, and Washington Irving lodged at No. 4 in 1821.—No. 2 Rue St-Florentin, once the *Hôtel de la Vrillière,* was built by Chalgrin in 1765-67; it was occupied by Lazare Carnot and by Tsar Alexander I in 1815; Talleyrand died there in 1838.

In the part of the Rue St-Honoré to the E. of the Rue de Castiglione is the baroque church of **St-Roch,** containing many interesting works of art of the 17–18th cent. and attended by a fashionable congregation. Begun under Louis XIV by *J. Lemercier* in 1653, the church was built for the most part in the reign of Louis XV by *Robert de Cotte,* and it was finished in 1740 by his son *Jules de Cotte,* who is responsible for the façade with its Doric and Corinthian columns.

Interior (413 ft. long). On the pillar to the left of the organ is a medallion of the dramatist Pierre Corneille, who died in 1684 at No. 18 in the neighbouring Rue d'Argenteuil and is buried in the church.—In the first bay of the E. Aisle (r.) are a bust of François de Créquy (d. 1687), by *Coysevox*, and a medallion of Mme Lalive de Jully, by *Falconet*. In the second bay: bust of the painter Pierre Mignard (d. 1695), by *Martin-Desjardins*, tomb of the Comte d'Harcourt (d. 1666), by *Renard*; statue of the diplomatic Card. Dubois (d. 1723), by *G. Coustou*. The fifth chapel, in the transept, has a painting by *Doyen* of the Healing of the 'Mal des Ardents.' Against the choir pillar to the left is a statue of St. Roch.—AMBULATORY. The marble *Group of the Nativity behind the altar is by *Michel Anguier*.—In the CHAPELLE DES CATÉCHISMES (open only during Holy Week; at other times apply to the keeper) is a marble Christ on the Cross by *Michel Anguier*, a kneeling figure by *Le Moyne* of the Comtesse de Feuquières, Mignard's daughter, as Mary Magdalen, and a statue of the Virgin by *Deseine*.—We return by the W. AISLE. On the last pillar of the ambulatory (r.) is a bust of the landscape-gardener André Le Nôtre (d. 1707), by the elder *Coysevox*. By the opposite pillar is a figure of Christ at Gethsemane, by *Falconet*. In the transept, the Preaching of St. Denis, by *Vien*. In the last chapel beyond the transept is a group of the Baptism of Christ by *Le Moyne*.

The neighbouring streets were the scene of Bonaparte's suppression of the royalist rising of Oct. 5th, 1795; some marks of his 'whiff of grape-shot' may still be detected on the front of the church. The Marché St-Honoré, N.W. of the church, stands on the site of the Dominican convent where the Jacobin Club met in 1789–94; and in the Rue Ste-Anne, to the N.E., Bossuet died in 1704.

The PLACE DU THÉÂTRE-FRANÇAIS, at the S. end of the Av. de l'Opéra, contains two fountains by Davioud. At the corner of the theatre is a marble monument to the poet Alfred de Musset (1810–57), by Antonin Mercié (1906).

The **Théâtre-Français,** which forms the S.W. wing of the Palais-Royal, was built in 1786–90 by *Victor Louis*. The façades were rebuilt in 1860–64, and the whole building was restored after a fire in 1900.

As an institution the Théâtre-Français or Comédie-Française dates from the amalgamation in 1680 of the Hôtel de Bourgogne actors with Molière's old company, which had already absorbed the Théâtre du Marais. In 1812 Napoleon signed a decree at Moscow reorganising the Comédie-Française, which is still a private company but is controlled by a director nominated by the government and enjoys an annual state subsidy.

The medallions of Corneille, Molière, Racine, and Victor Hugo under the portico in the Rue de Richelieu are by *Denys Puech*; on the Palais-Royal side is a bust of Larroumet by *Roussel*.

The vestibule contains a statue of Talma, the tragedian, by *David d'Angers*; statues of Tragedy (Rachel as 'Phèdre') by *Duret* and Comedy (Mlle Mars as Célimène in 'Le Misanthrope') by *Thomas*; and a statue of George Sand by *Clésinger*. The staircase and foyer are adorned with busts of eminent dramatists. In the foyer is the seated *Statue of Voltaire, by *Houdon*. The ceiling of the auditorium was painted by *Albert Besnard*; on the side nearest the stage are Molière, Racine, Corneille, and Victor Hugo.

The PLACE DU PALAIS-ROYAL, immediately S.E. of the Place du Théâtre-Français, is one of the busiest points in Paris. It has the *Palais-Royal* on its N. side, the *Grands Magasins du Louvre* on the E., the *Grand-Hôtel du Louvre* on the W., and the *Ministère des Finances*, a part of the Palais du Louvre, on the S.

The *RUE DE RIVOLI, a fine thoroughfare nearly 2 m. in length, running E. and W. from the Place du Palais-Royal, was constructed in 1811–56 and named in honour of Bonaparte's victory over the Austrians in 1797. For its E. portion, continued by the Rue St-Antoine to the Bastille, see p. 25. The W. portion, from the Palais-Royal to the Place de la Concorde, skirts the **Louvre** (Rte. 18) and the Tuileries Gardens. The N. side of the street, W. of the Rue du Louvre, is uniform in design, with covered arcades and balconies, and is lined with hotels and shops.

A short distance to the W. of the Place du Palais-Royal the Rue de Rivoli crosses the small *Place de Rivoli*, with a spirited bronze-gilt statue by Frémiet of Joan of Arc.

The ***Jardin des Tuileries** (closed in winter at 8 p.m., in summer at 10 p.m.), formal gardens of 63 acres adorned with a wealth of statues, extends from the Place du Carrousel to the Place de la Concorde, and is divided into two sections by the Avenue Paul-Déroulède. The E. part is laid out on the site of the Tuileries Palace.

The ARC DE TRIOMPHE DU CARROUSEL, a reduced copy of the Arch of Septimius Severus at Rome (47 ft. high instead of 75 ft.), begun in 1806 from the designs of *Fontaine* and *Percier* to commemorate the victories of Napoleon I in 1805, was formerly the main entrance to the courtyard of the Tuileries.

On the top are figures of Soldiers of the Empire and a bronze chariot-group by *Bosio* (1828) representing the Restoration of the Bourbons. The four sides are decorated with marble bas-reliefs: the Battle of Austerlitz; the Capitulation of Ulm; the Meeting between Napoleon and Alexander at Tilsit; the Entry into Munich; the Entry into Vienna; and the Peace of Pressburg.

The PLACE DU CARROUSEL, now enclosed on three sides by the buildings of the Louvre, was down to the middle of the 19th cent. a small square amidst a labyrinth of narrow streets. It derives its name from a kind of equestrian fête given by Louis XIV in 1662. The guillotine was set up here in 1793 but was later transferred to the Place de la Concorde. The archways on the S. side give on the Quai des Tuileries, opposite the Pont du Carrousel. On the E. side is the monument to Léon Gambetta (1838–82), the 'fiery tribune,' by Boileau and Aubé (1888). Behind this lies the *Square du*

Carrousel, which commands a renowned vista up to the Place de l'Etoile.

In the centre of the square is a bronze group, The Children of Cain, by *Landowski*, and in the further plot is an equestrian statue of Lafayette (1757–1834), by Paul Wayland Bartlett, presented to France in 1900 by the school-children of the United States. The principal entrance to the **Louvre Galleries** (see Rte. 18) is in the Pavillon Denon, on the S. side of the Square du Carrousel.

The Palais des Tuileries, once the centre and soul of Paris, which stood on the E. side of the present Avenue Paul-Déroulède, no longer exists, except for the *Pavillon de Flore* on the S. side and the *Pavillon de Marsan* on the N., both of which have been restored or rebuilt and now form the ends of the W. wings of the Louvre.

The palace was begun by *Philibert Delorme* in 1564 for Catherine de Médicis, widow of Henri II, on a site beyond the city walls known as the 'Sablonnière' and occupied by tile-kilns (tuileries). Delorme was succeeded by *Jean Bullant* and then, in 1595, by *Baptiste du Cerceau*, who built the Pavillon de Flore. The Pavillon de Marsan was built under Louis XIV in 1660–65, by *Louis Levau* or *Le Vau* and his son-in-law *François d'Orbay*. Louis XVI was brought from Versailles to the Tuileries by the Paris mob in 1789, and confined there (except during his ineffectual attempt to escape in 1791) until the riot of Aug. 10th, 1792, when the Swiss Guards were massacred. In 1793–96 it was the headquarters of the Convention. The Tuileries was later the permanent residence of Napoleon I, Louis XVIII, Charles X, Louis-Philippe, and Napoleon III. In May 1871, the Communards set fire to the building, which, like the Hôtel de Ville, was completely gutted. The walls stood until 1884, and the site of the ruins was converted into a garden in 1889.

The W. part of the Jardin des Tuileries was the private garden of the palace and has been little altered since it was laid out by Le Nôtre in 1664. It was the favourite promenade of the fashionable nobility of Paris until superseded by the Palais-Royal just before the Revolution.

Among the flower-beds are arranged groups of decorative sculpture, notably 18th cent. works by *Guillaume* and *Nicolas Coustou*, *Coysevox*, and *Le Paultre*. On the S. side is a monument to Waldeck-Rousseau (1846–1904), by *Marqueste* (1910).

The central avenue, beyond the round pond, is flanked with clumps of chestnuts and lime trees enclosing gravelled plots and lawns. The first two are known as the 'Carrés d'Atalante' or 'Jardins de Robespierre' and contain two semicircular marble benches set up under the Convention for the old men to watch the floral games.

Terraces extend along both sides of the gardens. On the S., overlooking the Quai des Tuileries, is the *Terrasse du Bord-de-l'Eau* or *Terrasse de l'Orangerie*, at the W. end of which is the *Orangery* (1853), now containing paintings by Monet (see Rte. 28). Beside the steps leading up to it is 'Hommage à Cézanne,' a sculpture by *Maillol*. The *Terrasse des Feuillants*, skirting the Rue de Rivoli on the N. side of the gardens, is a popular promenade named after a Benedictine monastery which in 1791 was the meeting-place of the Club des Feuillants, representing the moderate republicans, which included Lavoisier and André Chénier among its members. At the W. end of the terrace is the **Jeu de Paume** (Rte. 28), a real tennis-court built in 1861, now devoted to paintings of the Impressionist School of the Musée du Louvre.

The monument to Nurse Cavell, which formerly stood against the E. end of the building, was removed by the Germans during the Occupation. Near by to the E., stood the *Manège,* the riding-school of the palace, used as the meeting-place of the National Assembly in 1789–93, where Louis XVI was condemned to death in 1793.

From the terrace staircases descend to the *Allée des Orangers,* many of the orange trees in which are of great age. At the foot of the staircase at the W. end are fragments of the façade of the Tuileries and more groups of sculpture; while on the S. side of the Jeu de Paume is the sunny terrace known as *Petite-Provence,* adorned with a monument to Charles Perrault (1628–1703), the writer of fairy tales, at whose suggestion the gardens were thrown open to the public.

The large octagonal fountain-basin, surrounded by statuary of the 17–18th cent., by the *Coustous* and *Van Cleve,* is the 'Round Pond' of Paris, where children sail their model yachts (yachts for hire).

At the W. end of the gardens is a gateway leading to the Place de la Concorde, with pillars crowned by *Equestrian figures of Fame and Mercury, by *Coysevox* (brought from Marly). A tablet in a recess on the left commemorates the first balloon ascent from Paris (Dec. 1783).

The ***Place de la Concorde,** at the W. end of the Tuileries Gardens and the Rue de Rivoli, is one of the largest and most beautiful squares in the world.

The present appearance of the square dates from 1854. It was first laid out, in a vacant space outside the city, by Louis XV, after whom it was named, and to whom a bronze statue was erected in 1763. In 1792 the statue of Louis XV was replaced by a huge figure of Liberty, and the name of the square was changed to Place de la Révolution. Louis XVI was guillotined here (on the spot now occupied by the fountain nearest the river) on Jan. 21st, 1793, and between May 1793 and May 1795 nearly 3000 persons suffered the same fate, the most notable being Charlotte Corday (July 17th, 1793), Marie Antoinette (Oct. 16th), the Girondins (Oct. 31st), Philippe-Egalité (Nov. 6th). Mme Roland (Nov. 10th), Hébert (March 24th, 1794), Danton (April 5th), Mme Elisabeth (May 9th), and Robespierre (July 28th). The square first received its present name in 1795 at the end of the Reign of Terror.

The ***Obelisk of Luxor,** a monolith of pink syenite, 75 ft. high and 250 tons in weight, commemorates in its hieroglyphics the deeds of Rameses II (13th cent. B.C.) and originally stood before a temple at Thebes in Upper Egypt. It was presented to Louis-Philippe in 1831 by Mohammed Ali (the donor also of Cleopatra's Needle in London). The pedestal is of Breton granite. The two fountains, by *Hittorf,* are copies of those in the piazza of St. Peter's at Rome; the statues represent Inland (N.) and Marine (S.) Navigation.

The eight stone pavilions round the square, built by *Gabriel* in the 18th cent., support statues personifying the great provincial cities of France: Lyons and Marseilles by *Petitot,* Bordeaux and Nantes by *Callouet,* Rouen and Brest by *Cortot,* Lille and Strasbourg (easily the two finest) by *Pradier.* Strasbourg (as capital of the lost Alsace) was, from 1871, hung with crape and wreaths, and on a shield appeared the date of its capitulation (Sept. 27th, 1870) and the question 'When?' History answered this question on Nov. 22nd, 1918.

On the N. side of the Place de la Concorde are two handsome mansions designed by Gabriel in 1763–72 (with pediment sculptures by Slodtz and the younger Coustou) and originally intended for the reception of ambassadors and other distinguished foreigners. That to the right is now the *Ministère de la Marine* (Admiralty; entrance 2 Rue Royale), that to the left is divided between the *Automobile Club* and the *Hôtel de Crillon*. In this building was signed the treaty of 1778, by which France recognised the independence of the United States. Between these buildings passes the Rue Royale, at the end of which appears the Madeleine.—On the S. side of the Place is the Seine, here spanned by the *Pont de la Concorde* (p. 69).

2. FROM THE PLACE DE LA CONCORDE TO THE ARC DE TRIOMPHE.

MÉTRO stations: *Concorde* (lines 1, 8, 12); *Champs-Elysées-Clemenceau, Franklin D. Roosevelt, George V* (line 1); *Etoile* (lines 1, 2, 6).—MOTOR-BUSES: Concorde (routes 52, 72, 73, 84, 94); Champs-Elysées (routes 52, 72, 73, 84, 94); Etoile (routes 30, 31, 92).

To the W. of the Place de la Concorde extend the ***Champs-Elysées,** through which the wide *Avenue des Champs-Elysées* ascends to the Arc de Triomphe, c. 1¼ m. distant. On two lofty pedestals at the beginning of the avenue are the fine groups of the *Marly Horses* by G. Coustou—" ces marbres hennissants " as Victor Hugo calls them—which were brought from the Château de Marly in 1795 and now form pendant to the winged horses at the W. entrance to the Tuileries.

The area, drained and planted in 1670, was improved and rearranged by the Marquis de Marigny, brother of Mme de Pompadour, in 1764. Under the Second Empire it was the fashionable promenade of Paris.

The Champs-Elysées consist of two parts. The first, forming a park nearly ½ m. long and ¼ m. wide, extends to the Rond Point des Champs-Elysées; the second, the continuation of the Avenue des Champs-Elysées thence to the Arc de Triomphe, is flanked by wealthy private mansions, large shops, and hotels. At night the view of the brilliantly lighted avenue from the Place de la Concorde is very striking. The cafés-concerts and restaurants at the E. end are fashionable resorts in summer. The part between the main avenue and the Elysée Palace is a favourite children's playground, with roundabouts, puppet-shows, and cake-stalls. The drinking-fountains here and elsewhere in Paris were presented by Sir Richard Wallace (d. 1890).

Skirting the N. (r.) side of the Champs-Elysées is the AVENUE GABRIEL, at the E. end of which is the *American Embassy*, at the corner of the Rue Boissy-d'Anglas. Farther on are (r.) the gardens of the British Embassy and (l.) the monument to Alphonse Daudet (1840–97), by St-Marceaux. Next come the gardens of the *Palais de l'Elysée*, the official residence of the President of the Republic. To the S. of the Avenue Gabriel, among the trees, are the *Théâtre des Ambassadeurs* and the *Pavillon de l'Elysée*.

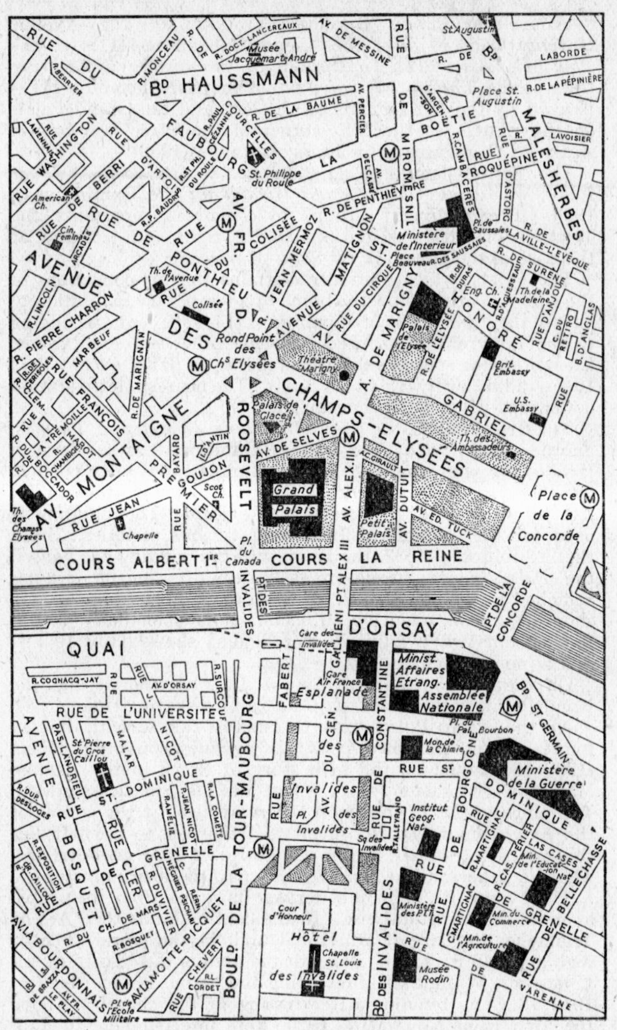

I, CHAMPS-ELYSÉES–INVALIDES

From the Place Georges-Clemenceau, the Avenue Marigny leads N., and the Avenue Alexandre-III S. to the *Pont Alexandre-III*. To the left of the former, among the trees, is the *Théâtre Marigny*, whilst the Av. Alexandre-III is flanked by the Petit Palais on the left, and the Grand Palais on the right. By the S.E. corner of the Place is a bronze statue of Clemenceau, by François Cogné (1932).

The **Petit Palais,** or *Palais des Beaux-Arts de la Ville de Paris*, was erected by *Charles Girault* for the Exhibition of 1900. The pediment group, by *Injalbert*, represents the Triumph of Paris; the groups to the right and left and at the base of the dome are by *Saint-Marceaux*.

The Palais, which normally contains the art-collections of the City of Paris, is now the home of a temporary exhibition of part of the French school of paintings (14–19th cent.) belonging to the Louvre, and is used also for other art exhibitions. Except during special exhibitions it is open daily (except Fri.) 10–5; adm. 30 fr. (15 fr. on Sun.). The nearest Métro station is Champs-Elysées-Clemenceau (line 1).

The **Grand Palais,** the work of *Deglane, Louvet,* and *Thomas*, another building of the 1900 Exhibition, has a classical façade, 200 yds. long, with Ionic columns and a lofty portico. On the great pillars flanking the portico are statues of (l.) Art by *Verlet* and (r.) Peace by *Lombard*. The building is used for the annual exhibitions of various societies. Since the Exhibition of 1937, the W. part of the building has housed the *Palais de la Découverte*, a centre of scientific studies attached to the University, in which are held lectures, cinema shows, etc., on scientific subjects. It is open daily 10–12, 2–4 (except Fri.); adm. 20 fr.; cinema shows daily at 3.30 and 5 (no extra charge).

On the N. side of the Grand Palais, between it and the Rond-Point, is the *Palais de Glace*, an ice-skating rink.

At the Rond-Point des Champs-Elysées, with its six fountains and its flower-beds, six avenues converge. Heine (1799–1856) died on the fifth story of No. 3 in the Avenue Matignon (r.), after years spent on his 'mattress-grave.' The office of *Le Figaro* is on the right also, at the corner of the Av. Franklin D. Roosevelt. Farther on, to the left, lies the wealthy *Quartier Marbeuf*. At No. 2 Rue de Berri (r.) Thomas Jefferson lived in 1785–89, as American minister.

The Place de l'Etoile derives its name from its twelve avenues radiating starwise. In the centre stands the ***Arc de Triomphe,** the largest triumphal arch in the world (147 ft. high and 149 ft. wide). Beneath the arch is the *Tomb of an Unknown Warrior, representing the heroic French dead of 1914–18. The remains, after resting in the chamber above the arch from Nov. 11th, 1920, were interred here in Jan.

1921, and now lie beneath a constantly burning flame which is revived every evening by a party of ex-service men. At the foot of the tomb is a bronze plaque presented by Allied Supreme Headquarters. The plaque bears a symbolic representation of the 'Shaef' shoulder-flash, and is dated Aug. 25th, 1945, the day of the liberation of Paris from the German invader.

Designed by *Chalgrin* and begun by Napoleon I in 1806, the Arc de Triomphe was not completed till the reign of Louis-Philippe (1836). The main façades are adorned with colossal groups in high-relief: facing the Champs-Elysées are (r.) the *Departure of the Army in 1792, by *Rude*, and (l.) the Triumph of Napoleon in 1810, by *Cortot*; facing the Av. de la Grande-Armée are (r.) the Resistance of the French in 1814 and (l.) the Peace of 1815, both by *Etex*. The four spandrels of the main archway contain figures of Fame by *Pradier*, and those of the smaller archway have sculptures by *Vallois* (S. side) and *Bra* (N. side). Above are panels in relief of the campaigns of 1792–1805. On the row of shields in the attic story are inscribed the names of the 172 battles of the Republic and the Empire, and below the side-arches are the names of the 386 generals who took part in the campaigns, the names of those who fell in action being underlined.

The platform on the top of the arch (open daily, except Tues., 10–4 or 5; 30 fr., 15 fr. on Sun.; lift, 20 fr. extra) commands a splendid panoramic *View of Paris.

3. THE GRANDS BOULEVARDS.

The ***Grands Boulevards,** a succession of wide thoroughfares extending in a curve from the Place de la Concorde to the Bastille (2¾ m.), have been laid out since the Revolution on the site of the inner fortifications or 'bulwarks', erected by Etienne Marcel in 1368 and demolished in the reign of Louis XIV. Though the Western Boulevards are no longer a centre of fashion, their animated and cosmopolitan street-life, and their tasteful and tempting shops, cafés, and restaurants make them still the chief attraction of Paris for the majority of visitors.

A. The Western Boulevards: from the Rue Royale to the Porte St-Martin.

MÉTRO stations: (lines 1, 8, 12); *Madeleine* (lines 8 and 12); *Opéra* (lines 3, 7, 8).—MOTOR-BUSES: Concorde (routes 52, 72, 73, 84, 94); Madeleine (routes 52, 84, 94); Opéra (routes 20, 21, 27, 66, 68, 95).

The short and broad RUE ROYALE, though not strictly one of the Boulevards, forms a convenient approach to them from the Place de la Concorde. As far as the Rue St-Honoré it is lined with uniform 18th cent. houses and with fine shops. Mme de Staël lived for a short time after 1816 at No. 8.

The ***Madeleine,** or church of *St. Mary Magdalen,* the most fashionable church in Paris, is built in the style of a Roman temple, surrounded by a majestic Corinthian colonnade. Begun in 1764 by *Contant d'Ivry* on the site of an earlier church, it was altered by *P. Vignon* after 1806 at the orders of Napoleon, who intended it as a Temple of Glory for the

'Grande Armée.' A royal decree of 1816 restored it to divine worship, and the church was finished by *Huvé* in 1842. In the pediment is a relief of the Last Judgment (restored) by *Lemaire*. The enormous bronze doors are adorned with bas-reliefs from the Decalogue by *Triqueti* (1838). The statue of St. Luke at the back of the church was decapitated in 1918 by a shell from 'Bertha,' the long-range gun with which the Germans bombarded Paris in the First World War.

The **Interior,** entered also by the little side-doors near the choir, consists of a domed cella, gorgeously decorated but somewhat inadequately lighted. The sculptured figures of the Apostles in the spandrels of the domes are by *Rude*, *Foyatier*, and *Pradier*. In the dark chapels on either side of the organ are the Marriage of the Virgin, by *Pradier*, and the Baptism of Christ, by *Rude*. In the first chapel (r.) is St. Amelia, by *Bra*; on the next pillar is a tablet to the Abbé Deguerry, a former curé, murdered in 1871 at La Roquette (p. 60). In the second chapel is the Saviour, by *Duret*; in the third chapel, St. Clotilda, by *Barye*. The graceful but somewhat affected group of the Ascension of the Magdalen, on the high-altar, is by *Marochetti*. Behind the altar are frescoes by *Raverat* and, above, a mosaic of Christ and New Testament characters, designed by *Lemaire* and executed by *Gilbert Martin*. The fresco, by *Ziegler*, in the semi-dome, represents the History of Christianity. In the chapels on the right as we return: first chapel, St. Augustin, by *Etex*; second chapel, Madonna, by *Seurre*; third chapel, a fine St. Vincent de Paul group, by *Raggi*.

The church stands in the centre of the **Place de la Madeleine,** on the W. side of which a flower market is held on Tues. and Fridays. On the N. side of the church is a monument (1900) to Lavoisier (1743–94), the famous chemist who died on the scaffold. The monument was despoiled of its bronze by the Germans in 1942.

On the left-hand side of the Madeleine is one of the chief entrances to the **Sewers** (*Egouts*) of Paris. The other is in the Place de la Concorde, near the statue of Lille. Visits (20 fr.; candle 20 fr.), starting from the Madeleine at 2 and 5, from the Concorde at 2.30 and 5.30, and lasting c. ¾ hr., and arranged every Thurs., July 1st–Oct. 15th; also on the 2nd and 4th Thurs. in May and June, and the last Sat. of each month in May–Sept. The interesting visit (very different from the trying experience of Jean Valjean in 'Les Misérables') is carried out in electric boats and cars under comfortable and entirely inoffensive conditions.

Marcel Proust (1871–1922) was born, and spent a great part of his youth in a house in the Boulevard Malesherbes, near the Madeleine, backing on to the Rue de Surène.

The BOULEVARD DE LA MADELEINE, the westernmost of the Grands Boulevards, runs E. from the Madeleine. Marie Duplessis, the 'Dame aux Camélias,' died at No. 15 in 1846 and Nos. 17–25 house the huge luxury shop, 'Aux Trois Quartiers.'

The *BOULEVARD DES CAPUCINES, the most aristocratic of the Boulevards and the centre of club-land and of journalistic

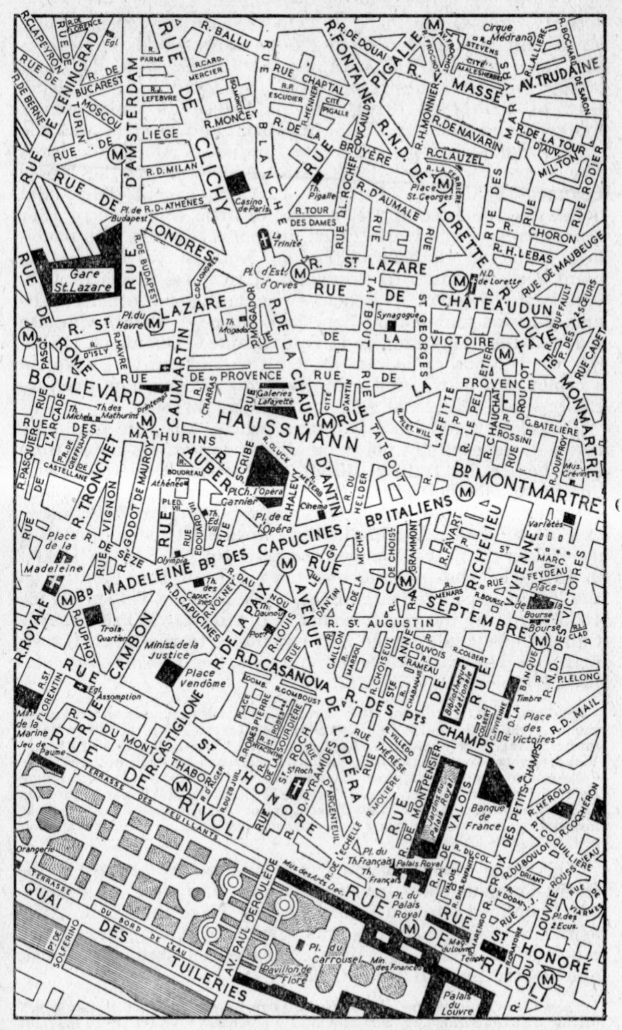

II. GRANDS BOULEVARDS WEST

activity, crosses the Place de l'Opéra, with the Opera House on the left. On the left of the boulevard, beyond *Olympia*, is the Rue Edouard-VII, with the *Théâtre Edouard VII* and, farther on, an equestrian statue (by Landowski) of King Edward VII (1841–1910), who as Prince of Wales was a frequent and popular visitor to Paris, and as king was the chief promoter of the 'Entente Cordiale.' An arcade leads thence to the Square de l'Opéra. At No. 25 is the **Musée Cognacq-Jay** (adm. 20 fr., 10–12, 2–5, except Tues. and holidays), which comprises a tasteful little collection of 18th cent. furniture and works of art, in rooms adorned with panelling from the château of Eu, in Normandy. Among the paintings are works by Reynolds, Lawrence, Gainsborough, Canaletto, Tiepolo, Boucher, Fragonard, and others. The museum was founded by Ernest Cognacq (d. 1928), who also founded the 'Magasins de la Samaritaine.' Offenbach (1819–80), the composer, died at No. 8 in the boulevard ; on No. 14 a tablet records the first exhibition of a cinema film given by the brothers Louis and Auguste Lumière in 1895.

The Boulevard des Italiens, whose cafés are gradually being superseded by office buildings, derives its name from the Théâtre des Italiens (1783), now replaced by the Opéra-Comique. On the right is the *Crédit Lyonnais*, a huge block extending to the Rue du Quatre-Septembre. Jefferson, in 1784–85, had a lodging in the Impasse Taitbout (now Rue du Helder ; l.), and Wagner occupied No. 25 Rue du Helder in 1840–41. The post office at the corner of Rue Laffitte, on the left, occupies the site of the house of Mme Tallien (1775–1835), wife of the revolutionist and afterwards Princesse de Chimay. Beyond, on the left, extending to the Boul. Haussmann, is the vast white building of the *Banque Nationale pour le Commerce et l'Industrie*.

The Rue Laffitte, named after a great banker, has a number of art-dealers' shops ; right at the end is seen Notre-Dame-de-Lorette, with the hill of Montmartre and the Sacré-Cœur in the background. No. 1 was the house of Sir Richard Wallace, where Lord Hertford accumulated the art-treasures now in the Wallace Collection in London. Napoleon III was born in 1808 at No. 17, at that time the residence of his mother, Queen Hortense of Holland ; and it was in the Rue Le Peletier, parallel to the E., that the conspirator Orsini, in 1858, flung a bomb at his carriage, killing and injuring many persons, but doing no harm to Napoleon or the Empress Eugénie.

The narrow Rue Marivaux (r.) leads to the entrance of the **Opéra-Comique** (box-office in the Rue Marivaux), in a somewhat confined position facing the tiny Place Boïeldieu. After a fire in 1887 the theatre was rebuilt by *Louis Bernier* and reopened in 1899. The ornate façade has statues of Music and Poetry by *Puech* and *Guilbert*.

The Opéra-Comique, now a subsidised theatre, originated in a company which produced pieces during local fairs, and in 1715 purchased from the Opéra the right of playing vaudevilles interspersed with lively airs. The founders of modern comic opera were the former directors, Charles Favart (1710–92) and his wife.

At the junction of the Boulevards des Italiens and Montmartre with the Boulevard Haussmann (extended to this point only in 1926) is the busy Carrefour Richelieu-Drouot. To the N. is the Rue Drouot, with the *Mairie of the 9th Arrondissement* (1750) on the right. No. 9 (l.) is the *Hôtel des Ventes Mobilières* or *Hôtel Drouot,* the 'Christie's' of Paris, where important sales are held from Feb. to June. To the S. is the Rue de Richelieu, leading to the Palais-Royal.

The short BOULEVARD MONTMARTRE, in spite of its name, is a long way from Montmartre. At No. 10 (l.) is the *Musée Grévin,* the Parisian Madame Tussaud's. On the right are the Rue Vivienne, leading to the Bourse, and the *Passage des Panoramas,* once noted for its panoramas. The busy Rue Montmartre (p. 24), at the end of the boulevard (r.), leads to the Halles, while the cheerful Rue du Faubourg-Montmartre (l.), ascending towards the 'suburb' of Montmartre, recalls the time when the boulevard formed the city boundary.

The Rue Geoffroy-Marie, a side-street of the Faubourg-Montmartre, commemorates a saddler and his wife, who in 1260 presented to the Hôtel-Dieu a little farm which in 1840 fetched 3¾ million francs.

The BOULEVARD POISSONNIÈRE ends at the Rue Poissonnière and Rue du Faubourg-Poissonnière, named after the fishmongers who used to pass through on their way to the Halles. No. 27 in the Boulevard was Chopin's first lodging in Paris (1831–32). The Rue Rougemont (l.) is continued by the Rue du Conservatoire, in which is *St-Eugène,* said to be the darkest church in Paris, much in favour for funerals.

The BOULEVARD DE BONNE-NOUVELLE, where the crowd begins to thin, ends at the Rue St-Denis (r.) and Rue du Faubourg-St-Denis (l.; leading to the Boul. de Magenta and Gare du Nord). On the left are the *Théâtre du Gymnase* and the Rue d'Hauteville, at the end of which is seen St-Vincent-de-Paul. In the Rue de la Lune, to the S., is *Notre-Dame-de Bonne-Nouvelle,* a church rebuilt in 1824. André Chénier (1762–94) lived in 1793 at 97 Rue de Cléry, close by. At the end of the boulevard (l.) is the **Porte St-Denis,** a triumphal arch 82 ft. high, designed by *Blondel* and erected in 1672 to commemorate the victories of Louis XIV in Germany and Holland. The pompous bas-reliefs on the arch were designed by *Girardon* and executed by the brothers *Anguier.*

The short BOULEVARD ST-DENIS stretches from the Porte St-Denis to the Porte St-Martin and is crossed by the busy thoroughfare formed by the Boul. de Strasbourg and Boul. de Sébastopol, the former leading to the Boul. de Magenta and the Gare de l'Est, the latter to the Châtelet. The **Porte St-Martin,** facing the Rue St-Martin and the Rue du Faubourg-

St-Martin, is a second triumphal arch in honour of Louis XIV, 60 ft. high, designed in 1674 by *Bullet* and decorated with bas-reliefs of contemporary campaigns.

B. The Eastern Boulevards: from the Porte St-Martin to the Bastille.

MÉTRO stations: *Strasbourg-St-Denis* (lines 4, 8, 9); *République* (lines 3, 5, 8, 9, 11); *Filles du Calvaire, St-Sébastien-Froissart* and *Chemin Vert* (line 8); *Bastille* (lines 1, 5, 8).—MOTOR-BUSES: République and Boul. St-Martin (routes 20, 52, 58, 65, 75); Bastille (routes 20, 66, 69, 76, 86, 91).

The BOULEVARD ST-MARTIN, over ¼ m. long, continues the series of the Grands Boulevards. On the left are the *Théâtre de la Renaissance*; the *Théâtre de la Porte-St-Martin* and the *Nouvel-Ambigu*, three famous theatres. The Porte-St-Martin is noted as the theatre of Frédérick Lemaître (1800–76), and here Coquelin aîné was seized by a mortal illness during a rehearsal in 1909. Paul de Kock (1794–1871), the 'Smollett of France,' died in the house No. 8. In front of the Ambigu is a monument to Baron Taylor (1789–1879), the author, by Tony Noël (1907).

The **Place de la République,** on the site of the Porte du Temple, is a very busy centre of traffic, at the junction of seven important thoroughfares. The *Monument de la République* (82 ft. high), in the centre, is a striking work by the brothers Morice (1883), the pedestal of which is adorned with sculptures by Dalou.

The *Caserne Vérines*, the barracks on the N.E. side, was re-named after a lieutenant-colonel in the Resistance, who was shot by the Germans at Cologne in 1942. There was considerable fighting in this area during the Liberation.

Beyond the Place de la République the boulevards are less interesting, and the cafés and shops change their character.

The BOULEVARD DU TEMPLE, ¼ m. long, owes its name, like the 'Quartier du Temple' (p. 34), to the Order of the Knights Templars, who owned most of the property in this region of Paris.

Gustave Flaubert occupied No. 42 in this boulevard in 1856–71 and there wrote 'Madame Bovary,' 'Salammbô' and 'L'Education Sentimentale.' A little to the N. is the site of the house whence Fieschi discharged his infernal machine at Louis-Philippe, in 1835. Marshal Mortier and fourteen others were killed, but the king was uninjured.—Béranger (1780–1857), the great ballad-writer, died at No. 5 in the street now called after him (parallel with the boulevard on the W.).

The short BOULEVARD DES FILLES-DU-CALVAIRE is named after an old convent (1633–1790). On the left is the *Cirque d'Hiver*.—The BOULEVARD BEAUMARCHAIS, nearly ½ m. long, is named after the famous dramatist Caron de Beaumarchais (1732–99), the site of whose house (at No. 2) is marked by a tablet. On the right are the Rue des Tournelles; the Rue du Pas-de-la-Mule, leading to the Place des Vosges ; and the house of Ninon de l'Enclos (Nos. 21–23).

The **Place de la Bastille** occupies a part of the site of the Bastille, the ground plan of which is marked by a line of white stones between the Boul. Henri-IV and the Rue St-Antoine. Beneath the pavement are large cellars once belonging to the famous prison.

The **Bastille,** or more correctly the *Bastille St-Antoine,* originated as a bastion-tower defending the E. entrance to Paris. It was developed under Charles V into a fortress with eight massive towers, immensely thick walls, and a wide moat. By the reign of Louis XIII the Bastille had become exclusively a state prison for political offenders, among whom were the mysterious 'Man in the Iron Mask' (1698–1703), Richelieu, and Voltaire. The arbitrary arrest of persons obnoxious to the Court, and their protracted imprisonment without trial, made the Bastille a popular synonym for oppression. Dr. Manette, in 'A Tale of Two Cities,' was a victim of this evil practice. In 1789, at the outbreak of the Revolution, the mob, aided by a few troops, attacked and overwhelmed the defenders. The prison was razed to the ground in the same year, and its key, presented by Lafayette to George Washington, is now at Mount Vernon. The anniversary of the fall of the Bastille (July 14th) is kept by the French as the Fête Nationale.

The **July Column** (*Colonne de Juillet*), 169 ft. high, in the centre of the square, is a bronze pillar, crowned by a figure of Liberty, erected by Louis-Philippe to commemorate the victims of the three days' street-fighting of July 1830, who are buried in vaults within the circular base of the column. The victims of the revolution of February 1848 were subsequently interred here, and their names added to the inscription.

Among the allegorical sculptures in bronze adorning the plinth, the most notable is a Lion, by *Barye,* symbolising the month of July. The gallery at the top (adm. 20 fr. daily, except Tues.. 10–4 or 5 ; 238 steps) commands a splendid view of Paris.

On the S.E. side of the Place is the *Gare de la Bastille* ; on the S. side is the *Gare d'Eau de l'Arsenal,* a dock at the end of the Canal St-Martin, which runs beneath the square. The Rue de la Roquette leads N.E. from the Bastille to Père-Lachaise. No. 34 bears the date 1377 ; at No. 70 is an 18th cent. fountain, and at 51bis is the charming little modern church of *Notre-Dame d'Espérance* (1930).—The Rue de Lyon leads S. to the Gare de Lyon.

4. THE CENTRAL QUARTERS BETWEEN THE BOULEVARDS AND THE LOUVRE.

This portion of central Paris, now largely given over to commerce, is bounded on the W. by the Av. de l'Opéra and on the E. by the Boul. de Sébastopol, and is crossed from W. to E. by three main parallel thoroughfares : on the N., the Rue du Quatre-Septembre and its continuation, the Rue Réaumur ; then the Rue des Petits-Champs and its continuation, the Rue Etienne-Marcel ; and lastly, on the S., the Rue de Rivoli. It is divided into a W. and E. half by the Rues Montmartre and du Louvre, while numerous cross-streets unite the boulevards with the Halles quarter and the Seine.

A. West Section: between the Avenue de l'Opéra and the Rues Montmartre and du Louvre.

MÉTRO stations: *Opéra* (lines 3, 7, 8); *Quatre-Septembre* and *Bourse* (line 3); *Pyramides* (line 7); *Palais-Royal* (lines 1 and 7); *Louvre* (line 1).—MOTOR-BUSES: Place du Théâtre-Français and Place de l'Opéra (routes 21, 27, 48, 67, 69, 72, 73, 74, 85, 95).

Starting from the Place de l'Opéra, the RUE DU QUATRE-SEPTEMBRE (named from the date of the foundation of the Third Republic) runs S.E., crossing the Rue de Richelieu (see below), to the *Place de la Bourse*. Both the Rue du Quatre-Septembre and its continuation, the Rue Réaumur, are modern thoroughfares, driven through an old quarter.

The ***Bourse** or *Stock Exchange* (open daily, except Sun. and holidays, 12–4; closed for business at 3, on most Sat. at 2), resembling the Temple of Vespasian at Rome, with a Corinthian peristyle, was built in 1808–27 by *Brongniart* and *Labarre*. The N. and S. wings were added in 1903 by *F. Cavel*. At the end of the great hall is the 'Parquet,' a railed-off space reserved for the 'agents de change' (stockbrokers), with a circular railing in the centre known as the 'Corbeille.' On the right is the 'Marché au Comptant,' where the prices are announced; on the left, the 'Coulisse de la Rente,' where government bonds are bought and sold. The best view of the scenes of bustle and excitement is from the upper gallery.

The RUE VIVIENNE, starting from the Boul. Montmartre and passing the Place de la Bourse and the Bibliothèque Nationale (Rte. 22), contains several fine houses of the 17th and 18th cent. At No. 4 Simon Bolívar lived in 1804.

The RUE DE RICHELIEU, over ½ m. long, laid out by the great cardinal, runs S. from the Grands Boulevards to the Louvre. Berlioz lived at No. 96 in 1830 and Meyerbeer at No. 91 in 1851. No. 101, with decorative masks in the court-yard, was the home of Abbé Barthélemy, the antiquary (1716–95). The carved coat-of-arms on the door of No. 75 (r.), a 17th cent. house S. of the Rue du Quatre-Septembre, should be noticed. On the left, at the corner of the Rue Colbert, stands the *Hôtel de Nevers*, once a royal residence. Farther on is (r.) the charming *Square Louvois*, with the **Fontaine Louvois* or *Fontaine Richelieu*, by the younger Visconti (1844), one of the prettiest fountains in Paris. Donizetti lived at No. 5 Rue Louvois in 1840. On the E. (l.) side of the Rue de Richelieu rises the W. façade of the **Bibliothèque Nationale** (see Rte. 22), on the site of a mansion of Cardinal Mazarin.

Just beyond is the crossing of the RUE DES PETITS-CHAMPS (the "New Street of the Little Fields" of Thackeray's 'Ballad of Bouillabaisse'), which runs E.

o the Place des Victoires (see below) and W. to the Rue de la Paix. No. 45 was the residence of Lulli; Mme Récamier died of cholera at No. 15 in 1849, and Stendhal at No. 78 in 1842.

No. 50 Rue de Richelieu was the early home of Jeanne Poisson (Mme de Pompadour). At the corner of the Rue Molière (at No. 25 in which lived Voltaire and his 'Emilie,' Mme du Châtelet) is the *Fontaine Molière*, another fountain by Visconti (1844), with a seated figure of the poet by Seurre and standing figures of Comedy by Pradier. No. 40 Rue de Richelieu stands on the site of the house in which Molière died in 1673; Diderot died in 1784 at No. 39, and Mignard in 1695 at No. 23.

At the end of the street, to the left, lies the Place du Palais-Royal, to the N. of which extends the **Palais-Royal,** one of the most attractive and interesting parts of Paris. The name is now applied not only to the original palace but also to the buildings and galleries surrounding the gardens beyond. The latter, freely open to the public and approached from the neighbouring streets by several passages, played an important rôle in the Revolutionary period, and in the more frivolous society of the early 19th cent. Now, however, it is little more than a quiet and pleasant backwater surrounded by the busy streets of the fashionable shopping centre near by.

The Palais-Royal proper, at the end of the first courtyard, was originally known as the 'Palais-Cardinal,' having been built by *J. Lemercier* in 1629–34 for Richelieu, who died there in 1642. Bequeathed to Louis XIII, it was first called 'Palais-Royal' during the residence of Anne of Austria (d. 1666). Richelieu's apartments were then occupied by Card. Mazarin. Queen Henrietta Maria of England found a refuge here in 1652. The palace dates its long connection with the Orléans family from 1672, when, after being enlarged by *Mansart*, it was presented by Louis XIV to his brother, Duc Philippe I, under whom the first exhibition of the Beaux-Arts was held here in 1673. The palace acquired a dissolute reputation from the 'petits soupers' of Duc Philippe II, the Regent (1674–1723). The building nearest the Place du Palais-Royal (now the Conseil d'Etat) was added after 1763 from the plans of *P. L. Moreau*. The houses and galleries around the gardens were built as a speculation by Philippe-Egalité, the Regent's grandson, in 1781–86, under pressure of debt, and let out as shops and cafés. He built the present Théâtre-Français, and the Théâtre du Palais-Royal, in the N.W. corner, dates from the same period. The cafés became a meeting-place for malcontents, and on July 13th, 1789, Camille Desmoulins delivered in the gardens the fiery harangue which brought about the fall of the Bastille on the following day. Under the Revolution the palace was renamed 'Palais-Egalité' and used as government offices. In 1814, however, it was handed back to the Orléans family, resuming the name of Palais-Royal, and Louis-Philippe lived there till 1832. After being plundered by the mob in 1848, it was occupied for a time by the 'Rights of Man' club. After some damage during the Commune, the Palais was rebuilt by *Chabrol* in 1872–76 and is now occupied by the Conseil d'Etat, the Under-Secretary for Fine Arts, and various government offices.

The buildings of the Cour de l'Horloge, the courtyard adjoining the Place du Palais-Royal, were erected by Moreau-Desproux, with sculptures by Pajou (l. wing) and Franceschi (r.; 1875). An inscription at the corner of the Rue de Valois marks the site of the *Salle du Spectacle*, occupied by Molière's company from 1661 to 1673 and by the Académie Royale de Musique (p. 1) from 1673 till the fire in 1763. The façade of the Cour d'Honneur was begun by Contant d'Ivry, continued by Louis, and finished by Fontaine, with statues by Pajou (l.) and Gérard (r.). The E wing is a part of Lemercier's original building; the W.

wing is by Fontaine. To the N., the Cour d'Honneur is separated from the gardens by a double Doric portico, by Fontaine (1829–31), which was restored and cleared of its shops in 1935.

The GARDENS of the Palais-Royal, behind the old Orléans palace, are surrounded by galleries and buildings (by Louis, 1781–84) and still occupied by shops. On the W. side is the *Galerie de Montpensier*; on the E., the *Galerie de Valois*; on the N., the *Galerie Beaujolais*; and on the S., the *Galerie d'Orléans*. In his rooms in one of the galleries John Howard Payne wrote 'Home, Sweet Home' in 1823.

Between the Rue de Valois on the E. side of the Palais-Royal, and the Rue des Bons-Enfants, the next street to the E., is the unspoiled little *Place de Valois*, entered by an archway.—At No. 7 in the RUE DES BONS-ENFANTS is the *Passage Henri-IV*, in the old buildings of the Théâtre Molière.

The **Banque de France** (entrance in the Rue de la Vrillière), founded in 1800, and in its present site since 1811, is one of the great banking institutions of the world. It occupies a huge building to the N.E. of the Palais-Royal, incorporating the former *Hôtel de la Vrillière*, which was built by Mansart in 1620 and restored by Robert de Cotte in 1719. Later known as the *Hôtel de Toulouse*, it became the residence of the Princesse de Lamballe, murdered in La Force in 1792. Mansart's projecting angle in the Rue Radziwill, supported by a bracket, is admired as a masterpiece of stonework, and within is the **Galerie Dorée* (shown to bona-fide research students only).

To the N. of the Bank lies the Place des Petits-Pères, in which is **Notre-Dame-des-Victoires,** or the church of the *Petits-Pères*, dedicated by Louis XIII in memory of the capture of La Rochelle from the Huguenots (1627) but not finished until 1740. In the second chapel on the left is the tomb of the composer Lulli (d. 1687), by Michel Cotton and Coysevox, and in the choir are elaborately carved stalls and seven paintings by C. Vanloo.

The circular **Place des Victoires,** immediately S.E. of the Place des Petits-Pères, was laid out by J. Hardouin-Mansart in 1685; the surrounding houses were designed by Pradot. The equestrian statue of Louis XIV by Bosio (1822) replaces the original, destroyed in 1792; the bas-reliefs on the pedestal depict the Passage of the Rhine and Louis XIV distributing decorations.

On the W. side of the Place des Victoires is the RUE DE LA FEUILLADE, continued by the Rue des Petits-Champs. No. 13 in the RUE CROIX-DES-PETITS-CHAMPS, which leads S. from the Place des Victoires to the Rue St-Honoré, was occupied by Malherbe in 1606–27. On the E. side is the RUE ETIENNE-MARCEL, leading to the Boul. de Sébastopol. In the RUE HÉROLD, formerly des Vieux-Augustins, which connects these two streets, Thackeray lived after his marriage in 1856. On the N.E. is the RUE DU MAIL, in which lived Colbert (at the richly decorated No. 7), Cagliostro, and Mme Récamier (at No. 12).

B. East Section: between the Rues Montmartre and du Louvre and the Boulevard de Sébastopol.

MÉTRO stations: *Louvre* (line 1); *Châtelet* (lines 1, 4, 7, 11); *Halles* and *Etienne-Marcel* (line 4); *Réaumur-Sébastopol* (lines 3 and 4); *Sentier* (line 3).—MOTOR-BUSES: Châtelet (routes 21, 47 58, 67, 69, 72, 73, 74, 75, 76, 77, 85, 96); Réaumur-Sébastopol (routes 38, 47, 52); Etienne-Marcel (routes 38, 58, 86); Sentier (routes 48, 52, 66, 67, 74, 85).

The RUE DU LOUVRE runs S. from about the middle of the Rue Montmartre, passing, at the corner of the Rue Etienne-Marcel, the **General Post & Telegraph Office** (*Hôtel des Postes et Télégraphes*), a huge block built in 1880–84. The long gallery entered from the Rue du Louvre contains most of the postal departments, with the exception of the poste-restante, telegraph office, and inquiry office, which are in the room on the right.

On the façade in the RUE JEAN-JACQUES-ROUSSEAU (where Rousseau lived with Thérèse in 1776) is an inscription marking the site of the *Hôtel d'Hervart*, occupied by La Fontaine at the time of his death (1695).

To the S. of the Post Office, in the Rue du Louvre, is the *Head Telephone Office*; opposite is the *Savings Bank* (*Caisse d'Epargne*), in the 18th cent. *Hôtel d'Ollone* (tablet).

A little to the E. of the Rue du Louvre is the **Bourse de Commerce** (shown Mon.–Fri. 9–6), formerly the corn exchange, a circular 18th cent. building remodelled in 1888.

The fine fluted Doric column (98 ft. high) adjoining the building is the sole relic of the *Hôtel de Soissons*, built for Catherine de Médicis in 1572 on the site of Blanche of Castille's Hôtel de Nesle.—The Rue de Sauval leads S. to the Rue St-Honoré, at the corner of which (No. 96) stood the house in which Molière was born in 1622. Wagner's first Paris lodging was close by, in a mean house in the vanished Rue de la Tonnellerie.

The Rue du Louvre now crosses the busy Rue St-Honoré and Rue de Rivoli.

In the former, to the W. of the Rue du Louvre, is the Protestant Reformed church of the **Oratoire**, designed by Clément Métezeau the younger and Jacques Lemercier, and built in 1621–30 by Louis XIII as the mother church in France of Card. Bérulle's Congregation of the Oratory, but assigned to the Calvinists by Napoleon in 1811. Against the apse of the church, under the arches in the Rue de Rivoli, is a monument, by Crauk, to Admiral Coligny (1517–72), the chief victim of the massacre of St. Bartholomew, who was murdered in the former *Hôtel de Ponthieu*, close by.

The Rue du Louvre runs S. to the Quai du Louvre on the bank of the Seine. On the right is the colonnade of the Louvre; on the left the PLACE DU LOUVRE, with the *Mairie of the 1st Arrondissement* (1859), which, according to Viollet-le-Duc, seems to have been intended as a caricature of the adjoining church.

***St-Germain-l'Auxerrois,** perhaps founded by St. Germanus of Paris about 560, is now a Gothic church of the 13–16th cent., drastically restored in the 18–19th. The flamboyant façade has a striking porch by *Jean Gaussel* (1435–39), with a rose window and a graceful balustrade above. The transeptal doorways (15th cent.) are noteworthy.

Molière was married and his first son was baptized in this church. Under the Revolution St-Germain was the Temple of Gratitude. The church was sacked by the mob in 1831, and was poorly restored after 1838, the conspicuous N. tower being added in 1860.

INTERIOR (256 by 128 ft.). The double aisles of the nave are continued round the choir. The 'restoration' of 1745, mingling the classicism of the 18th cent. with 14–15th cent. architecture, mangled the choir-arches, converted the piers into fluted columns, and heightened their capitals. Over the doors on either side of the porch are two rooms, of which the former *SALLE DES ARCHIVES, or muniment room, on the left, has preserved its original pavement, doors, panelling, carved ceiling, and 16th cent. triptych.—In the NAVE is (l.) the 'banc-d'œuvre,' or churchwardens' pew, a handsome piece of late 17th cent. carpentry, with a 16th cent. Flemish altarpiece in the aisle-chapel behind. Opposite the pulpit is a Christ by *Bouchardon*. The fine wrought-iron choir-railings date from 1767. The outer aisle on the S. side of the nave is occupied by the CHAPELLE DES CATÉCHISMES (14th cent.; apply to the sacristan). The reredos has 19th cent. bas-reliefs in which has been inserted a 14th cent. Tree of Jesse in stone, from a church in Champagne.—The TRANSEPTS have retained their *Stained Glass of the 15–16th centuries.—AMBULATORY (beginning on the S.). In the fourth chapel (beyond the sacristy) are marble statues of Etienne d'Aligre and his son, both Chancellors of France (d. 1635, 1677). Fifth chapel: Ancient bas-relief of the Entombment, and Pietà by *Bonnardel*. Seventh chapel: Effigies from the tomb of the Rostaing family (1582 and 1645). Next comes the state pew (1681) once used by the French court, St-Germain being the parish church of the Louvre. Thirteenth chapel: St. Peter of Nola, by *Sébastien Bourdon*.

The RUE DU PONT-NEUF, starting from the quays a little E. of St-Germain, passes between the departmental stores of *La Samaritaine* and *La Belle-Jardinière*, crosses the Rue de Rivoli, and the E. end of the Rue St-Honoré (comp. p. 21), and ends on the N. at the **Halles Centrales,** or *Central Markets*, called by Zola "le ventre de Paris."

There are twelve pavilions, designed by Baltard and begun in 1881, and divided into two parts by the Rue Baltard. The six on the E. side are used for fruit, vegetables, butter, fish, cheese, poultry, and game; those on the W. side for meat, poultry, and eggs. Two new pavilions were added on the W. in 1936 The best time for a visit to the Halles is between 5.30 and 8 a.m.

To the S.E. of the Halles, not far from the Boul. de Sébastopol, is the small *Square des Innocents*, on the site of the ancient Cimetière des Innocents, said to date from the Gallo-Roman period and until 1780 the chief burial ground of Paris.

Traces of the arches of the charnel-houses are still to be seen on the odd-number side of the Rue des Innocents. In the centre of the square is the charming Renaissance *FONTAINE DES INNOCENTS. Erected in 1550, in the neighbouring Rue St-Denis by *Pierre Lescot* with bas-reliefs by *Jean Goujon,* it was remodelled and set up here in 1850. At the N.W. corner of the square is the reconstructed doorway from the office of the *Marchandes Lingères* (1716). To the S. is the Rue de la Ferronnerie, where Henri IV was assassinated by Ravaillac in 1610, in front of No. 11.

On the N. side of the Halles, at the intersection of six streets, rises ***St-Eustache,** sometimes known as ' Notre-Dame des Halles,' one of the largest churches in Paris. In detail and decoration it is a Renaissance building, but in plan and in its general lay-out it is of medieval design.

Begun in 1532 by *Pierre Lemercier,* it was consecrated in 1637. The main W. doorway was rebuilt in 1755–88 in a completely inharmonious classical style. Both transepts have handsome round-headed doorways; the N. transept is approached by a passage from the Rue Montmartre. The open-work bell-tower (' Plomb de St-Eustache ') above the crossing has lost its spire. Above the Lady Chapel in the apse is a small tower built in 1640 and restored in 1875.—St-Eustache was the scene of the riotous Festival of Reason in 1793, and in 1795 it became the Temple of Agriculture. Molière was baptized in this church in 1622; in 1791 the body of Mirabeau lay in state here before its removal to the Panthéon; and among the notabilities buried here are Colbert, Louis XIV's minister of finance (d. 1683); Adm. de Tourville (d. 1701); the composer Rameau (d. 1764); and Mozart's mother (d. 1778).—St-Eustache is noted for its music, especially at the midnight mass on Christmas Eve and the services on Good Friday and St. Cecilia's Day (Nov. 22nd).

The INTERIOR is strikingly original in its combination of classical forms with a Gothic plan. The double aisles and chapels of the nave are continued round the choir. The square piers are flanked by three stories of columns in the different orders; the keystones are adorned with fine sculpture. The chapels are decorated with paintings, some dating from the time of Louis XIII, but restored. The eleven lofty windows of the apse, representing the twelve Apostles, the four Latin Fathers, and St. Eustace, were executed by *Soulignac* (1631) from the cartoons of *Philippe de Champaigne.* The churchwardens' pew dates from about 1720. The stalls came from the convent of Picpus.

SOUTH AISLE. Above the door is the Martyrdom of St. Eustace, by *Simon Vouet.* The fourth chapel contains the Marriage of the Virgin, a group by *Triqueti.* In the S. transept hangs a fine Savonnerie carpet (Louis XV) discovered in 1832 in a forgotten cupboard in the sacristy.—In the second choir-chapel (r.) is an Entombment, by *Luca Giordano.*—At the entrance of the LADY CHAPEL are statues of the Angel Gabriel and St. Michael; inside the chapel are Mary, Mother of Christ (in the centre), Mary, Star of the Sea (l.), and Mary the Consoler (r.), by *Couture*; above the altar is a *Virgin by

Pigalle.—North Aisle. In the first choir-chapel as we return is the tomb of Colbert, designed by *Lebrun*, with statues of Colbert and Abundance by *Coysevox* and of Religion by *Tuby*. Above the altar of the second chapel, the Disciples at Emmaus, a painting of the *Rubens* school; the third and fourth contain 17th cent. frescoes. In the fourth nave-chapel or baptistery, Adoration of the Magi, by *Vanloo*.

The Rue Montmartre is an ancient thoroughfare leading from St-Eustache to the Grands Boulevards, and crossing the Rue Réaumur. Emile Zola (1840–1902) was born at No. 10 Rue St-Joseph, on the right; and Molière was buried in the vanished Cimetière St-Joseph, near by. In 1778 Mozart and his mother lodged in the Rue du Sentier, opposite the end of the Rue du Croissant.

At St-Eustache begins the Rue de Turbigo, on its way to the Place de la République. This soon crosses the Rue Etienne-Marcel, in which, to the W. (l.), rises the *Tour de Jean-sans-Peur*.

This graceful embattled tower was added in the 15th cent. to the *Hôtel d'Artois* or *Hôtel de Bourgogne*, a mansion used in the 16–18th cent. as a theatre, where 'Le Cid,' 'Andromaque,' and 'Phèdre' were performed.

Farther on the Rue de Turbigo crosses the Rue St-Denis, one of the oldest and most entertaining streets in Paris, running from the Place du Châtelet to the Porte St-Denis (⅝ m.), parallel with the Boul. de Sébastopol.

No. 32, near the S. end, where the dramatist Eugène Scribe was born in 1791, is marked by his bust. No. 33 has an 18th cent. sign, 'Au Mortier d'Argent.' Next comes (l.) the Square des Innocents (p. 22). No. 92 is the church of St-Leu-St-Gilles (see below). No. 135 has an inscription showing the former position of the *Porte St-Denis* or *Porte aux Peintres*, a gateway in the walls of Philip Augustus. At the corner of the Rue Tiquetonne (then Rue du Petit-Lion), stood the old shop bearing the sign of the 'Cat and Racket,' celebrated in Balzac's story, 'La Maison du Chat qui Pelote.' On No. 142 is the little *Fontaine de la Reine* (1730); on No. 224, at the corner of Rue Tracy, is a cartouche with the head of Jules Michelet, the historian, who was born in 1798 in a house on this site.

A little farther on the Rue de Turbigo crosses the broad and ugly Boulevard de Sébastopol, which connects the Place du Châtelet (p. 25) with the Boul. St-Denis. A short distance down the boulevard to the S. (r.) is the little church of **St-Leu-St-Gilles,** built in 1320 for the abbey of St-Magloire, an institution for penitent women. The aisles and chapels were added in the 15–16th cent.; the choir and apse were rebuilt in 1617 in the Renaissance style; the Gothic façade was deliberately remodelled in the taste of the 18th cent.; and the ambulatory altered in 1858 to make way for the boulevard. Besides a number of frescoes, the church contains a portrait of St. Francis of Sales by Philippe de Champaigne (left of the altar), and 15th cent. alabaster bas-reliefs (in the sacristy entry). In the crypt is a fine sculpture of the dead Christ (15th or 16th cent.).—The municipal *Musée d'Hygiène*, housed in the former presbytery, 57 Boul. de Sébastopol, contains maps, plans, diagrams, and models of hygienic installations.

5. FROM THE PLACE DU CHÂTELET TO THE BASTILLE.

MÉTRO stations: *Châtelet* (lines 1, 4, 7, 11); *Hôtel de Ville* and *St-Paul* (line 1); *Bastille* (lines 1, 5, 8).—MOTOR-BUSES: Châtelet (routes 21, 38, 47, 58, 67, 69, 72, 73, 74, 75, 76, 77, 85, 96); Hôtel de Ville (routes 69, 72, 73, 74, 75, 76, 77, 96); Bastille (routes 20, 66, 69, 76, 86, 91).

The section of the RUE DE RIVOLI that lies to the E. of the Louvre was constructed by Napoleon III to open up a rapid access for troops to the Hôtel de Ville in case of emergency. Beyond the Rue du Pont-Neuf and the Rue des Halles it crosses the Boul. de Sébastopol (see above). To the right, at their intersection, is the *Square St-Jacques,* in the centre of which rises the **Tour St-Jacques,** the only relic of the church of St-Jacques-la-Boucherie, dating from 1508–22. This graceful and ornate Gothic tower is now used as a meteorological station.

On the ground floor is a poor statue (1854) of Blaise Pascal, who verified on this tower (or on that of St-Jacques-du-Haut-Pas) the barometric experiments he had caused to be made on the Puy de Dôme. The niches are filled with nineteen modern statues. At the corners of the roof are a statue of St. James the Apostle and figures of an eagle, a lion, and a bull, the symbols of the Evangelists (originals in the Musée de Cluny).

The adjoining **Place du Châtelet** is bounded on the S. by the Seine, which is here crossed by the Pont au Change. The square is named after the vanished *Grand Châtelet,* a fortress-gateway leading to the Cité, once the headquarters of the Provost of Paris and the Guild of Notaries. A plan of the gate may be seen on the front of the *Chambre des Notaires,* on the N. side of the square. On the E. side is the *Théâtre Sarah-Bernhardt*; on the W., the *Théâtre du Châtelet,* in which many Communards were court-martialled in 1871. A tablet on the S. side of the latter marks the site of the house in which the painter Louis David was born in 1748. In the centre of the square is the *Fontaine du Châtelet,* known also as the *Fontaine de la Victoire* or *Fontaine du Palmier,* dating from 1806 and 1858. An inscription indicates the position of the 'Parloir aux Bourgeois,' the seat of the municipality of Paris from the 13th cent. till 1357.

The wide AVENUE VICTORIA, so named in honour of Queen Victoria's visit to Paris in 1854, leads hence across the Rue St-Martin and past the *Assistance Publique* (Poor Law Offices) to the **Place de l'Hôtel-de-Ville,** which is bounded on the N. by the Rue de Rivoli, on the E. by the Hôtel de Ville, and on the S. by the Seine, crossed here by the *Pont d'Arcole.* On the S. side of the Hôtel de Ville is an equestrian statue of *Etienne Marcel* (d. 1358), the famous 'Prévôt des Marchands,' by Idrac and Marqueste.

Known until the Revolution of 1830 as the *Place de Grève*, this square was the usual site for public executions and has been the scene of many historic events. Among the famous executions (many of them incredibly barbarous) which took place in the square were those of Jean Hardi (1473), for an attempt to poison Louis XI; a long series of Protestants, including Briquemont and Cavagnes, the Huguenot leaders (1572); the Comte de Montgomery, captain in the Scottish Guard (1574), who accidentally caused the death of Henri II in a tournament; Ravaillac, the assassin of Henri IV (1610); Eléonore Galigaï, the favourite of Marie de Médicis, executed for sorcery (1617); the Marquise de Brinvilliers (1676), poisoner; Cartouche, the famous highwayman (1721); and Damiens (1757) who attempted to murder Louis XV. De Launay, governor of the Bastille, was beheaded, and Foullon, the controller-general of finance, and his son-in-law Bertier were hanged here by the mob in 1789. The last victim was Louvel, murderer of the Duc de Berri (1820).—The square has been enlarged, and adorned with flower-beds.

The ***Hôtel de Ville,** a splendid building in the style of the French Renaissance, adorned with statues of eminent Frenchmen, was built in 1874–84 from the plans of *Ballu* and *Deperthes*. It is an enlarged and enriched replica of its famous predecessor, begun c. 1532 on the same site, which was burned down by the Communards in 1871.

The first civil magistrate of Paris in the 12th cent. was the provost or 'Prévôt de Paris,' whose office was frequently bought and sold. The 'Echevins,' as the magistrates were called until 1789, were constituted by an edict of Philip Augustus, from which date also the arms of the city. About the middle of the 13th cent. the head of the 'Hanse des Marchands' (merchant-guild) received the title of 'Prévôt des Marchands' or 'Maître des Echevins,' and this guild became the chief municipal authority. The first meeting-place of this body, known simply as the 'Parlouer aux Bourgeois' was situated near the Grand-Châtelet; later the merchants met at the Grand-Châtelet itself; until finally, in 1357, the Provost Etienne Marcel bought the 'Maison aux Piliers' or 'Maison du Dauphin,' a large house in the Place de Grève. In 1532 plans for a new building were adopted, but the work was stopped at the second floor, and the new designs approved by Henri II in 1549 were not completed till 1628.

The historical importance of the building dates more especially from 1789, when it became the meeting-place of the 300 electors nominated by the districts of Paris. On July 17th, 1789, Louis XVI received the tricoloured cockade from the hands of Bailly, mayor of Paris. In 1792 the 172 commissaries elected by the sections of Paris gave from here the signal for the insurrection of Aug. 10th. In 1794 Robespierre took refuge at the Hôtel de Ville with his friends, but was arrested on July 27th (the 9th Thermidor, An II) and was dragged thence, his jaw shattered by a bullet, to the guillotine. After it had become the seat of the Préfet de la Seine and his council in 1805, a number of brilliant fêtes were given to celebrate Napoleon's marriage with Marie-Louise (1810), the birth of the King of Rome (1811), and numerous other great occasions. During the days of 1830 the Swiss Guards put up a stout defence in the Hôtel de Ville. It became the seat of the provisional government of 1848 under Louis Blanc, and on May 15th it witnessed the arrest of the leaders Barbès and Blanqui. During the dark days of June the building was saved by the courage of a handful of men. On Sept. 4th, 1870, the Republic was proclaimed at the Hôtel de Ville, and in the following year, on March 26th, the Commune was proclaimed here by the Committee of Public Safety; on May 24th the beautiful building was set on fire by its defenders, many of whom perished in the flames.

In August 1944 the area around the Hôtel de Ville was the centre of the Resistance movement's attack against the German forces of occupation. On the 19th the headquarters of the movement was established in the building itself, and managed to repel the attacks of the enemy until the arrival of Gen. Leclerc's division on the 24th. Plaques commemorating the peace of 1919 and the cessation of hostilities in April 1945 are affixed to the balustrade outside the main entrance.

Intending visitors should apply to the office of the Accueil de Paris, 14, Rue François-Miron (4e.).

The magnificent interior is interesting for its mural paintings, sculptures, carvings, etc., lavishly illustrating the official taste in art of the third quarter of the 19th century. The panels of the Seasons, by *Puvis de Chavannes*, in the room at the head of the S. staircase, are noteworthy ; and a curiosity, in the Salle des Cariatides (off the main banqueting hall), is the huge malachite vase, weighing 4 tons, presented by Alexander III of Russia in 1893, to commemorate the exchange of visits by the French and Russian fleets.

On the E. side of the Hôtel de Ville, beyond the Rue Lobau, are two large barracks built by Napoleon III (now occupied as annexes of the Hôtel de Ville). Between them lies the *Place St-Gervais.* At the E. end of the square is the church of **St-Gervais-St-Protais,** founded in the 6th cent. but in its present form an edifice of the 16th cent., mainly in the flamboyant Gothic style. The façade, however, built in 1616–21, is the earliest example in France of the simultaneous use of the Doric, Ionic, and Corinthian orders. The N. tower is Gothic, with a classical top story. In 1793 the church was converted into a Temple of Youth. Bossuet preached here ; Mme de Sévigné was married here ; and here are buried Philippe de Champaigne, Scarron, and Crébillon.

The INTERIOR is impressive from its loftiness and its unity of style. The chapels contain frescoes and paintings and 16th cent. stained glass (fifth and sixth S. chapel, Lady Chapel, and choir). The first chapel on the right has a Crucifixion ascribed to *Ph. de Champaigne* ; in the second chapel is an altar commemorating the victims of the bombardment of Good Friday, 1918, when a German shell struck the church and killed fifty of the congregation. In the ninth chapel are the tomb of Chancellor Michel Le Tellier (d. 1685), by *Mazeline* and *Hurtrelle* (part of this monument is in the Louvre), and a 14th cent. statue of the Madonna. The Lady Chapel, a remarkable example of flamboyant Gothic (1517), has a fine pendent keystone.—The entrance to the sacristy is closed by fine iron gates of the 17th century.—In the choir the stalls are of the 16th and 17th cent. In the N. transept is a painting of the Passion, ascribed to *Aldegrever*, a pupil of Dürer ; the two succeeding chapels contain notable woodwork.—Over the churchwardens' pew, on the S. side of the nave, is a semicircular painting of God the Father, by *Perugino* (part of the Ascension at Lyons).

The famous Chanteurs de St-Gervais sing in this church on certain festivals during the year (unaccompanied plain-song). François Couperin (1668–1733), and several members of his family, served as organist here, and their organ, restored, still survives.

The region to the S., between our main thoroughfare and the Seine, a picturesque old quarter which is fast disappearing beneath the housebreaker's hammer, may be explored before we resume our eastward course viâ the Rue St-Antoine.

In the RUE FRANÇOIS-MIRON, leading N.E. from St-Gervais, No. 10 was the birthplace of Ledru-Rollin, the Radical politician (1807–74). No. 68, the *Hôtel Beauvais* (1665), has a fine courtyard, an ornate circular vestibule, and a carved staircase by Martin van Bogaert of Breda, called Desjardins. Anne of Austria and Card. Mazarin watched the entry of Louis XIV and Marie Thérèse into Paris in 1660 from its balcony. Christina of Sweden was a later tenant, and here in 1763 Mozart was the guest of the Bavarian ambassador. No. 82, the *Hôtel du Président Hénault*, has a beautiful balcony.—No. 26 in the neighbouring RUE GEOFFROY-L'ASNIER is the *Hôtel de Chalons-Luxembourg*, built for the Constable de Montmorency and once occupied by Gabriele d'Annunzio; tastefully remodelled in the early 17th cent., the mansion has a handsome door and knocker, and an attractive Louis XIII pavilion at the end of the courtyard.—No. 7 RUE DE JOUY, the **Hôtel d'Aumont*, by Levau (1648) and Fr. Mansart (1656), was bought by the city in 1936, and is now undergoing restoration.—At the corner of the RUE DU FIGUIER and the RUE DE L'HÔTEL-DE-VILLE is the ***Hôtel de Sens**, built c. 1474–1519 for the Archbishops of Sens, at a time when the bishopric of Paris was suffragan to the metropolitan see of Sens (before 1623); it is older than the Hôtel de Cluny, the only other example in Paris of the domestic architecture of the 15th cent., and after a long period of neglect is undergoing restoration (1950).—In the RUE CHARLEMAGNE the two masks in the courtyard of No. 21 and the graceful door of No. 25 should be noted.

The QUAI DES CÉLESTINS continues the Quai de l'Hôtel-de-Ville to the E., opposite the Ile St-Louis. An inscription on No. 32 marks the site of the tennis-court of the Croix-Noire where Molière and the other actors of the *Illustre Théâtre* performed in 1645. Another tablet commemorates the *Tour Barbeau* in the walls of Philip Augustus. Still another, on No. 28, at the corner of the Rue des Jardins, records that Rabelais died in that street in 1553 (at No. 9, according to tradition).

He was buried in the churchyard of *St-Paul-des-Champs*, a little to the N. (demolished in 1794). In this church were also the tombs of Nicot, the Mansarts, Biron, and the 'Man in the Iron Mask.'

At No. 4, on the quay, the sculptor Barye died in 1875. No. 2, the stately *Hôtel Fieubet*, with an interesting courtyard, was built by J. H. Mansart (1676–81); it is now the 'Ecole Massillon.'

In the RUE BEAUTREILLIS, which lies to the N., No. 7 has an old wooden staircase; No. 6 has a curious clock in the courtyard; No. 16 is the birthplace of the dramatist Victorien Sardou (1831–1908); and beneath the carriage-entrance of No. 22, the *Hôtel de Charny*, are some wood-carvings in the purest Louis XIII style. Baudelaire stayed here in 1858–9.—No. 12 in the RUE CHARLES-V was the *Hôtel d'Aubray*, the imposing residence of the Marquise de Brinvilliers, the poisoner.

At the end of the Quai des Célestins is the BOULEVARD HENRI-IV, which leads on the left to the Bastille and on the right is carried by the *Pont de Sully* across the river and the E. end of the Ile St-Louis to join the Boul. St-Germain (the dome of the Panthéon is seen in the distance). At the junction of the quay and boulevard lies the *Caserne des Célestins*, the barracks of the Garde Républicaine, built on part of the site of a famous Celestine monastery founded in 1365.

The **Quartier de l'Arsenal,** named after the arsenal established here by Henri IV, extends from the Seine to the Bastille. At Nos. 1–3 Rue de Sully is the **Bibliothèque de l'Arsenal** (open 10–5, except on Sun., holidays, and the first fortnight in Sept.), founded in 1757 by Antoine d'Argenson de Paulmy, governor of the Arsenal, and installed in the former residence of the Grand Master, of which several rooms with their furniture have been preserved.

The library possesses 12,000 MSS., 1,000,000 printed vols., and 120,000 engravings; it is noted especially for its incomparable series of illuminated MSS. and its almost complete collection of French dramatic works. Among the interesting documents are the papers of the Bastille, souvenirs of the 'Man in the Iron Mask,' the documents of the 'Affair of the Diamond Necklace,' and the letters of Henri IV to the Marquise de Verneuil. St. Louis's Book of Hours and Charles V's Bible are shown also.—Nodier, Hérédia, Mérimée, and Anatole France were librarians here.

The RUE ST-ANTOINE, an ancient and busy thoroughfare, continues the Rue de Rivoli to the E., beyond the Rue François-Miron and Rue Pavée. At No. 101 is the entrance to the *Lycée Charlemagne*, which occupies a house of the Jesuits (17th cent.).

The adjoining church of **St-Paul-St-Louis,** or the *Grands-Jésuites*, was built for the Society of Jesus by Louis XIII in 1627–41, and was originally dedicated to St. Louis only, the name of St. Paul being added in 1801 to commemorate the demolished church of St-Paul-des-Champs. It was designed by Père Fr. Derrand, and its florid style, founded on that of the Italian churches of the 16th cent., is the earliest example of the Jesuit school of architecture in France. The dome is the oldest in Paris after that of the Carmes. Richelieu said his first mass here. The handsome baroque portal is by Père Martel Ange. The interior is over-decorated but imposing. The shell-shaped holy-water basins were presented by Victor Hugo at the christening of his first-born son. In the left transept is a painting of Christ in the Garden of Olives, a fine early work by *Delacroix* (1827); in the right transept is a painting of Louis XIII with a model of the church, and St. Louis, by *Simon Vouet*; and on the left of the high altar is a Mater Dolorosa, by *Germain Pilon*.

No. 62, farther on in the Rue St-Antoine, is the **Hôtel de Sully*, built by Jean du Cerceau in 1624–30 on part of the site of the Palais des Tournelles and purchased in 1634 by Sully, the minister of Henri IV. No. 21, the *Hôtel de Mayenne* or *Hôtel d'Ormesson* (now the Ecole Commerciale des Francs-Bourgeois), with its turret and charming staircase, is likewise by Du Cerceau (1613). The Rue de Birague, on the left, leads viâ a charming gateway to the Place des Vosges. The *Temple de Ste-Marie*, now a Protestant church, farther on in the Rue St-Antoine, was originally the chapel of the convent of the

Visitation, a circular building of graceful outline, erected by Fr. Mansart in 1632. Fouquet (d. 1680) and Charles de Sévigné (killed in a duel in 1651) were buried here. Balzac's first Paris lodging was a garret (at 3 sous a day) at No. 9 Rue Lesdiguières, on the right.—The Rue St-Antoine ends at the Place de la Bastille.

Near their junction was the barricade of 1848, where Abp. Affre was shot while urging the people to peace. This spot was also one of the last strongholds of the Communards in 1871.

6. THE DISTRICTS TO THE NORTH OF THE RUE DE RIVOLI AND RUE ST-ANTOINE.

MÉTRO stations: *Bastille* (lines 1, 5, 8); *St-Paul* and *Hôtel de Ville* (line 1); *République* (lines 3, 5, 8, 9, 11); *Temple* (line 3); *Arts et Métiers* (lines 3 and 11); *Réaumur-Sébastopol* (lines 3 and 4).—MOTOR-BUSES: Place de la Bastille (routes 20, 66, 69, 76, 86, 91); Hôtel de Ville (routes 69, 72, 73, 74, 75, 76, 77, 96); Place de la République (routes 20, 52, 58, 65, 75); Arts et Métiers (routes 52 and 58).

The ***Quartier du Marais,** a fashionable district down to the 18th cent. and one of the most interesting parts of old Paris, forms a triangle with its apex at the Place de la République and its sides defined by the Rue du Temple on the W., the Rue de Rivoli and Rue St-Antoine on the S., and the boulevards on the E. Many of its interesting old mansions have fallen from their high estate and are occupied as factories, offices, and shops, and much of the old quarter is now in process of being demolished and modernised.

Parallel with the S. part of the Boul. Beaumarchais is the RUE DES TOURNELLES, No. 28 in which is a fine mansion built for himself by Jules Hardouin-Mansart (1646–1708). It was partly occupied at one time by the cultured and fascinating courtesan Ninon de l'Enclos. The Rue du Pas-de-la-Mule, farther on, leads (r.) to the Boul. Beaumarchais and (l.) to the Place des Vosges.

The ***Place des Vosges,** the heart of the Marais, a large square surrounded by houses in red brick with stone facings, was built on a uniform plan with arcaded ground floors, and, though now somewhat lonely and neglected, it has preserved its ancient aspect. It is approached direct from the Rue St-Antoine viâ the Rue de Birague.

The square occupies the site of the royal *Palais des Tournelles*, the residence of the Duke of Bedford, regent of France after the death of Henry V; in 1559 this was the scene of the tournament fatal to Henri II and was abandoned in consequence by his widow Catherine de Médicis. The square was laid out in its present form probably by Baptiste du Cerceau for Henri IV as the *Place Royale* and opened in 1605; the king's pavilion was above the gateway in the centre of the S. side, while the queen's was the corresponding building opposite. In the reign of Louis XIV this was one of the most fashionable addresses in Paris and the centre of the 'Nouvelles Précieuses' satirised by Molière. It acquired its present name in 1799, the department of the Vosges having been the first to discharge its liabilities for the Revolutionary Wars.

At the corners of the square are fountains, and in the centre is a poor equestrian statue of Louis XIII, by Cortot and Dupaty.—Adjoining No. 1, the *Hôtel de Coulanges* (1606), is the pavilion in which Mme de Sévigné was born in 1626. No. 3 is the *Hôtel d'Estrades*; No. 7 the *Petit-Hôtel de Sully*. No. 9, the *Hôtel de Chaulnes*, was the residence of Rachel (d. 1858), the tragedian. No. 21 was the mansion of Card. de Richelieu (1615), in front of which was fought in 1627, on the very day after the cardinal's edict against duelling, the famous duel of François de Montmorency and Des Chapelles against Bussy and Beuvron. No. 24, the *Hôtel de Vitry*, was the first house in the square to be completed. No. 14 occupies part of the *Hôtel Dangeau*, the home of the Marquis de Dangeau (1638–1720), the historian (comp. p. 163). Théophile Gautier and Alphonse Daudet lived for a while at No. 8.

No. 6 in the Place des Vosges is the ***Musée Victor-Hugo,** installed in 1903 in the house of which the poet Victor Hugo occupied the second floor from 1833 to 1848. The house, built in 1610 for the Maréchal de Lavardin (d. 1619), was subsequently the residence of the courtesan Marion Delorme (d. 1650). The museum is open daily 10–12.30, 2–5 (except Tues. and holidays); adm. 25 fr.; free on Sun.

On the staircase and landings are drawings and water-colours to illustrate Hugo's works.

First Floor. Ante-Room. Paintings by *Willette, Carrière, Rioult*, and others. The bust of Hugo is by *Schœnewerk* (1879). R. 1 contains a series of the most interesting of Hugo's drawings. Bust of Hugo by *Rodin*.—R. 2. Drawings by Hugo, and MSS and first editions of his works.—R. 3. Portraits and souvenirs of Juliette Drouet. Paintings by *Fantin-Latour, Henner*, and others.

Second Floor. Ante-Room. Bust of Paul Meurice, who commissioned most of the paintings in the museum; bust of Hugo by *David d'Angers* (1838). *Raffaelli*, Fête on Hugo's 80th birthday; *Jeanniot*, Hauteville, Hugo's home in Guernsey.—The Dining Room contains furniture designed by Hugo and a table with inkstands belonging to Hugo, George Sand, Dumas père, and Lamartine, with their autographs.—R. 3 (the former drawing-room) contains the furniture from the dining-room in Juliette Drouet's house at Guernsey. Woodwork and fireplace by Hugo.—RR. 4–6. Decorations, and portraits and souvenirs of the Hugo family; in R. 6, portraits of Hugo's children, including his daughter Léopoldine, who was drowned on her honeymoon.—R. 7. Sketches, portraits, and photographs of Hugo. Head of the author by *Dalou*, modelled the day after his death.—R. 8 is a reconstitution of the room where Hugo died, with portraits by *Bonnat* and *Falguière*.—The Library (on the 3rd floor, at present closed) contains a complete set of first editions, many with interesting dedications.

Near the N.W. corner of the Place des Vosges we reach the Rue des Francs-Bourgeois and the Rue de Turenne, two of the chief streets of the Marais, both full of interest for the lovers of old French architecture and history.

The Rue de Turenne, which begins at the Rue St-Antoine on the S., runs due N. In the court of No. 23 is the *Hôtel de Villacerf*, built c. 1660, with a fountain. At No. 41 is the *Fontaine de Joyeuse* (1687). No. 54 is the *Hôtel de Gourgues*, dating from the early 18th cent. No. 56 was for a time the home of Scarron (1610–60) and his wife Françoise d'Aubigné (1635–1719), afterwards Mme de Maintenon. No. 60 is the *Hôtel du Grand-Veneur*, with a boar's head on the façade.—The church of **St-Denis-du-St-Sacrement,** built by Godde in the Grecian style of 1835, occupies the site of the mansion of Marshal Turenne. The interior, of the Ionic order, has a fine Pietà by Delacroix (floodlit on application to the sacristan), wall-paintings by Abel de Pujol, a statue of St. Geneviève by Perraud (1868), and other sculptures.

No. 5 Rue Thorigny (reached by the small street opposite the church) is the magnificent *Hôtel de Juigné*, built in 1656 for Aubert de Fontenai, the financier, and popularly known as the 'Hôtel Salé' on account of the profits its owner had made out of the salt tax. The grand staircase is especially fine. Part of the Archives Nationales will eventually be housed here.

The *RUE DES FRANCS-BOURGEOIS leads N.W. from the Place des Vosges to the Rue des Archives. It takes its name from the citizens who, being vassals to a feudal lord, were exempt from municipal taxes. At the corner of this street and the Rue de Sévigné is the **Musée Carnavalet** (Rte. 23), in a house once occupied by Mme de Sévigné.

In the RUE DE SÉVIGNÉ, to the right, No. 29, formerly the *Hôtel Le Peletier de St-Fargeau*, built by P. Bullet in 1687, is now the **Bibliothèque Historique de la Ville de Paris** (open daily, except holidays, 9.30–12, 1.30–5). The library contains over 400,000 vols. and 100,000 MSS. relating to the history of Paris and the Revolution. It is also the seat of the Service des Travaux Historiques de la Ville de Paris.

In the RUE PAYENNE, the next turning to the right (N.) from the Rue des Francs-Bourgeois, is the 18th cent. house (No. 5) in which died Clotilde de Vaux (1846), the friend of Auguste Comte. Since 1905 it has been used as a *Positivist Chapel* on the lines laid down by Comte (adm. 10–6, except. Mon.). Nos. 11 and 13 are good examples of early 18th cent. mansions.

The RUE PAVÉE, leading left (S.) from the Rue des Francs-Bourgeois, has several fine old houses, including (at the corner) the **Hôtel Lamoignon* (No. 24), built in 1594 for Diane de France, the legitimised daughter of Henri II, but named after Lamoignon, president of the Parlement de Paris (1658), a later occupant. In this street stood the notorious prison of *La Force* (demolished 1851), where many victims of the Revolution were massacred.

No. 16 RUE ELZÉVIR, the next turning on the right (N.), was the home of Ninon de l'Enclos in 1642.

Farther on in the Rue des Francs-Bourgeois are the handsome red brick *Hôtel de Jean de Fourcy* (No. 30), with a bust of Henri IV, and the *Hôtel d'Albret* (No. 31), dating from c. 1550 but rebuilt in the 18th century. Farther on the Rue Vieille-du-Temple diverges on the right and left.

The RUE VIEILLE-DU-TEMPLE, connecting the Rue de Rivoli with the Boul. du Temple, is another street with many interesting old houses, such as No. 15 (the *Hôtel de Vibray*), No. 36 (with a charming door), No. 43 (the *Hôtel de Bragelonne*), and No. 44 (door and staircase). No. 47, the **Hôtel de Hollande*, stands on the site of the house of the Maréchal de Rieux, in front of which the Duke of Orleans was assassinated in 1407 by the hired bravos of the Duke of Burgundy. The present house, built by Cottard in 1638–55, with a finely carved oaken door and a large bas-relief of Romulus and Remus in the courtyard, was the residence of the Dutch ambassador in the reign of Louis XIV. Later it was the home of Beaumarchais, who wrote his 'Mariage de Figaro' here and in 1788 turned the house into a provident institution for poor nursing mothers. A few houses beyond No. 54 (15th cent.; at the corner of the Rue des Francs-Bourgeois) stood the *Hôtel Barbette*, the favourite residence of Queen Isabeau de

Bavière, of which the pretty Gothic turret of the *Hôtel Hérouët* (1528; restored in 1886) is sometimes considered to be a relic. The building is in course of restoration after damage by enemy action in 1944. No. 87, the **Hôtel de Rohan,** known also as the *Hôtel de Strasbourg* and the *Palais Cardinal,* was begun in 1704. It was successively occupied by four cardinals of the Rohan family, all of whom were bishops of Strasbourg; the most famous was the Cardinal de Rohan implicated in the 'affair of the diamond necklace' (1784–5). From 1809 to 1925 the mansion was occupied by the Imprimerie Nationale, and it now contains certain departments of the Archives Nationales (for adm., apply to the concierge). In 1928–38 the building and gardens underwent a thorough restoration. In the second court is a good relief, the Horses of Apollo, by *Robert Le Lorrain*; and the 'Cabinet des Singes' contains paintings of apes by *Chr. Huet* (1745–50).

In the Rue Barbette, opposite the Hôtel de Rohan, No. 8 is the *Hôtel de Choisy* and No. 17, the *Hôtel de Brégis*, has a door with two medallions.—In the Rue des Quatre-Fils, beyond the Hôtel de Rohan, Nos. 16 and 20 have fine doorways, and No. 22 was the residence of the celebrated Marquise du Deffand (1697–1780), whose salon was frequented by Voltaire, Montesquieu, D'Alembert, Horace Walpole, and other distinguished men.—In the Rue Charlot are several 16–18th cent. houses and the church of **St-Jean-St-François,** built in 1623 as a Capuchin chapel and enlarged in 1828–55. In the choir are statues of St. Francis of Assisi by Germain Pilon and St. Denis by Jacques Sarrazin. In the sacristy are preserved the sacred ornaments used at the celebration of mass at the Temple on the morning of Louis XVI's execution.—In the parallel Rue de Saintonge, Robespierre lived at No. 64 in 1789–91.

Farther on in the Rue des Francs-Bourgeois is the head office of the *Crédit Municipal* or *Mont-de-Piété,* the chief government pawnbroking establishment, founded by Louis XVI in 1777 and reorganised by Napoleon III. In the Cour de l'Horloge are lines marking the course of the city walls of Philip Augustus. Adjacent is *Notre-Dame-des-Blancs-Manteaux,* a church of little interest, apart from its pulpit, a work of the most florid Flemish style of the mid-18th century.

The Rue des Francs-Bourgeois ends at the Rue des Archives, and at the right-hand corner stands the **Archives Nationales,** or *Record Office,* founded in 1795 and housed since 1808 in the old *Hôtel de Soubise, the greater part of which was built by *Delamair* in 1706–12, on the site of the mansion of the Ducs de Guise. The gateway, with a figure of History, after *Delacroix,* in the tympanum, leads to the Cour d'Honneur, which is surrounded by a splendid colonnade and has copies of the 'Four Seasons,' by *Robert Le Lorrain,* on the façade.

The Musée Documentaire de l'Histoire de France, in which some of the outstanding documents, MSS., etc., belonging to the Archives are exhibited, is open daily 2–5, adm. 50 fr.

The exhibition rooms, on the first floor, have preserved much of their 18t, cent. decoration, including paintings by *Boucher, Carle Vanloo, Natoire, Restout* and others. The documents usually on view include letters and wills of French royal personages, from Philip Augustus onwards, and many letters from foreign potentates (including the Emperor Charles V, Christina of Sweden, and Tamerlane) and statesmen (Benjamin Franklin and Washington). Among the state documents are the Treaties of Bretigny, Westphalia, and the Pyrenees; the Report of the Council of the Parlement of Paris, with a contemporary sketch of Joan of Arc; the Edict of Nantes (with the signature of Henri IV) and its Revocation. Among the rich collection of Revolutionary relics may be mentioned the Oath of the Tennis Court; Marie Antoinette's last letter and Louis XVI's will; the official report on the execution of Louis XVI; a letter of Charlotte Corday; and the keys of the Bastille. The furniture includes the table on which the wounded Robespierre was laid in July 1794, and the chair of Bailly, President of the National Assembly (1789).

The Rue des Archives begins on the S. at the Rue de Rivoli, opposite the Rue Lobau. On the right (No. 24) is the *Temple des Billettes,* built in 1756 for the Carmelites, but used since 1812 as a Lutheran church. A pretty 15th cent. cloister on the N. is a relic of the former convent. The handsome Gothic gateway flanked with turrets at No. 58 was formerly the entrance to the *Hôtel de Clisson,* built by the Constable in 1371, known as the *Hôtel de Guise* from 1553 to 1688, and now belonging to the Archives. Bolingbroke, afterwards Henry IV, gave a farewell banquet there in 1399 before setting forth to win the crown of England. Opposite, at the corner of the Rue des Haudriettes, is a pretty fountain, with a naiad by Mignot (1765). Next comes the *Central Telephone Exchange* (1934), in sharp contrast with the 17th cent. No. 70, the house where Lamennais (1782–1854), the independent religious writer, died. No. 78, built by P. Bullet, with a beautiful staircase, was the residence of Marshal Tallard (1712), vanquished at Blenheim; it has a fine staircase at the end of the court. The street ends at the Square du Temple (see below).

The densely populated **Quartier du Temple,** which derives its name from the house of the Knights Templars (see below), lies to the S. of the E. part of the Rue de Turbigo. Its chief streets are the Rue du Temple and Rue St-Martin.

The Rue du Temple, parallel with the Rue des Archives, unites the Place de l'Hôtel de Ville with the Place de la République and contains several interesting buildings. The square turret on No. 24 dates from 1610. At No. 62 Anne de Montmorency, Constable of France, died in 1567. No. 71, the *Hôtel de St-Aignan,* built by Lemuet in 1640–50, has a fine gate and courtyards. No. 79, the *Hôtel de Montmor,* dates from c. 1620 and has a great gateway and a charming pediment in the courtyard.

No. 28 Rue Michel-le-Comte, a turning on the left, is a notable 18th cent. mansion, the probable birthplace of Mme de Staël (1766).

Nos. 101–103 are the *Hôtel de Montmorency* (entrance, No. 5 Rue de Montmorency). No. 115 was the residence of

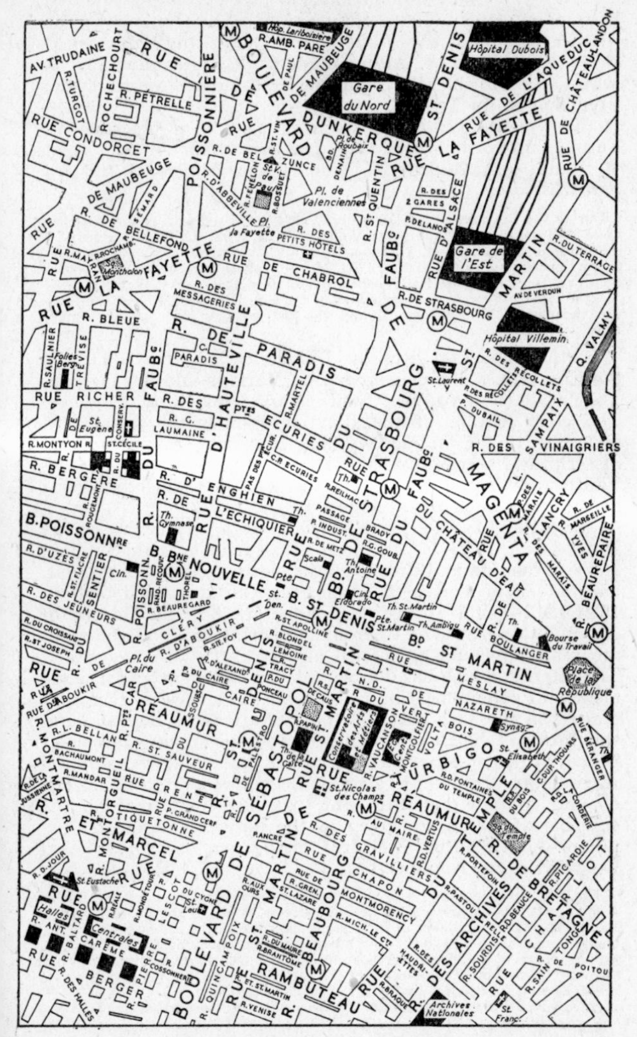

III. GARE DU NORD—TEMPLE

Jean Bart (1650–1702), the famous privateer, who was created Admiral of the Fleet by Louis XIV; and Balzac lived at No. 122 after 1814. After passing the Rue Réaumur and its continuation to the right, the Rue de Bretagne, we reach the large **Square du Temple,** on the site of the old stronghold of the Knights Templars, the headquarters of the order in Europe, occupied after 1313 by the Order of St. John of Jerusalem. On the E. side is the *Mairie of the 3rd Arrondissement.*

During the Revolution the TOUR DU TEMPLE was used as a prison, and here Louis XVI and the royal family were brought in Aug. 1792. The king went hence to the guillotine on Jan. 21st, 1793; on Aug. 2nd Marie Antoinette was removed to the Conciergerie; on May 9th, 1794, Mme Elisabeth was carried off to execution; the Dauphin (Louis XVII) is believed to have died here on June 9th, 1795 and the sole survivor, Mme Royale, was released on Dec. 19th, 1795. The tower was demolished by Napoleon I, and the last vestiges were removed under Napoleon III.

Farther on in the Rue du Temple, beyond the square, is **Ste-Elisabeth,** a church founded by Marie de Médicis in 1628. The façade is a copy of Santa Maria Novella at Florence. The chief feature of the Ionic interior is the woodwork, including, in the ambulatory, late 16th cent. *Woodcarvings of scriptural scenes from the abbey of St-Vaast at Arras.—The Rue du Temple now joins the Rue de Turbigo and ends at the Place de la République.

The straight RUE ST-MARTIN, leading from the Pont Notre-Dame to (⅘ m.) the Porte St-Martin, was the original Roman road from Lutetia to the north. Near the S. end, half-hidden by houses, is **St-Merri,** a Gothic church built in 1520–1612 on the alleged site of the grave of St. Mederic of Autun (7th cent.). The W. front and portal, though unfinished, are remarkable for their rich and eccentric ornamentation. The interior, which has double aisles on the right and a single aisle with communicating chapels on the left, was somewhat marred in the 18th cent. by the alterations of *Boffrand* and the brothers *Slodtz*; but the carved keystones, the vault beneath the crossing, the transeptal rose windows, and the fragmentary 16th cent. glass, still deserve admiration. The chapels contain mid-19th cent. paintings and frescoes, the subjects of which are given in the notices hanging on the pillars.—No. 89 Rue St-Martin, farther on, has a 17th cent. bas-relief of the Annunciation.

The old quarter around St-Merri, between the Rue St-Martin and the Rue du Temple, with its narrow and picturesque streets, is one of the poorest parts of Paris; it retains a number of interesting old houses, which, however, are fast being demolished.—The RUE DE VENISE, which used to be the home of the usurers, is one of the oldest and most curious streets in Paris and retains in part (W. end) its cut-throat appearance of the 14th cent.; No. 27 was the *Cabaret de l'Epée-de-Bois,* frequented by Louis Racine and Marivaux.

No. 13 RUE CHAPON (on the right, farther N.), with an interesting court, was the house of the Archbishops of Reims. In the RUE QUINCAMPOIX parallel with

boyant Gothic church with Renaissance details, built in the 15–17th cent. but completely remodelled in 1862–66, when a bay was added to the nave and the Gothic façade and graceful spire constructed. Mme du Barry (Jeanne Bécu ; 1746–93) was married here in 1764. In the tympanum of the main doorway are paintings on enamelled lava by Paul Balze representing scenes from the life of St. Lawrence. The roof has elaborately carved pendentives.—Just beyond the church the Boulevard de Strasbourg diverges on the right for the **Gare de l'Est,** the terminus of the line to Strasbourg, etc.

The Boulevard de Strasbourg, uniting the Gare de l'Est with the Boul. St-Denis, forms with its S. extensions, the Boul. de Sébastopol, the Boul. du Palais, and the Boul. St-Michel, one of the chief arteries of N. to S. traffic in Paris.

Farther on the Boul. de Magenta passes close to the former *Prison de St-Lazare* which was entirely renovated in 1935, and converted into a clinic. This was the headquarters from 1632 of the Congregation of Lazarist Missionaries, founded in 1625 by St. Vincent de Paul (1576–1660).—The boulevard then crosses the Rue de La Fayette (see below) at the point whence the short Boul. Denain leads N.E. (r.) to the **Gare du Nord,** the terminus of the line from Calais, Boulogne, etc., in the Rue de Dunkerque. The statues on the top of the central building represent some of the principal cities of Northern Europe. To the N.W. is the *Hôpital Lariboisière* (1846–53), the largest hospital in Paris (1200 beds).

The Rue de La Fayette, one of the longest streets in Paris, stretches from the Rue de la Chaussée-d'Antin on the S.W. to the Place Stalingrad on the N.E. A little to the W. of its intersection of the Boul. de Magenta is the small *Place de La Fayette,* dominated on the N. by **St-Vincent-de-Paul,** a large church on the basilican plan, built by *Lepère* and *Hittorf* in 1824–44. A wide flight of steps and two curved roadways ascend to the portico of twelve Ionic columns, above which is a pediment with a bas-relief of St. Vincent de Paul with Faith and Charity. The square towers are 177 ft. in height.—The chief decoration in the interior is the huge processional frieze (558 ft. in length and 10 ft. high) in the nave, painted, in imitation of the mosaics of Ravenna, by *Hippolyte Flandrin,* on a gold background. The other furnishings, good of their kind, were carried out by noted artists of the early 19th cent. ; the choir-stalls have a peculiar interest of their own, as they show portraits of the Orleans princes in the costumes of their patron-saints.

Following the Rue de La Fayette towards the S.W., we cross the Rue du Faubourg-Poissonnière, where Corot died in 1875 (at No. 56), and farther on, at the Square Montholon (r.), the Rue Montholon, where No. 9 was the residence of Franz Liszt in 1831. The Rue de La Fayette beyond the Rue de

Châteaudun is noted for its art-dealers' and old curiosity shops, and the side streets on the S. leading to the Grands Boulevards are a centre of high finance. The pavement on the right between the Rue de Châteaudun and the Rue Buffault is an open-air diamond-market. The street then crosses the Rue du Faubourg-Montmartre, the Rue Laffitte, and the Rue de Provence, likewise noted for its curiosity shops, and ends at the junction of the Rue de la Chaussée-d'Antin with the Boul. Haussmann.

The important RUE DE LA CHAUSSÉE-D'ANTIN leads N. from the Boulevard des Italiens to the conspicuous church of La Trinité.

Rossini lived at No. 2 from 1857 onwards. No. 5 was the residence of Chopin from 1832 until he left for Majorca in 1838 with George Sand. No. 7 (demolished) was the residence of the Neckers, who entertained Gibbon here; Mirabeau died at No. 42 in 1791. In the Rue Taitbout, the next street to the E., Chopin lived at No. 80 in 1842–49.

The conspicuous and ugly church of **La Trinité** was built in 1863–67 by *Ballu*, in a hybrid Renaissance style. The porch is surmounted by a tower 206 ft. in height.

The three streets behind La Trinité (E. to W. the Rue Pigalle, Rue Blanche, Rue de Clichy) are all convenient approaches to Montmartre; each with a theatre, but not otherwise very interesting. Victor Hugo lived at No. 21 Rue de Clichy in 1880, and Daniele Manin (1804–57), the hero of the Risorgimento in Venice, died an exile at No. 70 Rue Blanche.

At No. 14 Rue de La Rochefoucauld, a short distance to the E. of La Trinité, is the **Musée Gustave-Moreau** (open 10–4, except Sun. and Tues.), a collection of works (1000 paintings, over 7000 drawings, etc.) by the painter Gustave Moreau (1826–98), bequeathed by him, together with his residence, to the state.

The dull RUE DE CHÂTEAUDUN, running E. from the Place de la Trinité to the Rue de La Fayette, crosses the Rue St-Georges, where Auber lived for thirty years and died in 1871 (at No. 24), and Henri Murger, the son of a concierge, was born in 1822 (at No. 19). **Notre-Dame-de-Lorette,** another of the drearily magnificent basilican churches of the early 19th cent., was built in 1823–36 by *Hippolyte Lebas*, with a portico of four Corinthian columns. The chief attraction of the luxuriously fitted-up interior is its frescoes, though many of them are almost indistinguishable. Attractive musical services are held here in the evenings during May, the month of Mary. Behind the church are (r.) the Rue des Martyrs, an approach to Montmartre (Balzac once lived at No. 47 and Géricault died at No. 49 in 1824), and (l.) the Rue Notre-Dame-de-Lorette, leading N.W. to the PLACE ST-GEORGES. The 'Lorettes' of this quarter, a favourite subject of the caricaturist Gavarni (1801–66), are represented, with other types of his, on his monument here. No. 27 in this square is the *Hôtel Thiers*, the residence of President Thiers (1797–1877). Burned down by the Communards, the building was re-constructed and bequeathed in 1905 to the Institut de France.

It now contains the BIBLIOTHÈQUE THIERS (80,000 vols. dealing with the history of France from the Revolution to the present day) and the Napoleonic collection of Frédéric Masson (30,000 vols., drawings by *David*, bust of Josephine by *Houdon*, etc.). The former is open on Tues. and Thurs., from 1–5; adm. on the recommendations of two members of the Institut. The Masson collection is open on request to Mlle Ginot (tel. TRU. 14–33).

At the end of the Rue Notre-Dame-de-Lorette is the Rue Chaptal (l.), at No. 16 in which Charles Dickens sat for his portrait to Ary Scheffer in 1856. The Rue Fontaine goes on thence to the Place Blanche, crossing the Rue de Douai, which leads (l.) to the Place de Clichy, viâ the *Place Vintimille*, with a bronze statue of the composer Berlioz (1803–69), who died at 4 Rue de Calais, close by. Zola died in 1902 at 21bis Rue de Bruxelles (which crosses the Place); while at 30 Rue de Douai (the house of Turgenev and Mme Viardot, the singer) Dickens met George Sand in 1856.

B. Montmartre.

MÉTRO stations: *Clichy* (lines 2 and 13); *Blanche* (line 2); *Pigalle* (lines 12 and 2); *Barbès-Rochechouart* (lines 2 and 4); *Abbesses*, *Lamarck-Caulaincourt*, and *Joffrin* (line 12); *Château-Rouge* (line 4).—MOTOR-BUSES: Place Clichy (routes 30, 68, 74, 80, 95); Place Pigalle (routes 30, 67); Barbès-Rochechouart (routes 30, 31); for the Sacré Cœur, route 30 to the Place d'Anvers.

The **Place de Clichy** is one of the busiest centres of traffic in the N. of Paris. Here stood the 'Barrière de Clichy,' heroically defended against the Russians by the Invalides and the Garde Nationale under Marshal Moncey on March 30th, 1814. In the centre is the monument to Moncey, a bronze group ('The Defence of Paris') 20 ft. high (1869). On the E. side of the Place begins the wide BOULEVARD DE CLICHY, one of the outer line of boulevards, forming, together with its E. continuation the Boul. de Rochechouart, the S. boundary of Montmartre. This lively thoroughfare is the centre of the night life of Montmartre with most of the cabarets and night-cafés. On the left, beside the *Gaumont Palace*, the largest cinema in Europe (5000 seats), diverges the RUE CAULAINCOURT, which is carried over the cemetery by a viaduct and is the most convenient approach for motorists to the Butte Montmartre.

Towards the middle of the 19th cent. the construction of large new thoroughfares through the N. slums rendered access to **Montmartre** more convenient, and the poorer artists, migrating to the cheap little streets on the Mount, made it for about thirty years a real centre of artistic endeavour, where poor living and high thinking were combined with unconventional gaiety. About 1885 the famous 'cabaret artistique' 'Le Chat Noir' (closed in 1897) was opened, and the advertisement thus given to the artistic attractions of the district invited a tide of pseudo-

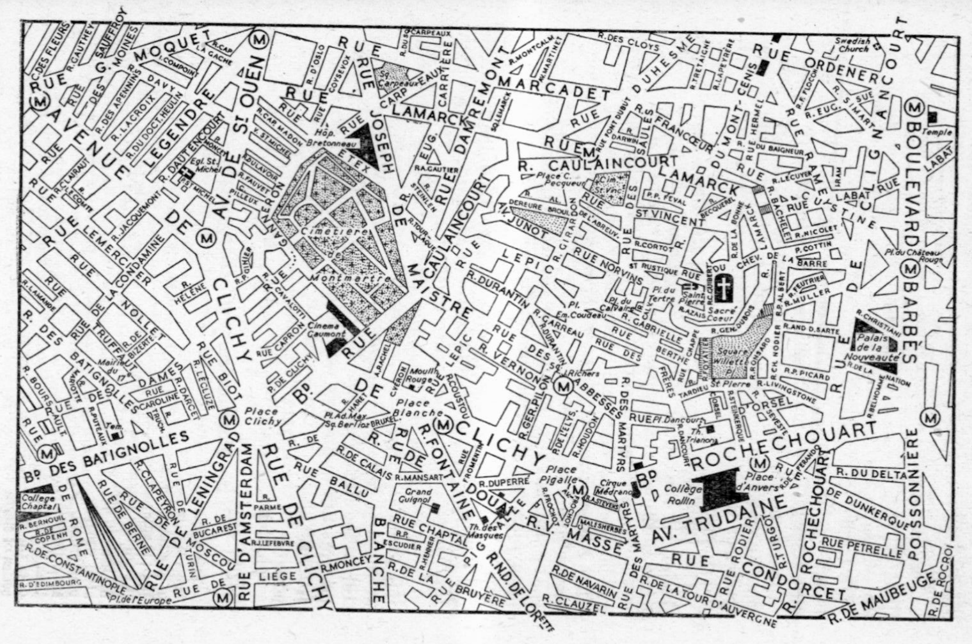

IV. MONTMARTRE

bohemians, foreign tourists, and less desirable hangers-on, before which the serious workers retired. The motley crowds to be seen in the cafés and 'cabarets artistiques' of the Place Pigalle, etc., have now but a shadowy connection with art or letters, and are apt to include elements against which the tourist should be on his guard. The personalities of Montmartre in its great days were vividly depicted by Henri de Toulouse-Lautrec (1864–1901), whose studio was at 5 Av. Frochot, near the Place Pigalle. Perhaps the best-known painter of the present-day Montmartre is Maurice Utrillo.

The Av. Rachel, on the left of the Boul. de Clichy, is the direct approach to the **Cimetière de Montmartre,** or *Cimetière du Nord,* on the W. slopes of the Butte, less important than Père-Lachaise but containing the graves of many famous people of the 19–20th cent., notably authors, artists, actors, and musicians.

The Boul. de Clichy goes on E. to the Place Blanche. On the left are the rebuilt *Moulin Rouge,* converted into a cinema, while the Rue Lepic ascends the steep slope of the Butte.

The **Place Pigalle** is surrounded by night-cafés and restaurants. The Passage de l'Elysée-des-Beaux-Arts, on the N., leads to the church of *St-Jean-l'Evangéliste,* built of reinforced concrete in 1894–1904.

The BOULEVARD ROCHECHOUART continues the Boul. de Clichy beyond the Rue des Martyrs. On the left rises the Butte Montmartre, while on the right are the *Cirque Médrano,* the *Collège Rollin* (entrance at 12 Av. Trudaine), and the little *Place d'Anvers.* In the centre of the gardens is a column with a figure of Armed Peace, by Coutan.

From the Place d'Anvers the Rue Steinkerque leads N. to the *Place St-Pierre.* The lower part of the square, at the foot of the first terrace, is known as the Square Willette; on the left is the little *Fontaine des Innocents,* by Derré. A series of terraces and pathways were added to the steep slope during 1924–29, and in the centre a handsome double staircase ascends to the terrace at the foot of the Sacré Cœur, which is reached also by a funicular railway from the W. side of the square.

The ***Butte Montmartre,** the 'butte sacrée,' rises 423 ft. above sea-level and 335 ft. above the level of the Seine.

The name of Montmartre has been variously derived from Mons Mercurii, Mons Martis, and Mons Martyrum. Of these the two first presuppose the existence of a Roman temple on the hill; the last is based on the legend that St. Denis and his companions, SS. Rusticus and Eleutherius, were beheaded at the foot of the hill, St. Denis afterwards walking to the site of the Basilica of St-Denis with his head in his hands. The *Chapelle du Martyre* (in the convent at 9 Rue Antoinette) occupies the probable position of a chapel erected on the site of the martyrdom. It was in the crypt beneath this that St. Ignatius de Loyola and his six companions, including St. Francis Xavier, took the first Jesuit vows, in 1534, thus founding the Society of Jesus.—The Butte Montmartre, commanding as it does the entire city, was the military key to Paris, and its history is one long series of sieges and battles. It was occupied by Henri of Navarre in 1589; here in 1814 took place the final struggle between the French and the Allies; and in 1871 it was held for two months by the Communards.

The ***Basilique du Sacré-Cœur,** crowning the Butte Montmartre and visible from almost every part of Paris, though hardly beautiful, is a conspicuous, oriental-looking church of white stone in the Romanesque-Byzantine style of the 12th century. The building of the church was decreed by the National Assembly in 1874 as a national votive offering of humiliation and repentance after the war of 1870–71 and was begun in 1876 from the plans of *Abadie*. Though used for service since 1891 the church was not consecrated as a basilica until Oct. 16th, 1919. The church is 328 ft. long, 164 ft. wide (246 ft. across the ambulatory), and is surmounted by a dome 197 ft. high and by a square bell-tower (308 ft. high), the latter being the work of *Magne* (1913).

On the façade are bas-reliefs of Jesus and the Woman of Samaria, by *A. d'Houdain*, and Mary Magdalen at the house of Simon, by *Louis Noël*; in the tympana, a Crucifixion by *Barrias*, Moses striking the rock by *Fagel*, and the Incredulity of St. Thomas by *H. Lefebvre*. The statue of the Sacred Heart above the main portal is by *Michel*. On the angles of the W. portico are two huge equestrian statues in bronze, of St. Louis and St. Joan of Arc, by *Lefebvre*.

The imposing **Interior** is richly decorated. On the right, facing the aisle, is the CHAPELLE DE L'ARMÉE, with mosaics of St. Joan of Arc and St. Louis and a statue of Joan of Arc by *Fagel*. The CHAPELLE DE ST-BENOÎT-LABRE, the first in the ambulatory on the right, contains a monument by *Fagel* to Louis Veuillot (1813–83), the Ultramontane journalist (the nun is a portrait of Veuillot's daughter). The first chapel in the left aisle (nearest the entrance) is the CHAPELLE DE LA MARINE, with a lamp in the form of the stern of a ship.

The fine CRYPT extending under the aisles, transepts, and choir is open 9–12 and 2–6 (adm. 10 fr.). The central CHAPELLE DES MORTS contains statues of Card. Guibert (d. 1886), offering the completed church to the Virgin, by *L. Noël*, and of Card. Richard (d. 1908) and Card. Amette (d. 1923), both by *Lefebvre*; the Pietà on the altar is by *Coutan*.—In the BELL-TOWER hangs the *Savoyarde*, or *Françoise-Marguerite*, a great bell presented by the four dioceses of Savoy and remarkable for its sonorous timbre; it was cast at Annecy in 1895 and weighs nearly 17¾ tons.—The DOME is open 9–11.30 and 2–5.30 (adm. 30 fr.). We first ascend to a platform overlooking the church of St-Pierre, where we find the guide. From the second gallery, or Galerie des Vitraux, we view the whole of the interior of the Sacré-Cœur. From either the exterior Galerie des Colonnes or the lantern at the top of the dome we obtain a magnificent * *View* of Paris and its environs, extending over a radius of 30 m.

To the W. of the Sacré-Cœur is a massive building belonging to a reservoir. In the Rue du Mont-Cenis is the old church of **St-Pierre-de-Montmartre,** the successor of the earliest Christian church in Paris, erected to commemorate the martyrdom of St. Denis. The present church, a relic of a Benedictine nunnery founded by Adélaïde de Savoie (d. 1154), was erected by Louis VI, her husband, in 1137–47. The simple façade dates from the 18th century. Inside, against the W. wall, are two ancient columns with capitals regarded as Merovingian, as are likewise the small capitals in the triforium. The nave has 15th cent. vaulting, but the aisles have wooden roofs. Behind the altar is the foundress's tomb. The apse itself, the exterior view of which is very picturesque, dates from the end of the 12th century. Several of the curious capitals of the columns in the nave, and most of their bases, are obvious reconstructions.

In the old graveyard behind the church, on the left (open only on Nov. 1st), are the tomb of Bougainville (1729–1811), the famous navigator, and a Calvary from the old convent on Mont Valérien.

Not much remains of Old Montmartre, with its cottages and little gardens; but the PLACE DU TERTRE, with the former Mairie (No. 3), is still attractive, as are also the Rue St-Rustique and the Rue du Mont-Cenis. No. 22 in the last was the home of Berlioz in 1834–37.

C. Quartier de l'Opéra, Quartier de l'Europe, and Batignolles.

MÉTRO stations: *Opéra* (lines 3, 7, 8); *Havre-Caumartin* (lines 3 and 9); *St-Lazare* (lines 3, 12, 13); *St-Augustin* (line 9); *Europe* (line 3); *Villiers* (lines 2 and 3); *Malesherbes* (line 3); *Rome* (line 2); *Clichy* (lines 2 and 13).—MOTOR-BUSES: Place de l'Opéra (routes 20, 21, 27, 52, 66, 68, 95); Havre-Caumartin (routes 20, 21, 27, 66, 94, 95); St-Lazare (routes 20, 21, 26, 27, 28, 32, 43, 49, 66, 80, 94); Malesherbes (routes 31, 94); Rome (routes 30, 66); Place Clichy (routes 30, 68, 74, 80, 95).

This district is bounded on the S. by the Boul. de la Madeleine and Boul. des Capucines, on the W. by the Boul. Malesherbes and Av. de Villiers, and on the E. by the Rue de la Chaussée-d'Antin and the Rue and Av. de Clichy. Between the Grands Boulevards and the Gare St-Lazare lies a district of high-class shops and stores, important business offices, and hotels of every grade; to the N.W. of the station is a favourite middle-class and even fashionable residential district; and beyond the Boul. des Batignolles the railway forms a sharp division between the middle-class streets on the W. and a poorer neighbourhood on the E.

The RUE AUBER leads from the Place de l'Opéra to the Boul. Haussmann and is continued thence to the Gare St-Lazare by the Rue du Havre. On the right of the Rue Auber are the opera house and the monument to Charles Garnier; the Rue Boudreau (l.) leads to the *Square de l'Opéra*. In the Rue Caumartin (r.) is the church of *St-Louis-d'Antin* (1783), by Brongniart. The Rue Auber ends at the junction of the Rue Tronchet with the Boul. Haussmann. The *Lycée Condorcet*, No. 8 Rue du Havre, is perhaps the leading boys' school in Paris.

The BOULEVARD HAUSSMANN (c. 1½ m. long), one of the main streets of Paris, was begun by Baron Haussmann in 1857 as part of a scheme to construct an unbroken thoroughfare from the Boul. Montmartre (Rue Drouot) to the Place de l'Etoile, a distance of 1⅝ m. The E. portion of this design, from the Rue Drouot to the Rue Taitbout, was not completed until 1926.

Near its E. end, at the corner of the Chaussée-d'Antin, are the *Galeries La Fayette*, and at the busy junction with the Rue Auber and Rue Tronchet are the large *Magasins du Printemps*. Chopin lived at No. 5 Rue Tronchet in 1839–42.—Following the Boul. Haussmann towards the W., we pass, in the gardens (l.), the **Chapelle Expiatoire** (open daily, except Tues., 12–4 or 5; adm. 20 fr., 10 fr. on Sun.; entrance in the Rue Pasquier), erected in 1815–26 from the plans of *Percier* and *Fontaine*. The chapel was built by order of Louis XVIII and dedicated to the memory of Louis XVI and Marie Antoinette, whose remains, interred in the graveyard of the Madeleine on this site, were removed to St-Denis in 1815. In the interior are two marble groups: Louis XVI and his confessor the Abbé Edgeworth, by *Bosio* ("Fils de St. Louis, montez au ciel"; below is inscribed the king's will, dated Dec. 25th, 1792); and Marie Antoinette supported by Religion, by *Cortot* (the latter figure bearing the features of Mme Elisabeth; below is inscribed the letter said to have been written by the queen in the Conciergerie to her sister-in-law on Oct. 16th, 1793). The bas-relief by *Gérard* above the doorway represents the removal of the royal remains to St-Denis.

In the open space in front of the chapel rest the bodies of nearly 3000 victims of the Revolution, including Charlotte Corday and nearly 1000 Swiss Guards killed on Aug. 10th, 1792.—At No. 8 Rue d'Anjou Gen. Lafayette died in 1834 (tablet); Benjamin Constant died at No. 29 in 1830. No. 102 Boul. Haussmann was Proust's home in 1905–19, with his notorious 'sound-proof' room lined with cork.

At the *Place St-Augustin* the Boul. Haussmann crosses the Boul. Malesherbes. On the N. side is the fashionable church of **St-Augustin,** an early and tasteless example of the use of iron in church-construction (1860–71). In the ornate interior the cupola is decorated with paintings, and the transept-chapels have frescoes by Bouguereau and Boisset. The stained glass is worth examination.

The statue of *Joan of Arc* in front of the church is a replica of the statue at Reims by Paul Dubois.—In the *Square de Laborde* (r.) are a statue of Paul Déroulède (1846–1914), the statesman, by *Landowski*, and '*Quand Même,' a marble group by *Mercié*, a copy of the group at Belfort commemorating the defence of that city in 1870–71. It formerly stood in the Tuileries Gardens.

At the corner of the Rue de la Pépinière, on the E. side of the Place, is the *Cercle Militaire*. This street is continued E. by the Rue St-Lazare to the huge *Hôtel Terminus*, behind which lies the **Gare St-Lazare,** the terminus of the lines from Dieppe, Rouen, Le Havre, etc.

Mme Vigée-Le Brun died at No. 29 Rue St-Lazare in 1842. No. 89 in the Rue de Rome was the home of the poet Stéphane Mallarmé from 1875. In the Rue d'Amsterdam lived Edouard Manet (in 1879–83; at No. 77), Jules Favre (in 1868–75; at No. 91) and Alexandre Dumas (from 1854; at No. 97).

The continuation of the Rue St-Lazare, between the station and La Trinité, is the S. boundary of the QUARTIER DE L'EUROPE, the streets of which are named after the chief cities of Europe. The Rue de Londres leads from La Trinité across the Rue d'Amsterdam to the *Place de l'Europe*, formed by a huge iron bridge over the railway lines. Beyond this, at No. 14 Rue de Madrid, formerly a Dominican college, is the **Conservatoire National de Musique et de Déclamation,** founded in 1765 as the Académie Royal de Chant, and intended primarily for the training of singers and actors for the state theatres.

The COLLECTION OF MUSICAL INSTRUMENTS (open Thurs. and Sat. 1.30–4, closed Aug. 15th–Sept. 15th.) at the end of the courtyard, on the first floor, originated in the fine collection of the late M. Clapisson. It includes the violins of Lulli, Kreutzer, and Sarasate, Beethoven's clavichord, Marie Antoinette's harp, and many other instruments of great historical and artistic value. The library, on the second floor, possesses the most complete series in existence of musical scores, books on music, and valuable MSS.

The Rue de Lisbonne continues the Rue de Madrid W. to the BOULEVARD MALESHERBES, a fine modern thoroughfare leading from the Madeleine past St-Augustin to the Porte d'Asnières (1⅝ m.). We follow the boulevard (r.) past the Av. Vélasquez, which leads to the Musée Cernuschi and Parc Monceau, and cross the Boul. de Courcelles. At the junction of the Boul. Malesherbes with the busy Av. de Villiers is the *Place Malesherbes*. On the N.W. side is the bronze statue of *Alexandre Dumas père* (1802–70), by Gustave Doré, with figures of D'Artagnan and three readers on the pedestal; on the S.E. is the statue of *Alexandre Dumas fils* (1824–95), by St-Marceaux, with the 'Dame aux Camélias' among the figures on the pedestal. Here also is a monument to *Sarah Bernhardt*, by F. Sicard (1926).

Shortly before it reaches the Porte d'Asnières, the Boul. Malesherbes crosses the *Place de Wagram*. Sarah Bernhardt (1844–1923) died at 56 Boul. Pereire, a little to the right.

Farther off to the right is the **Quartier des Batignolles,** which gave its name to a school of impressionist painters under the leadership of Manet.

The AVENUE DE VILLIERS, which bears to the left at the Place Malesherbes, leads to the *Place Pereire* and the Porte Champerret. At No. 43 (l.) is the **Musée Henner** (adm. 10 fr.; Sat. and Sun., 2–5), an admirably arranged gallery illustrating the work of *Jean-Jacques Henner* (1829–1905), the Alsatian painter. The house and paintings, mainly studies in the nude, were bequeathed to the nation by M. and Mme Jules Henner, nephew and niece of the artist, in 1924.—The painter Puvis de Chavannes (1824–98) died at 89 Av. de Villiers. The striking church of *Ste-Odile* (1938–46), to the r. (N.) of the Porte Champerret, was designed by *J. Barge*, with fine stained glass by *M. Décorchemont*.

8. THE WESTERN DISTRICTS.

A. To the North of the Champs-Elysées.

MÉTRO stations: *Villiers* (lines 2 and 3); *Monceau, Courcelles* and *Ternes* (line 2); *Etoile* (lines 1, 2, 6); *Argentine, Porte Maillot, Sablons, Pont de Neuilly* (line 1).—ELECTRIC TRAINS every 10 min. from the Gare St-Lazare to *Neuilly-Porte Maillot* (change at Pont Cardinet).—MOTOR-BUSES: Villiers, Monceau, Courcelles (routes 30 and 94); Ternes (routes 31, 36, 43, 83); Etoile (routes 30, 31, 52, 73, 92); Obligado (route 73); Porte Maillot (route P.C.); Pont de Neuilly (route P.C. 43, etc.).

From the Place St-Augustin the long BOULEVARD HAUSSMANN leads W. in the direction of the Place de l'Etoile. The AVENUE DE MESSINE, diverging on the right, is continued by the Av. Ruysdaël to the S. entrance of the Parc Monceau. No. 7 Av. de Messine is the *Musée du Cinéma,* with a library of films, and interesting collections illustrating the history of the film (adm. free 6.30–10 p.m.). In the Rue de Monceau (l.) No. 28, belonging to Prince Murat, was the residence of President Wilson during the Peace Conference of 1919; No. 32 was the birthplace of Oscar I of Sweden (1799–1859), son of Bernadotte (tablet).

The ***Parc Monceau,** a charming little park of 217 acres, surrounded by the handsome private houses of this elegant quarter, derives its name from a vanished village and is a remnant of the private park laid out by Carmontelle in 1778 for Philippe-Egalité d'Orléans, the father of Louis-Philippe.

Various 'picturesque' details in the taste of the 18th cent. have survived from the Orléans park, such as the brook, the tomb in the woods, and the *Naumachie,* a large oval basin in the N.E. part of the park. The Corinthian colonnade on this lake is supposed to have come either from the Château du Raincy or from the great rotunda begun to the N. of the cathedral of St-Denis by Catherine de Médicis as a mausoleum for Henri II and herself. At the main entrance in the Boul. de Courcelles is the round *Pavillon de Chartres,* a toll-house of the 18th cent. city wall erected by the Farmers-General, now used as the keeper's lodge. Near the Naumachie are a large Renaissance arcade from the old Hôtel de Ville. The park is adorned with sculpture, and there are monuments to Maupassant (1850–93), by R. Verlet and H. Deglane; to the composer Ambroise Thomas (1811–96), by Falguière; to Gounod (1818–93), by A. Mercié; to the poet and dramatist Edouard Pailleron (1834–99), by Bernstamm; and to Chopin (1809–49), by J. Froment-Meurice.

No. 7 in the Av. Vélasquez, leading E. from the park to the Boul. Malesherbes, is the **Musée Cernuschi,** an interesting collection of Chinese and Japanese art formed by M. Cernuschi, who, in 1895, bequeathed it, together with his house, to the city of Paris. The bronzes are specially valuable, but the whole collection is surpassed by the Musée Guimet. Many valuable additions have been made since the foundation of the museum, and interesting temporary exhibitions are frequently held. Adm. 25 fr. At No. 63 Rue de Monceau, behind it, is the **Musée Nissim de Camondo** (Rte. 29).

To the N. of the Parc Monceau is a quarter favoured by the wealthier literary and artistic set, with specially fine houses in the Rue de Prony, Rue Jacques de Bingen, and Rue Fortuny. National styles of architecture have been used for the *Swedish Church* (1913) in the Rue Médéric, and for the *Russian Church* (1859–61) in the Rue Daru (W. of the park).

Beyond the Av. de Messine the Boul. Haussmann passes (No. 158; r.) the **Musée Jacquemart-André** (Rte. 27), and crosses successively the Rue de Courcelles and the Rue du Faubourg St-Honoré.

The very long RUE DE COURCELLES runs N.W. from St-Philippe-du-Roule (see below), viâ the Place Pereire, to the Porte de Courcelles. No. 38 in this street (then No. 48) was Dickens's lodging in 1846; at No. 45 Proust lived in 1901–5.

The RUE DU FAUBOURG-ST-HONORÉ, the N.W. continuation of the Rue St-Honoré, with many 18th cent. mansions, stretches from the Rue Royale to the Place des Ternes (1¼ m.). It intersects an aristocratic quarter and contains several fashionable dress shops, as well as jewellery, print, and curiosity shops. Near its S.E. end is the **British Embassy** (No. 39), purchased for £32,000 by Wellington in 1814 from Pauline Bonaparte, Princesse Borghèse, much of whose furniture remains. The *Embassy Church* is in the Rue d'Aguesseau, opposite. No. 41 (l.) is the *Hôtel Pontalba*, built by Visconti and restored by M. de Rothschild; No. 45 was the residence of Thiers at the end of his term as President, in 1874. Farther on are the *Ministère de l'Intérieur* (Home Office; r.) and the **Palais de l'Elysée** (no adm.), the official residence of the President of the Republic (l.), at the corner of the Av. Matignon.

This mansion (since greatly altered and enlarged) was built as the Hôtel d'Evreux in 1718. It was occupied later by Mme de Pompadour, Murat, Napoleon I (who signed his abdication here in 1815), Wellington, and Napoleon III, who lived here as President until he went to the Tuileries as Emperor.

Beyond the Av. Matignon (recently extended) is the Rue de Penthièvre (r.), No. 26 in which is believed to have been Benjamin Franklin's city office. In the Rue Jean-Mermoz (l.), formerly Rue Montaigne, Gambetta lived at No. 12, and Meyerbeer died in 1864 at No. 2. At the busy crossing of the Rue La Boétie, where the Av. Franklin-Roosevelt comes in on the left, is the classical church of ST-PHILIPPE-DU-ROULE, built in 1769–84 by *Chalgrin*, and later enlarged. The *Salle Gaveau*, at 45 Rue La Boétie, is one of the most important concert halls in Paris. The new Av. Myron T. Herrick (r.; 1938–41) commemorates a much-loved American ambassador. Just beyond the end of the Boul. Haussmann is the *Ecole Pratique des Gardiens de la Paix* (police school); in the garden is a monument to members of the force who fell in the Liberation of Paris in 1944. The buildings are those of the old *Hôpital Beaujon* (1784), removed in 1935 to new premises at Clichy. It was in this new building that Eleutherios Venizelos (1864–1936), the Greek statesman, died. No. 252 (r.), beyond the Av. Hoche, is the *Salle Pleyel*, the largest and most modern concert hall in Paris. A little farther is the Place des Ternes, whence the Av. de Wagram leads left to the Etoile.—Alfred de Vigny died at No. 6 Rue d'Artois (l.) in 1863.

Beyond the Rue du Faubourg-St-Honoré the line of the Boul. Haussmann is continued by the AVENUE DE FRIEDLAND to the Place de l'Etoile (p. 10). At No. 11 in this avenue Pres. Doumer was assassinated in 1938. Balzac died in 1850 at No. 12 in the cross-street that bears his name (formerly Rue Fortunée).—Beyond the Etoile we follow the wide AVENUE DE LA GRANDE-ARMÉE. This is the continuation of the Champs-Elysées towards Neuilly and contains numerous motor and cycle shops. No. 65 (l.) is the headquarters of the *Touring-Club de France*.

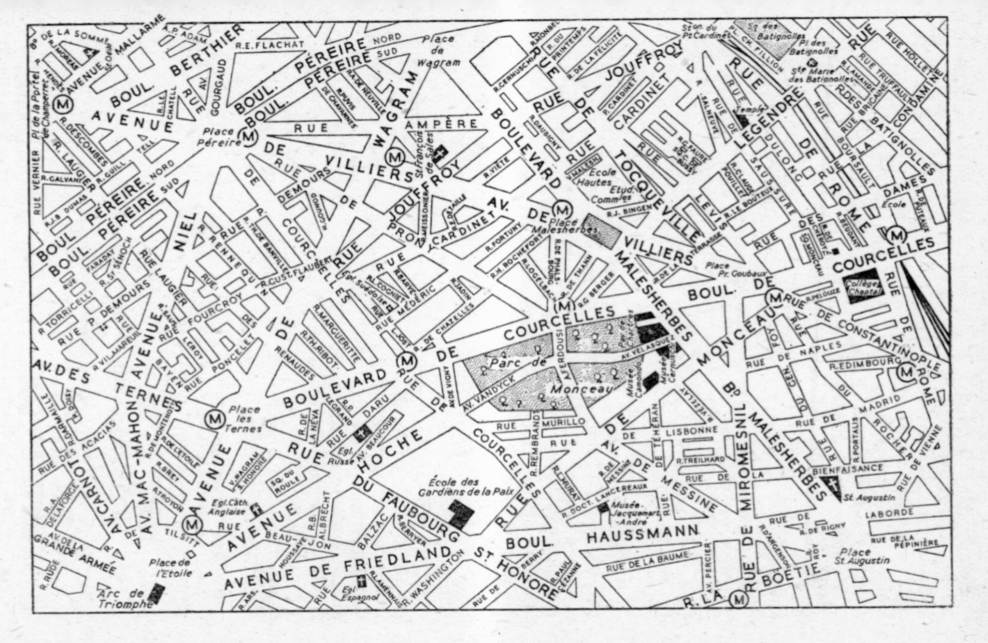

V. PARC MONCEAU

Neuilly (60,172 inhab.) is the most fashionable suburb of Paris. Its N. half, now a colony of elegant houses, was formerly the park of Louis-Philippe's château, built in 1740 and burned down by the mob in 1848. In recent years the tendency to build large blocks of flats threatens to overwhelm the distinctive character of the neighbourhood.

We leave Paris by the *Porte de Neuilly*. On the left is the *Porte Maillot*, the N.E. entrance to the Bois de Boulogne, and on our right is the semi-circular PLACE DE VERDUN, with the Boulevard Pershing leading N. to the Place des Ternes.

On the right in the Boul. Pershing is the **Chapelle St-Ferdinand,** a Byzantine mausoleum erected in 1843 on the site of the inn in which Ferdinand, Duc d'Orléans, son of Louis-Philippe, died as the result of a carriage accident on July 13th, 1842. Within (apply at No. 13; gratuity), on the right, is the cenotaph of the duke, who is buried at Dreux. It was designed by Ary Scheffer and sculptured by Triqueti.

From the Place des Ternes the AVENUE DU ROULE runs W. to the *Place Winston-Churchill*; in front of the neighbouring church of ST-PIERRE (1898) is a marble statue of Joan of Arc by Péchiné. The central porch and the two side doors of the church were re-decorated in 1946–48 with sculptures by students of the Atelier Saupique of the Beaux Arts. On the N. side of the Place is the *Boulevard d'Inkermann*, with the huge red buildings of the *Lycée Pasteur* on the left. Beyond the church, to the W., is the *Hôtel de Ville*, with a bust of Mermoz, the famous French aviator, and a statue of Parmentier (1737–1813), who made his first experiments in potato growing at Neuilly.

The wide AVENUE DE NEUILLY continues the Av. de la Grande-Armée N.W. to the handsome *Pont de Neuilly*, almost entirely rebuilt in 1935–39. The *Ile du Pont*, which is traversed by the bridge, will eventually be laid out in decorative gardens. Beyond the bridge, the *Av. du Général de Gaulle*, between *Puteaux* (l.) and *Courbevoie* (r.), ascends to the Place de la Défense.

Théophile Gautier died in 1872 at a house on the site of No. 33 Rue de Longchamp, on the left a little short of the bridge; and in the old cemetery, a little nearer Paris, is the grave of Anatole France (1844–1924).

B. To the South of the Champs-Elysées.

MÉTRO stations: *Champs-Elysées-Clemenceau, Franklin D. Roosevelt, George V* (line 1); *Etoile* (lines 1, 2, 6); *Victor-Hugo, Porte Dauphine* (line 2); *Boissière* (line 6); *Trocadéro* (lines 9 and 6); *Passy* (line 6); *Egl. d'Auteuil* (line 10); *Michel-Ange-Auteuil* (lines 9 and 10); *Porte d'Auteuil* (line 10); *Michel-Ange-Molitor* (lines 9 and 10); *Mirabeau* (line 10). All stations from *Franklin D. Roosevelt* to *Porte de St-Cloud* on line 9.—MOTOR-BUSES: Etoile (routes 30, 31, 52, 73, 92); Victor-Hugo (route 52); Boissière (route 30); Trocadéro, Passy (route 32); Mirabeau, Egl. d'Auteuil (route 72); routes 30, 32, 52, 63, 72, 126 and the P.C., correspond roughly to the Métro stations on line 9 mentioned above.

The broad COURS-LA-REINE, laid out under Marie de Médicis in 1616 and leading due W. from the Place de la Concorde to the Place d'Alma, is called in its W. part the COURS ALBERT PREMIER. At the beginning of the Cours-la-Reine, in the Place de la Concorde, is an equestrian statue (1938) of Albert I, King of the Belgians, by Armand Martial. The parallel QUAI DE LA CONFÉRENCE, on the Seine, takes its name from the Porte de la Conférence (demolished in 1730), through which the Spanish ambassadors entered Paris in 1660 to discuss with Mazarin the projected marriage between Louis XIV and Maria Theresa. On the right are the *Petit-Palais* and the *Grand-Palais* ; on the left is the *Pont Alexandre III*.

At the corner of the Av. FRANKLIN D. ROOSEVELT, which leads to the Rond-Point des Champs-Elysées, are a monument to Alfred de Musset (1810–57), by Moncel, with a relief of the Dream of the Poet and a bust of Jacques Cartier (1491–1557), discoverer of the St. Lawrence river, by Drivier. Opposite is the *Pont des Invalides*.

The RUE FRANÇOIS-PREMIER, which diverges here (r.), is crossed at the *Place François-Premier* by the Rue Jean-Goujon and the Rue Bayard. In the Rue Jean-Goujon (l.) are the *Armenian Church*, built by A. Guilbert in 1903–5, and **Notre-Dame-de-Consolation** (open daily 2–5 Apr.–Oct.), a sumptuous chapel in the Louis-Seize style, designed likewise by Guilbert and dedicated to the memory of the 130 victims of the fire at the Charity Bazaar (May 4th, 1897) on this spot. Gustave Doré had a studio at No. 1 Rue Bayard, and in the flat above lived Jules Ferry.

At the corner of the Cours Albert Premier and Rue Bayard is the ***Maison de François Premier,** a small Renaissance mansion in the Venetian style, built by the king in 1523–27 at Moret, near Fontainebleau, either for his sister Margaret of Navarre or for his son's mistress Diane de Poitiers. It was re-erected on its present site for Mlle Mars in 1824. The façade (partly modernised) has three round arches on the ground floor and three square windows above. The pilasters, corner-ornamentations, frieze, genii, and medallions (ascribed to Jean Goujon) form a charming decorative ensemble. In the centre are the arms of France and Navarre.

At the end of the Cours Albert Premier is the **Place de l'Alma,** whence the *Pont de l'Alma* crosses the Seine to the Quai d'Orsay, while several handsome modern streets radiate on the N. bank. Here are the Monument of Belgium's Gratitude for French aid during the First World War and a statue of Adam Mickiewicz, the Polish poet, by *Bourdelle*.

At the beginning of the AVENUE MONTAIGNE, which leads N.E. to the Rond-Point des Champs-Elysées, is the attractive *Théâtre des Champs-Elysées*, a reinforced concrete building (1911–13), with bas-reliefs and frescoes by Bourdelle.

In the AVENUE GEORGE-V, leading N., is the American Episcopal Church of **Holy Trinity,** with a graceful tower, built in the early-English Gothic style by G. S. Street (1885–88), with fine glass illustrating the Te Deum. On the left is the

Memorial Battle Cloister, designed by Bertram Goodhue (1923), in honour of the U.S. army units who suffered casualties in France in 1917–18.

The QUAI DE NEW-YORK (formerly the Av. de Tokio) continues the Quai de la Conférence towards Passy, passing between the *Pont d'Iéna* and the Palais de Chaillot (see below).—The AVENUE MARCEAU leads N.W. from the Place de l'Alma to the Etoile, passing the Rue Georges-Bizet (l.), in which is the Orthodox Greek church of *St. Stefanos*, with a handsome interior and marble iconostasis. The church of *St-Pierre-de-Chaillot* (1935) by E. Bois, with front sculptured by Bouchard, and the wealthy *Quartier Chaillot* take their name from a vanished village.

From the Av. Marceau the AVENUE DU PRÉSIDENT-WILSON diverges almost immediately on the left. On the right is the main façade of the **Musée Galliéra** (now given up exclusively to temporary exhibitions; entrance at No. 10 Av. Pierre 1er de Serbie).

On the left is the entrance to the **Musée National d'Art Moderne** (adm. daily except Tues. 10–5, 30 fr.; Sun. free). This enormous building, which lies between the Av. du Président-Wilson and the Quai de New York, was constructed for the Exhibition of 1937 by Aubert, Dondel, Viard and Dastugue.

The two wings are separated by a square giving on to the Quai de New York, and a high portico with a double colonnade on the N. side. The ornamental lake on the S. side is decorated by four bronze figures, and the wall of the terrace has a fine bas-relief by Janniot, depicting the legends of antiquity. On the terrace is a statue by *Bourdelle* of 'La France,' in honour of French patriots who fell in the Second World War. On either side of the peristyle are figures of 'La Force' and 'La Victoire,' by *Bourdelle.*

The museum is devoted to a very extensive collection of recent and contemporary schools of French painting and sculpture. The exhibits are mostly arranged under the schools or coteries of their creators. The rooms devoted to painting are indicated by numbers; those containing sculptures by letters. Only a few of the best-known artists are mentioned in the list which follows.

GROUND FLOOR. The large hall on the right is reserved for temporary exhibitions.—ROOM A. Sculptures by *Aristide Maillol* (1861–1944).—Paintings: R. 1. Neo-Impressionists: *Paul Signac.*—R. 2. School of Pont-Aven: *Louis Anquetin, Paul Bernard.*—RR. 3, 4. Les Nabis: *Pierre Bonnard, Maurice Denis.*—R. 5. *Maurice Utrillo, Suzanne Valadon.*—R. 6. *Félix Vallotton.*—R. 7. Les Fauves: *André Derain, Othon Friesz, Georges Rouault, Maurice de Vlaminck.*—R. 9. *Kees van Dongen.*—R. 10. *Raoul Dufy, Albert Marquet.*—R. 11. *Henri Matisse.*—R. 12. 20th Century 'Primitives.'—R. 14. *Juan Gris, Fernand Léger.*—R. 15. *Georges Braque.*—R. 18. Cubists.—R. 19. *Pablo Picasso.*—R. 20. *A. Dunoyer de Segonzac, J. L. Boussingault.*

FIRST FLOOR. R. 23bis. Expressionism and the 'Ecole de Paris': *Marc Chagall.*—R. 24. The Abstracts.—R. 25 shows the modern artist at his most attractive, in decorative art, with tapestries by *Raoul Dufy* and *Jean Lurçat*; ceramics, jewellery, goldsmiths' work, enamels, ivories, furniture, and decorative sculpture.—RR. 26–30. Contemporary painters.—R. 31. Second World War: *F. R. Bernard* (d. 1944), *Eric Peters* (shot by the Germans in 1942).—On the grand staircase, tapestry, 'The Woodmen of the Forest of Mormal,' by *Marcel Gromaire.*

LOWER GROUND FLOOR. ROOMS B–J. Sculpture, including works by *Charles Despiau* (1874–1946; Room E), *Antoine Bourdelle* (1861–1929; Room G), and *Paul Landowski* and *François Sicard* (Room H).—R. 32. Paintings of 1900–14: *Aman-Jean, Giovanni Boldini*; glassware and ceramics.—R. 33.

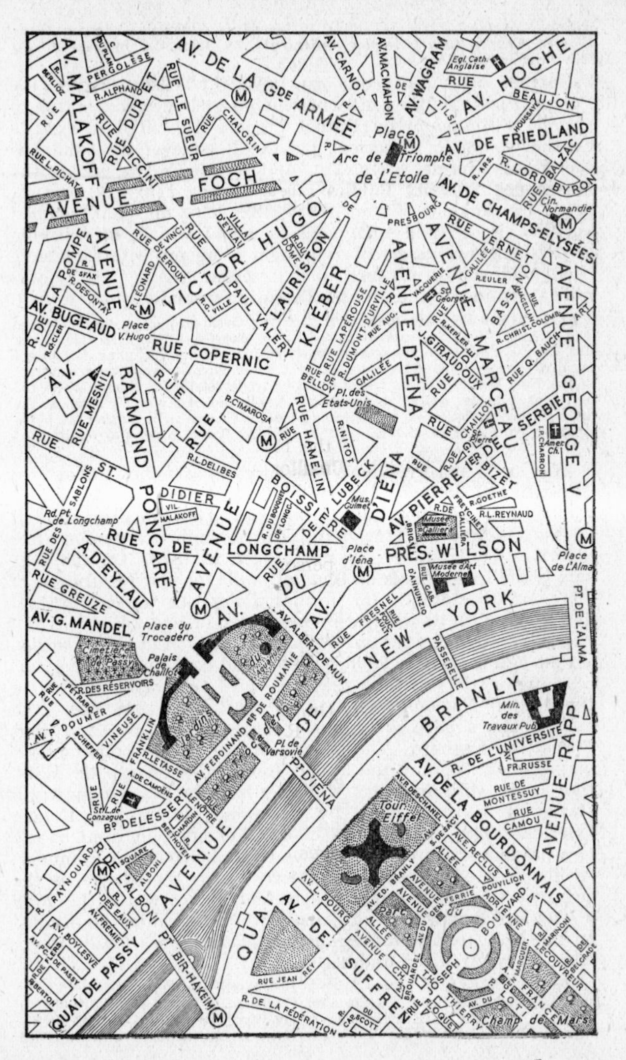

VI. ETOILE–PASSY

the Rue St-Martin on the W., Nos. 10, 12, and 14 have rococo façades; No. 34, the *Hôtel de la Reynie*, has 17th cent. ironwork. At No. 43 John Law (1671–1729), the celebrated Scottish financier, established his Mississippi bank which ended (1720) in a bankruptcy even more catastrophic than the 'South Sea Bubble.'

Farther on the Rue St-Martin crosses the Rue de Turbigo. At the corner of Rue Réaumur is the large Gothic church of **St-Nicolas-des-Champs,** built mainly in 1420 but enlarged in 1541–75, when the choir and the E. part of the nave were rebuilt in the Renaissance style. On the S. side rises a square tower. The elaborate Renaissance S. portal was built c. 1575 from a design found among the papers of *Philibert Delorme*. The Assumption and the Apostles at the tomb of the Virgin (above the high-altar, which is by *Mansart*) is by *Simon Vouet*.

Budæus (d. 1540), the Renaissance scholar, Gassendi (d. 1655), the astronomer, and Mlle de Scudéry (d. 1701), the 'précieuse,' are buried in this church.

Beyond the Rue Réaumur, on the E. side of the Rue St-Martin, is the **Conservatoire des Arts-et-Métiers** (Rte. 21). Opposite, between the Rue St-Martin and the Boul. de Sébastopol, lies the *Square Emile-Chautemps*, in the centre of which is a column, with fountains, commemorating the Crimean War (1854–55). On the S. side of the square is the *Théâtre de la Gaîté-Lyrique*.

At the N.W. corner of the Conservatoire is the *Fontaine du Vertbois*, erected in 1712 and restored in 1886, at the same time as the adjoining tower of *St-Martin-des-Champs* (tablet).

7. THE DISTRICTS TO THE NORTH OF THE GRANDS BOULEVARDS.

A. Between the Canal St-Martin and the Rue de la Chaussée-d'Antin.

MÉTRO stations: *République* (lines 3, 5, 8, 9, 11); *Jacques Bonsergent* (line 5); *Gare de l'Est* (lines 4, 5, 7); *Poissonnière, Cadet, Le Peletier* (line 7); *Chaussée-d'Antin* (lines 7 and 9); *Trinité, N.-D. de Lorette,* and *St-Georges* (line 12).—MOTOR-BUSES: Place de la République (routes 20, 52, 65, 75); Gare de l'Est (routes 30, 31, 38, 47, 65); Carrefour Gluck-Haussmann (routes 20, 21, 27, 66, 68, 95).

From the Place de la République the long BOULEVARD DE MAGENTA, intersecting various important streets, leads N.W. to the line of the outer boulevards. In the RUE DU FAUBOURG-ST-MARTIN, which crosses it diagonally, is (l.) the handsome *Mairie of the 10th Arrondissement*, with a relief of *International Brotherhood, by Dalou, in the Salle des Fêtes. Beyond the little *Square St-Laurent* (r.), in which is a group (Brother and Sister) by A. Lefeuvre, the Boul. de Strasbourg (see below) crosses the Boul. de Magenta. At the corner is **St-Laurent,** one of the oldest foundations in Paris, a flam-

Salon des Artistes Français.—R. 34. Salon de la Nationale: *Jacques-Emile Blanche, Charles Cottet, Antoine Villard.*—R. 35. Salon des Indépendants.—RR. 36–38. Salon d'Automne.

Farther on the Avenue du Président-Wilson crosses the PLACE D'IÉNA, in the centre of which is an equestrian statue of *George Washington*, by Daniel French, presented to France by the women of America. On the N. side of the square is the **Musée Guimet** (Rte. 26), and on the S.W. side is the **Musée des Travaux Publics** (adm. 20 fr., 1.30–5.30, except Fri.), by Auguste Perret (1937–38). The museum, opened in 1939, is devoted to models (some of which are working models) of various great civil engineering projects that have been achieved in France during recent years. The model railway trains on the ground floor are especially worth a visit.

At No. 24 Rue Boissière, to the N.W., the poet Henri de Régnier died in 1936.—The Avenue d'Iéna leads direct to the Etoile, passing (l.) the agreeable PLACE DES ETATS-UNIS. Here are several American monuments, including *Bartholdi's* group of Washington and Lafayette (1895); a monument to American Volunteers of the First World War, by *Victor Boucher*; and busts of Dr. Horace Wells, the first dentist to use gas as an anæsthetic (1844) and of Myron T. Herrick, the distinguished ambassador, by *Bertrand Bouthée.* On the right, farther on, is the Anglican church of *St. George,* built in 1887–88 at the expense of Sir Richard Wallace.

The Av. du Président-Wilson ends at the PLACE DU TROCADÉRO, 550 yds. across and nearly circular in shape, whence five avenues radiate fanwise. The Place is situated on the 'Colline du Trocadéro,' a little eminence named after a fort at Cadiz, taken by the French in 1823. On the S.E. side is the huge **Palais de Chaillot**, built for the Exhibition of 1937, on the site of the former *Palais du Trocadéro,* and described, with its interesting museums, in Rte. 24.

Underneath the central square is the *Théâtre de Chaillot,* a vast hall seating c. 2900 persons, and containing a magnificent organ. It was here that the third General Assembly of the United Nations was held in Sept.–Dec. 1948. On each side of the square are gilded bronze statues by Couturier, Cornet, and others. The S. side of the square commands a magnificent view of the Eiffel Tower, the Champ de Mars, the Ecole Militaire, etc. On the N. side is an equestrian statue of *Marshal Foch,* by Raymond Martin and Robert Wlerick (1949), and on the E. and W. sides, in front of the two pavilions, are bronze groups by Bouchard and Pommier. At the foot of the terrace, directly below the square, is the entrance to the theatre, and stretching S. towards the *Pont d'Iéna* are handsome gardens, with ornamental fountains. In the N.E. part is the *Aquarium du Trocadéro* (daily 10–6; adm. 20 fr., children under 10, 10 fr.).

The AVENUE KLÉBER (where Aristide Briand, the statesman, died at No. 52 in 1932), leads N.E. from the Place du Trocadéro to the Place de l'Etoile. It passes on the right the Rue Hamelin, where Marcel Proust died in 1922 (at No. 44); and on the left the Rue Paul-Valéry (formerly de Villejust), No. 40 in which was the home of Paul Valéry (1871–1945) from 1902; in the same house, from 1883, was the studio of Berthe Morisot (1841–95), a favourite rendezvous of the literary and artistic society of the day. Near its farther end is the former Hôtel Majestic, now the European headquarters of U.N.E.S.C.O. The AVENUE RAYMOND-POINCARÉ leads N., crosses the *Place Victor-Hugo* and the Avenue Foch, and is continued to the Porte Maillot by the AVENUE MALAKOFF. No. 124 AVENUE VICTOR-HUGO (which leads S.W. from the Etoile to La Muette) marks the site of the house where Hugo died in 1885.

At the beginning of the RUE FRANKLIN, which leads S.W. from the Place du Trocadéro towards Passy, is a statue to Benjamin Franklin (minister plenipotentiary to France 1776–85), by John Boyle, presented to Paris in 1906 by an American banker. Georges Clemenceau lived at No. 8 in 1896–1929, and the house has been preserved in its original state as a memorial (open Thurs., Sat. and Sun.; adm. 10 fr., free on Sun.).—Close by are steps ascending to the small **Cimetière de Passy** (entrance at 2 Rue des Réservoirs), which contains a number of interesting monuments, including those of Debussy (d. 1918) and Manet (d. 1883).

The shady AVENUE GEORGES-MANDEL leads W. to the *Rue de la Pompe*, and is continued W. to the Porte de la Muette by the AVENUE HENRI-MARTIN, in which, near the Square Lamartine, the poet Lamartine died in 1869 (house demolished). The *Porte de la Muette*, one of the chief entrances to the Bois de Boulogne, is dominated on the S. side by a huge block of flats, while on the N. side is a bronze and granite statue to Peter I of Serbia and Alexander I of Yugoslavia, erected in 1936. To the E. of the Av. Suchet are the remains of the ancient royal park of **La Muette,** where the first balloon ascent in France was made in 1783 by Pilâtre de Rozier and the Marquis d'Arlandes. The royal Château de la Muette, originally a hunting-lodge but rebuilt by Louis XV, has completely disappeared; and the present mansion, built by Baron Henri de Rothschild, is now the property of the European Council of Economic Co-operation.

From the Place de la Muette, the BOUL. SUCHET runs S to the *Porte d'Auteuil*. On the left the Avenue Raphaël leads into the *Jardin du Ranelagh*, which, just before the Revolution, was a fashionable resort in the style of its namesake in London. At No. 2 in the Rue Louis-Boilly (l.) is the **Musée Marmottan** (adm. 30 fr.; Sun. and Thurs., 2–5), which is devoted to furniture and objets d'art of the Renaissance and the First Empire. The museum was founded by Jules Marmottan, and left to the Institut de France by his son, Paul (d. 1932).

The residential district of **Passy,** though quiet and pleasant enough, is of little direct interest to-day. In the middle of the last century, however, it was a favourite residence of artists and literary men, but modern blocks of flats have largely replaced their villas and gardens. Benjamin Franklin, who lived here in 1777–85, erected on his house the first lightning conductor seen in France. Among distinguished 19th cent. residents were Balzac, Rossini, Lamartine, and, at a later period, Maeterlinck, René Boylesve, Gabriel Fauré, Henri Bergson, and Jacques-Emile Blanche; and here

Maupassant died insane in 1893 in a private hospital. No. 47 Rue Raynouard is *Balzac's House* (open daily, except Tues., 1.30–5; adm. 20 fr.), containing a museum of souvenirs of the great novelist, who lived here in 1841–47.

From the Chaussée de la Muette the Avenue Mozart runs S. to **Auteuil,** another residential district with an agreeable atmosphere and several large private hospitals. Boileau and Molière both lived at Auteuil, and later residents were Alfred de Musset and Marshal Joffre. The church of *Notre-Dame-d'Auteuil* was rebuilt by Vaudremer in 1877–88 in the Romanesque-Byzantine style. In front of it is the tomb of the chancellor D'Aguesseau (d. 1751) and his wife, a pyramid of red marble, crowned with a globe and cross of gilded copper.

The Rue d'Auteuil leads W. from the parish church to the *Porte d'Auteuil*. the S.E. entrance to the Bois de Boulogne. Beyond, the Avenue de la Porte d'Auteuil is bordered on its S. side by the **Jardin Fleuriste** (open daily 10–5 or 6). Farther W. is the *Stade Roland-Garros*, famous for the many Davis Cup matches that have been played there. Facing the Avenue du Général-Sarrail (S.) are the new *Lycée Fontaine* (l.), and, farther on, the huge *Vélodrome du Parc des Princes*, built in 1936.

9. The Bois de Boulogne.

MÉTRO stations: *Porte Maillot* (line 1); *Sablons* (line 1); *Porte Dauphine* (line 2); *Ranelagh* (line 9); *Porte d'Auteuil* (line 10).—Electric trains from the Gare St-Lazare to *Neuilly-Porte Maillot, Av. Foch, Av. Henri-Martin, Passy, Auteuil-Boulogne* (change at Pont-Cardinet).—MOTOR-BUSES: Porte Maillot (routes 73, P.C.); Porte de la Muette (route 63); Porte d'Auteuil (routes 52, P.C.).

There are five entrances to the Bois from Paris, namely the *Porte Maillot* and *Porte Dauphine* (the two main entrances), and the *Porte de la Muette, Porte de Passy,* and *Porte d'Auteuil.*

The usual approach to the Bois is the handsome AVENUE FOCH, ⅝ m. long and 110 yds. wide, leading from the Etoile to the Porte Dauphine. Opened in 1855 as the Avenue de l'Impératrice, it is composed of a central roadway with a path for pedestrians on the left and a riding-track on the right. No. 80 was the residence of Claude Debussy (1862–1918). Not far from the Etoile is (r.) a monument to Adolphe Alphand (1817–91), who laid out the Bois and most of the other parks of Paris in their present form. Anatole France died in 1924 at No. 5 Villa-Saïd (r.), and Raymond Poincaré died ten years later at 26 Rue Marbeau, just to the N. At the end of the Av. Foch, above the Bois, Mont-Valérien and the hills of St-Cloud, Bellevue, and Meudon come into sight. On the left (No. 59) is the **Musée D'Ennery** (open Thurs. and Sun. afternoon; adm. 20 fr.), a collection of Oriental art formed by the dramatist D'Ennery (1811–99) and bequeathed by him to the state together with his house.

The ***Bois de Boulogne,** familiarly known as the 'Bois,' lies just outside Paris on the W., and is bounded by the former fortifications on the E., the Seine on the W., Neuilly on the N., and Boulogne on the S. Though the châteaux of La Muette, Madrid, and Bagatelle and the abbey of Longchamp were erected on its borders, until 1852 the Bois was utterly neglected. In that year it was handed over by the state to the city of Paris and was transformed into the present splendid park of 2155 acres, the favourite promenade of the Parisians.

Between the Porte Maillot and the Porte d'Auteuil, the former fortifications skirting the E. side of the Bois have been replaced since 1930 by handsome modern streets adorned with memorial and other sculpture.

From the Porte Dauphine we follow the Route de Suresnes, straight in front of the gate, past the Pavillon Dauphine (café-restaurant) to (½ m.) the ROND ROYAL or CARREFOUR DU BOUT-DES LACS (Pavillon-Restaurant du Rond-Royal), whence two roads follow respectively the right and left (W. and E.) banks of the Lac Inférieur to (¾ m.) the Carrefour des Cascades at its other end. The road on the W. bank skirts the *Pelouses de la Croix-Catelan* (Arnaud Catelan was a troubadour murdered here c. 1300), with the sports-grounds of the *Racing Club* ; that on the E. bank passes the starting-point of the ferry to the island in the lake (boats for hire).

The Route de Suresnes, which diverges at the Rond Royal, leads S.W. to the Carrefour de Longchamp, crossing the *Carrefour de la Croix-Catelan* (18th cent. pyramid of stones), and skirts the enclosure of the **Pré-Catelan,** in which is a fashionable café-restaurant (dancing, etc.).

The LAC INFÉRIEUR, or *Grand Lac*, has two islands, linked together by a bridge, on the larger of which is the Chalet des Iles, a café-restaurant. The *Carrefour des Cascades*, with a waterfall under which one may walk, divides it from the LAC SUPÉRIEUR. The *Butte Mortemart*, beyond the S. end of the latter, overlooks the *Hippodrome d'Auteuil*, a racecourse devoted to steeplechasing (second half of June).

From the Carrefour des Cascades the Avenue de l'Hippodrome leads W. to the famous racecourse of Longchamp and to the CARREFOUR DE LONGCHAMP, at the S.W. end of the long Allée de Longchamp. Here the *Grande Cascade*, an artificial waterfall c. 30 ft. high, descends from the Mare de Longchamp. In a pathway behind the lake is a monument to 35 young men who were shot by the Germans in August, 1944.

The **Hippodrome de Longchamp,** opened in 1857, is one of the premier racecourses of the world, and has stands accommodating 10,000 spectators. It is seen at its gayest on the day of the 'Grand Prix' in June. The Route des Tribunes, which skirts the N. and W. sides of the racecourse, passes the windmill (restored), which is practically the only relic of the *Abbey of Longchamp*, founded in 1256 by St. Isabella of France, sister of St. Louis.—The Route de Suresnes, going on from the Carrefour to the Pont de Suresnes, passes the Polo Ground and the *Abbey Pool* (r.) and the Restaurant de l'Ermitage de Longchamp (l.).

From the Carrefour de Longchamp the Rue de Longchamp runs N., passing (l.) the *Champ d'Entraînement*, dating from 1856, now used for football, tennis, etc., beyond which appears the Seine with the little *Ile de la Folie* and the large

Ile de Puteaux, part of which is leased to the Société des Sports. On the right is the beautiful park (59½ acres) of **Bagatelle** (adm. 20 fr.), the former residence of Lord Hertford (d. 1870) and Sir Richard Wallace (d. 1890), purchased by the city in 1904 and open to the public till dusk (cars not admitted). Art exhibitions are sometimes held in the little palace, which was built for a wager in one month by Belanger for the Comte d'Artois (1779), brother of Louis XVI. During the season the rose-garden is worth a visit.

The broad ALLÉE DE LONGCHAMP or *Allée des Acacias*, nearly 2 m. long, which leads from the Carrefour de Longchamp to the Porte Maillot, is a favourite forenoon resort in spring. About ½ m. from the Carrefour it is crossed by the *Allée de la Reine-Marguerite*, another wide drive.

This leads, right, to the Porte de Boulogne (1⅓ m.) and, left, to the Porte de Madrid (⅜ m.). Beside the latter once stood the *Château de Madrid*, built in 1528 by Francis I, who is said to have named it in memory of his captivity in Spain. It was gradually demolished between 1793 and 1847, but has given its name to the S.W. quarter of Neuilly.

Farther on the Allée de Longchamp passes (l.) the enclosure of *Les Acacias*, with pigeon-shooting and skating clubs, between which and the Jardin d'Acclimatation lies the *Mare de St-James*, a pond surrounded by charming woods. Beyond the *Pavillon d'Armenonville*, a fashionable café-restaurant, the Allée de Longchamp joins the road leading from the Porte Maillot to the Jardin d'Acclimatation.

At the N. end of the Bois, between the Porte des Sablons and the Porte de Neuilly is the **Jardin d'Acclimatation** (open daily 9–7 or dusk; adm. 30 fr., children under 7, 15 fr.; a miniature railway runs from the Porte Maillot to the entrance, fare 15 fr.). The gardens, founded in 1854 with the idea of introducing and acclimatising exotic animals and plants, have since 1919 developed into a high-class playground for children, with a small-scale zoo. Besides the main entrance at the Porte des Sablons, there is another at the W. end., at the Porte de Neuilly (Av. de Madrid).

10. THE EASTERN DISTRICTS.

MÉTRO stations: *La Chapelle* (line 2); *Stalingrad* (lines 2, 5, 7); *Jean-Jaurès* (lines 2, 5, 7); *Col. Fabien* (line 2); *Belleville* (lines 11 and 2); *Riquet, Crimée, Corentin-Cariou, Porte de la Villette* (line 7bis); *Bolivar, Buttes-Chaumont, Botzaris* (line 7); *République* (lines 3, 5, 8, 9, 11); *Parmentier, St-Maur* (line 3); *Père Lachaise* (lines 2 and 3); *Martin-Nadaud, Gambetta* (line 3); *Bastille* (lines 1, 5, 8); all stations between Bastille and Daumesnil on line 8; *Gare de Lyon, Reuilly-Diderot* (line 1); *Nation* (lines 1, 2, 6, 9); *Vincennes* (line 1); *Daumesnil, Bercy* (line 6).—MOTOR-BUSES: Av. Jean-Jaurès (route 26); Porte de la Villette (route P.C.); Buttes-Chaumont (routes 26, 75); Place de la République (routes 20, 52, 58, 65, 75); Ménilmontant (route 96); Père-Lachaise (routes 69, 26); Charonne (route 76); Bastille (routes 20, 66, 69, 76, 86, 91); Place Felix-Eboué (routes 62, 66); Gare de Lyon (routes 20, 63, 65, 91); Nation (route 86); Porte de Vincennes (routes 26, 86, P.C.).

The populous industrial quarters in the E. of Paris, with the exception of the Buttes-Chaumont and Père-Lachaise, have little to offer that is of interest to the average visitor.

The BOULEVARD DE LA CHAPELLE, continuing the Boul. de Rochechouart, one of the outer boulevards, to the E., is the S. boundary of the thickly populated QUARTIER DE LA

CHAPELLE, which contains numerous workshops and foundries. On the right is the Hôpital Lariboisière. The Rue Marx Dormoy (l.), leads N. to the quaint old parish church of *St-Denis-de-la-Chapelle* (13th cent., but much restored). At the side of the entrance is Charpentier's statue of Joan of Arc, who received Communion in this church in Nov. 1429. The ugly monumental basilica erected on the same site is as yet unfinished. The Boul. de la Chapelle is continued by the BOULEVARD DE LA VILLETTE, which soon turns S. at the Place de Stalingrad, or Rond Point de La Villette. The *Rotonde* here is one of the toll-houses built by Ledoux in 1789.

To the N.E. extends the dreary QUARTIER DE LA VILLETTE, with the RUE DE FLANDRE (1⅛ m. long), the continuation of the Rue du Faubourg-St-Martin, and the AVENUE JEAN-JAURÈS ($1\frac{1}{10}$ m. long), the prolongation of the Rue de La Fayette, as its main thoroughfares.

Between the two lies the **Bassin de la Villette,** a large dock, serving as the terminus of the *Canal de l'Ourcq* and *Canal de St-Denis,* and connected also with the Seine (Bassin de l'Arsenal) by the *Canal St-Martin.*—At the end of the Rue de Flandre, beyond the Canal de St-Denis, are the **Abattoirs de la Villette,** the largest slaughter-houses in Paris (visitors apply to the porter ; gratuity). Foot-bridges over the Canal de l'Ourcq connect the abattoirs with the *Cattle Market* (*Marché aux Bestiaux*), which is busiest on Mon. and Thurs. mornings.

From the Av. Jean-Jaurès the Av. Laumière leads S. to the Place Armand-Carrel in which are the main entrance to the Buttes-Chaumont and the *Mairie of the 19th Arrondissement.* The ***Parc des Buttes-Chaumont,** the most picturesque of the Paris parks (59½ acres), is situated in the midst of the industrial district of BELLEVILLE. It was laid out under Haussmann's régime in 1866–67 on the bare hills (' monts chauves ' ; 275–330 ft.) of Belleville, which had till then been used as the rubbish-dump of Paris. The great quarries of gypsum (' plaster of Paris ') were ingeniously transformed into rock-scenery.

These heights were the scene of the Battle of Paris in 1814 and were held in 1871 by the Communards, who were, however, dislodged by bombardment from Montmartre (of which the park commands a notable *View). The park contains a lake with an island, a sports-ground and stadium, three cafés-restaurants, a marionette theatre, etc.

The Rue Fessart leads S.E. from the park to the handsome Gothic-revival church of *St-Jean-Baptiste,* in the RUE DE BELLEVILLE, erected by Lassus in 1854–59. To the E. the Rue de Belleville passes the *Cimetière de Belleville,* the highest point in Paris (419 ft.), and crosses the Rue Haxo, No. 79 in which, to the right, is the **Chapelle des Otages,** built in 1936–38 on the site of the *Villa des Otages.* We walk through the little passage to the right of the chapel and turn left. Here, on May 26th, 1871, fifty-two hostages held by the Commune, including Jesuit priests, National Guards, and police, were shot in front of the wall at the end of the garden. In front is the ditch into which their bodies were flung. In a little courtyard (r.) are a statue of Père Olivaint, the Jesuit superior ; the balcony of the council-room in which the fate of the victims was decided ; and a door leading to a small building where the five cells of the Jesuit priests in the Prison de la Roquette have been reconstituted.

Beyond the Place de Stalingrad the Boul. de la Villette turns S., crossing the Place du Colonel-Fabien, with the new Av. de Verdun leading S.W. to the Gare de l'Est.

In the block of houses immediately to the W. was the site of the *Gibet de Montfaucon*, the 'Tyburn' of Paris, set up in the 13th cent., and finally removed in 1790.—In the RUE DE LA GRANGE-AUX-BELLES, which leads hence towards the Place de la République, is the large *Hôpital St-Louis* (1450 beds), a hospital for skin diseases founded by Henri IV and built by Claude Vellefaux (1607–12). The fine courtyards and chapel may be viewed on Thurs. and Sun. 1–3.—At the corner of the Rue des Ecluses-St-Martin was a small graveyard for foreign Protestants (now built over). Paul Jones was buried here in 1792, but his body was subsequently exhumed and is now in the Naval Academy at Annapolis.

At the end of the Boul. de la Villette the Rue de Belleville and the RUE DU FAUBOURG-DU-TEMPLE, crossing the quarter of BELLEVILLE, diverge left and right. The Boul. de la Villette is continued by the Boul. de Belleville and the Boul. de Ménilmontant to Père-Lachaise (see below).

From the Place de la République the AVENUE DE LA RÉPUBLIQUE leads E.S.E. to (1 m.) the N.W. corner of Père-Lachaise. On the left is the BOULEVARD JULES-FERRY and on the right is the BOULEVARD RICHARD-LENOIR, running above the Canal St-Martin to the Bastille. The 'Foire aux Jambons' and 'Foire à la Ferraille' (noted for spurious antiques) are held here during Holy Week. The Avenue de la République ends at the Place Auguste-Métivier, crossed by the BOUL. DE MÉNILMONTANT.

In the latter, opposite the main entrance of Père-Lachaise, is (r.) the Rue de la Roquette, on the N. side of which is the *Prison de la Petite-Roquette* (for women), built in 1899 on the site of the **Prison de la Roquette**. Outside, the five stones on which the guillotine used to be set up are still to be seen. It was in La Roquette, used for condemned prisoners awaiting execution, that Abp. Darboy, M. Deguerry, curé of the Madeleine, and other hostages of the Commune were shot in 1871.

***Père-Lachaise,** or the *Cimetière de l'Est*, is the largest (106 acres) and most fashionable cemetery in Paris; its tombs form an open-air sculpture-gallery with examples of most of the French sculptors of the 19th century. Father La Chaise, from whom it derives its name, was the confessor of Louis XIV and lived in the Jesuit House built in 1682 on the site of the chapel. The property, situated on the side of a hill, was bought by the city in 1804 and laid out by Brongniart. The cemetery has since been considerably extended on the E. and is said to contain as many graves as there are houses in Paris (c. 90,000). On All Saints' and All Souls' Days ('Jour de la Toussaint' and 'Jour des Morts'; Nov. 1st and 2nd) Père-Lachaise is visited by over 100,000 persons. The first interments were those of *La Fontaine* and *Molière*, whose remains were transferred hither in 1804 (Section 25). The popular monument of the 12th cent. lovers *Abélard and Héloïse* (Section 7) was set up in 1779 at their abbey of the Paraclete and removed hither in 1817; the canopy is composed of sculptured fragments collected by Lenoir from the abbey of Nogent-sur-Seine. In the E. corner of the cemetery (Section 97) is the *Mur des Fédéres*, against which the last of the Communards were shot in 1871 and to which the Socialists of Paris bring tributes every year on the anniversary (May 28th). Most visitors will be impressed by Bartholomé's sublime *Monument aux Morts* (Section 4).

The names of the illustrious dead interred here are too numerous to list in a brief guide; in addition to those already noted, however, the following monuments are outstanding: to the authors *Alfred de Musset* (d. 1857), *Alphonse Daudet* (d. 1897), *Beaumarchais* (d. 1799), *Béranger* (d. 1857), *Balzac* (d. 1850; bust by David d'Angers), *Henri de Régnier* (d. 1936), *Oscar Wilde* (d. 1900; monument by Epstein); to the composers *Rossini* (d. 1868), *Chopin* (d. 1849), *Bizet* (d. 1875); to the painters *Ingres* (d. 1867), *Daubigny* (d. 1878), *Daumier* (d. 1879), *Delacroix* (d. 1864), *Corot* (d. 1875); also *Sarah Bernhardt* (d. 1923); *Thiers* (d. 1887); *Marshal Ney* (d. 1815); and *Sir Sidney Smith* (d. 1840). For further details a guide-plan of the cemetery may be obtained for a nominal sum from the keeper's lodge at the main entrance.

In the Rue de Bagnolet, to the E. of the cemetery, is *St-Germain-de-Charonne*, an interesting little church of the 12–15th cent., the centre of the former village of Charonne. To the S. of the cemetery lies the Rue Planchat with the impressive modern church of *St-Jean-Bosco* (1937). The lofty tower contains a remarkable carillon of 28 bells.—The Rue de Charonne, still preserving a few 17–18th cent. houses, prolongs the Rue de Bagnolet westwards towards the Bastille.

The AVENUE GAMBETTA (1⅓ m. long), beginning at the Place Auguste-Métivier, skirts the N. side of the cemetery, leaving on the left the hilly quarter of *Ménilmontant*. In the Square Gambetta (r.) are a number of sculptures, including 'Le Mur,' a bas-relief by Moreau-Vauthier (1909), dedicated to the victims of the Revolutions. The avenue crosses first the Place Martin-Nadaud, and then the Place Gambetta, with the *Mairie of the 20th Arrondissement*. The Av. Gambetta goes on N.E. to the *Porte des Lilas*.

The BOULEVARD VOLTAIRE runs S.E. from the Place de la République to (1¾ m.) the Place de la Nation. Beyond the church of *St-Ambroise*, a pseudo-Romanesque work by Ballu, the boulevard crosses the Place Voltaire, with the *Mairie of the 11th Arrondissement* on the N. The Rue de la Roquette leads hence E. to Père-Lachaise and W. to the Place de la Bastille.

Almost due E. from the Place de la Bastille issues the RUE DU FAUBOURG-ST-ANTOINE, leading to the (c. 1 m.) Place de la Nation and forming the main artery of the FAUBOURG ST-ANTOINE, a quarter memorable in the history of the Revolution and now noted for its manufacture of furniture. It was the scene of a skirmish during the Fronde (1652), when Turenne defeated Condé. To the left, at the corner of the Rue de Charonne (see above) is the *Fontaine Trogneux* (1710). To the right, at the junction of the Av. Ledru-Rollin, is the statue, by Boverie, of Baudin, representative of the people for the department of the Ain, killed in 1851 on a barricade in front of No. 151 (tablet). Farther on (r.) the *Square Trousseau* occupies the site of the *Hospice des Enfants-Trouvés* in the graveyard of which the Princesse de Lamballe (p. 20) was buried, after her corpse had been paraded through the streets. On the same side is the *Hôpital St-Antoine,* rebuilt in 1905 by François Renaud, with a pediment by Boverie.

The Rue St-Bernard, nearly opposite, leads N. to the church of **Ste-Marguerite,** built in 1624 and almost entirely rebuilt after 1712. It is believed that Louis XVII, who in all probability died at the Temple, aged 10, was buried in the graveyard with other victims of the Revolution.

The spacious circular **Place de la Nation,** formerly the *Place du Trône* (named after the throne erected for Louis XIV's triumphal entry with Maria Theresa), is the meeting-place of the chief thoroughfares of the E. districts of Paris. No fewer than 1300 victims of the Terror were guillotined on this spot. From the ornamental basin in the centre rises the **Triumph of the Republic,* a colossal bronze group by Dalou. Round the basin are bronze crocodiles. On the E. side of this 'circus' are two pavilions, built as toll-houses by Ledoux in 1788, each surmounted by a Doric column 100 ft. high. On the columns are statues of Philip Augustus (by Dumont) and of St. Louis (by Etex), with allegorical sculptures below.

On the S.W. side of the Place is the *Ecole Arago,* behind which is the Rue de Picpus, leading S.E. from the Boul. Diderot. At the end of the garden of No. 35, formerly a convent of Augustinian nuns, is the little ***Cimetière de Picpus** (gratuity), a private burial-ground for 'émigrés' and descendants of victims of the Revolution; the tombstones display the names of the most illustrious families of France. In the first section lie *Gen. Lafayette* (d. 1834; American soil was specially sent to cover his coffin, and the United States flag surmounts his grave), Montalembert (d. 1870), and members of the families of Chateaubriand, Crillon, Gontaut-Biron, Tascher de la Pagerie, Choiseul, La Rochefoucauld, Du Plessis, Montmorency, Talleyrand-Périgord, Rohan-Rochefort, Noailles, Quélen, etc., as well as sixteen Carmelites of Compiègne martyred in 1794. In the second section are buried members of the house of Salm-Kyrburg and 1306 persons executed at the Barrière du Trône in 1795–96. Here, too, was the common trench into which the body of André Chénier, the poet, was flung in 1794.

The spacious COURS DE VINCENNES leads E. from the Place de la Nation, and is prolonged by the Av. Gallieni and the Av. de Paris beyond the line of the old fortifications to the *Château de Vincennes* (see p. 200).

From the Place de la Bastille (p. 17) the RUE DE LYON, on the right of the Gare de Vincennes, leads S. to the handsome **Gare de Lyon,** the terminus of the railways to Geneva, Lyons, Marseilles, etc. The BOULEVARD DIDEROT, which passes the front of the station, leads from the Pont d'Austerlitz to the Place de la Nation.

The AVENUE DAUMESNIL, diverging from the Rue de Lyon (l.), leads to the Porte Dorée and the ($1\frac{3}{4}$ m.) Bois de Vincennes. On the way it passes the Place Felix-Eboué, at the junction with the Rue and Boul. de Reuilly, embellished with a fountain removed from the Place de la République. Just beyond (r.) is the striking modern church of *St-Esprit*

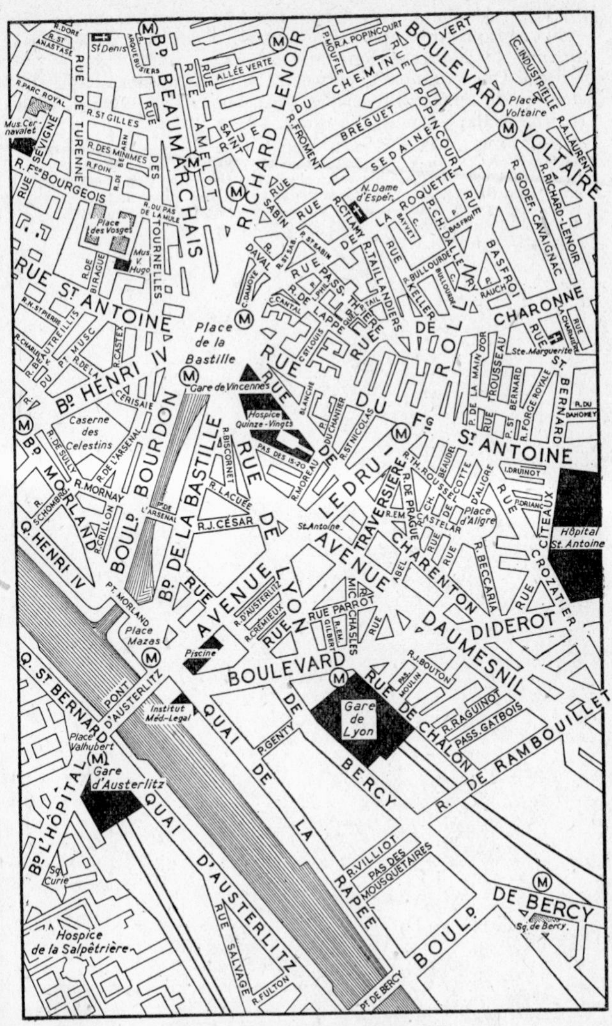

VII. BASTILLE–GARE DE LYON

(1928–35), by Paul Tournon, with flat domes recalling St. Sophia at Constantinople. The interior is adorned with mural paintings by Maurice Denis and others.

In the Bercy quarter, between the Av. Daumesnil and the Seine, is the huge *Entrepôt des Vins*, bonded warehouses with 115 wine-cellars, facing the quay.

In the Rue de Charenton, which runs S.E. from the Place de la Bastille, is the *Hospice des Quinze-Vingts*, an asylum for 300 blind persons founded by St. Louis in 1260. The building was before 1780 the Hôtel des Mousquetaires-Noirs. Hundreds of Protestants were massacred in this street in 1621, as they were leaving church. Farther on we intersect the Av. Ledru-Rollin, leading (r.) to the Pont d'Austerlitz.

II. THE SEINE, THE CITÉ, AND THE LEFT BANK

In its curved course through Paris (from E. to W.), the **Seine** divides the capital into two unequal parts, the smaller of which lies on the S. or left bank, while it forms two islands, the *Ile St-Louis* and the larger *Ile de la Cité*. The CITÉ was the site of the original Gallic settlement of Lutèce or Lutetia Parisiorum, the Paris of the Romans and the Franks, and it remained the royal, legal, and ecclesiastical centre long after the town had extended to the river-banks. It retains important relics of its pristine glory, notably the two gems of medieval religious art, Notre-Dame and the Sainte-Chapelle, and the Palais de Justice. Paris on the LEFT BANK (Rive Gauche) comprises rather more than one-third of the area of the capital. The numerous learned and scientific institutions in the Latin Quarter make it, now as in the past, the literary, artistic and academic quarter. Farther W. is the aristocratic Faubourg St-Germain, with the somewhat gloomy mansions of the old nobility, government offices and embassies, and a number of large military establishments. The Panthéon, the Cluny Museum, the Jardin des Plantes, and the Invalides are the chief points of interest on the left bank.

11. THE SEINE.

"The Seine," said Napoleon, "is the high road between Paris, Rouen, and Havre," and Paris owes much of its prosperity to its river. It enters the capital at a point over 300 m. from its source (1426 ft.) in Burgundy, and the low-water mark at the Pont-Royal is only 80 ft. above sea-level. The river, flanked within the city by broad quays, is subject to periodic rises, which flood the lower parts of Paris. In its course of 7 m. through Paris the Seine is spanned by thirty-two bridges and footbridges, as compared with the twenty bridges over the Thames in London ; but here railway bridges are found only on the outskirts of the city.

The **Port of Paris,** accessible to small sea-going vessels, has its centre in the wharves and quays between the Pont d'Arcole and Pont d'Austerlitz, and is the most important commercial harbour in France, clearing some 12,000,000 tons of merchandise annually.

A STEAMER TRIP is interesting and attractive. Beautiful views (especially at sunset) are obtained as the vessel emerges from beneath the bridges. But the best idea of the quays of Paris is obtained by a drive, or still better by a walk, along them (most interesting section between the Pont de Sully and Pont d'Iéna).

RIVER STEAMERS. The 'Bateaux Omnibus' have been discontinued since the war, but the 'Bateaux Mouches' run a service for visitors in spring and summer. Information about times of embarkation, etc., can be obtained from 17, Rue d'Astorg (Tel. ANJ. 22–56).

MÉTRO stations near the Seine (going downstream): *Quai de la Gare* (line 6); *Quai de la Rapée* (line 5); *Gare d'Orléans* (lines 5 and 10); *Châtelet* (lines 1, 4, 7, 11); *Cité* (line 4); *St-Michel* (line 4); *Sully-Morland, Pont-Marie, Pont-Neuf* (line 7); *Concorde* (lines 1, 8, 12); *Chambre des Députés* (line 12); *Invalides* (lines 8 and 14); *Alma-Marceau* (line 9); *Passy* and *Grenelle* (line 6); *Javel* and *Mirabeau* (line 10).

MOTOR-BUSES: Quai de la Rapée (routes 63, 65, 91); Gare d'Orléans (routes 63, 65, 91); Châtelet (routes 21, 38, 47, 58, 67, 69, 72, 73, 74, 75, 76, 77, 85, 96); Cité (route 67); St-Michel (routes 21, 27, 38, 77, 85, 96); Sully-Morland (route 86); Pont-Neuf (routes 21, 58, 67, 69, 72, 73, 74, 75, 76, 85); Concorde (routes 52, 72, 73, 84, 94); Chambre des Députés (routes 63, 83, 84, 94); Invalides (routes 63, 69, 83); Alma-Marceau (routes 63, 72, 80, 92); Passy (routes 32 and 72); Javel (route 62); Mirabeau (routes 62 and 72).

A. From the Louvre to the Pont National.

This route is described in the upstream direction; 'r.b.' and 'l.b.' refer to the right and left bank as seen when proceeding downstream.—Distances from the Louvre are given at each bridge.

In midstream, nearly level with the E. front of the Louvre, the Square du Vert-Galant on the Ile de la Cité with its charming little garden, points downstream like the prow of a ship. On the QUAI DE CONTI (l.b.) are the *Institut* and the *Monnaie*. The smaller arm of the Seine branches off to the right.—The ***Pont-Neuf** ($\frac{1}{5}$ m.), in spite of its name the oldest bridge in Paris, and the most picturesque, was begun by Baptiste du Cerceau in 1578, in the reign of Henri III, finished under Henri IV, and several times repaired since then. It crosses the 'Pointe de la Cité,' on which stands the famous statue of Henri IV. Above the pillars runs a fine row of masks.

CHANNEL TO THE S. OF THE CITÉ. The QUAI DES ORFÈVRES, on the bank of the Cité, has a number of jewellers' shops in the old houses backing on the Place Dauphine. Then comes the *Palais de Justice.* Opposite (l.b.) is the QUAI DES GRANDS-AUGUSTINS, with many bookshops, ending at the Place St-Michel.—The **Pont St-Michel** has been rebuilt several times since the 14th cent. (last in 1857). Opposite the short QUAI ST-MICHEL (l.b.) is the QUAI DU MARCHÉ-NEUF, with the *Préfecture de Police.*—The **Petit-Pont** (1853) occupies the site of one of the two Roman bridges of Paris. Down to 1782 it was defended at the S. end by the *Petit-Châtelet*; a tablet on No. 2 Place du Petit-Pont commemorates the *Tour de Bois* defended by a handful of citizens against the Normans in 886.—On the Cité is the *Place du Parvis-Notre-Dame*, with the *Hôtel-Dieu* in the background and the statue of Charlemagne on the river-bank. Behind the QUAI DE MONTEBELLO (l.b.) is seen the little church of *St-Julien-le-Pauvre.*—The **Pont au Double** (1881) takes the place of a 17th cent. bridge for crossing which the toll of a 'double' ($\frac{1}{12}$*d.*) was charged. The QUAI DE L'ARCHEVÊCHÉ, skirting the S. side of Notre-Dame and the gardens beyond, is named after the archbishop's house pulled down in 1831.—At the end of the smaller arm of the Seine is the **Pont de l'Archevêché** (1827).

Beyond the Pont-Neuf is the QUAI DE LA MÉGISSERIE (r.b.), once known as Quai de la Ferraille from its sword-makers and scrap-iron merchants. The characteristic shops now are those of the corn-chandlers, bird-fanciers, and dealers in fishing-tackle and sporting goods. Here, too, are the *Belle-Jardinière* stores and the *Théâtre du Châtelet.* It ends at the *Place du Châtelet.* On the bank of the Cité is the QUAI DE L'HORLOGE, skirting the N. side of the *Palais de Justice* as far as the clock-tower whence it derives its name.

The **Pont au Change** ($\frac{2}{5}$ m.) was built in 1858–59 to replace a stone bridge (slightly lower down) which dated from 1639 and was lined with moneylenders' shops. At the beginning of the QUAI DE GESVRES (r.b.) is the *Théâtre Sarah-Bernhardt.* Opposite, on the QUAI DE CORSE, are the *Tribunal de Commerce* and the *Marché aux Fleurs.*—The **Pont Notre-Dame** ($\frac{1}{2}$ m.), rebuilt in 1913, occupies the site of the chief Roman bridge. The QUAI AUX FLEURS, with the N. front of the *Hôtel-Dieu,* is connected with the *Place de l'Hôtel-de-Ville* (r.b.) by the **Pont d'Arcole** ($\frac{2}{5}$ m.), built under the Restoration and named after a young man killed in 1830, while leading a band of insurgents against the Hôtel de Ville. Behind the QUAI DE L'HÔTEL-DE-VILLE is the statue of Etienne Marcel, on the S. side of the Hôtel de Ville. At this point, the junction of the two channels encircling the Ile St-Louis, a miniature ' Pool of London ' is formed, a busy centre of barge and steamboat traffic.

CHANNEL TO THE N. OF THE ILE ST-LOUIS. The **Pont Louis-Philippe** was rebuilt in 1862. On the Ile St-Louis is the QUAI DE BOURBON. Beyond the **Pont Marie** (1614–28), which is named after its builder, are the QUAI DES CÉLESTINS (r.b.), with the striking *Hôtel Fieubet,* and, on the Ile St-Louis, the QUAI D'ANJOU. Beyond is the Pont Sully (see below).

The two islands are connected by the **Pont St. Louis** ($\frac{4}{5}$ m.; 1877), damaged by a lighter in 1939 and at present replaced by a footbridge. The QUAI DE LA TOURNELLE (l.b.) is mainly engaged in the wine trade ; at No. 47, however, is the *Musée de l'Assistance Publique* (open daily 10–12, 2–5, except. Tues. and holidays ; adm. 20 fr.), in a wing of the Pharmacie Centrale des Hôpitaux (see p. 82). This interesting little museum contains many documents and other objects from the various charitable institutions of Paris, as well as from the archives of the Assistance Publique. At Nos. 55–57 is the *Hôtel de Nesmond* (c. 1636).—On the Ile St-Louis are the QUAI D'ORLÉANS and QUAI BÉTHUNE.

The old **Pont de la Tournelle** (1 m.), originally (1369) built of wood, was rebuilt in 1634, again under Louis-Philippe, and finally, in reinforced concrete, in 1925–28. The imposing statue of St. Geneviève (the patron saint of Paris) at the S. end is by Paul Landowski. The **Pont Sully** ($1\frac{1}{5}$ m.), built in

1874–76 to unite the Boul. Henri-IV with the Boul. St-Germain, crosses obliquely both arms of the Seine and the E. end of the island.

On the Quai Henri-IV (r.b.), occupying with its port what was till c. 1840 the *Ile Louviers*, are the *Magasins de la Ville* and the *Archives de la Seine*. At the farther end of the quay is the dock-entrance of the *Gare de l'Arsenal*, crossed by the *Pont Morland*. Behind the Quai St-Bernard (l.b.), with its busy wharves, are the *Halle aux Vins* and the railings of the *Jardin des Plantes*.

The **Pont d'Austerlitz** ($1\frac{3}{4}$ m.), inscribed with the names of the chief officers who fell at Austerlitz (1805), was built in 1802–7, rebuilt in stone in 1855, and widened in 1884–86. On the Quai d'Austerlitz (l.b.) are the *Gare d'Orléans* and a number of yards and factories. A remarkable railway viaduct (Métro) here crosses the river in a single span of 450 ft. The busy Quai de la Rapée (r.b.) is lined with wine-merchants' offices, workshops, forage stores, etc. At No. 12 is the *Institut Médico-Légal* (no adm.) which takes the place of the old Morgue that stood at the S. end of the Ile de la Cité.

Beyond the **Pont de Bercy** ($2\frac{1}{4}$ m. ; 1864) is the Quai de Bercy (r.b.), lined with the vast *Entrepôts de Bercy*, warehouses for wine, spirits, vinegar, and oil, which extend beyond the **Pont de Tolbiac** ($2\frac{3}{4}$ m. ; 1879–84) to the Pont National. Opposite is the Quai de la Gare, with timber-wharves and railway works. Just within the old fortifications is the **Pont National** ($3\frac{1}{4}$ m. ; 1852, enlarged in 1939–42), used by the Ceinture railway as well as by road traffic.

B. From the Louvre to Auteuil.

Immediately below the Rue du Louvre is the **Pont des Arts** (for foot-passengers only), built in 1802–4, which derives its name from the 'Palais des Arts,' as the Louvre was called at that time. It commands a noted view of the W. end of the Ile de la Cité.—The chief feature of the Quai du Louvre (r.b.) is the beautiful S. front of the *Louvre*, with the Jardin de l'Infante. On the Quai Malaquais (l.b.) is the *Ecole des Beaux-Arts*.—The **Pont du Carrousel**, originally built in 1834, was entirely rebuilt in 1935–39. At the ends of the bridge are four seated stone figures by Petitot and Pradier, from the original bridge. Behind the Quai des Tuileries (r.b.) is the long gallery between the Louvre and the Pavillon de Flore. At the *Port des Tuileries* cargoes of sand and grindstones are discharged. Opposite is the Quai Voltaire.—The **Pont-Royal** ($\frac{3}{8}$ m.) is a five-arched bridge built by Père F. Romain and Mansart in 1685–89 and commands a splendid view. The last pillar on either bank has a hydrographic scale indicating the low-water mark (zero), besides various flood-marks.

Below the Pont-Royal is the QUAI ANATOLE-FRANCE (l.b.) with the *Caisse des Dépôts et Consignations*, the imposing *Gare d'Orsay*, and the *Palais de la Légion d'Honneur*. Behind the QUAI DES TUILERIES (r.b.) lie the *Tuileries Gardens*.—On the cornice of the **Pont de Solférino** (¾ m.; 1858–59) are the names of the French victories in the Austrian war of 1859.—The **Pont de la Concorde** (1 m.; fine views) unites the *Place de la Concorde* with the *Palais-Bourbon*. It was built by Perronet in 1788–90, and stone from the Bastille was used in the construction of the upper part. The bridge was widened in 1930–32. The river now flows between the QUAI DE LA CONFÉRENCE and the QUAI D'ORSAY (l.b.), with the *Ministère des Affaires Etrangères* and the *Gare* and *Esplanade des Invalides*. Beyond the Esplanade is the *American Church*.—The ***Pont Alexandre-III** (1⅕ m.; 1896–1900), the first stone of which was laid by Tsar Nicolas II, is a single steel arch, 350 ft. in span and 150 ft. wide.

The pillars at either end are surmounted by gilded figures of Fame and Pegasus, by Frémiet, Steiner, and Grenet. At the base are statues of the France of Charlemagne, by Lenoir, and Modern France, by Michel (r.b.); Renaissance France, by Coutain, and the France of Louis XIV, by Marqueste. The shields in the centre of the bridge bear the arms of Leningrad (facing upstream) and of Paris (facing downstream).

The **Pont des Invalides** (1⅖ m.), constructed in 1827–29 and rebuilt in 1879–80, has on its central piers stone figures of Victory by Land and Victory by Sea.—The **Pont de l'Alma** (1⅘ m.), built in 1854–57, with the *Place de l'Alma* at its N. end, is adorned with stone figures of a Grenadier and a Zouave, by Diéboldt, and a Chasseur and an Artilleryman, by A. Arnaud. The Zouave is a familiar gauge for estimating the height of the Seine in flood.

Between the Pont de l'Alma and the Pont de Bir-Hakeim (see below) is the QUAI DE NEW-YORK (r.b.; formerly the Quai de Tokio); opposite is the QUAI EDOUARD-BRANLY. A little above the *Passerelle Debilly* are the two huge buildings of the *Palais d'Art Moderne* (r.b.) and part of the *Ministry of Works* with the *Ministry of Economic Affairs* farther on (l.b.). We now pass between the gardens of the *Palais de Chaillot* (r.b.) and the *Champ-de-Mars* (l.b.) with the *Eiffel Tower*. The **Pont d'Iéna** (2⅕ m.), which spans the river here, was built in 1806–13 and widened in 1914, and again in 1936. The **Pont de Bir-Hakeim** (2⅗ m.; 1903–6) is a double bridge, the upper story being used by the Métro. The four groups, by G. Michel, represent the Boatmen of the Seine and the Ironworkers of France. The centre of the bridge rests on the E. end of the long and narrow *Allée* or *Ile des Cygnes* ('Isle of Swans'). On the right bank is the QUAI DE PASSY; on the left, the QUAI DE GRENELLE. The river and island are crossed also by an oblique railway-viaduct (1900) and by the **Pont de Grenelle** (3¼ m.), rebuilt in 1875. On the extremity of the island, facing downstream, is a reduced bronze copy of Bartholdi's famous statue, *Liberty enlightening the World*, presented by the French Republic to the United States, where it stands at the entrance to New York Harbour.

Beyond the Pont de Grenelle are the QUAI LOUIS BLÉRIOT (r.b.) and the QUAI DE JAVEL (l.b.). The **Pont Mirabeau** (3½ m.), built in 1895–97, is adorned with sculptures by Injalbert. On the right is the *Institution de Ste-Périne*. The ***Pont-Viaduc d'Auteuil** (4 m.) is a fine work by Bassompierre (1866), consisting of a double carriage-way and the track of the Ceinture railway.

12. THE CITÉ AND THE ILE ST-LOUIS.

MÉTRO stations: *Cité* (line 4); *Châtelet* (lines 1, 4, 7, 11); *St-Michel* (line 4); *Sully-Morland*, *Pont-Marie* (line 7).—MOTOR-BUSES: Cité (route 67); Châtelet (routes 21, 38, 47, 58, 67, 69, 72, 73, 74, 75, 76, 77, 85, 96); St-Michel (routes 21, 27, 38, 77, 85, 96); Sully-Morland (route 86).

The **Ile de la Cité,** the oldest part of Paris, lies in the river like a ship, moored to the banks by numerous bridges, with Notre-Dame as its poop and the 'Pointe,' pointing downstream, as its prow. A ship has figured in the arms of Paris from time immemorial.

The Pont-Neuf leads from the Quai du Louvre to the W. extremity of the Cité, occupied by the *Square du Vert-Galant*, with its pleasant garden. Here, close to the bridge, stands the fine equestrian *Statue of Henri IV*, by Lemot, set up in 1818 in place of a statue by Giambologna and Tacca which stood here from 1635 to 1792. On the pedestal are bronze reliefs of Henri IV sending bread to the besieged Parisians and Henri IV's entry into Paris.

To the E. of the bridge, in front of the Palais de Justice, is the *Place Dauphine*, with two rows of houses dating for the most part from Louis XIII's reign. Mme Roland (1754–93) spent her early youth here (tablet on 41 Quai de l'Horloge).

During the 17th and 18th cent. the Place du Pont-Neuf and the bridge were frequented by pedlars and mountebanks. Tabarin, the famous mountebank, set up his 'theatre' in the Place Dauphine. Here, too, was the original site of the Samaritaine, one of the earliest hydraulic pumps. The second-hand booksellers now open their stalls ('boîtes') on the parapets of the quays.

The ***PALAIS DE JUSTICE,** a huge block of buildings occupying the whole width of the island, includes within its precincts the Sainte-Chapelle, the Conciergerie, the Dépôt des Prévenus (remand prison), and the Cour de Cassation (supreme court of appeal). Its oldest surviving portion includes the

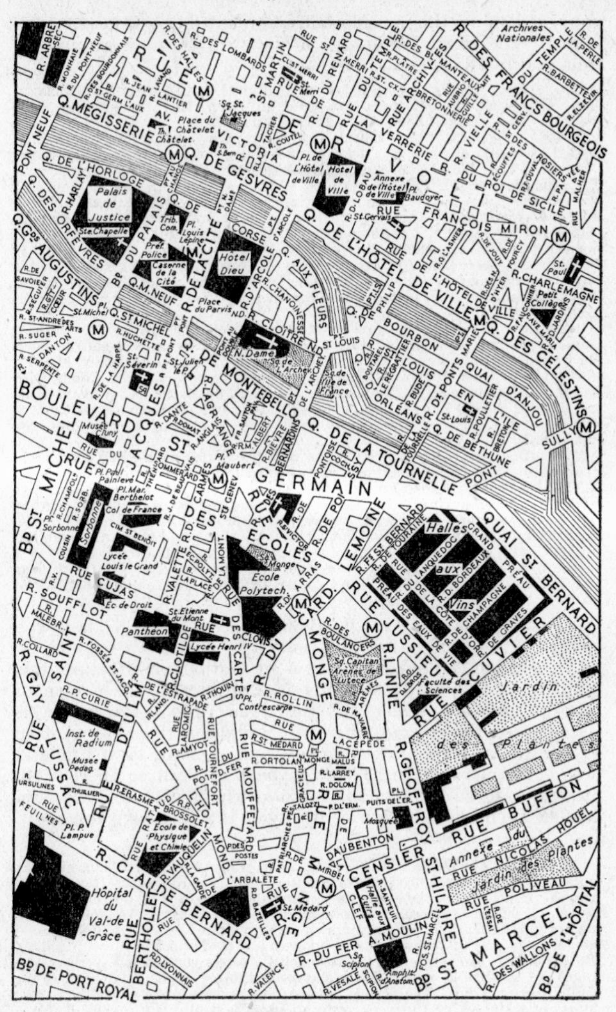

VIII. CITÉ–QUARTIER LATIN

four towers on the N. side and the Sainte-Chapelle (13–14th cent.). The main buildings, of the 18th cent., were greatly enlarged in 1857–68 and 1911–14.

ADMISSION. The *Palais* is open daily (free) from 11–6, except Sun. and holidays. The *Sainte-Chapelle* and the *Conciergerie* are open daily (except Tues. and holidays) 10–12, 1.30–4 or 5. Adm. 30 fr. (15 fr. on Sun.).

HISTORY. The site of the Palais de Justice was occupied as early as the Roman period by a palace, which was a favourite residence of the Emperor Julian the Apostate. The Merovingian kings divided their time between the Thermes, in the country, and this Palais de la Cité, which was inside the walls. Louis VI died in the palace in 1137, Louis VII in 1180; and in the 13th cent. Philip Augustus was married there to the King of Denmark's sister. St. Louis, the "father of the Cité," altered the palace and built the Sainte-Chapelle. Francis I was the last king to reside in the Palais de la Cité. From the reign of Henri II onwards the whole palace was occupied by the Parlement, which had shared it with the reigning sovereign since the time of St. Louis. Since then the palace, which has suffered from frequent fires, has been repeatedly rebuilt, enlarged, and restored.

EXTERIOR. The imposing COUR DU MAI, named after the maypole set up here annually by the 'Basoche,' or society of law-clerks, is separated from the Boul. du Palais by handsome iron railings, erected in 1787 and reconstructed in 1877. A flight of steps ascends to the Galerie Marchande, above which rises a dome with sculptures by *Pajou*.—The buildings in the Boul. du Palais, between the Cour du Mai and the clock-tower, are in the 14th cent. style and serve in part as the façade of the Salle des Pas-Perdus, which may be entered directly from the boulevard.

The 14th cent. TOUR DE L'HORLOGE or clock-tower, on the N., completely renewed in 1852, has an enormous clock copied from the original dial designed c. 1585 by *Germain Pilon*. Fronting the Quai de l'Horloge is a block of buildings of 14th cent. origin (upper stories rebuilt in the original style). Between the TOUR DE CÉSAR and TOUR D'ARGENT, a pair of projecting round towers, is the entrance to the Conciergerie, and farther on is another round tower, the TOUR DE BONBEC, with the 19th cent. wing of the Cour de Cassation beyond.

The handsome façade in the Place Dauphine (1857–68) is adorned with lions and statues, while to the S., on the Quai des Orfèvres, are the new courts added in 1914.

A vaulted gateway in the Boulevard du Palais leads to the great COUR DE LA SAINTE-CHAPELLE.

The ****Sainte-Chapelle,** a gem of Gothic architecture was built in 1245–48 by St. Louis as a shrine for the Crown of Thorns and a fragment of the True Cross. Its design is ascribed to *Pierre de Montereau*. Royal marriages were often celebrated at the Sainte-Chapelle, and Richard II of England was betrothed here in 1396 to Isabella of France. In 1837–40 it was restored by *Duban*, *Lassus* (who built the successful leaden flèche in the 15th cent. style, 108 ft. above the roof), and *Viollet-le-Duc*.

EXTERIOR. The chapel, 118 ft. long, 56 ft. wide, and 138 ft. high, gives an impression of great height in proportion to its length and breadth. It consists of two chapels, one above the other, the lower chapel being used by the retainers and servants, while the elaborately decorated upper chapel was reserved for the royal family and the court. The lofty windows are surmounted by delicately sculptured gables and a graceful balustrade. The modern lead roof is picked out with gilding. By the fourth window on the right is a little recess constructed (perhaps) by Louis XI so that he could hear mass without being seen. Below this is the Oratory of St. Louis. The portal consists of two porches, one above the other; most of the statues are 19th cent. restorations. The flamboyant rose window was reconstructed under Charles VIII.

CHAPELLE BASSE. The interior is very low (21 ft.), with 40 single shaft columns and admirable bosses of carved oak. The pavement consists entirely of tombstones.

CHAPELLE HAUTE. A staircase leads from the lower chapel to the porch of the upper chapel, which communicates on the N. side with the palace. The whole of the dim interior (67 ft. high) has been repainted and regilded, but its outstanding decoration is the *Stained Glass (restored in 1845) which glows with the radiance of jewels. The 1st window on the right represents the Legend of the Cross and the removal of the relics. The other windows in the nave and apse depict scenes from the Old and New Testaments; the large rose window, with 86 panels from the Apocalypse, dates from Charles VIII. Beneath the windows on either side runs a blind arcade and a bench, with sculptured quatrefoils (scenes of martyrdom); against the pillars are figures of the Apostles with consecration crosses (the 4th, 5th, and 6th on the left and the 3rd, 4th, and 5th on the right are original). The two deep recesses under the windows of the 4th bay were the seats reserved for the royal family. In the 5th bay on the right is Louis XI's recess. Behind the altar in the centre of the arcade across the apse is a lofty wooden canopy beneath which the sacred relics used to be exhibited on Good Friday. The spiral staircase on the right is original.

From the Cour du Mai, the main entrance-courtyard, we ascend the steps to the GALERIE MARCHANDE, at the right end of which is the *SALLE DES PAS-PERDUS, the great hall of the medieval palace, where, in 1431, the coronation banquet of Henry VI of England was celebrated. This magnificent hall, divided by a row of arches, was rebuilt by *Salomon de Brosse* in 1622, burned by the Communards in 1871, and restored in 1878. It is adorned with monuments to distinguished lawyers, and a memorial to advocates who fell in the First World War, by *Bartholomé* (1922). At the far end on the right is the entrance to the Première Chambre Civile, formerly the GRAND' CHAMBRE or CHAMBRE DORÉE (restored), perhaps originally the bedchamber of St. Louis. Later it was used by the Parlement, and it was here that Louis XIV coined his famous epigram " L'Etat, c'est moi." The Revolutionary Tribunal sat here in 1793 and condemned to death many famous persons, including Charlotte Corday, Marie Antoinette, the Girondists, and Mme Roland.

The GALERIE DES PRISONNIERS and the GALERIE LAMOIGNON traverse the whole length of the building, on the left of the great hall, and are approached from the Boul. du Palais by a late 18th cent. staircase, revealed by alterations in 1932. To the right is the GALERIE ST-LOUIS, with a painted statue of St. Louis, by *Guillaume*, and two wall-paintings from the life of St. Louis, by *L. O. Merson*. At the end (l.) the GALERIE DES BUSTES, leads to the CHAMBRE CIVILE DE LA COUR DE CASSATION (when the court is not sitting, apply to the usher), elaborately decorated, with a ceiling-painting, the Glorification of Law, by *Paul Baudry*. When the court is sitting the entrance is by the VESTIBULE DE HARLAY, to the right at the end of the Galerie Lamoignon. In the vestibule, at the ends, are statues of St. Louis, Philip Augustus, Napoleon I, Charlemagne, and a bust of Duc by *Chapu*. The grand staircase leads (l.) to the Assize Court and (r.) to the Court of Criminal Appeal; while from the S. end of the Vestibule de Harlay the GALERIE DE LA PREMIÈRE PRÉSIDENCE, with the Première Chambre de la Cour d'Appel on the right, leads back to the Galerie Marchande or entrance-vestibule.

The ***Conciergerie** (entered from the Quai de l'Horloge), one of the famous prisons of the world, originally the residence of the 'Concierge' or chief executive of the Parlement, occupies the lower floor of the right (N.) wing of the Palais. Part of it is still used for prisoners awaiting trial.

The historical associations of the Conciergerie are innumerable. In 1418 the Comte d'Armagnac was massacred with many of his partisans by the hired assassins of the Duke of Burgundy. During the Revolution, first Marie Antoinette, then Bailly, Malesherbes, Mme Élisabeth, Mme Roland, Mme du Barry, Camille Desmoulins, Danton, André Chénier, and Robespierre passed their last days in the Conciergerie. In the massacres of Sept. 1792 288 prisoners perished here. Later prisoners were Georges Cadoudal (d. 1804), the Chouan leader, Marshal Ney and the Duc d'Orléans (1890).

On the right side of the courtyard is a door leading to the SALLE DES GARDES, where visitors await the guide, a handsome 14th cent. double room restored in 1877. On the window side are two small staircases (no adm.), that on the right leading to the Tour de César, where Ravaillac, the murderer of Henri IV (1610), and Prince Jérôme Bonaparte (1883) were imprisoned. The other stair leads to the Tour d'Argent, which served as a prison for Damiens, who attempted the life of Louis XV (1757). The little staircase on the left of the room in the right-hand corner was ascended by Marie Antoinette and over 2700 other prisoners on the way from their cells to the Tribunal.

The wide gallery known as the RUE DE PARIS served as a prison during the Revolution for the 'pailleux' (prisoners who slept on straw, being unable to bribe their gaolers). The fine Gothic SALLE DES GENS-D'ARMES (or de St-Louis; l.) was restored in 1877.

This is the original 'Salle des Pas-Perdus,' said to be so called because the victims of the Revolution walked through it on their way to the Cour du Mai and execution; the name has since been transferred to the hall above and to the waiting-halls of other public buildings.

The CUISINES DE ST-LOUIS (so called) really date from the 14th cent. The Rue de Paris ends at the GALERIE DES PRISONNIERS, the windows of which look out on to the COUR DES FEMMES, where the women prisoners were allowed to take exercise, the scene of the massacres of Sept., 1792. The corner exactly opposite the windows of the Galerie des Prisonniers was divided off for the men by a railing that still exists. To the left in the Galerie des Prisonniers is a little room where condemned prisoners had their hair shorn and awaited their departure for the guillotine, and at the end is the iron wicket which was the sole entrance to the prison in Revolutionary times. In front of this was the registrar's office (now a restaurant). At the opposite end of the Galerie des Prisonniers is (l.) the original door (but in a different position) of MARIE ANTOINETTE'S CELL, which was converted into a chapel of atonement in 1816. Next to the queen's cell, and now communicating with it, is ROBESPIERRE'S CELL. Next comes the SALLE DES GIRONDINS, where the Girondists spent their last night on earth. Once the chapel of the Conciergerie and used again as a chapel during the Restoration, it has preserved its original appearance, with its gallery for the prisoners. Here are now collected souvenirs of the Revolutionary period, including the lock of Robespierre's cell, a letter written by Marie Antoinette after her trial and a crucifix found in her cell.

On the opposite side of the BOULEVARD DU PALAIS are the *Préfecture de Police* (the ' Scotland Yard ' of Paris), the headquarters of the *Régiment des Sapeurs-Pompiers* (fire brigade), and the *Tribunal de Commerce* (open on weekdays, 10–4), built by Bailly in 1860–65. In the *Marché aux Fleurs* (Place Louis-Lépine), behind the Tribunal, a flower market is held on Wed. and Sat., and a bird market on Sun. afternoons. The Rue de la Cité (r.) leads to the PLACE DU PARVIS-NOTRE-DAME, which is bounded on the S. by the Seine, on the W. by the *Caserne de la Cité* (barracks of the Garde Républicaine ; 1865), the scene of considerable fighting during the liberation of Paris. On the N. is the *Hôtel-Dieu* (a hospital founded on the S. side of the Parvis by St. Landry, Bishop of Paris, c. 660 and rebuilt on its present site in 1868–78), while on the E. is the cathedral of Notre-Dame. At the S.E. corner of the square is a colossal group of Charlemagne, Roland, and Oliver, by the brothers Rochet (1882).

The ****CATHEDRAL OF NOTRE-DAME** is archæologically the most interesting of the Gothic cathedrals of France, though for beauty it ranks after Chartres, Reims, Amiens, and Bourges. Taken in hand at the time when Gothic art was beginning to throw off the traditions of the Romanesque style, Notre-Dame was completed during the 13th cent., so that it is possible to follow, step by step, the progress of the new style until its decadence in the 14th century.

HISTORY. The idea of converting into a single building, on a much larger scale, the two basilicas of Notre-Dame (founded by Childebert, 6th cent.) and St-Etienne (perhaps the mother-church of Paris, 4th cent.), which replaced a pagan temple more or less on the site of the present cathedral, was due to Maurice de Sully, Bishop of Paris. The foundation-stone of the new building was laid by Pope Alexander III in 1163. The choir was finished in 1177 (except for the great roof), the nave in 1208, and the W. front and its towers c. 1225–50. A girdle of chapels was added in 1240–1315. The S. porch was begun in 1257, and the N. porch a few years later. In 1431, in the choir of Notre-Dame, Henry VI of England was crowned King of France at the age of ten, and in 1560 Mary Stuart was crowned queen-consort of Francis II. Until the end of the 17th cent. Notre-Dame had preserved intact its appearance of the 14th cent., but the reigns of Louis XIV and Louis XV brought deplorable alterations (especially the destruction of the tombs and stained glass). The baptistery of *St-Jean-le-Rond*, adjoining the N. tower, was demolished in 1748. During the Revolution many of the sculptures and treasures of the cathedral were destroyed, and an opera-singer was here enthroned as the Goddess of Reason. Napoleon I and Josephine were crowned by Pius VII in Notre-Dame in 1804, and other grand ceremonies were the baptism of the King of Rome, the marriage of Napoleon III and Eugénie de Montijo (1853) and the baptism of the Prince Imperial (1857). In 1845 a thorough restoration, guided by technical knowledge and good taste, was begun under the direction of Lassus and Viollet-le-Duc. In 1914 the church was slightly damaged by a bomb from a German aeroplane. The classic description of the cathedral is that in Victor Hugo's 'Notre Dame.'

EXTERIOR. The *WEST FRONT, in three distinct stories, forms one harmonious whole. The *Porte du Jugement*, or central portal (23 ft. high), ruined by Soufflot in 1771, has a modern statue of Christ on the pier and the Last Judgment in the tympanum; only the upper tier of sculptures is ancient. The *Portail de la Vierge* (l.) has the most striking sculptures. On the pier is the Virgin trampling the serpent underfoot (restored). In the lower part of the tympanum are three prophets (l.), three kings (r.), and the Resurrection of the Virgin (centre); above is the Coronation of the Virgin. The sculptures of the *Portail de Ste-Anne* (r.) are mostly 12th cent. work, designed for a narrower portal with additions of c. 1240. On the pier is St. Marcellus trampling on the dragon. Above, scenes from the lives of St. Anne and the Virgin; Louis VII, and Maurice de Sully. The wrought-iron *Hinges, especially those of the Portail de Ste-Anne, are masterpieces of medieval work, restored. On the buttresses between the doors are four beautiful niches with modern statues.—Above the portals is the *Gallery of the Kings of Judah*, the 28 statues of which, destroyed in 1793, were reconstructed by Viollet-le-Duc. The balustrade above this is the *Gallery of the Virgin*, with modern statues. The magnificent rose window, 31 ft. in diameter, is flanked by double windows within arches. Higher still is a fine open arcade with graceful columns.—The TOWERS, 223 ft. high, originally intended to be crowned with spires are open daily (except Tues.) 10–5. Entrance at the door of the N. tower; adm. 30 fr., 15 fr. on Sun. The platforms at the top command a superb *View of Paris. The balustrades are adorned with the famous *Gargoyles ('chimères') designed by Viollet-le-Duc, grotesque figures of devils, birds, and beasts. In the S. tower hangs the great bell ('Emmanuel-Marie-Thérèse'), recast in 1686 and weighing 13 tons.

The side façades and the apse likewise consist of three distinct and receding stories. The flying-buttresses of the apse are especially admired for their boldness and elegance. The *South Porch*, according to the Latin inscription at the base, was begun in 1257 under the direction of Jean de Chelles. The ancient sculptured medallions are believed to depict a student's life in the 13th century. The *North Porch* dates from about the same period. On the pier is a fine original statue of the Virgin and Child. Beyond the N. door is the graceful **Porte Rouge*, a masterpiece of 14th cent. carving, reserved for the canons. To the left of the Porte Rouge, below the windows of the choir chapels, are seven bas-reliefs of the 14th cent. (life of the Virgin, and story of Theophilus). The apse chapels were built after 1294. The sacristy, on the S. side of the choir, is by Lassus and Viollet-le-Duc.—The *Flèche* (312 ft. above the ground) of lead-covered oak, was rebuilt

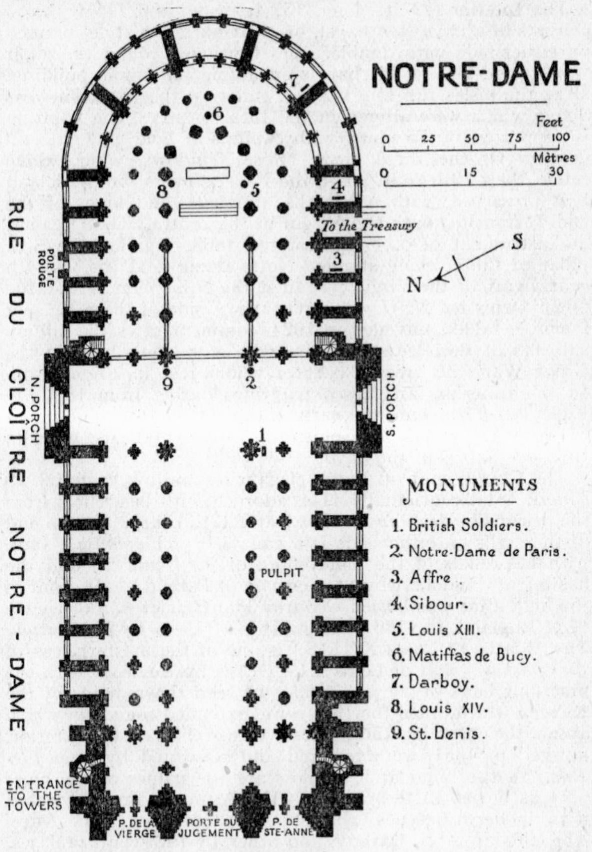
NOTRE-DAME
Feet
0 25 50 75 100
Mètres
0 15 30
To the Treasury
S
N
RUE DU CLOÎTRE NOTRE-DAME
PORTE ROUGE
N. PORCH
S. PORCH
PULPIT
ENTRANCE TO THE TOWERS
P. DE LA VIERGE
PORTE DU JUGEMENT
P. DE STE-ANNE
PLACE DU PARVIS
MONUMENTS
1. British Soldiers.
2. Notre-Dame de Paris.
3. Affre.
4. Sibour.
5. Louis XIII.
6. Matiffas de Bucy.
7. Darboy.
8. Louis XIV.
9. St. Denis.

by Viollet-le-Duc in 1859–60. The ball below the cross contains relics of the True Cross and the Crown of Thorns.

The **Interior** (427 ft. long, 157 ft. wide, and 115 ft. high) consists of a nave (ten bays), of great purity of style, flanked on either side with double aisles continued round the choir (five bays), and of 37 chapels encircling the whole building. Over the aisles run fine vaulted galleries, the nave windows above which were altered in the 13th century. The vaulting is supported by 75 piers, with capitals of bold and graceful design. Of the three great *Rose Windows, which alone retain their 13th cent. glass, the N. window is the finest and best preserved, with patriarchs, prophets, and kings of the Old Testament, with the Virgin in the centre. The Organ is an instrument of c. 1730, restored 1868. Against the S.E. pillar of the crossing stands 'Notre-Dame de Paris,' a 14th cent. figure of the Virgin; against the N.E. pillar is a statue of St. Denis by *N. Coustou*. On the S. side of the S.W. pier a simple tablet, unveiled in 1924, commemorates the million subjects of the British Empire who gave their lives in the Great War, the greater part of whom rest in French soil. In the transepts are fresco paintings dating from 1869–70. Eight late-17th cent. and early-18th cent. pictures, presented to Notre-Dame by the Goldsmiths' Guild of Paris, hang in the side-chapels of the nave.

The CHOIR, shut off by an elegant low railing, contains 78 superb *Stalls (originally 114), adorned with bas-reliefs from the designs of *Jean du Goulon* (early 17th cent.). At the end of the stalls on either side is a canopied archiepiscopal stall, with bas-reliefs of the martyrdom of St. Denis (r.) and the healing of Childebert by St. Germain of Paris (l.).—In front of the high altar was buried Geoffrey Plantagenet, son of Henry II of England, in 1186. Behind it is a *Pietà by *N. Coustou*. The *Statue of Louis XIII (S.) is one of the masterpieces of *G. Coustou*; that of Louis XIV (N.) is by *Coysevox*.—In the first four bays of the choir may be seen the remains of the *Screen which, until the 18th cent., extended round the whole apse; the charming and expressive bas-reliefs on the exterior, finished in 1351, were restored and repainted by *Viollet-le-Duc*. In the blind arches below are the names of the chief persons buried in the church.—The AMBULATORY, decorated with modern frescoes, contains the tombs of Abp. Affre, Abp. Sibour, Abp. Darboy, and other 18–19th cent. prelates. Behind the high-altar is the tomb-statue of Bp. Matiffas de Bucy (d. 1304).

On the right in the ambulatory is the entrance to the SACRISTY, which contains the *Treasury* of the cathedral (open daily except Sun. and feast days; adm. 20 fr.).

Road mileages in France are calculated from the W. door of Notre-Dame.

Behind the apse lies the *Square de l'Archevêché* in which is a bust of Goldoni, the Italian dramatist, who died in Paris in 1793. The name of the square recalls the archbishops' palace, which stood on the quay until 1831.

The **Ile St-Louis,** named after Louis XIII and known familiarly as 'L'Ile,' the quietest and loneliest part of Paris, is connected with the right bank of the Seine by three bridges and with the left bank by two. Formerly two islets, it was not built over till the 17th cent., under Richelieu. It is reached from the Cité by the Pont St-Louis (temporary footbridge, see above).

No. 51 in the Rue St-Louis-en-l'Ile, with a balcony, is the *Hôtel Chenizot* 1730), formerly the archbishop's house. The church of *St-Louis-en-l'Ile* was begun by Levau in 1664 and finished by Jacques Doucet in 1726. The tower and curious openwork spire, 98 ft. high, were added in 1741. The ornamental stone carving in the interior was executed under the direction of J. B. de Champaigne.—At No. 12 in this street Philippe Lebon first introduced the principle of lighting by gas in France (1799 ; tablet). No. 7 has an arch of the *Hôtel de Bretonvilliers,* built by Jean I du Cerceau in 1640. Fénelon lived at No. 3. No. 2 is the splendid *Hôtel Lambert* (no adm.), built c. 1650 by Levau and decorated by Lebrun, and later the residence of Voltaire and Mme du Châtelet. For over 100 years it has been the home of the Czartoryski family and a centre of Polish life in Paris. In the Quai d'Anjou (N. side of the island) is the *Hôtel Lauzun* or *de Pimodan* (No. 17 ; 1657), after 1682 the residence of the Duc de Lauzun, commander of the French troops at the battle of the Boyne and now the property of the City of Paris. Gautier and Baudelaire lived together here in 1847. Princess Elizabeth and the Duke of Edinburgh were received here during their visit to Paris in 1948. Nos. 13 and 15 in the Quai de Bourbon (N. side) were the *Hôtel Le Charron* (17th cent.). In the Quai d'Orléans, on the S. side of the island, are the *Polish Library,* with souvenirs of Adam Mickiewicz (No. 6 ; the interior and most of the collection were destroyed by the Germans during the summer of 1940) ; and the birthplace (No. 12 ; with medallion) of Félix Arvers, the poet (1806–50), who died in the Quai de Béthune. In the latter (S. side of the island) is the mansion of the Duc de Richelieu, nephew of the cardinal (No. 18). At the E. end of the island is the little Square Henri IV with a monument to Barye (1793–1875), the sculptor of animals who had a studio on the Quai d'Anjou.

13. THE LATIN QUARTER.

Métro stations : *St-Michel* (line 4) ; *Odéon* (lines 4 and 10).—Motor-buses: St-Michel (routes 21, 27, 38, 77, 85, 96) ; Odéon (routes 88 and 96).

The **Latin Quarter,** or *Quartier Latin,* is the district to the S. of the Ile de la Cité, on either side of the Boul. St-Germain and Boul. St-Michel. Originally known as the *Université* this has always been the learned quarter of Paris, deriving its present name (conferred by Rabelais) from the language spoken by the early students. Though most of the old streets and buildings have been swept away, the Latin Quarter still contains the chief educational and scientific institutions of Paris, and it is still famous for the careless Bohemian life of its students.

The Pont St-Michel links the Boul. du Palais in the Cité with the **Place St-Michel** at the beginning of the Boul. St-Michel. The *Fontaine St-Michel,* 85 ft. high on the S. side of the Place, was erected by Davioud in 1860. At the base is a memorial to the inhabitants of the 5th and 6th Arrondissements who lost their lives during Resistance operations in the summer of 1944.

Adjoining the Place St-Michel on the S.W. is the *Place St-André-des-Arts,* connected with the Boul. St-Germain by the new Rue Danton, No. 8 in which, at the corner of the Rue Serpente (r.), is the *Hôtel des Sociétés Savantes* (lectures). The Rue Serpente (l.) crosses the RUE HAUTEFEUILLE, in which is the *Hôtel des Abbés de Fécamp* (No. 5), with a pretty turret. Charles Baudelaire (1821–67), the poet, was born at No. 15.—Several other interesting streets lead N. from the RUE ST-ANDRÉ-DES-ARTS; in the RUE DES GRANDS-AUGUSTINS Nos. 3–7 are the old *Hôtel d'Hercule,* occupied by Francis I in his youth; No. 21 was the birthplace of Littré (1801–81), and Heine lived at No. 25 in 1841.—In the ancient COUR DU COMMERCE-SAINT-ANDRÉ, leading hence S. to the Boul. St-Germain, is the bookshop (No. 9) where Dr. Guillotin perfected his "philanthropic beheading machine"; opposite (No. 8) is the shop where Marat's journal 'L'Ami du Peuple' was printed; and at No. 4 is the basement of one of Philip Augustus's towers. An alley leads hence (l.) to the 16–17th cent. *Cour de Rohan,* originally part of the palace of the Archbishop of Rouen.

To the E. of the Place lies an interesting corner of Old Paris, of which the quaintest streets are the Rue Xavier-Privas, the Rue de la Huchette, and the Ruelle du Chat-qui-Pêche, named after an old shop-sign. In the Rue de la Huchette, Bonaparte lodged at No. 8 in 1795; and the *Théâtre de la Huchette* is the smallest in Paris. At the end of the Rue St-Séverin is ***St-Séverin,** one of the architectural gems of Paris, rebuilt in the 13–16th cent. on the site of an oratory of the time of Childebert I. The lower part of the W. front, the first three bays of the nave and the triforium of the first four bays, and the vaulting of the first three bays of the inner S. aisle all date from the early 13th cent.; the outer aisles and the apse were in construction during the 15th cent., the chapels in 1500–20. The main W. portal, of the early 13th cent., was brought piecemeal in 1837 from St-Pierre-aux-Bœufs in the Cité. The two upper stories date from the 15th century. On the left is a tower of the 13–14th cent., with a door which was long the sole entrance; the tympanum is modern but on the frame is a 15th cent. inscription: "Bonnes gens qui par cy passés, Priez Dieu pour les trespassés."—The striking features of the interior are the ribs of the vaulting and the choir triforium, which approaches English Perpendicular in style. The apse was classicised in the 17th cent. at the expense of Mlle de Montpensier. The windows of the nave, from the fourth bay onwards, contain 15th and 16th cent. glass; one of the subjects is the murder of St. Thomas Becket. In the W. rose window is a Tree of Jesse.—To the S. of the choir are the remains of a 15th cent. charnel-house, resembling a cloister but irregular in plan.

About 100 yds. E. of St-Séverin, beyond the Rue St-Jacques, is **St-Julien-le-Pauvre,** a tiny church rebuilt c. 1160 and used from 1655 as the chapel of the old Hôtel-Dieu. Since 1889 it has been used by the Melchites, Greek Catholics subject to Papal authority. The portal and tower were taken down in 1675, but the interior, in which is the tomb of Baron de Montyon, still retains some attractive features.—To the N. of the church is the little SQUARE RENÉ-VIVIANI, which commands a magnificent view of Notre-Dame. To the S. lies the RUE GALANDE, probably the oldest existing street in Paris (14th cent.). The RUE DU FOUARRE (perhaps named from the 'straw' on which the students sat), behind St-Julien, was the centre of the four 14th cent. schools of the University and is referred to by Dante (who was once supposed to have attended lectures here).

The BOULEVARD ST-MICHEL (popularly the 'Boul. Mich'), the chief thoroughfare in the Quartier Latin, begins at the Place St-Michel and leads S. to (⅘ m.) the Carrefour de l'Observatoire, passing the Cluny Museum, the Sorbonne, and the Luxembourg Gardens. Laid out by Haussmann as a direct continuation of the Boul. de Strasbourg and Boul. de Sébastopol, it is now a very busy street, especially in its lower part, which swarms with students' cafés.—At a busy traffic-centre, 300 yds. S. of the Place St-Michel, the Boul. St-Michel crosses the BOULEVARD ST-GERMAIN, an important thoroughfare, the E. sections of which we now visit.

For the continuation of the Boul. St-Michel to the S., see p. 88.

In the Boul. St-Germain just to the W. of this point is the imposing façade (1878) of the **Ecole de Médecine,** a huge block erected by Gondouin in 1769–76 on the site of the *Collège de Bourgogne* (especially devoted to natural philosophy) and the *Collège des Prémontrés* and greatly enlarged in recent years. The older part, considered the most classical work of the 18th cent., faces the Rue de l'Ecole-de-Médecine.

In the handsome courtyard are a bronze statue of Bichat, the anatomist (1771–1802), by David d'Angers, and (l.) a marble monument to Dr. Brouardel (1837–1906) by Denys Puech.

INTERIOR (apply to the concierge at the door on the right of the railings in the Rue de l'Ecole-de-Médecine; gratuity). The great *Lecture Hall* (800 seats) has a fresco by Urbain Bourgeois depicting the chief masters of the medical art, ancient and modern. The *Library* (open to doctors and students daily 11–7 and 7.30–10.30, except Aug. 1st–Oct. 15th) contains c. 300,000 vols. and the interesting commentaries of the heads of the faculty from 1395 onwards. The *Salle du Conseil* (adm. on application to the secretary) is hung with four magnificent *Gobelins of the Louis XIV period, after Charles Lebrun.

The *Musée Orfila* (open daily 12–4 or 5 to medical men with a permit from the secretary), a museum of comparative anatomy, with interesting historical collections, is entered from the end of the outside gallery to the left of the railings.

Opposite the Ecole de Médecine at Nos. 17–21 Rue de l'Ecole-de-Médecine is the *Ecole Pratique* or laboratories, a modern building. On the left of the entrance is the former refectory of the *Couvent des Cordeliers,* a 15th cent. Franciscan convent; during the Revolution this was the meeting-place of the extremist Club des Cordeliers, the leaders of which were Marat, Camille Desmoulins, and

Danton. On the first floor is the ***Musée Dupuytren*** (open to medical men on Tues., Thurs. and Sat., 3-4.30), an important museum of pathological anatomy.

No. 5 Rue de l'Ecole-de-Médecine is the ***Institut des Langues Modernes***, occupying the old Amphitheâtre de St-Côme (1691-94), with a beautiful portal. At No. 20 (demolished) Marat was stabbed in his bath by Charlotte Corday in 1793.

Farther W. in the Boul. St-Germain, beyond the Ecole de Médecine, is a bronze statue by A. Pâris, of the revolutionist Danton (1759–94), on the site of his house, where he was arrested. A few yards farther on we reach the Carrefour de l'Odéon.

To the E. of its intersection with the Boul. St-Michel, the Boul. St-Germain passes the gardens of the Hôtel de Cluny (Rte. 25) and crosses the Rue St-Jacques. At the corner of the Rue Thénard is the new *Ecole Spéciale des Travaux Publics*. Farther on is the Place Maubert. The large modern building on the S. side of the square occupies the site of the former *Marché des Carmes*. No. 15 Rue des Carmes (also to the S.) is the *Syrian Catholic Church*, which was formerly the chapel (1760) of a community of Irish priests, who established themselves in the 17th cent. in the buildings of the *Collège des Lombards*.

Beyond the Place Maubert the Boul. St-Germain passes the Rue de Bièvre (l.), where Dante is said to have written part of the 'Divina Commedia.' On the right of the boulevard is the apse of **St-Nicolas-du-Chardonnet** ('of the thistle-field'), an unfinished Renaissance church built in 1656–1709, from the plans of Charles Lebrun. The clumsy tower (13th cent.) is a relic of an earlier edifice.

The 2nd chapel on the right of the choir, beyond the transept, contains the monument of Bignon, the jurist (d. 1656), by *Girardon*, and a painting of St. Francis of Sales after *Philippe de Champaigne*. In the 8th chapel (around the apse) is the striking tomb of Lebrun's mother, by *Tuby* and *Collignon*, designed by *Lebrun* in the theatrical style of Bernini; against the window is a monument to Lebrun (d. 1690) and his widow, by *Coysevox*. The wall and ceiling paintings are likewise by *Lebrun*. The 11th chap. contains a 17th cent. wood relief of St. Peter repentant. The fine 18th cent. organ-case should be noted.

To the E. of the church is the huge mass of the *Maison de la Mutualité*, built in 1931 on the site of the former seminary connected with the church. The Boul. St-Germain now crosses the Rue de Pontoise, in which (l.), facing the Quai de la Tournelle, is the *Pharmacie Centrale des Hôpitaux*, formerly the convent of the 'Miramiones' or Filles de Ste-Geneviève, founded by Mme de Miramion (d. 1696). The firemen's barracks at No. 24 Rue de Poissy (r.) occupy the 14th cent. refectory of the *Collège des Bernardins*. The boulevard ends at the Pont de Sully.

The dreary RUE MONGE, ¾ m. long, runs S.E. from the Place Maubert across the old Faubourg St-Marceau to the Av. des Gobelins. In the triangular *Square Monge*, below the Ecole Polytechnique, is a bronze statue of *François Villon*, by

Etcheto ; also two statues from the old Hôtel de Ville and a Louis XV fountain. The new buildings of the school, to the S. (see below), are conspicuous.

The Rue Monge crosses the Rue du Cardinal-Lemoine, at No. 32 in which (l.) was the *Collège des Bons-Enfants*, where St. Vincent de Paul founded his congregation of mission-priests. No. 49 is a fine mansion, built by Boffrand in 1700 and occupied by Watteau and Buffon. The passage-way under the house leads into the Arènes de Lutèce (see below). The Institution Chevalier, opposite the Rue Clovis, is the old **Scots College** (*Collège des Ecossais* ; apply to the concierge), founded in 1325 by David, Bp. of Moray. The building was erected in 1665 by Robert Barclay. The chapel, on the first floor, contains the tomb of the Duchess of Tyrconnel (d. 1731) ; a memorial erected to James II (who bequeathed his brain to the college) by the Duke of Perth, with a long Latin epitaph ; the tomb of Sir Patrick Menteith, who died in 1675 in the service of Louis XIV ; etc. The Rue du Cardinal-Lemoine, going uphill, passes (l.) the Rue Rollin, at No. 2 in which (tablet) Blaise Pascal died in 1662, and ends on the S. at the *Place de la Contrescarpe*. No. 1 in this square has a tablet commemorating the Cabaret de la Pomme-de-Pin, immortalised by Rabelais and the 'Pléiade.' The populous and animated Rue Mouffetard, to the S., intersects a squalid district which has retained in part its ancient aspect.

In the Rue de Navarre, diverging to the left from the Rue Monge, are the ruins of **Arènes de Lutèce** (2nd or 3rd cent.), the amphitheatre of Roman Paris, discovered in 1870 and fully excavated since 1883. It is 62 yds. long and 51 yds. wide. To the E. of the arena, the gardens of the Square Capitan look on to the Rue des Arènes.

St-Médard, farther on (r.), dedicated to the 'St. Swithin' of France, is one of the most picturesque churches in Paris. The nave and aisles are Gothic of the 15th cent. ; the Renaissance choir (1562–86) was disfigured in the 18th century. The church was sacked by Huguenots in 1561 and but little of the 16th cent. glass survives. The charming painting of St-Geneviève in one of the choir chapels on the left is by Charles Eisen (not Watteau). The churchyard, now a garden, was once notorious for the fanatical orgies of the Jansenist pilgrims ('convulsionnaires') at the tomb of the Abbé Pâris (d. 1727).

The Rue Mouffetard (see above) leads N. from the front of the church. Taking the Rue de l'Arbalète (l.) in which No. 3 was the birthplace of Auguste Rodin (1840–1917) and Nos. 9–16 the buildings of the *Institut National Agronomique*, we reach the Rue Lhomond (r.) which leads back to the Panthéon. Beyond the Place Lucien-Herr (r.) is the old Rue Tournefort with the new *Sanctuaire du Christ-Roi* (1935–40). To the left is the modern Rue Pierre-Brossolette, over-shadowed by the huge brick building of the Ecole de Physique et de Chimie Industrielles. Nos. 12–24 in the Rue Lhomond are taken up by the new laboratories of the *Ecole Normale* and the *Hôpital Curie*. At the corner of the Rue des Irlandais (r.) is the *Collège des Irlandais*, founded in 1578, and established here as a seminary in 1769. At No. 17 Rue d'Ulm, on the left, is the Maronite church of *Notre-Dame-du-Liban*. No. 29 is the *Musée Pédagogique*, No. 31 is the *Ecole Nationale Supérieure des Arts Décoratifs*, and No. 45 is the *Ecole Normale Supérieure* (see p. 115).

The Rue Clovis, leading out of the Rue du Cardinal-Lemoine (see above), is crossed by the Rue Descartes, No. 34 in which was the residence of Paul Verlaine (1844–96). At

Nos. 5 and 21 are the entrances to the *Ecole Polytechnique,* founded by Monge in 1794 for the training of artillery and engineer officers and transferred hither in 1805 to the buildings of the *Collège de Navarre,* which were considerably enlarged in 1929–35. At No. 23 Rue Clovis is the entrance to the *Lycée Henri-IV,* the tower of which (restored) has a Romanesque base and two Gothic upper stories (14–15th cent.) and is a relic of the church of the *Abbaye de Ste-Geneviève.* Practically the whole of the conventual buildings were rebuilt in the 18th cent., but the former refectory (now the chapel), adjoining the Place Ste-Geneviève, is a pleasant but over-restored 13th cent. building and the kitchens are likewise medieval.

The Rue Clovis ends at the *Place Ste-Geneviève,* on the E. side of which is the remarkable and interesting church of ***St-Etienne-du-Mont,** a mainly Renaissance building with a Gothic choir and a N. tower partly of the 15th century.

The original 13th cent. church was rebuilt 1517–38; and Margaret of Valois laid the foundation stone of the portal in 1610. Under the Revolution it became the Temple of Filial Piety. The N. side, with its picturesque porch, is especially attractive.

The INTERIOR has lofty columns, a wide ambulatory and ribbed vaulting with pendent keystones. On the floor near the entrance a marble slab marks the spot where Abp. Sibour was assassinated in 1857 by an inhibited priest named Verger. The beautiful **Rood Screen,* built in 1525–35, is a masterpiece of design and carving; the date 1605 on the side refers only to the spiral staircases by which it is ascended. The organ-case dates from the 17th cent.; the pulpit from 1651. The **Stained Glass* ranges in date from c. 1550 to c. 1700; the oldest windows are those in the apse; perhaps the best is that in the fourth chapel of the S. aisle (Parable of the Great Supper; 1568).—Between the sixth and seventh chapels in the S. aisle is a marble tablet in memory of the Jacobins, an order of preaching friars established in the Rue St-Jacques in 1218, of which SS. Dominic and Thomas Aquinas were members.—In the N. aisle are bronze busts of Racine and Pascal, whose graves are at the entrance to the Lady Chapel; and on either side of the first S. chapel in the choir are their epitaphs (nearly opposite).

The *Chapelle de Ste-Geneviève* (S. of the choir), much visited by the faithful, especially during the 'neuvaine' of St. Geneviève (Jan. 3rd–10th), contains the modern copper-gilt shrine of the saint. Inside the modern plaster sarcophagus is a fragment of the saint's tomb; her bones were burned by the mob in the Place de Grève in 1801. In the next bay are an exit to the Rue Clovis and (l.) a corridor leading to the sacristy and charnel house. At the end of the corridor (r.) is the *Presbytery,* once the residence of the Regent Orléans, where he died in 1723. On the left is the gallery of the *Charnel House,* with twelve superb **Windows* of 1612–22, with portraits of Pope Paul III, Charles V, Francis I, Henry VIII, and other celebrities.

To the W. of the Place Ste-Geneviève rises the ***PANTHÉON,** situated on the 'Mont de Paris,' the highest point on the left bank (200 ft.) and the burial-place of St. Geneviève, patron-saint of Paris (422–509 or 512).

The present building was begun by Louis XV in 1764 to replace the former church of Ste-Geneviève (see above). The architect *Soufflot* died of anxiety in 1780 owing to a subsidence of the walls. In 1791 the Constituent Assembly decided that the church should be used as a Pantheon, or burial-place for distinguished citizens, and on the pediment were inscribed the words 'Aux Grands Hommes La Patrie Reconnaissante.' The building was again a church from the Restoration to 1830 and from 1851 to 1885, but on the occasion of Victor Hugo's interment it reverted to the name and purpose decreed in 1791.

The Panthéon is an imposing building in the shape of a Greek cross, 360 ft. long, 270 ft. wide, and 270 ft. high to the top of the majestic dome. The pediment above the portico of 22 Corinthian columns is a masterpiece of *David d'Angers*, representing France between Liberty and History distributing laurels to famous men. Flanking the central entrance are marble groups by *Maindron*: the Baptism of Clovis, and St. Geneviève and Attila.

ADMISSION. The Panthéon is open daily (except Tues.) 10–4 or 5; adm. 30 fr. Visits to the crypt (gratuity) every 15 min.

The INTERIOR, coldly baroque, is adorned with paintings on a gold ground representing saints and notabilities of France, together with monuments to those who have deserved the gratitude of their country. Among the paintings the Scenes from the Life of St. Geneviève, by *Puvis de Chavannes* (S. aisle of nave, and N. aisle of choir), are outstanding, though pallid in colouring. In the S. transept is a monument to unknown and unrecognised heroes, by *Landowski*. By the same artist is the monument to unknown artists, in the N. transept. The colossal group of the Convention, at the E. end of the choir, is by *Sicard*.

The DOME is supported by four piers united by great arches. There are three distinct cupolas, of which the first is open in the centre to reveal the second, which has a fresco by *Gros*, the Apotheosis of St. Geneviève, including the chief kings of France. By the first pillar (r.) is the monument of Jean Jacques Rousseau, by *Bartholomé*, with figures of Music, Truth, Philosophy, Nature, and Fame. By the first pillar (l.) is a monument to Diderot and the Encyclopædists by *Terroir*.

Within the dome, in 1852, Léon Foucault, the physicist, gave the first public demonstration of his pendulum experiment proving the rotation of the Earth.

CRYPT (entrance in the apse to the left of the choir). Before the entrance, shrine containing the heart of Gambetta (d. 1882), brought hither in 1920. On the right is the tomb of *Jean-Jacques Rousseau* (d. 1778; transferred hither in 1794); on the left, *Voltaire* (d. 1778; transferred in 1791), with his statue by Houdon; opposite, *Soufflot* (d. 1780), the architect.

Between the four central pillars a curious echo may be awakened. Of the well-known men whose remains have been re-interred in the vaults, the most famous are probably *Victor Hugo* (d. 1885) and *Emile Zola* (d. 1902), whose removal hither from Montmartre Cemetery in 1908 created something of a riot; *Berthelot*, the chemist (d. 1907), *Jean Jaurès* (assassinated in 1914), socialist politician; and *André Maginot* (d. 1932), originator of the Maginot Line.

Mirabeau (d. 1791) and *Marat* (d. 1793) were interred here with great state but their remains were soon cast out with ignominy; the former now rests in the cemetery of Ste-Catherine, the latter in the graveyard of St-Etienne-du-Mont.

In the N.W. corner of the PLACE DU PANTHÉON is the *Ecole de Droit*, begun by Soufflot in 1771 and enlarged in 1892–97. The *Mairie of the 5th Arrondissement*, opposite, is in the same style.—The **Bibliothèque Ste-Geneviève,** on the N. side of the Place, originated in the library of the famous Abbey of Ste-Geneviève (p. 84). The present building, on the site of the 14th cent. Collège de Montaigu, was designed by Labrouste and completed in 1850.

The library contains c. 700,000 vols. (nearly 4000 MSS.) and over 30,000 prints and engravings (10,000 portraits). The large reading-room is open daily 10–10. The reserve reading-room is open 10–12 and 1–4, but prospective students must make written application to M. le Conservateur. The library is closed annually from Aug. 15th–30th inclusive.—The rooms devoted to Scandinavian literature (c. 90,000 vols.; entrance, 6 Place du Panthéon) are open daily (except Sun. and holidays) 2–5. The *Bibliothèque Littéraire Jacques Doucet*, bequeathed to the University of Paris in 1929, has been installed in the reserve of the library (open 2–5 on Mon. and Fri. on application). This collection comprises c. 8000 vols. of late 19th and 20th cent. French authors, and includes MSS. of Rimbaud, Verlaine, Baudelaire, Gide, Paul Valéry, and others.

Among the most valuable illuminated MSS. in the library, which are exhibited from time to time, are an English Bible, copied by Manerius in the 12th cent.; the Chronicles of St-Denis (end of 13th cent.); several MSS. of the Carlovingian period; the 'De Proprietatibus Rerum' of Barthélemy l'Anglais (Catalan translation of the 15th cent.), and 'La Cité de Dieu' of St. Augustine (late 15th cent.).

In the Rue Valette, on the right of the library, are the interesting remains of the *Collège Fortet* (No. 21), dating from 1397, where Calvin was a student.—To the left of the library, at the beginning of the Rue Cujas, is the *Collège Ste-Barbe*, founded in 1460, the oldest existing public educational establishment in France, at which SS. Ignatius Loyola and Francis Xavier were scholars.

The broad RUE SOUFFLOT leads W. from the Panthéon to the Boul. St-Michel, opposite the Luxembourg Gardens. A tablet on No. 14 commemorates the Dominican or Jacobin convent (1217–1790), where Albertus Magnus and St. Thomas Aquinas taught.

The Rue Soufflot is crossed by the RUE ST-JACQUES, which is nearly 1 m. long. Near the corner (l.) is No. 151 bis, a charming Louis XV mansion. Turning to the N., we pass the *Lycée Louis-le-Grand* (r.), formerly the Jesuit *Collège de*

Clermont, founded in 1560 and rebuilt in 1887–96. Molière, Voltaire, Robespierre, and Desmoulins studied here. On the left is the Sorbonne.

In the Place Marcelin-Berthelot (r.) is the **Collège de France** (apply to the concierge; gratuity), founded by Francis I in 1530. The present building was begun in 1610, finished by *Chalgrin* c. 1778, and enlarged in recent years. Above the gateway of the Cour d'Honneur are the words 'Docet Omnia,' an enterprise provided for by forty professorships. In the courtyard, with its graceful portico, are a marble statue of Guillaume Budé (Budæus; 1467–1540) and tablets with the names of all the professors since the foundation.

In the garden on the N. side of the college are a statue of Claude Bernard (1813–78) and a bust of Ronsard, and bordering the Rue Jean-de-Beauvais are the two huge science blocks belonging to the college.

The **SORBONNE,** the seat of the University of Paris, was founded as a modest theological college in 1253 by Robert de Sorbon, chaplain to St-Louis. It was rebuilt at Richelieu's expense by *Jacques Lemercier* in 1629, but, with the exception of the church, the present buildings, designed by *Nénot* on an imposing scale, date from 1885–1901.

The University of Paris, which disputes with Bologna the title of the oldest university in Europe, arose in the first decade of the 12th cent. out of the schools of dialectic attached to Notre-Dame. Transferred by Abélard to the Montagne Ste-Geneviève, it obtained its first statutes in 1208, and these served as a model for Oxford and Cambridge and other universities of Northern Europe. By the 16th cent. it comprised no fewer than forty separate colleges. Before the end of the 13th cent. the Sorbonne had become synonymous with the faculty of theology, overshadowing the rest of the University and possessing the power of conferring degrees. Though it has the honour of having introduced printing into France, by allowing Ulrich Gering and his companions to set up their presses within its precincts in 1469, the Sorbonne was distinguished for its religious rancour, supporting the condemnation of Joan of Arc, justifying the massacre of St. Bartholomew, and refusing its recognition to Henri IV. The University was suppressed at the Revolution but was refounded by Napoleon in 1808.

The Sorbonne is now the chief seat of the *Faculté des Lettres* and the *Faculté des Sciences*. It houses the University Library (700,000 vols.), the *Académie de Paris*, whose rector is the head of the whole educational system of France, and other minor learned institutions. The University, the largest in the world, with 17,000 students, confers degrees of 'bachelier,' 'licencié,' and 'agrégé.'

Visitors are admitted to the great lecture-hall (Grand Amphithéâtre) on application to the Secrétariat, Rue des Ecoles. The other lecture-halls are open during lecture hours (consult the notice-boards). The library is open to students and those with special permission from the conservateur 9–12.30, 1.30–6, and the church of the Sorbonne is open 9–12, 1–4 or 6.

The massive block of buildings, between the Rue de la Sorbonne (W.), the Rue des Ecoles (N.), and the Rue St-Jacques (E.), is effective if somewhat ponderous; the successful *Cour d'Honneur*, entered from the Rue de la Sorbonne.

follows the lines of the courtyard of the old college. The chief rooms of the INTERIOR, entered from the Rue des Ecoles, are lavishly decorated in the style of 1900. From the *Vestibule*, with statues of Homer and Archimedes, the *Grand Staircase*, with paintings illustrating the history of the University, ascends to the *Banqueting Hall* and the *Grand Amphithéâtre*, or great lecture-hall, with 2700 seats. Here are seated statues of the founder, and of benefactors and teachers of the University; and at the end of the hall is the Sacred Grove, a huge and popular painting by Puvis de Chavannes.

The Church of the Sorbonne, on the E. side of the Place de la Sorbonne, was founded as the college chapel in the 13th cent. and rebuilt by *Lemercier* in 1635–59 at the expense of Card. Richelieu, whose family still has the right of being married and buried here. The dome was the first example of a true dome in Paris, those of the Carmes and St-Paul-St-Louis being but half-hearted attempts.

INTERIOR. The spandrel-paintings in the cupola, by *Philippe de Champaigne*, represent Four Fathers of the Church, with angels. On the right is the tomb, by *Ramey*, of the Duc de Richelieu (d. 1822). The marble group by *Sinding*, in the chapel on the left, was presented by Norway to the University. In the S. transept is the dramatic *TOMB OF CARDINAL RICHELIEU (d. 1642), designed by *Lebrun* and sculptured by *Girardon* (1694); the cardinal is represented in an attitude of grief, supported by Religion and Science. In the crypt are the bodies of twelve students of the University killed during the Resistance of 1940–45.

At the N. end of the Rue de la Sorbonne is the *Square Paul-Painlevé*, with a monument to Puvis de Chavannes, by Desbois, a memorial fountain, and a marble statue of Montaigne, by Landowski (1933). Thence a few steps along the Rue du Sommerard, past the entrance of the **Musée de Cluny** (Rte. 25), bring us to the Boulevard St-Michel, just S. of its intersection with the Boul. St-Germain.

Following the BOULEVARD ST-MICHEL to the S., we have on the right the Rue de l'Ecole-de-Médecine and the Rue Racine (see below), where George Sand lived at No. 3, on the 4th floor. Farther on (r.) is the *Lycée St-Louis*, built by Bailly on the site of the *Collège d'Harcourt*, the earliest and greatest of the University colleges (1280). Beyond its monumental gateway (1916) begins the Rue de Vaugirard, leading to the Luxembourg. Opposite lies the Place de la Sorbonne, with a monument to Auguste Comte (1798–1857), founder of Positivism. Comte spent the last years of his life at No. 10 in the Rue Monsieur-le-Prince, just beyond on the right. The composer Saint-Saëns lived at No. 14 in 1877–89, and Longfellow had lodgings at No. 49 in 1826, and, in a subsequent winter, at No. 5 Rue Racine. Farther on, opposite the Rue Soufflot, is the *Place Edmond-Rostand*, on the edge of the Luxembourg Gardens, with a fountain and a bronze group by Crauk. In the Rue de Médicis, which leads (r.) to the Luxembourg, André Gide (1869–1951) was born at No. 19.

We next pass (r.) the ECOLE SUPÉRIEURE DES MINES, occupying the Hôtel Vendôme, an 18th cent. building enlarged in the 19th cent. The *Museum of Mineralogy and Geology* is open on Tues., Thurs., and Sat., 2.30–4. César Franck died at No. 95, nearly opposite, in 1890. The Rue Auguste-Comte (r.) leads to the AVENUE DE L'OBSERVATOIRE, opposite the S. side of the Luxembourg Gardens, of which it once formed part. It was laid out under the Convention in 1795 and has flower-beds and lawns adorned with ornamental sculpture. On the W. side of the avenue are the Moorish-looking *Ecole Coloniale* (1896), the *Ecole de Pharmacie* (1876–85), and, beyond the Rue Michelet, the *Institut d'Art et d'Archéologie* (1927), another mock-oriental edifice (entrance 3 Rue Michelet; library open daily 2–6, except Sun. and in vacation). Farther S. is the **Fontaine de l'Observatoire*, a charming fountain by Davioud (1875), with bronze sea-horses and turtles by Frémiet and, in the centre, the four Quarters of the Globe, supporting an armillary sphere, a masterpiece by Carpeaux.

The Av. de l'Observatoire and the Boul. St-Michel converge, and end together in the Carrefour de l'Observatoire (p. 117).

14. THE JARDIN DES PLANTES AND FAUBOURG ST-MARCEL.

MÉTRO stations: *Jussieu* (lines 7 and 10); *Gare d'Orléans-Austerlitz* (lines 5 and 10; these two stations for the Jardin des Plantes); *St-Marcel, Campo-Formio* (line 5); *Place d'Italie* (lines 5, 6, 7); *Quai de la Gare, Chevaleret, Nationale* (line 6).—MOTOR-BUSES: Jussieu (route 67); Gare d'Orléans-Austerlitz (routes 63, 65, 91); Saint-Marcel (route 91); Campo-Formio (route 67); Place d'Italie (routes 27, 47, 67).

From the Pont de Sully and the E. end of the Boul. St-Germain the QUAI ST-BERNARD leads S.E. past the **Halle aux Vins,** a huge bonded warehouse for wine, on the site of the Abbaye de St-Victor. The quay then skirts the Jardin des Plantes and ends at the semi-circular PLACE VALHUBERT, with the main entrance of the Jardin des Plantes. On the E. is the *Gare d'Austerlitz* or *Gare d'Orléans*, the terminus of the railway to Toulouse, etc.

The **JARDIN DES PLANTES,** officially the *Muséum National d'Histoire Naturelle*, 60 acres in area, combining the attractions of a menagerie, botanical gardens, and natural history galleries, is one of the most popular of Paris resorts, in spite of its out-of-the-way situation. Its collection of wild and herbaceous plants is unrivalled ; in May and June the peonies make a magnificent show.

The *Gardens* are open free daily from sunrise to sunset ; besides the main entrance (see above) there are other entrances in the Rue Cuvier (N.W. side) and Rue Geoffroy-St-Hilaire (W. side). The *Galleries* are open daily (except Tues. and holidays which do not fall on a Sun.) 1.30–5. The *Menagerie* is open daily 9–5 or 6. The *Musée Cynégétique* on Thurs. and Sat. 1.30–5.

ADMISSION. *Galleries* 15 fr. ; *Musée Cynégétique* 10 fr. ; *Menagerie* 20 fr. ; *Reptile House* 10 fr. ; *Vivarium* 10 fr. ; combined ticket for the last three 40 fr.

Founded under Louis XIII as a ' physic garden ' for medicinal herbs by the royal physician Guy de la Brosse, the garden was first opened to the public in 1650. Its present importance is due mainly to the great naturalist Buffon, who was superintendent in 1739–88, and in 1793 it was reorganised by the Convention under its present official title, and provided with 12 professorships. Many distinguished French naturalists have taught and studied here, and are commemorated by monuments in the garden or near by.

Facing the main entrance is a statue of Lamarck (1744–1829) and on the right is a pond with water-plants and a bronze group, the Cub-Stealer, by Frémiet. To the left, along the Allée Buffon, are the *Anatomical and Palæontological Galleries* and, farther on, the *Botanical Gallery*. At the far end of the last is the trunk of one of the first locust-trees (Robinia pseudoacacia) in Europe, introduced from N. America by Jean Robin in 1601. To the left a special exit in the Rue Buffon leads to the *Musée Cynégétique* or Hunting Museum (No. 43bis, opposite), the principal attraction of which is the zoological collection of the Duke of Orleans (d. 1926), bequeathed by him to the nation.

On the left of the Allée Haüy, which prolongs the Allée Buffon, are the *Mineralogical and Geological Galleries*, with the *Library* (c. 250,000 vols., and 2000 MSS.) at the far end, and *Buffon's House*, occupied by him from 1773 to his death, beyond. Commanding the W. end of the gardens are the *Zoological Galleries*, in the N. wing of which is the tomb of Guy de la Brosse (d. 1641). In front are a pond with aquatic plants, and a statue of Buffon. Between the Allée Centrale and the Allée de Cuvier, an avenue of chestnut-trees skirting the menagerie, is the *Ecole de Botanique*, with about 13,000 species.

The *Menagerie*, or zoological garden, has two entrances in the Allée de Cuvier. Passing through the gardens (the monkey house is especially worth a visit), we proceed W. towards the exit, on the left of which is a monument to Bernardin de St-Pierre (1737–1814). On the right are *Cuvier's House*, where the great naturalist died in 1832, and the *Amphithéâtre*. On the lawn in front of the administrative office is a statue of Chevreul (1786–1889). To the W. lies the *Butte*, a hillock with a maze, the first cedar of Lebanon to be planted in France (by Bernard de Jussieu, 1753), a column in memory of Daubenton (1716–99), and, on the summit, a bronze belvedere. To the E., bordering the W. side of the Allée Edmond Perrier, are the glass houses of the Winter Gardens and tropical plants.

Opposite the exit at the corner of the Rue Linné and Rue Cuvier is the *Fontaine Cuvier* (1840), with groups of animals, including an anatomically impossible crocodile. Thence the Rue Geoffroy-St-Hilaire leads S. to the *Institut Musulman* (entr. in the Place du Puits de l'Ermite, behind), opened in 1925, with a **Mosque,** the first to be erected in France, in the 14th cent. Moorish style (open daily 2–5 or 6, except Fri. and Muslim holidays ; adm. 20 fr., gratuity to guide).

The Rue Geoffroy-St-Hilaire ends at the Boul. St-Marcel (see below). Near their junction was the *Cimetière Ste-Catherine,* where the bodies of Mirabeau and other revolutionaries were reburied after being ejected from the Panthéon.

The Boulevard de l'Hôpital extends in a straight line from the Place Valhubert to (c. 1 m.) the Place d'Italie, intersecting the busy artisan quarter of the Faubourg St-Marcel and passing the Square Marie-Curie. On the S. side is the huge **Hospice de la Salpêtrière** founded by Louis XIV, a charitable institution for aged or insane women. The main building, by Levau and others, dates from 1660 ; the domed *Church* was built by Libéral Bruant in 1670 ; and the whole is a notable example of the austere magnificence of the architecture of the period. Dr. Charcot (1825–93), the hypnotist, is commemorated by a monument to the left of the gateway.

Farther on in the boulevard, on the same side, is the *Hôpital de la Pitié,* transferred in 1911 from the Rue Lacépède, where it had been founded by Marie de Médicis in 1612.

To the right (W.) of the Boul. de l'Hôpital, opposite the Salpêtrière, diverges the Boulevard St-Marcel, leading to (½ m.) the Av. des Gobelins and continued by the Boul. Arago.

15. THE FAUBOURG ST-GERMAIN.

The district still known as the **Faubourg St-Germain** lay until the end of the 17th cent. outside the walls of Paris. It stretches S. from the river opposite the Louvre and the Tuileries, between the Pont des Arts on the E. and the Pont de la Concorde on the W. Its chief thoroughfares are the wide and modern Boul. St-Germain and Boul. Raspail, but the most characteristic streets of the once 'noble faubourg' are the Rue de Lille, Rue de l'Université, Rue St-Dominique, and Rue de Grenelle, with their secluded 18th cent. mansions of the old aristocracy, with handsome courtyards in front and spacious gardens behind.

A. East Part of the Faubourg St-Germain.

Métro stations : *St-Germain-des-Prés* and *St-Sulpice* (line 4) ; *Odéon* (lines 4 and 10) ; *Mabillon* (line 10).—Motor-buses : St-Germain-des-Prés (routes 48, 63, 86, 95, 96) ; St-Sulpice (routes 84, 86, 95, 96) ; Odéon (routes 86 and 96) ; Mabillon (route 86).

At the S. end of the Pont des Arts, facing the Louvre, is the Place de l'Institut, at the meeting of the Quai Malaquais and the Quai de Conti, with a marble statue of the Republic (1850). The quays in the neighbourhood are lined with bookstalls.

The **Palais de l'Institut,** or *Institut de France,* is surmounted with a dome which is one of the outstanding features of this part of the quays.

The courtyards are open daily from sunrise to sunset (except Sun. and holidays), and the assembly rooms and dome may be visited on Sat. 10–12, 1.30–4.30; Sun. 10–12 (apply at the secretary's office in the second courtyard, door D, on the left).

The left wing of the Institut and the Hôtel de la Monnaie cover the site of the *Hôtel de Nesle* (13th cent.) in which was incorporated the 12th cent. *Tour de Nesle* (tablet on the left wing of the Institut), or *Tour Hamelin*, the river bastion of Philip Augustus's wall. The tower is notorious in legend as the scene of the amours of Margaret and Joan of Burgundy, wives of Louis X and Philip the Tall, who used to have their lovers thrown into the river. Later occupants were Isabeau de Bavière, Charles the Bold, and Henry V of England. The W. part, with the tower, known as *Petit-Nesle*, was the workshop of Benvenuto Cellini in 1540 and was demolished in 1663. The E. part, or *Grande-Nesle*, rebuilt in 1648 by Fr. Mansart, became the *Hôtel de Conti* (1670) and in 1770 the Mint.—The present building was erected in accordance with the will of Card. Mazarin, who bequeathed 2,000,000 fr. in silver and 45,000 fr. a year for the establishment of a college for sixty gentlemen of the four provinces acquired by the Treaties of Münster and the Pyrenees, viz.: Flanders, Alsace, Roussillon, and Italy (Pinerolo and the States of the Church). The building, designed by Louis Levau, was erected in 1662–74. The official name of the new college was the *Collège Mazarin*, but its popular name was the *Collège des Quatre-Nations*, perhaps not only in allusion to Mazarin's foundation, but also to the 14th cent. division of the old University into the Ecoles des Quatre-Nations (France, Normandy, Picardy, and England). The Institut, founded in 1795 and installed at first in the Louvre, acquired the former Collège Mazarin in 1806.

The Institut de France comprises five academies: the ACADÉMIE FRANÇAISE, founded by Richelieu in 1635 and restricted to forty members, whose special task is the editing of the dictionary of the French language; the ACADÉMIE DES BEAUX-ARTS, founded by Mazarin in 1648; the ACADÉMIE DES INSCRIPTIONS ET BELLES-LETTRES, founded by Colbert in 1664; the ACADÉMIE DES SCIENCES, founded by Colbert in 1666; and the ACADÉMIE DES SCIENCES MORALES ET POLITIQUES, founded in 1832. The Académie Française holds special receptions for newly elected members, tickets of admission to which (apply to the secretary) are much sought after. The five academies meet together at an annual general meeting on Oct. 25th (adm. by ticket only).

We pass through the door on the left of the dome into an octagonal courtyard. The portico on the right is the main entrance to the Salle des Séances Solennelles beneath the dome, while that on the left leads to the Bibliothèque Mazarine (see below). There are two further courtyards, of which the third is the attractive little *Kitchen Court* of the old Collège Mazarin.

From the second court we enter (l.) the ground-floor Vestibule and ascend, past the secretary's office, to the upper Vestibule. On the right is the Library (adm. on personal introduction only); on the left the *Salle des Pas-Perdus* leads to the *Salle des Séances Ordinaires des Trois Académies* (Science, Beaux-Arts, Inscriptions) and the *Salle des Séances Ordinaires de l'Académie Française* (used also by the Académie des Sciences Morales). All these rooms are decorated with statues and busts (of no outstanding merit) of academicians and other distinguished men.

We return to the first courtyard and pass through the portico on the right, and two Vestibules, with further statues.

The SALLE DES SÉANCES SOLENNELLES, restored by the elder *Vaudoyer*, is the former college chapel, where Mazarin (tomb in the Louvre) and his niece, the Duchesse de Mazarin (d. 1699), the famous beauty of the court of Charles II, were buried. Here are held the receptions of the members of the Académie Française and the annual general meetings of the five academies and the Institut. It contains about 400 seats (green for members of the Académie Française, red for the other academies).

The Palais de l'Institut contains also the BIBLIOTHÈQUE MAZARINE (open daily 10–4 or 5, except Sun. and holidays, and from Sept. 15th to Oct. 1st), a library of c. 275,000 vols., 5800 MSS., and 1900 incunabula; and the small *Musée de Mme de Caen* (entrance, 1 Rue de Seine; apply to the concierge; gratuity) containing a number of sculptures, paintings, etc., contributed by winners of the Prix de Rome, in accordance with the will of the Comtesse de Caen (d. 1870), the foundress of the prize.

The QUAI DE CONTI, named after the Hôtel de Conti, runs. E. from the Place de l'Institut, opposite the lock and weir at the W. end of the Ile de la Cité. No. 13 is the *Hôtel de Sillery-Genlis,* often visited by Bonaparte when on leave from the Ecole Militaire. At No. 5, on the corner of the Rue Guénégaud, Col. de Marguerittes of the Resistance set up his headquarters while he was conducting operations for the liberation of Paris, Aug. 19–28th, 1944.

The ***Hôtel des Monnaies,** or '*La Monnaie,*' the French mint, is a large and dignified building, adjoining the Institut on the E. It was built by *J. D. Antoine* in 1771–75. The handsome doorway is ornamented with Louis XVI's monogram and elegant bronze knockers; on the impost is the fleur-de-lys escutcheon with Mercury and Ceres as supporters.—The **Musée Monétaire,** or *Museum of the Mint,* is entered from the second landing of the double staircase, on the right of the vestibule, a notable example of 18th cent. architecture. It is open free daily (except Wed.) 2–5. Visits to the workshops take place twice weekly, on Tues. and Thurs. at 5; adm. free. The *Bureau de Vente* (sale-room for medals) is open on weekdays 9–12, 2–5 (Sat. 9–11).

In the ANTECHAMBER are show-cases containing plaster models of modern medals. On the right is the 'mouton,' a special stamping press; on the left is a press used for coining 50-centime pieces from Russian bronze cannon taken at Austerlitz.—The SALLE GUILLAUME DUPRÉ, in the centre of the building, is in the best Louis XVI style. Above the doors are four medallions with the initials of four of the civil servants who first organised the Monnaie. The room is devoted to temporary exhibitions. SALLE SAGE: New acquisitions.—SALLE JEAN VARIN: Portraits of directors of the mint; French medals of the 16–18th cent.—SALLE DENON: Medals of the Consulate, Empire and Louis XVIII periods.—SALLE DUVIVIER : Coins of Great Britain, Denmark, Spain, Portugal, Italy, etc. ; examples of coins illustrating the evolution of French currency from Merovingian times to the present day. On the chimneypiece is a small gilt bronze reproduction of the famous group in the Tuileries, by Coysevox.—The SALLES PISANELLO and ARNAUNE are temporarily closed.

On the right of the second courtyard is the door of the 'Ateliers' or WORKSHOPS, in which the interesting processes in the production of coins and medals are seen. Visitors are escorted through by a guide (no gratuity). The presses in the large *Atelier du Monnayage* are capable of producing about 850,000 coins in a day.

On the QUAI MALAQUAIS, to the W. of the Institut, are some charming 17–18th cent. mansions ; No. 9 was the residence of Charles Perrault ; No. 15 is the *Hôtel de Chimay* ; a tablet records the residence here in 1844–53 of Anatole Thibault (1844–1925), better known as Anatole France (born at No. 19 on the quay). At the corner of the Rue Bonaparte (l.) is the **Ecole des Beaux-Arts,** begun in 1820 and finished in 1862. It replaces the convent of the Petits-Augustins, founded in 1608, of which the only important relics are the convent-chapel and the small chapel of Margaret of Valois. In 1885 the school was enlarged by the acquisition of the *Hôtel de Bouillon,* built by Mansart in the 17th cent. and later known as the Hôtel de Chimay.

The courtyards and principal rooms are open to visitors on Thurs. 2–4 (closed July 1st–Oct. 15th) ; entrance No. 17 Quai Malaquais. Parties are conducted by a guide (gratuity). The library may be used on written application to the Director.

From the entrance on the quay steps ascend to the SALLE DE MELPOMÈNE (by *Duban,* 1860–62), which is used for the display of students' works at the time of the competition for the Grands Prix de Rome (annually for painting, sculpture, and architecture ; less frequently for engraving, etching, medal design, and gem engraving). An annual exhibition of prize-winners' works is held in the Galerie d'Exposition, on the first floor. Normally the rooms contain copies of the chief paintings in the galleries of Europe.

A staircase descends to the pleasant little COUR DU MÛRIER (Mulberry Tree Court), with porticoes in the Renaissance style on three sides, and sculptures by Rome Prize winners. In the W. portico is a good monument, by *Ernest Coquard,* to Henri Regnault and other pupils of the Beaux-Arts who fell in 1870–71, and on the S. wall is a memorial for 1914–18. Passages lead hence into the VESTIBULE DES ECOLES (monument to Ingres, on the right), which opens into the FIRST COURTYARD, with the main entrance from the Rue Bonaparte on the left. In the centre is a Corinthian column with a bronze statue of Abundance, in the style of Germain Pilon and on the farther side are 15–16th cent. sculptures from the demolished Hôtel de La Trémoille. To the left is the former CONVENT CHAPEL, the present *Doorway of which, a masterpiece of *Jean Goujon* and *Philibert Delorme* (16th cent.), was brought from the inner court of the Château d'Anet; the figure of Cupid bending his bow, after the antique, is a later addition. The chapel (c. 1600) contains casts of sculpture. In the so-called CHAPEL OF MARGARET OF VALOIS, a small domed hexagon on the S. side of the main chapel, are casts of the chief works of Michelangelo.

A graceful stone screen brought from the Château de Gaillon (1500–10) in Normandy separates the first from the Second Courtyard, which leads up to the main façade of the school, a successful work by *Duban,* begun in 1834. In and about the court are fragments of French architecture and sculpture, e.g.: carved capitals and friezes from the church of Ste-Geneviève (12th cent.); large stone basin, with masks of pagan gods, from the refectory of the Abbey of St-Denis (13th cent.). In the garden on the right is a charming arcade of the Hôtel de Torpane (c. 1570), from the Rue des Bernardins.

A VESTIBULE, with fragments of antique sculpture, admits to the INNER COURT, in the bays of which is a valuable collection of original antique marbles. Opposite the entrance is a monument to Duban, by *Guillaume* and *Bernier.* Two short staircases ascend to the *HÉMICYCLE, used for important functions, on the wall round which is a huge and celebrated painting by *Paul Delaroche,* representing the chief masters of every school of art of every period. At the back of the platform is a painting by *Ingres* of Romulus bringing back the spolia opima.

The LIBRARY (comp. above) on the first floor contains about 30,000 vols. and about one million engravings, drawings by famous artists, etc.

The RUE BONAPARTE runs S. to join the Boul. St-Germain at the Place St-Germain-des-Prés. Edouard Manet (1832–83) was born in the *Hôtel de Persan* (Nos. 7–9), and at No. 16 is the **Académie de Médecine,** founded in 1920, which has no connection with the Academies of the Institut. This street, narrow and busy, with its numerous antique shops, is one of the most pleasant and characteristic in the ' business ' part of the Faubourg.

Prosper Mérimée (1842–46) and Corot (1849–55) lived at No. 10 in the RUE DES BEAUX-ARTS, Fantin-Latour at No. 8; at No. 13 Oscar Wilde died in utter destitution in 1900.—In the narrow RUE VISCONTI (then Rue des Marais) Racine lived from 1693 till his death in 1699 (house demolished); at No. 21 Adrienne Lecouvreur died in 1730, in the arms of Marshal Saxe; at No. 17 Balzac had a printing business, liquidated in 1828, and on the 2nd floor is a studio once occupied by Paul Delaroche (1827–34) and Delacroix (1838–43).—Laurence Sterne put up in the RUE JACOB on his arrival on Paris in 1762, and later was a guest of Mme de Rambouillet at No. 46. Wagner lodged at No. 14 in 1841–42, and Mérimée at No. 18 (rebuilt) in 1848.

The RUE DE SEINE, which leads S. from the little Square Honoré-Champion, crossing the Boul. St-Germain, to the Luxembourg, contains several noteworthy houses. The RUE MAZARINE, on the E., is noted for its curiosity shops. No. 12 is on the site of the former tennis-court, where the *Illustre Théâtre* was opened in Dec., 1643, by Molière's company. No. 42 marks the site of the *Théâtre de Guénégaud*, occupied by the Opéra in 1671–72, by Molière's company in 1673–80, and by the Comédie-Française in 1680–89.—The RUE DE L'ANCIENNE COMÉDIE, straight on, takes its name from the Comédie Française of 1689–1770, which occupied No. 14. The *Café Procope*, opposite, was a favourite haunt of Voltaire and the Encyclopædists, Musset, George Sand, and Gambetta. Just beyond is the CARREFOUR DE L'ODÉON, a busy cross-roads just S. of the Boul. St-Germain. Thence the Rue de l'Odéon runs S. to the Place de l'Odéon and the former Théâtre de l'Odéon. The PLACE DE L'ODÉON, with the chief façade of the theatre, is lined with uniform rows of houses by Servandoni. The *Café Voltaire* (No. 1) was the resort of Mallarmé, Verlaine, and their circle. At No. 2 Camille Desmoulins was arrested in 1794.

The **Salle du Luxembourg** of the Comédie Française (formerly the Théâtre de l'Odéon), built in the form of a classical temple by Wailly and Peyre, on the gardens of the Hôtel de Condé (see below), was opened in 1782 with the title of Théatre-Français, and rebuilt by Chalgrin after a fire in 1807. The colonnades round the building are filled with bookshops.

The vestibule and foyer on the first floor contain busts and portraits of contemporary actors and playwrights, and eight panels depicting famous scenes from the French Drama. The auditorium (1264 seats) is one of the finest in Paris.

The S. side of the Odéon looks on the RUE DE VAUGIRARD, the longest street in Paris, stretching from the Boul. St-Michel to the Porte de Versailles (2¾ m.). Following it to the right (W.), we pass the Rue de Condé and the Rue de Tournon opposite the entrance to the Luxembourg.

The RUE DE CONDÉ, like the Rue Monsieur-le-Prince, finds the source of its name in the vanished *Hôtel de Condé*, the home of the princely family of Condé in 1612–1764. Lucile Duplessis lived at No. 22 before her marriage to Desmoulins; No. 26 was the home of Beaumarchais in 1763–76, the period of 'Le Barbier de Séville.'

At No. 2 in the RUE DE TOURNON Balzac lived in 1827–30. Marie Lenormand, the fortune-teller consulted by so many Revolutionary celebrities, lived at No. 5 for over fifty years and died there in 1843. No. 6, the *Hôtel de Brancas*, reconstructed by Bullet during the Regency, now contains the *Institut Tessin*, with a museum and library of Swedish art (open 2–6, except Sat., Sun., and holidays). Gambetta lived on the top story of the *Hôtel du Sénat* (No. 7). No. 10, a fine 18th cent. mansion, is now used as the barracks of the Garde Républicaine. Paul Jones died in 1792 on the first floor of No. 19.

The **Palais du Luxembourg,** once a royal residence and since 1946 the seat of the Conseil de la République, is noted especially for its beautiful gardens.

The Luxembourg was built by *Salomon de Brosse* in 1615–27 for Marie de Médicis, widow of Henri IV. The building was altered in 1804 and enlarged in 1831–44. Marie de Médicis bequeathed the palace to her second son Gaston, Duc d'Orléans, and the 'Palais Médicis' became the 'Palais d'Orléans.' Subsequently the palace belonged in succession to Mlle de Montpensier, the Duchesse de Guise (1672), Louis XIV (1694), and the Orléans family. Among the famous prisoners confined here during the Revolution were Marshal de Noailles, executed at the age of 79 with his wife; the Vicomte de Beauharnais and his wife Joséphine, future empress; Hébert, Danton, Desmoulins, Fabre d'Eglantine, and David, who here drew the first sketch for the painting of the Sabine Women. Tom Paine was imprisoned here in 1793 for voting in the Assembly against the king's execution and escaped the guillotine only by an accident. In 1794 the Directory transferred the seat of government from the Tuileries to the Luxembourg, and here Gen. Bonaparte presented the treaty of Campo Formio. In 1800 the 'Palais Directorial' became the 'Palais du Consulat'; under the Empire it was the 'Palais du Sénat' and, later, the 'Palais de la Pairie.' Marshal Ney was confined here in 1815. The ministers of Charles X were tried here under Louis-Philippe in 1830, and Louis Napoléon Bonaparte after his landing at Boulogne in 1840. From 1852 to 1940 the Palais was the meeting-place of the Senate, the upper chamber of the French Republic, except in 1871–79, when it was the seat of the Préfecture de la Seine. In 1940–44 it was occupied by Marshal Sperrle, commander-in-chief of the Luftwaffe on the Western Front. In 1946 the Conseil de la République replaced the Senate as the second chamber of the French parliament.

The N. front of the Palais du Luxembourg is the original, and the architect is supposed to have made an effort to recall the style of the Palazzo Pitti at Florence, where Marie de Médicis was born. The main entrance from the Rue de Vaugirard is surmounted by an eight-sided dome, and the two wings, terminating in steep-roofed pavilions, with three orders of columns superimposed, are connected by a one-storied gallery. The S. façade overlooking the gardens is a 19th cent. copy. The entrance-doorway is at the back of the great court, to the left.

ADMISSION. The Palais is open on Sun. 2–3.30 (conducted parties only). Visitors wishing to attend a session of the Conseil should apply through their diplomatic representative.

The interior, remodelled by *Chalgrin* under Napoleon I, is decorated in the sumptuous 19th cent. manner, with statues and historical and allegorical paintings, mostly of no great merit. The principal rooms on the first floor may be visited. Especially conspicuous are the Apotheosis of Napoleon I, by *Alaux*, on the ceiling of the SALLE DES CONFÉRENCES (the former throne-room), and the statues of statesmen behind the president's chair facing the hemicycle in the SALLE DES SÉANCES, where the Conseil meets, and which is notable for its fine woodwork. The LIBRARY contains the best paintings in the palace, by *Eugène Delacroix*: in the central cupola, the Limbo of Dante's Inferno; above the window, Alexander placing Homer's poems in the golden casket of Darius after the Battle of Arbela.—The CABINET DORÉ was formerly Marie de Médicis's audience chamber; the BUVETTE, or BUREAU DE TABAC, was her bedchamber.

The adjoining **Petit-Luxembourg** (no adm.), the mansion of the Prince de Tingry-Luxembourg in 1570–1612, was presented to Richelieu by Marie de Médicis in 1626 and is now the residence of the president of the Conseil de la République. It includes the cloisters and chapel of the Filles du Calvaire, for whom Marie de Médicis built a convent adjoining her palace. The cloisters now form a winter-garden; the chapel, at the end of the courtyard in the Rue de Vaugirard, is a charming example of the Renaissance style. Farther W. is the former orangery, until recently occupied by the Musée du Luxembourg.

The ***Jardin du Luxembourg,** though deplorably mutilated in 1867 and less regular in shape than the Tuileries, is still one of the most beautiful gardens in Paris. It is the only Renaissance garden in the capital, having been laid out by Salomon de Brosse, the palace architect, and three of the elms planted by Marie de Médicis in 1612 still survive. Its numerous statues, mostly well above the average standard of public monuments, make it a veritable open-air sculpture gallery.

Entering by the gate in the Rue de Vaugirard on the E. side of the palace, we have on the left a pleasant garden in the English style with monuments to Théodore de Banville by *Roulleau* and *Courtois-Suffit* and to Henri Murger by *Bouillon*. Then comes an avenue of plane trees with an oblong pool, at the end of which is the ***Fontaine Médicis,** by *Salomon de Brosse* (c. 1627), removed hither in 1861. In the central niche is Polyphemus about to crush Acis and Galatea; on either side are Pan and Diana; and at the back is a bas-relief, the Fontaine de Léda, brought from the Rue du Regard in 1855.

We now ascend to the EASTERN TERRACE, with its statues of famous women, including Mary, Queen of Scots, Jeanne d'Albret, Mlle de Montpensier, by *Demesmay*, and Margaret of Anjou. Amongst the clumps of trees in this part of the gardens are monuments to Leconte de Lisle, by *Denys Puech* and *Scellier de Gisors*; *George Sand, by *Sicard*, etc.

In the beds between the two terraces, to the S. of the ornamental basin, is a monument to Scheurer-Kestner, the Alsatian patriot, by *Becker*, with figures by *Dalou* and *Formigé*. To the E. of the basin are Marius on the ruins of Carthage; and David, a graceful statue on a column.

On the WESTERN TERRACE is continued the series of famous women, comprising statues of eight royal ladies of France and Petrarch's Laura. Among the clumps of trees on this side are a marionette theatre and a café. Amid the fine plane trees at the N. end, near the private garden of the Petit-Luxembourg, is a monument to Eugène Delacroix, by *Dalou* and *Menuel*. To the W. of the Petit-Luxembourg is a fine copy of the Venus of Medici, placed on fragments of the ruins of the Tuileries. In the flower-beds to the S., along the Rue Guynemer, are monuments to Paul Verlaine, by *Rodo de Niederhausern*, and to Chopin, by *Boucher*.

In the ENGLISH GARDEN (the former nursery-ground) are numerous statues including a monument to Watteau, by *Gauquié* and *Guillaume*.

Farther on in the Rue de Vaugirard, opposite the Petit-Luxembourg, is the Rue Garancière, with the *Hôtel de Sourdéac* (No. 8; 1640). Jules Massenet lived and died (1912) at 48 Rue de Vaugirard (first floor). Opposite the former Musée du Luxembourg diverges the picturesque Rue Férou, leading to the Place St-Sulpice (see below); No. 50, at the corner, was once the *Hôtel de La Trémoille*; at No. 15, Fantin-Latour's house, Whistler painted his famous portrait. The next street on the right is the Rue Bonaparte. We then cross the Rue

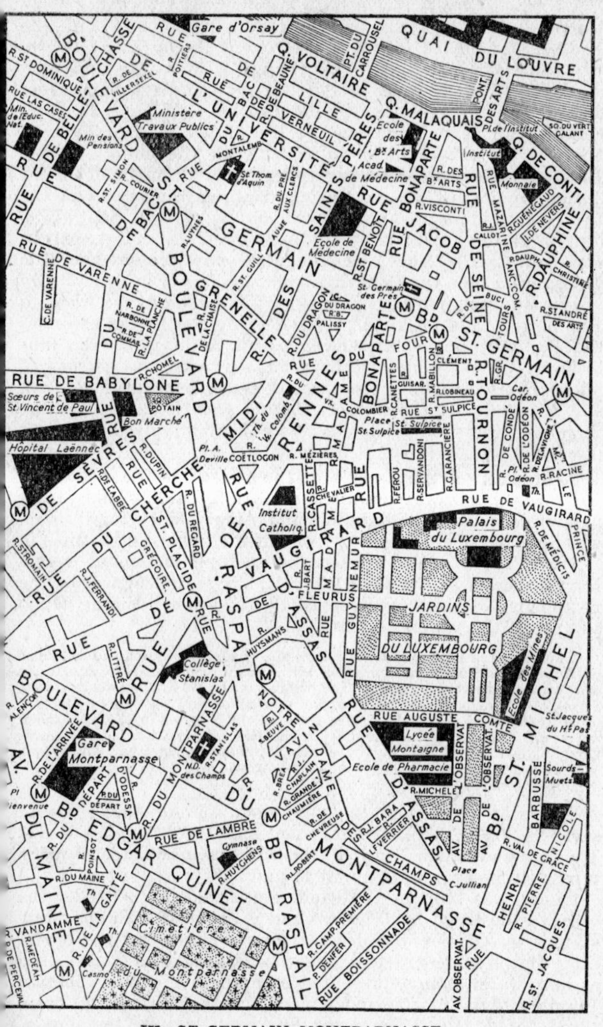

IX. ST-GERMAIN–MONTPARNASSE

Madame ; No. 25, at the corner, was the home in 1832 of Mlle George, Napoleon's mistress. At No. 23 in the Rue Cassette (r.) Taine wrote his history of English literature and died in 1893. At the corner of the Rue Vaugirard and the Rue d'Assas are the buildings of the *Institut Catholique de Paris* (enlarged in 1930 ; entrance, 21 Rue d'Assas). No. 70, next door, is the *Séminaire des Carmes* with the church of St-Joseph-des-Carmes, once the chapel of a Carmelite convent dating from 1613–20. The crypt contains the bodies of the 151 priests massacred in the convent garden in Sept. 1792 (apply to the concierge for adm. ; open daily 2–4, except Tues and Sat.). The Rue Vaugirard now crosses the Rue d'Assas and then the Boul. Raspail.

The Rue Bonaparte, bordered by the garden of the Allée du Séminaire, leads N. to the Place St-Sulpice. In the centre is the Fontaine des Quatre-Evêques, or fountain of the four bishops, by *Visconti* ; it is decorated with the statues of four famous preaching bishops: Bossuet, Fénélon, Massillon, and Fléchier. At the former *Séminaire de St-Sulpice*, on the S. side of the square, Renan was educated ; the building is now used by the Finance Ministry.

St-Sulpice, on the E. side of the square, is the wealthiest and most important church on the left bank. This rather ponderously classical building, imposing mainly for its size, was described by Gibbon as " one of the noblest structures in Paris." The W. front consists of an Ionic colonnade over a Doric. The N. tower, 240 ft. high, has seated figures of the Evangelists ; the S. tower is 16 ft. lower. Victor Hugo compared the towers to clarionets.

It was begun in 1646 by *Gamard* on the site of an older church and continued by *Levau* in 1655 and *Gittard* in 1670. After an interval from 1675 to 1719 the work was resumed by *Oppenordt*. The building of the W. front was entrusted to *Servandoni*, who, however, failed to give satisfaction and was replaced in 1745 by *Maclaurin*. His successor, *Chalgrin*, rebuilt the N. tower in 1777, but the S. tower was left incomplete. Camille Desmoulins was married here to Lucile Duplessis in 1790. Under the Convention St-Sulpice became the Temple de la Victoire, and in 1799 a public banquet was given here to Gen. Bonaparte.—St-Sulpice is noted for its music.

The stately **Interior,** a noted example of the ' Jesuit ' style, is 360 ft. long, 184 ft. wide, and 108 ft. high.—NAVE. The famous organ, one of the largest in existence (6588 pipes ; to be heard on Sun. at 11 and 3.30, except in Lent and Advent), was built in 1781 and remodelled in 1860–62 ; the case was designed by *Chalgrin* and is adorned with charming statues by *Clodion* and decorations by *Duret*. At the beginning of the nave are two huge shells (Tridacna gigas) used as holy-water stoups, presented to Francis I by the Venetian Republic ; the marble rocks on which they rest were sculptured by *Pigalle*. The late 18th cent. pulpit, by *Wailly*, bears gilded figures of Faith and Hope, by *Guesdon*, and Charity, by *Dumont*. In the paving of the S. transept is a bronze tablet connected by a meridian line with a marble obelisk in the N. transept; at noon the sun's rays, passing through a small opening in a blind window in the S. transept, strike the meridian at different points according to the time of year.

The CHAPELS encircling the church are decorated with frescoes. In the first chapel (r.) are *Paintings by *E. Delacroix*: on the ceiling, St. Michael and the Devil; l., Jacob wrestling with the angel; r., Expulsion of Heliodorus from the Temple (best view from the aisle, near the pulpit); and four angels, in grisaille. Fifth chapel, Tomb of the curé Languet de Gergy (1674–1750), founder of the Enfants Malades, by *Slodtz*, a disciple of Bernini.—CHOIR. Scourging of Christ, Mater Dolorosa, and eight Apostles, by *Bouchardon*.

LADY CHAPEL. In a niche behind the altar is a marble Madonna, by *Pigalle*, with little angels, by *Mouchez*, floating among the clouds. The paintings on the walls are by *Carle Vanloo*, and in the dome is the Assumption, by *Lemoyne*.

Under the church is a large crypt, with considerable remains of the 16th cent. church (apply to the 'Vicaire de garde').

B. West Part of the Faubourg St-Germain.

MÉTRO stations: *St-Germain-des-Prés* (line 4); *Sèvres-Babylone* (lines 10 and 12); *Bac, Solférino, Chambre des Députés* (line 12); *St-François-Xavier* (line 14).—MOTOR-BUSES: St-Germain-des-Prés (routes 48, 63, 86, 95, 96); Varenne (route 69); Croix-Rouge (routes 84 and 86); Mabillon (route 86); Sèvres-Babylone (routes 68, 83, 84, 86, 94); Bac (routes 63, 68, 83, 84, 94); Solférino (routes 63, 69, 83, 84, 94); Chambre des Députés (routes 63, 83, 84, 94); St-François-Xavier (routes 28, 92, 96).

The Pont du Carrousel connects the Louvre with the QUAI VOLTAIRE, which continues the Quai Malaquais to the W. and was formerly the Quai des Théatins. Voltaire died in 1778 at the house of the Marquis de Villette (No. 27; tablet), Ingres at No. 11 in 1867. Alfred de Musset lived at No. 23 in 1841–49, and No. 13 was occupied successively by Delacroix, Pradier, Corot, and Horace and Carle Vernet. The quay is lined with bookstalls and old curiosity shops, at one of which Balzac's hero bought the 'peau de chagrin.'

The RUE DES SAINTS-PÈRES, running S. from the E. end of the Quai Voltaire, near the Beaux-Arts, across the Boul. St-Germain to the Rue de Sèvres, is also noted for its curiosity shops. At the corner of the Rue de Lille is the *Ecole des Langues Orientales*, founded by the Convention in 1795. Farther S., stretching from the Rue Jacob to the Boul. St-Germain, is the enormous building of the *Ecole Pratique de la Faculté de Médecine* (1937; unfinished), on the site of the Hôpital de la Charité, founded in 1602 (see p. 104). Opposite is the *Ecole des Ponts et Chaussées*, a civil engineering school (1747).

The QUAI ANATOLE-FRANCE, and, farther to the W., the QUAI D'ORSAY, are the centre of the foreign and diplomatic affairs of the Republic. Beyond the Rue du Bac, and between the Pont Royal and the Pont de Solférino, lies the *Gare d'Orsay*, built in 1898–1900 for the Paris–Orléans railway, on the site of the old Cour des Comptes.

To the W., beyond the Rue de Bellechasse, is the charming **Palais de la Légion d'Honneur,** the entrance to which is flanked by a colonnade with bas-reliefs by *Roland* on the attic story. The Corinthian portico in the courtyard is adorned with a frieze of arabesques with the device 'Honneur et Patrie.' Facing the quay is a rotunda with Corinthian columns and symbolical busts; on the gallery above are six mythological statues.

Built by *Rousseau* in 1782–86 for the Prince de Salm-Kyrburg, at the Revolution this elegant 18th cent. mansion was raffled and won by a wigmaker's apprentice. Mme de Staël gave her famous receptions here under the Directory, and in 1804 it was bought by the government for the grand chancellery of the Legion of Honour.

On the E. side, in the Rue de Bellechasse, is the entrance to the **Musée de la Légion d'Honneur,** which is devoted to medals, decorations, documents, paintings, etc., relating to the history of the Orders of the Legion of Honour. At the time of writing the museum is closed.

The building is well seen from the back, in the quiet RUE DE LILLE, which retains several 18th cent. mansions, notably the *Hôtel Beauharnais* (No. 78), the former German Embassy. Lafayette lived at No. 123 in 1799.

Opposite the Pont de la Concorde, at the beginning of the Quai d'Orsay, is the **Palais-Bourbon,** the seat of the Assemblée Nationale. This is the lower house of the French parliament, which took the place of the Chambre des Députés in 1946, and corresponds approximately to the House of Commons.

In 1722 a mansion was erected on this site for the dowager Duchess of Bourbon, of which only the inner courtyard and main entrance at 128 Rue de l'Université have survived. Her grandson, the Prince de Condé, enlarged the palace in 1789 and incorporated the Hôtel de Lassay. In 1795 it became property under the name of Maison de la Révolution, the meeting-place of the Council of Five Hundred and later was occupied by the Archives (1799–1808), and it has been used as the House of Parliament since 1815. The quay façade was built in 1804–7, and the present assembly-room dates from 1828–32.

In 1940–44 the Palais-Bourbon was the headquarters of the German military administration of the Paris region, and at the time of the liberation considerable fighting took place here, causing some damage to the building and the destruction by fire of over 30,000 vols. from the library.

ADMISSION. Intending visitors should apply in writing to the Questeur. Permission to attend a session of the Assembly must be obtained in writing from a Deputy. The entrance is in the Place du Palais-Bourbon, on the S. side.

The façade consists of a portico, by *Poyet* (1804–07), with twelve Corinthian columns, and statues of statesmen on either side. The bas-relief on the pediment, by *Cortot*, represents France, standing between Liberty and Order, beckoning to Commerce, Agriculture, Peace, War, and Eloquence.

The decorations in the interior are, with certain exceptions, of no great artistic merit. The SALON DE LA PAIX, or SALLE DES PAS-PERDUS has ceiling paintings by *Horace Vernet*, while the most notable adornment of the SALLE DES SÉANCES, where the Assembly meets, is the bas-relief of Fame and History, by *Lemot*, on the speakers' tribune. Historical paintings, by *Ary Scheffer, Horace Vernet*, and others, adorn the SALLE DES CONFÉRENCES and the VESTIBULE, or SALLE DES DISTRIBUTIONS; and the great gallery of the LIBRARY (300,000 vols., including many rarities) contains an admirable set of twenty religious or historical *Paintings by *Eugène Delacroix*: showing the progress of the civilised arts, with illustrations from classical mythology and ancient history: at the N. end, Attila and his hordes trampling under foot Italy and the arts; S. end, Orpheus instructing the Greeks in the arts of peace. In the centre is a collection of tokens, medals, and identity cards of deputies, from the Constituent Assembly (Nov. 9th, 1789) to the present day.—SALON PUJOL. Paintings in grisaille by *Abel de Pujol*.—SALLE CASIMIR-PÉRIER. Large bronze bas-relief by *Dalou* of the Constituent Assembly (June 23rd, 1789).—SALON DU ROI. *Paintings and grisailles by *Delacroix* (1833).

Farther along the quay, between the Palais-Bourbon and the Esplanade des Invalides, are the *Hôtel de Lassay* (1724), the official residence of the President of the Assemblée, and the *Ministère des Affaires Etrangères* (Foreign Office), built by Lacornée in 1845. King George VI and Queen Elizabeth were received here during their official visit to Paris in 1938, and the area was a scene of heavy fighting during the liberation of Paris (Aug. 1944). By the railings of the garden bordering the Quai d'Orsay is a monument to Aristide Briand (d. 1931), by Bouchard and Landowski.

In the *Place du Palais-Bourbon*, to the S. of the Palais, is a statue of Law, by Feuchères.—The RUE DE L'UNIVERSITÉ, coming from the Invalides, crosses the Place and then the Boul. St-Germain. Alphonse Daudet died at No. 41 in 1897 (tablet). Chateaubriand lived at No. 25 in 1816–21. Berthe Albrecht, a young heroine of the Resistance, lived at No. 16 (tablet). No. 13, the *Dépôt de la Marine*, is an 18th cent. building by Lassurance. Franklin's first lodging on his arrival in Paris in 1776 was at the Hôtel Hambourg in this street.

We now follow the BOULEVARD ST-GERMAIN, 1 m. long, which extends in a shallow curve from the Pont de la Concorde to the Pont de Sully. No. 288, at the corner of the Quai d'Orsay, is the *Cercle Agricole*. At the extreme W. end of the building the bullet holes are a reminder of the fighting during the liberation of Paris. The *Ministère de la Guerre* (War Office; No. 231), built by Bouchot in 1867–77, has a clock-tower at the corner of the Rue de Solférino. Looking down this street to the left, we can see the Sacré-Cœur at Montmartre.

In the *Place de Bellechasse*, behind the Ministère de la Guerre, is **Ste-Clotilde,** an uninspired Gothic-revival church (1846–56). The two spires are 226 ft. high.

In the gardens in front is a monument to the composer ***César Franck*** (1822–91), who was organist of Ste-Clotilde for 30 years from 1860.—The Rue St-Dominique runs W. to the Esplanade des Invalides and Champ-de-Mars. Nos. 1, 3, and 5 (E. end) date from c. 1710; No. 3 was occupied by Jean-Baptiste Dumas, the chemist (d. 1884). No. 5 was the home of Gustave Doré from 1849 till his death in 1883. Nos. 14 and 16, the *Hôtel de Brienne* (1714 and 1730), are now part of the War Office. The *Maison de la Chimie*, founded in 1934, occupies the *Hôtel de la Rochefoucauld-d'Estissac* (1710; enlarged), at No. 28; and No. 57, the *Hôtel de Sagan*, built by Brongniart in 1784 for the Princess of Monaco, is now the *Polish Embassy*.

The Rue de Bellechasse, which the Boul. St-Germain next crosses, runs from the Rue de Lille to the Rue de Varenne. At No. 41 the Conseil National de la Résistance and the Comité Parisien de la Libération organised operations for the rising of Aug. 19th, 1944.

No. 5 Rue Las Cases (r.) is the **Musée Social** (open daily 2–6, except Sun. and holidays), founded by the Comte de Chambrun in 1894 to provide facilities for the study of social legislation. It comprises a special library of 6000 vols. and the *Institut Léonard de Vinci*, which is intended as a national academy of Industrial Art.

Nos. 244–248 in the Boul. St-Germain are the *Ministère des Travaux Publics* (Ministry of Public Works), occupying a modern and two early 18th cent. houses. No. 246, the *Hôtel de Roquelaure* (1722), has a fine courtyard.

The Rue du Bac is one of the oldest streets in the quarter, extending from the Pont-Royal to (¾ m.) the Rue de Sèvres. It is named after the ferry by which the Seine was crossed before the construction of the Pont-Royal. No. 46, the former *Hôtel de Boulogne*, has a fine courtyard. No. 98, the *Café des Deux-Anges*, with gilt angels above the door and good iron balconies, was the secret rendezvous of the Chouans (c. 1800). At No. 108bis Laplace, astronomer and mathematician, died in 1827. At No. 110 Whistler (from 1892) was visited by Beardsley and Mallarmé, and got into trouble with his landlord for letting his child-models run about naked in the garden. Nos. 118 and 120, with doors designed by Toro, are the *Hôtel de Clermont-Tonnerre*, where Chateaubriand lived from 1838 till his death in 1848; on the 3rd and 4th floors Mrs. Clarke and her daughter Mary (later Mme Mohl) had their famous salon, and here they were visited by Dean Stanley, Mrs. Gaskell, and Florence Nightingale. No. 128 is the *Séminaire des Missions Etrangères*, founded in 1663, with relics of martyred missionaries in its 'Chambre des Martyrs' (daily 2–4 except Tues.). Nos. 136–140 are the *Hôtel de Chatillon*, built by Mansart, with two handsome portals, now occupied by the Sœurs de Charité. At the S. end of the street is the 'Bon Marché.'

A short distance to the N. of the Boul. St-Germain is **St-Thomas-d'Aquin,** begun in 1682 by *Pierre Bullet*, in the Jesuit style, and completed, with the construction of the façade, in 1787. The ceiling painting in the Lady Chapel (Transfiguration) is a characteristic 18th cent. work by Lemoyne. Farther on the Rue Saint-Guillaume runs S. from the Boulevard, and at No. 27, in the 16th cent. *Hôtel de Mesmes* (enlarged in 1933), is the *Institut National des Sciences Politiques*. At the corner of the Rue des Saints-Pères (l.) are the enormous new buildings of the *Ecole de Médecine* (p. 101), and bordering them on the S. side is the little *Chapelle St-Pierre*, rebuilt in 1611, the sole relic of the Hôpital de la Charité, which stood on this site from 1605 to 1937. It is now the seat of the Ukrainian Catholic Mission in Paris (High Mass on Sun. 10.30). In the small Square de la Charité, before the church, is a bust of Dr. Laënnec.

No. 184 Boul. St-Germain is the *Hôtel de la Société de Géographie,* founded in 1821, and beyond that (l.) are two cafés noted for the artistic and literary set that frequents them: the *Deux Magots* and the *Café de Flore.* The Action Française was founded in the latter in 1898. The *Place St-Germain-des-Prés* is a busy cross-roads at the junction of the Rue Bonaparte and Rue de Rennes with the boulevard.

***St-Germain-des-Prés,** on the E. side of the square, is the oldest church in Paris and the only one with any considerable remains of Romanesque architecture.

This church, the chief relic of a great Benedictine abbey founded by Childebert I in the 6th cent. to receive the tunic of St. Vincent which he had captured at Saragossa, and the burial-place of St. Germanus, Bp. of Paris (d. 576), was built at the beginning of the 11th cent. (body of the W. tower) and at two periods in the 12th (nave, and then the choir), and was dedicated by Pope Alexander III in 1163. The massive flying buttresses of the choir are among the earliest in France. The W. porch dates from 1607, but preserves the jambs of a Romanesque door and a 12th cent. lintel depicting the Last Supper. The transepts were remodelled c. 1644. The bell-chamber of the tower was added in the 17th cent., the spire in the 19th. Flanking the choir are the bases of two towers, pulled down in 1822. A single 14th cent. tower of the abbey's fortifications survives at No. 15 Rue St-Benoît, on the N.W. side of the Place St-Germain.

By the S.E. corner of the church is a bust of the scholar monk Mabillon (1632–1707). In the porch is an excellent plan indicating the position of the monuments, etc.

The ***Interior** (213 ft. by 69 ft., and 62 ft. high) is especially interesting for the combination of the Romanesque style in the nave with the first attempts at the Gothic style in the choir. The 17th cent. roof of the nave has been remodelled of recent years. The pillars are each flanked by four columns, the sculptured capitals of which were mostly removed to the Cluny Museum about 1824 and replaced by copies. One original remains in the N.W. corner. Both nave and choir are adorned with large wax and fresco *Paintings by *Hippolyte Flandrin* (1854–63; superb but inappropriate and badly lighted), finished by *Sébastien Cornu.*

NAVE. Above each arch are two paintings by *Flandrin,* one a subject from the Old or New Testament, the other representing the corresponding dogma or mystery. On the right: Preparations for the Last Judgment and Ascension of Our Lord (painted by *Paul Flandrin* after his brother's death); Dispersion of the Apostles and the Tower of Babel; Resurrection of Christ and Jonah thrown up by the whale; Death of Christ and Abraham's Sacrifice; Treason of Judas and Sale of Joseph. On the left: Annunciation and the Burning Bush; Nativity of Christ and Promise of a Redeemer; Adoration of the Magi and Prophecy of Balaam; Baptism of Christ and Passage of the Red Sea; Institution of the Eucharist and Priesthood of Melchizedek. The intervals between the windows above are filled with the figures of Prophets and Judges of Israel.

SOUTH AISLE. Large marble statue of Notre-Dame de Consolation, presented to the Abbey of St. Denis by Queen Jeanne d'Evreux in 1340. The W. chapel of the S. transept

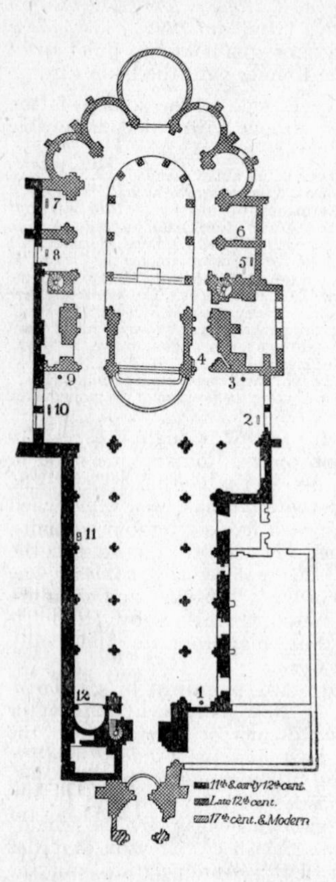

TOMBS AND WORKS OF ART

1. N.D. de Consolation.
2. Castellan.
3. St. Margaret.
4. Montmorency-Laval.
5. James Douglas.
6. Marriage of St. Catherine.
7. Boileau.
8. Wm. Douglas.
9. St. Francis Xavier.
10. John Casimir of Poland.
11. Flandrin.

was consecrated by St. Francis of Sales in 1619 and contains a cupola-painting by *Restout* (Apotheosis of St. Maur, 1756). In the transept itself are a statue of St. Margaret (1705) and the tomb of Olivier and Louis de Castellan, killed in the king's service in 1644 and 1669, by *Girardon*. On the left, against the choir wall, is a coloured relief presented by French Canadians, commemorating the consecration in this church (1658) of François de Montmorency-Laval (1628–1703), first bishop of French Canada. In the first ambulatory-chapel is the tomb of Lord James Douglas (d. 1645; son of the first Marquis of Douglas), a Scottish gentleman in the service of Louis XIII; the altar-piece is an 18th cent. copy of *Raphael's* St. Michael. Second chapel: opposite the altar are the Mystic Marriage of St. Catherine, ascribed to *Erasmus Quellyn,* and the tombstones of Descartes, removed from Ste-Geneviève, and Mabillon (see above). Third: Two marble medallions of the 17th cent., with profiles of Christ and the Virgin. Fourth: Fragments of 13th cent. stained glass.

CHOIR. The little marble columns in the triforium are re-used material from the 6th cent. abbey of St. Vincent; their bases and capitals are of the 12th cent.—The LADY CHAPEL was rebuilt at the beginning of the 19th cent., Pope Pius VII laying the first stone of the altar.

NORTH AISLE (as we return). First chapel: Holy Sepulchre of the 16th cent. (cast). Third: Tombstone of Boileau, removed from the Sainte-Chapelle. Fourth: Tomb of William Douglas, 10th Earl of Angus (d. 1611), who died in the service of Henri IV. In the N. transept are a statue of St. Francis Xavier, by *Guillaume Coustou*; the tomb of John Casimir, King of Poland, who became abbot of St-Germain in 1669 and died in 1672. In the second bay of the nave is a marble monument to Hippolyte Flandrin, by *Oudiné* (1866).

In the little garden to the N. of the church are fragments of sculptures from the great lady-chapel built in 1212–55 by Pierre de Montereau within the precincts of the abbey. In the Rue de l'Abbaye, to the N. of the garden, is the former *Abbot's Palace,* erected c. 1586 by Cardinal de Bourbon; it is now occupied by a dispensary. Behind it was the *Prison de l'Abbaye,* where Mme Roland wrote her memoirs and Charlotte Corday spent her last days. Delacroix died in 1863 at 6 Rue Furstemberg, which now contains a little museum of souvenirs, sketches, etc. (open daily 10–5 in Apr.–Nov., adm. 50 fr.); and No. 1 Rue Bourbon-le-Château, a few yards E., was Whistler's first home in Paris (1855–56). To the N. of the Abbey lay the *Pré-aux-Clercs,* a favourite promenade of medieval students.—In a garden adjoining the boulevard, S. of the church, is a statue of Bernard Palissy (1510–89), whose workshop is said to have been in the Rue du Dragon. This latter street, doomed to destruction, runs parallel to the busy RUE DE RENNES, a modern thoroughfare leading S.W. to Montparnasse. At No. 30 Rue du Dragon Victor Hugo lived in 1822.

We continue to follow the boulevard to the E. On the right the Rue Montfaucon leads to the *Marché St-Germain,* on a site on which the Foire St-Germain was held from 1176 to 1790. Farther on the boulevard skirts on the S. the interesting quarter described on pp. 96, 81 and reaches (r.) the *Carrefour de l'Odéon.*—For the Boul. St-Germain to the E. of this point, see p. 81.

From the junction of the Boul. St-Germain and the Rue du Bac the wide BOULEVARD RASPAIL leads S.E. in a straight line to the Place Denfert-Rochereau, crossing several interesting streets.

It first crosses the RUE DE GRENELLE, which extends from the Av. de la Bourdonnais, on the W., to the Rue de Sèvres, on the E. No. 36, *A la Petite Chaise*, with an interesting railing, dates from 1681. Jean Ampère lived at No. 52 in 1840–46. On Nos. 57 and 59 is the fine **Fontaine des Quatre-Saisons*, designed by Bouchardon in 1739, with sculptures of the Seasons and the City of Paris with the Seine and Marne at her feet. Alfred de Musset lived at No. 59 from 1824 to 1840. No. 71, a 17th cent. house, is now an annex of the Italian Embassy. No. 73, seen from the gate of 71, is a fine mansion with an Ionic peristyle, built by Legrand in 1775. No. 75, the *Hôtel d'Estrées*, and No. 79, the *Russian Embassy*, were built by Robert de Cotte in 1713. No. 85, the *Hôtel d'Avaray*, is now the Netherlands Embassy. No. 106, dating from 1755, is the *Temple de Pentemont*, once the chapel of a convent where Josephine de Beauharnais lived for several years. Its main building (37–39 Rue de Bellechasse) housed an aristocratic school for girls, where Jefferson's daughter was a pupil during her father's embassy.

No. 110, the *Ministère de l'Education Nationale*, was the Hôtel de Courteilles, (1778); No. 116, the old Hôtel de Brissac, built by Boffrand and Leroux (1731), is now the *Mairie of the 7th Arrondissement*. No. 101, the former Hôtel d'Argenson, built by Lassurance in 1700, is now the *Ministère du Commerce*. Nos. 138 and 140 were built by Jean Courtonne in 1724. Marshal Foch died at No. 138 in 1929. No. 127, the *Ministère du Travail* (Ministry of Labour), was the Hôtel du Châtelet, one of the finest examples of the Louis XIV style; it was at one time used as the Archbishop's House.

The RUE DE VARENNE, which next diverges on the right from the Boul. Raspail, leads to the Boul. des Invalides. No. 47 is the *Italian Embassy*. No. 57 is the fine *Hôtel de Matignon*, built by Courtonne about 1721 and altered in the 19th cent.; having served as the Austro-Hungarian embassy in 1888–1914, since 1935 it has been the *Hôtel de la Présidence du Conseil*. No. 69, the *Hôtel d'Orsay*, is now the seat of the Haut Commissariat à l'Energie Atomique. No. 77, at the corner of the Boul. des Invalides, is the *Hôtel Biron*, built in 1730 by Gabriel, after 1820 the aristocratic convent of the Sacré-Cœur, and from Oct. 1907 the studio of Auguste Rodin, who, however, continued to reside at Meudon. Here is now installed the ***Musée Rodin** (Rte. 30).—André Gide died in 1951 at No. 1bis Rue Vaneau, which leads out of the Rue Varenne (l.), just beyond the Hôtel de Matignon.

To the right (W.) of the Boulevard Raspail, between the Rue Babylone and the Rue de Sèvres, is the large *Square Potain* or *Boucicaut*, with a monument to *Mme Boucicaut* (founder of the Bon Marché) and *Baroness Hirsch*, benefactresses of the city of Paris. On the W. side of the gardens are the *Grand Magasins du Bon Marché*, with annexes on the other side of the Rue du Bac.

The RUE DE SÈVRES, which the boulevard crosses here, begins at the *Carrefour de la Croix-Rouge*, and leads S.W. to the junction of the Boul. Pasteur and Boul. Garibaldi.—At No. 42 Rue de Sèvres, to the W. of the boulevard, is the *Hôpital Laënnec*, formerly a home for incurable women, founded by Cardinal de La Rochefoucauld about 1635, with an interesting courtyard and chapel. Farther on is the *Eglise des Lazaristes*, with a silver shrine containing the body of St. Vincent de Paul. In the Rue St-Romain (l.), in the 18th cent. *Hôtel Choiseul-Praslin*, is the interesting *Postal Museum* (daily except Tues. 2–6; 20 fr., Sun. 10 fr.).

The RUE DU CHERCHE-MIDI, which the Boul. next crosses, derives its name from an 18th cent. sign on No. 19 (E. part), representing an astronomer tracing a sundial. To No. 37 Victor Hugo came to woo his cousin, Adèle Foucher, and here their marriage was celebrated in 1823.—No. 38 is the *Prison Militaire du*

Cherche-Midi, where many French patriots were imprisoned during the war.—David d'Angers and the historian Michelet lived in the Rue St-Placide; Parmentier in the Rue de l'Abbé-Grégoire; and at No. 3bis Rue de Bagneux was the studio of Augustus Saint-Gaudens, the American sculptor (1897–1900). All these are side-streets on the S.

The Boul. Raspail then crosses the Rue de Rennes and the Rue de Vaugirard and ends at the Carrefour Vavin (p. 118).

16. THE INVALIDES, CHAMP-DE-MARS, AND S.W. DISTRICTS.

MÉTRO stations: *Invalides* (lines 8 and 14); *Tour-Mauborg, Ecole Militaire, Champ-de-Mars* (line 8); *St-François-Xavier* (line 14); *Duroc* (lines 10 and 14); *La Motte-Picquet-Grenelle* (lines 6, 8, 10); *Emile-Zola, Charles-Michels, Javel* (line 10): *Quai de Grenelle, Cambronne, Sèvres-Lecourbe* (line 6); *Place Balard* (line 8).—MOTOR-BUSES: Invalides (routes 63, 69, 83); Tour-Maubourg (routes 28, 49, 69); Ecole Militaire (routes 28, 49, 80, 86, 92); Champ-de-Mars (route 80); St-François-Xavier (routes 28, 86, 92); Duroc (routes 28 and 92); La Motte-Picquet-Grenelle (route 80); Charles-Michels, Pl. Balard (route 69); Javel (route 62); Dupleix (route 69); Cambronne (routes 49 and 80).

The districts to the W. of the Faubourg St-Germain are overshadowed by the dome of the Invalides and the Eiffel Tower.

The ESPLANADE DES INVALIDES is a large open space, 490 by 270 yds., planted with trees along the sides. The symmetry of its appearance is spoilt by the **Gare des Invalides,** which since 1946, has become the 'gare aérienne' or reception centre for passengers travelling by air from the airports at Orly and Le Bourget. The electric railway to Versailles still starts from here, however. From the N. side of the Esplanade the *Pont Alexandre-III* crosses the Seine to the Champs-Elysées. On the S. side, the Esplanade is bounded by two little squares; on the E., the Square des Invalides, and on the W., by the Square de la Tour-Maubourg.

The ***HÔTEL DES INVALIDES** was founded by Louis XIV in 1671 as a home for disabled soldiers, the first of its kind, and at one time housed as many as 7000 pensioners. At present about 150 war-wounded live in the buildings. Built from the designs of *Libéral Bruant*, and continued by *Hardouin-Mansart*, the Invalides was restored under Napoleon I and Napoleon III and now covers an area of about 31 acres. The chief things to see are the **Musée de l'Armée** (Rte. 19) and Napoleon's tomb. The Invalides is the headquarters of the military governor of Paris.

The courtyards of the Invalides are open daily 7–5; the *Dôme*, with *Napoleon's Tomb* (main entrance in the Place Vauban), is open daily 9.30–5; adm. 30 fr.

Passing through the iron entrance-gates, we enter the FORECOURT, with its radiating flower-beds. On either side of the gates are two German Panther tanks, captured by the Leclerc Division in Alsace during the liberation. Facing the Esplanade is a row of forty pieces of captured artillery, of which the eight on gun-carriages form the *Batterie Triomphale* (removed by the Germans during the war). Arranged on either side of each half-battery are twenty unmounted pieces.

In the flower-bed to the left of the entrance is a statue of *Prince Eugène de Beauharnais* (1781–1824), by Dumont.

The plain and dignified FAÇADE is 230 yds. long and has no less than 133 windows in its three stories. Flanking the entrance are statues of Mars and Minerva, by *Guillaume Coustou* (1735), who was responsible also for the equestrian bas-relief above the central door of Louis XIV accompanied by Justice and Prudence. By the two corner-pavilions are four groups of conquered nations by *Desjardins*, removed from the Place des Victoires.

The COUR D'HONNEUR, 140 by 68 yds., is bordered by galleries adorned with unfinished frescoes (the Military Annals of France), begun by *Bénédict Masson* in 1867. Opposite the entrance is the door of the church of St-Louis, above which are *Seurre's* original bronze statue of Napoleon, formerly on the Vendôme Column, and an astronomical clock (1781). On either side of the courtyard are the entrances to the **Musée de l'Armée** (weapons and armour on the W., historical collection on the E.; see Rte. 19).

The **Church of St-Louis,** or chapel of the Invalides, was built by *Bruant*. The interior is decorated with captured ensigns. On the night of May 30th, 1814, at the moment of the Allies' entry into Paris, Marshal Sérurier, governor of the Invalides, ordered 1400 enemy flags to be burned in the courtyard. Those remaining were brought from other buildings or are trophies of later wars.

On the right is a monument to the generals killed in the First World War; the small stone post in front of it contains earth from a battlefield of the Second World War. On the left is the *Chapelle du Soldat de la Grande Armée* in which are deposited the tablets, palms, and other offerings brought from the Tomb of the Unknown Soldier. Here also is a stone containing earth from an American cemetery of the Second World War. A series of these posts ('bornes') crosses France from Cherbourg to Metz, and recalls the campaign of Gen. Patton and his troops in June–Nov. 1944. Farther on is the hearse used to transport Napoleon's remains at St. Helena, and, near the end of the aisle, the monument to French Airmen who lost their lives in the First World War. On the pillars are monuments to marshals of France and governors of the Invalides. The *Chapelle Napoléon*, at the end of the right aisle, contains three stone slabs from the tomb at St. Helena, the copper coffin and the velvet pall used for the removal of the remains in 1840, and a plaster mask of Napoleon made by Antommarchi. The stained glass behind the high-altar separates the church from the Dôme des Invalides.

In the *Vaults* (no adm.) are the graves of marshals and generals of France, including Turenne (d. 1675), Bertrand (d. 1844), Grouchy (d. 1847), and Franchet d'Espèrey (d. 1942). Here, too, are buried the hearts of Vauban (d. 1707) and Kléber (d. 1800), and the remains of Gen. Guillaumat (d. 1940), Gen. Giraud (d. 1949), and Gen. Leclerc (de Hautecloque; d. 1947), commander of the famous Division Leclerc, which fought with the Allies in the invasion of Europe, and liberated Paris and Strasbourg.

From the Cour d'Honneur we pass through the Corridor de Metz (on the right as we leave the church) to reach the entrance to the Dome and Napoleon's tomb.

The ***Dôme des Invalides,** begun by *J. Hardouin-Mansart*

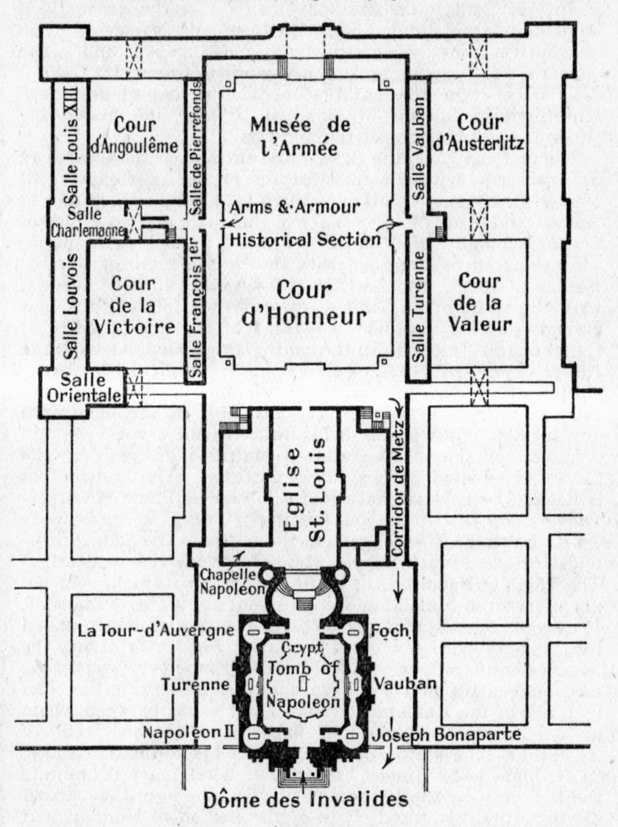

in 1675 and finished in 1706, was added to the church of St-Louis as a chapel royal. It is separated from the Place Vauban by a large courtyard enclosed by handsome iron railings. In the niches on the ground floor are statues of Charlemagne and St. Louis. The ribbed dome is roofed with lead, adorned with gilded trophies, and crowned with a flèche 345 ft. above the ground.

The ***Interior,** 184 ft. square, is in the form of a Greek cross. The most striking features are its admirable proportions, its sculptures, and its mosaic pavements. In the centre is a large circular opening above the tomb of Napoleon. The pendentives are painted with the four Evangelists, and in the cupola is St. Louis presenting his sword to Christ, by *Charles de Lafosse.* On the entablature below the windows are sculptured medallions of kings of France, and above the windows are paintings of the apostles.

The first chapel on the right of the entrance is the CHAPELLE ST-AUGUSTIN, with the tomb of Joseph Bonaparte, King of Naples (d. 1844).—Tomb of Vauban (d. 1707), with statues of Science and War, by *Etex*; above the doors are bas-reliefs of St. Louis founding the Quinze-Vingts and the Fall of Damietta. —CHAPELLE ST-AMBROISE, with the bronze tomb of Marshal Foch (d. 1929), by *Landowski.*—CHAPELLE ST-GRÉGOIRE, with the heart of La Tour d'Auvergne (d. 1800; "the first grenadier of the Republic").—Tomb of Turenne (d. 1675).—CHAPELLE ST-JÉRÔME. In the centre is the sarcophagus of the Roi de Rome (1811–32), or Napoleon II, the great Napoleon's only son. Originally buried in Vienna, his remains were brought hither by the Germans in 1940, on the hundredth anniversary of the burial of his father in the crypt.

On either side of the altar a staircase descends to the CRYPT (conducted parties only; gratuity). The bronze door is flanked by colossal statues of Civil and Military Power, by *Duret.* The inscription on the impost may be translated: "I desire that my ashes rest on the banks of the Seine, in the midst of the French people whom I have loved so dearly." The **Tomb of Napoleon,** 13 by 6½ ft., and 15 ft. high, is of red porphyry from Finland and was presented by Tsar Nicholas I. It rests on a pedestal of green Vosges granite and is surrounded by a gallery with ten bas-reliefs after *Simart,* typifying the benefits conferred on France by the Emperor. Facing the sarcophagus are twelve colossal figures representing the chief victories of the Emperor, *Pradier's* last work, between which are six trophies of fifty-four flags taken at the Battle of Austerlitz. The statue of Napoleon in his coronation robes, 8½ ft. high, is by *Simart.* In front is a reliquary containing the hat worn by the Emperor at Eylau, the sword he carried at Austerlitz, his grand chain of the Legion of Honour, and other relics.

In the semi-circular Place Vauban, to the S. of the Dôme, are statues to Marsha Fayolle (1852–1928) and Marshal Galliéni (1849–1916), both by *Jean Boucher.*

The district to the W., between the Invalides and Champ-de-Mars, is intersected by the Boul. de la Tour-Maubourg and by the wide Av. de La Motte-Picquet, Av. Bosquet, and Av. Rapp. At the corner of the Rue Jean-Nicot and the Quai d'Orsay is the *American Church in Paris* (1927-31). Jean Giraudoux (1882–1944), the playwright, died at No. 89 Quai d'Orsay, and at No. 1 Quai Branly are the pleasing white buildings of the *Ministère des Travaux Publics, des Transports, et du Tourisme*. Here also are the seat of the *Secretariat Général à l'Aviation Civile et Commerciale* and the *Météorologie Nationale*. No. 41 Quai Branly is a fine new building belonging to the *Ministry of Economic Affairs*.

The E. side of the Invalides, the charming domestic architecture of which contrasts with the formal façade on the Esplanade, is skirted by the BOULEVARD DES INVALIDES. On the left diverge the Rue de Grenelle and the Rue de Varenne. Near the beginning of the latter is the Musée Rodin (Rte. 30). Farther on in the boulevard is the church of **St-François-Xavier** (1875). In the Rue Duroc (r.) is the *Blind Asylum* or *Maison des Aveugles* (Nos. 5–9), built in 1907, with a sale-room, workshops, museum, and library. The *Institut National des Jeunes Aveugles*, on the right side of the boulevard, was founded by Valentin Haüy in 1793 and transferred to this building in 1843.—The Boul. des Invalides ends at the Rue de Sèvres and is continued by the Boul. du Montparnasse.

The AVENUE DE TOURVILLE, leading W. from the Boul. des Invalides to the Champ-de-Mars, passes between the Dôme des Invalides and the *Place Vauban*, from the S. side of which radiate the Av. de Villars, the wide Av. de Breteuil, and the Av. de Ségur.

The wide AVENUE DE BRETEUIL crosses the *Place de Breteuil*, in which rises a lofty monument to *Pasteur* (1822–95), by Falguière and Girault, erected in 1904 by public subscription. At the end of the Av. de Breteuil begin the Boul. Garibaldi and the BOULEVARD PASTEUR, with the buildings of the *Institut d'Optique* (1924–27) on the left.

In the part of the RUE DE SÈVRES between the Av. de Breteuil and the Boul. des Invalides are (l.) the *Hôpital des Enfants-Malades*, founded in 1724, and the *Hôpital Necker*, once a Benedictine nunnery, founded in 1779 by Louis XVI, directed at one time by Mme Necker, and rebuilt in 1840.

From the Place de Breteuil the Av. de Saxe leads N.W. to the *Place de Fontenoy*, in front of the huge courtyard of the Ecole Militaire. On the right of the Place are the large modern buildings of the *Ministry of the Merchant Marine* and other government offices. In the centre is a granite monument to Frenchmen who have lost their lives in defence of their country. The **Ecole Militaire**, a handsome structure covering 29 acres, was built by Gabriel for Louis XV and enlarged in 1856. It is separated from the Place de Fontenoy by a fine 18th cent. railing, and on either side of the entrance gates are two captured German tanks. The school was founded in 1751 for the training of noblemen as army officers; after 1792 it was used as barracks; and it is now occupied by the *Ecole Supérieure de Guerre*, or staff college.

On the N.W. side of the Ecole Militaire, in the Place Joffre, is a monument to Marshal Joffre (d. 1931), by Réal del Sarte.

Between the Ecole Militaire and the Seine lies the **Champ-de-Mars,** about 1000 yds. long and from 200 to 500 yds. wide. It was laid out about 1770 as a parade-ground and made into a park after 1913, and is now the centre of a select but dull residential quarter.

Here were held numerous festivals, the most famous of which was the Fête de la Fédération on July 14th, 1790, when the king, the Assembly, and the delegates from the provinces and the army took the oath at the Autel de la Patrie to observe the new Constitution; the 'Champ de Mai,' held by Napoleon on his return from Elba; and many International Exhibitions. Bailly, president of the Constituent Assembly, was brutally executed here in 1793, and Capt. Dreyfus was publicly degraded here in 1894.

At the river end of the Champ-de-Mars, facing the Palais de Chaillot, rises the ***Eiffel Tower** or *Tour Eiffel* (984 ft. high; the third tallest building in the world), dominating the W. end of Paris.

The tower was constructed by the engineer Alexandre Eiffel in 1887–89. It weighs 7000 tons and is composed of 12,000 pieces of metal, fastened by 2,500,000 rivets. The base of the tower is supported by four huge masonry piers, sunk 30–45 ft. in the ground, the surface of each measuring 31 sq. yds. The ascent, which is not recommended in misty, windy, or cold weather, is made in lifts (the first platform may be reached also by staircases). The lift starts working at 10.45 and continues till 5. To the first platform, 70 fr.; second platform, 110 fr.; third platform, 150 fr. On the first platform (187 ft. high) is the restaurant 'En Plein Ciel,' and there are bars on both the other two (377 ft. and 902 ft., respectively). The *View, extending over a radius of 60 m. from Paris, is usually clearest about 1 hr. before sunset. At the top of the tower is a powerful wireless installation. Underneath the N. leg of the tower is a bust of Eiffel, by Bourdelle.

To the S.W. of the Champ-de-Mars, opposite the Pont de Passy (now Pont de Bir-Hakeim), where the Quai Branly becomes the Quai de Grenelle, is the BOULEVARD DE GRENELLE, which is continued E. by the BOULEVARD GARIBALDI. At the junction of these boulevards is the PLACE CAMBRONNE, with a statue of Garibaldi (1807–82). From the Place Cambronne the Rue de la Croix-Nivert leads S.W. to the new Square St-Lambert, laid out on the site of the old gasworks.

The chief point of interest in the district to the S.W. of the Ecole Militaire is the **Imprimerie Nationale,** or government printing-works, moved in 1925 from the Hôtel de Rohan to the Rue de la Convention. In front is a statue of Gutenberg, by *David d'Angers*. Visitors are admitted to the workshops on the last Thurs. of each month at 2.30, on previous application.

Facing the Imprimerie is **St-Christophe-de-Javel,** a modern church (1926–34) by *C. H. Besnard*, dedicated to the patron saint of travellers and sportsmen and decorated outside with frescoes in cement, by *H. M. Magne*, of St. Christopher as the averter of accidents. The mural decorations in the interior, by *J. M. Ferrières*, are also noteworthy. A short distance to the N.W. the *Pont Mirabeau* crosses the Seine to Auteuil.

The Rue Gutenberg leads S. from the Imprimerie to the Boul. Victor, in which are various buildings of the *Ministère de l'Air* and the *Marine Militaire*. The *Musée de l'Air*, opened in 1936 in the building facing the Place Balard, is not at present open to the public. It contained many interesting historic flying-machines, models of modern aircraft, engines of various types, etc.

17. THE SOUTHERN QUARTERS.

MÉTRO stations: *Montparnasse* (lines 4, 6, 12, 14); *Vavin* (line 4); *Raspail* (lines 4 and 6); *Denfert-Rochereau* (lines 4, 6, S.); *Mouton-Duvernet*, *Alésia*, *Porte d'Orléans* (line 4); *Edgar-Quinet*, *St-Jacques*, *Glacière*, *Corvisart* (line 6); *Pl. d'Italie* (lines 5, 6, 7); *Gobelins* (line 7); *Port-Royal*, *Cité Universitaire* (S.).—MOTOR-BUSES: Montparnasse (routes 28, 48, 91, 92, 94, 95, 96); Vavin (routes

58, 68, 91); Raspail (route 68); Denfert-Rochereau (routes 38 and 68); Mouton-Duvernet (routes 38 and 68); Alésia (routes 28, 38, 62, 68); Porte d'Orléans (routes 28, 38, 68, P.C.); Edgar-Quinet (route 91); Glacière (route 77); Pl. d'Italie (routes 27, 47, 67); Gobelins (routes 27, 83, 91); Port-Royal (routes 38, 83, 91); Cité Universitaire (P.C.).

The quarter lying E. of the S. part of the Boul. St-Michel and S. of the Quartier Latin contains a notable number of scientific institutions. At the E. corner of the Luxembourg Gardens diverges the RUE GAY-LUSSAC, in which, at the corner of the Rue St-Jacques, is the *Institut Océanographique,* founded by Prince Albert I of Monaco in 1910.

Adjacent are the *Institut de Géographie,* and, in the Rue Pierre-Curie, the *Institut de Biologie Physico-Chimique* (Fondation S. de Rothschild), the *Institut Henri-Poincaré,* the *Institut du Radium,* the *Laboratoire de Chimie-Physique* and the *Institut de Chimie Appliquée.*

The Rue Gay-Lussac ends at the Rue Claude-Bernard and Rue d'Ulm. At the corner (45 Rue d'Ulm) is the *Ecole Normale Supérieure,* established in 1795 for the training of teachers. On the wall of the building is a medallion of Pasteur commemorating the site of the laboratory where he worked from 1864 to 1888.

To the S.W. is the winding and picturesque RUE ST-JACQUES, with many booksellers' shops, in medieval times the main thoroughfare of the left bank. No. 218 occupies the site of the house of Jean de Meung, part-author of the 'Roman de la Rose' (c. 1300). *St-Jacques-du-Haut-Pas,* a plain classical building (1630–84), was the favourite church of the Jansenists. No. 254, at the corner of the Rue de l'Abbé-de-l'Epée, is the *Deaf and Dumb Asylum* (*Institution des Sourds-Muets*), founded by the Abbé de l'Epée about 1770 and taken over by the state in 1790; the building, once the seminary of St-Magloire, was reconstructed in 1823. In the courtyard is a statue of the Abbé, by Felix Martin, a deaf-and-dumb sculptor (1789).—A little farther on (Nos. 269 and 269bis; l.) is the **Schola Cantorum** (visitors admitted; gratuity), a free conservatoire of singing and music, established by Vincent d'Indy (d. 1931).

The buildings (1674) are those of the English Benedictine monastery of St. Edmund, founded in France in 1615, and established on this site from 1640 to 1818; they still belong to the English Roman Catholic authorities. The salon and the staircase are good examples of the Louis XIV style; the lower part of the chapel is now the concert hall; and the 'chapelle ardente,' where James II's body lay in state, is now a bedroom.

James II (d. 1701), his daughter Louisa (d. 1712), and the Duke of Berwick (d. 1734), his son by Arabella Churchill, are buried here; the bodies, hidden at the Revolution, are probably in the catacombs, which were once accessible from the house. The last burial here was that of Berwick's second son Charles (d. 1787). Dr. Johnson (1775) and Benjamin Franklin were guests of the English monks here.

The door between columns, at the end of the courtyard of No. 284, was once an entrance to the Carmelite convent to which Louise de la Vallière, mistress of Louis XIV, retired in 1675. Another relic of the convent is a crypt beneath No. 25 Rue Denfert-Rochereau, at the back. Chateaubriand lived at No. 92 in this street in 1826–35.

At Nos. 277–279 Rue St-Jacques (l.) the **Val-de-Grâce,** since 1790 a military hospital, was once the house of the Benedictine nuns of Val-Profond, whose patroness was Notre-Dame du Val-de-Grâce. The present buildings, including the church, were erected by Anne of Austria in thanksgiving for the birth of Louis XIV. In the courtyard is a bronze statue of Baron Larrey (1766–1842), the surgeon, by *David d'Angers.* The church, in the style of St. Peter's at Rome, was built in 1645–65 by *Fr. Mansart* and his successors. The façade is a fine example of the Jesuit style, and the *Dome is one of the finest in France. Inside the dome is a huge painting by *Pierre Mignard.* The high-altar is a copy of Bernini's in St. Peter's, with six huge twisted columns in Brabançon marble. On the right of the choir is a painting of Anne of Austria. In the church are buried the hearts of Queen Henrietta Maria (daughter of Henri IV of France and wife of Charles I of England), Anne of Austria, and many other royal persons.

The Musée du Service de Santé (entrance 277bis Rue St-Jacques; adm Mon.–Fri. 9–12, 2–6, closed holidays), illustrating military hygiene, consists of five sections, of which only two, the Museé du Matériel Sanitaire and the Musée Historique, are at present open.

Val-de-Grâce was only one of the religious houses with which this district abounded until the Revolution. Just to the N. are the Rue des Ursulines and Rue des Feuillantines, whose names recall vanished convents; almost opposite were the Carmelites; to the S. stood Port-Royal (see below); and, in the Boul. d'Arago beyond, the *Hôpital Broca* stands on the site of a 13th cent. Franciscan nunnery.

The Rue St-Jacques ends on the S. at the Boulevard de Port-Royal, which continues the line of the Boul. du Montparnasse S.E. from the Carrefour de l'Observatoire to the Av. des Gobelins, opposite the Boul. St-Marcel. At the W. end, on the S. side, is the *Hôpital de la Maternité,* which has occupied since 1814 the buildings of *Port-Royal,* a branch of the Jansenist abbey of Port-Royal-des-Champs. In the chapel, built by Lepautre in 1647, is the tomb of Antoine Lemaistre (d. 1658), the first hermit of Port-Royal.

From the E. end of the Boul. de Port-Royal the Avenue des Gobelins leads S. On the right is the ***Gobelins** (adm. free, 2–4 on Thurs.), the famous tapestry factory which has been a state institution for over three hundred years. Most of the buildings have retained their 17th cent. aspect. The museum building (1914), facing the avenue, contains a good collection of ancient and modern tapestries, but has not yet been reopened to the public.

The original royal tapestry factory at Fontainebleau was removed to Paris by Henri II. Suspended during the 16th cent. Religious Wars, the industry was revived by Henri IV and installed in 1601 in the buildings of the Gobelins (two brothers Gobelin, who had set up dye-works here on the banks of the Bièvre, a small stream now covered over, at the end of the 15th cent.). In 1667 Louis XIV added the royal furniture factory, and Lebrun and then Pierre Mignard were appointed as directors. In 1662 the royal carpet factory of the *Savonnerie*, started in 1604 in the galleries of the Louvre and subsequently moved to a 'savonnerie' (soap-factory) at Chaillot, was placed under the same management, and it transferred its workshops to the Gobelins factory in 1826.

In the Cour d'Antin is a marble statue of Lebrun, by *Cordier* (1907). On the left are the two WORKSHOPS, separated by a staircase. The tapestry is woven on high-warp looms, several of which date from the time of Louis XIV. The weaver works on the reverse side of the tapestry, having the painting which he is copying behind him and reflected in mirrors. The average amount of tapestry that a weaver can produce in a day is 2⅕ sq. inches.—A passage beyond the second workroom leads to a staircase descending to the workshops for Savonnerie carpets.

A covered passage leads hence to the Cour Colbert, with a bronze statue of Colbert, and the CHAPEL, which has been fitted out as a small historical museum with documents relating to the Gobelins, and portraits of various celebrated craftsmen who have worked there, etc. In the Sacristy is exhibited the treasury of the chapel.

At No. 7 in the Rue Berbier-du-Mets, behind the factory, is a little 18th cent. hunting lodge (at present masked by a protective covering). This is to be re-erected in the SQUARE RENÉ LE GALL, a garden laid out on the former allotments of the tapestry workers, the N. end of which is occupied by the huge, but not unpleasing, building of the new *Mobilier National* (1935). The entrance is decorated by two fine mastiffs, by Abbal. The charming garden, bordering the Rue Croulebarbe and Rue Corvisart, is strictly formal in its adherence to the 16th cent. style.

The Av. des Gobelins ends on the S. at the **Place d'Italie,** the meeting place of seven great thoroughfares. On the N. side is the *Mairie of the 13th Arrondissement* (1867–77).

At the S. end of the Boul. St-Michel, and crossed by the Av. de l'Observatoire, is the **Carrefour de l'Observatoire,** with a monument to the explorer François Garnier (1839–73), by Puech. On the E. was the *Bal Bullier*, once the most famous of the public dance-halls of the Left Bank. On the W. is Rude's **Statue of Marshal Ney* (1769–1815; "le brave des braves"), near the spot where the marshal was shot for espousing Napoleon's cause on his return from Elba. Beyond the Boul. du Montparnasse, in the Avenue de l'Observatoire, is a monument to Théophile Roussel (1816–1903), politician, physician, and philanthropist. Balzac lived in 1830–36 at 3 Rue Cassini and wrote 'Le Peau de Chagrin' here. In the garden at the end of the avenue is a statue of the astronomer

Le Verrier (1811–77), by Chapu, situated exactly on the meridian of Paris and facing due N. To the E., at No. 38 Rue du Faub. St-Jacques, the Société des Gens de Lettres occupies the *Hôtel de Massa* (1784), removed from the Champs-Elysées in 1927.

The **Observatoire** was founded by Louis XIV and built by Claude Perrault in 1667–72.

The four sides of the Observatoire face the cardinal points of the compass, and the latitude of the S. side is the recognised latitude of Paris (48° 50′ 11″ N.). A line bisecting the building from N. to S. is the meridian of Paris (2° 20′ 14″ E. of Greenwich), which was till 1912 the basis for the calculation of longitude on French maps. The Observatoire is the headquarters of the *Bureau International de l'Heure*, which sends out the correct time by wireless.—Visitors who have obtained permission from the director are shown round on the 1st Sat. of the month, at 2 p.m.

On the first floor of the main building is a *Museum* of instruments, and the contents of the *Rotunda* in the W. tower illustrates the history of astronomy. The room on the second floor, on the pavement of which is traced the Paris meridian, contains old physical and astronomical instruments.—A shaft descending from the roof of the main building into the catacombs has been used for the study of falling bodies. In the E. cupola is the great equatorial telescope of 14 in. ape ture.

From the Carrefour de l'Observatoire the BOULEVARD DU MONTPARNASSE, 1 m. long, leads N.W. to the Rue de Vaugirard and Rue de Sèvres, crossing the Boul. Raspail at the busy Carrefour Vavin. Here stands the famous **Statue of Balzac*, by Rodin, erected here in 1939. The statue was commissioned in 1898 by the Société des Gens de Lettres, but rejected by them as unsuitable.

The cross-roads may be regarded as the centre of the quarter of **Montparnasse.** Its well-known cafés, *Le Dôme* and *La Rotonde*, succeeded those of Montmartre as the principal artistic and bohemian rendezvous of Paris, but, like Montmartre, the district was invaded by a horde of pseudo-bohemians and would-be artists. The cafés and 'boîtes' of the neighbourhood, however, still attract a variegated and polyglot crowd.

The neighbouring streets are full of associations with the artists of the late 19th and early 20th cent., from Whistler and Rodin to Picasso and Braque. Trotsky and his fellow-revolutionists frequented the Rotonde in the years before 1917. No. 3 RUE CAMPAGNE-PREMIÈRE was one of Whistler's earliest homes in Paris; he and Rodin had studios in the same building (demolished) at 132 Boul. du Montparnasse. In 1892–1900 Whistler's studio was at No. 86 RUE NOTRE-DAME DES CHAMPS, and his academy of painting was in the Passage Stanislas (now Rue Jules-Chaplain). An earlier dweller in the Rue Notre-Dame des Champs was Victor Hugo (at No. 11 in 1827). Sainte-Beuve, the critic, lived at No. 19 in this street, and died at No. 11 RUE DU MONTPARNASSE in 1869.

Beyond the church of *Notre-Dame des Champs* (1867–76), the boulevard crosses the *Place de Rennes*, on the S. side of which is the **Gare Montparnasse,** the left-bank terminus of the western region of the S.N.C.F.

From the PLACE BIENVENUE, on the S. side of the station, the Boul. de Vaugirard leads W. to the Boul. Pasteur. In the Rue du Docteur-Roux, to the left of the latter, is the **Institut Pasteur,** founded by Louis Pasteur in 1887–89, and built by private subscription. It is devoted not only to scientific research (carried on also in the *Institut de Chimie Biologique*, opposite) but also runs a hospital (Hôpital Pasteur, 213 Rue de Vaugirard) for the free treatment of infectious diseases. The Institut also carries out research work on tuberculosis in special laboratories at No. 96 Rue Falguière. In front of the Institut is a bronze sculpture by Truffot, the shepherd Jupille wrestling with a mad wolf. Jupille, who later became concierge of the institute, was one of the first to be inoculated by the Pasteur method. In the *Crypt* (open on 1st and 3rd Sat. of each month, 2–4) is the *Tomb of Pasteur* (1822–95). In the gardens is the tomb of Dr. Emile Roux (1853–1933), inventor of the treatment of diphtheria by serum-injection.

On the left of the Av. du Maine, just N. of the Place Bienvenue, is the Rue Antoine-Bourdelle. Here the *Musée Antoine-Bourdelle* (daily except Tues. 10–12, 2–5; 25 fr., Sun. free) occupies the house (No. 16) of the famous sculptor (1861–1929) and contains his furniture, many works of art, and personal souvenirs, bequeathed by Mme. Bourdelle.

In the BOULEVARD EDGAR-QUINET, which runs E. from the Place Bienvenue to the Boul. Raspail, is the main entrance of the **Cimetière Montparnasse,** laid out in 1824 and ranking third in size (45 acres) and interest among the Paris cemeteries. Like that of Montmartre, this cemetery contains the graves of many musicians, artists, and writers, including Baudelaire, Maupassant, and César Franck.

From the Av. de l'Observatoire the Av. Denfert-Rochereau leads S.W. to the **Place Denfert-Rochereau,** a busy centre of traffic. Known as the Place d'Enfer until 1871, it received its present name in honour of the brave defender of Belfort, Col. Denfert-Rochereau (1823–78). In the centre is the *Lion of Belfort*, a reduced copy of Bartholdi's splendid sculpture at Belfort, and the gardens are adorned with statues.

The BOULEVARD ST-JACQUES runs E. from the Place Denfert-Rochereau to be continued by the Boul. Auguste-Blanqui. In the Rue de la Tombe-Issoire (r.) is the church of *St-Dominique* (1913–21), by Gaudibert.

On the S.W. side of the Place Denfert-Rocherau, in one of the octroi pavilions of the old Barrière d'Enfer (1784), is the main entrance to the **Catacombs.** These are a vast series of underground, rat-infested quarries dating from the time of the Romans and extending from the Jardin des Plantes to the Porte de Versailles and into the suburbs of Montrouge, Montsouris, and Gentilly. Some of them are still worked. In the 18th cent. they were converted into a charnel-house for bones removed from disused Paris graveyards. Among the remains transferred hither were those of Mme de Pompadour (d. 1764) and of victims of the massacres under the Terror.—Visitors are escorted round the catacombs on the 1st and 3rd Sat. of each month, from Oct. 16th to June 30th ; every Sat. from July 1st to Oct. 15th ; adm. 20 fr. ; candles 20 fr. each.

The tour lasts over an hour and is apt to be a trifle monotonous. We descend a spiral staircase and follow a narrow passage for about ten minutes, leading to the huge charnel-house (ossuaire), which is said to contain the remains of nearly three million persons and consists of a labyrinth of galleries lined with bones and rows of skulls. The exit is in No. 36 Rue Remy-Dumoncel, E. of the Av. du Général-Leclerc.

The AVENUE DU GÉNÉRAL-LECLERC, which runs S. from the Place Denfert-Rochereau, is the main thoroughfare of **Petit-Montrouge,** a typical middle-class quarter. On the left of the avenue is the *Hospice La Rochefoucauld,* a 'maison de retraite' founded by the Frères de la Charité under the title of Maison Royale de Santé. At the Place Victor-Basch, farther on in the Av. Leclerc, is *St-Pierre-de-Montrouge,* built in the style of the early Italian basilicas, with a tower 165 ft. high.

The Av. du Parc de Montsouris leads S. from the Place Denfert-Rochereau to the **Parc de Montsouris,** some 40 acres in area. The *Bardo* (100 yds. N. of the Boul. Jourdan) is a reproduction of the Bey's Palace at Tunis, which was made for the exhibition of 1867 and is now used as a meteorological observatory. In the N.E. corner of the park is a lake with a pleasant summer-restaurant (Pavillon du Lac).

Facing the park on the opposite side of the Boul. Jourdan, is the **Cité Universitaire** (founded 1923), a group of large hostels for students, extending some three-quarters of the length of the boulevard towards the Porte d'Orléans, with a station on the railway to Sceaux. The twenty different foundations, each built in the characteristic architecture of its own country, present a wide diversity of styles. The enormous *Maison Internationale* (1936) and the Swiss foundation (by Le Corbusier) are especially noteworthy. Opposite the United States foundation (1928) is a bronze statue of Tom Paine (1737–1809). The British hostel was opened in 1937. To the S. of the Maison Internationale, in the Av. de Montrouge, is the church of the *Sacré-Cœur* (1936).

Historical Plan of the Louvre

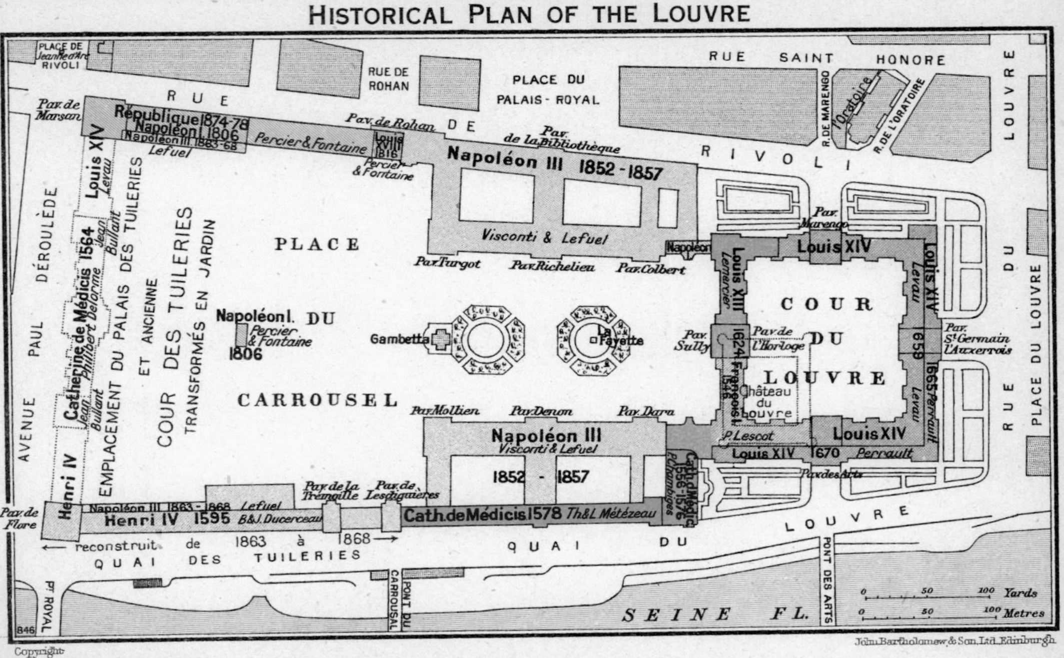

III. THE LOUVRE AND OTHER GREAT COLLECTIONS.

WITH the exception of the Musée de l'Armée, the Musée Cluny and the Musée Rodin, the Great Public Collections of Paris are situated on the N. side of the river. All (with the exception of the Musée Jacquemart-André) are closed on Tuesday. But all (with the exception of the Bibliothèque Nationale) are open on Sunday and other days of the week. Exact details of days and hours of admission will be found in the table on page xxxviii.

In addition to the collections described in the present section, the visitor may be reminded of the Musée des Archives, and the scientific museums at the Jardin des Plantes, as well as the important collections at Chantilly, Fontainebleau, and Versailles.

18. THE LOUVRE AND ITS COLLECTIONS.

MÉTRO stations. *Palais-Royal* (lines 1 and 7).—MOTOR-BUSES: 27, 48, 95 to the Musée du Louvre.

The **Palais du Louvre,** situated between the Rue de Rivoli on the N. and the Seine on the S., is the most important public building in Paris and one of the largest (40 acres) and most magnificent palaces in the world. The construction of the building, which extended over three centuries, is of great architectural and historical interest.

HISTORY. The name of the Louvre is derived either from an early wolf-hunters' rendezvous known as 'Lupara' or 'Louverie,' or from a 'Louver,' a blockhouse, and the building first appears in history as one of Philip Augustus's fortresses (c. 1204). Charles V made it an official royal residence. The W. and S. sides were rebuilt under Francis I (1515–1547) and extended by his successor Henri II. Catherine de Médicis, Henri II's widow, began the Long Gallery, facing the river, to connect the Louvre with her new palace at the Tuileries. The building was considerably extended during the reigns of Henri IV and Louis XIII, and the quadrangle was completed, at Colbert's orders, during the minority of Louis XIV. However, the king soon lost interest in the new buildings, and they were left in a state of complete disrepair until Louis XV commissioned his architect Gabriel to renovate and repair the palace in 1754. Under Napoleon I the W. part of the gallery on the N. side of the Cour du Louvre was erected, and under Napoleon III the main wings which enclose the Place du Carrousel on the N. and S. were built. The Pavillon de Marsan and Pavillon de Flore (at the extreme W. end) have been rebuilt since their destruction by fire under the Commune.

Catherine de Médicis was resident in the palace after the death of her husband. Here Henry of Navarre (afterwards Henri IV) was married to Marguerite de Valois, sister of Charles IX, and here, five days later, Catherine de Médicis extorted from Charles IX the order for the Massacre of St. Bartholomew (Aug. 25th, 1572). In 1591, during the Wars of the League, the Duc de Mayenne hanged three members of the 'Council of Sixteen' in the Salle des Gardes (now the Salle des Cariatides). Henrietta Maria, the widowed queen of Charles I of England, found refuge in the Louvre. In 1658 Corneille's tragedy 'Nicomède' was performed in the Salle des Gardes by command of Louis XIV. In 1793 the Musée de la République was opened in the Louvre, and the palace has remained a national art gallery and museum ever since. During the Revolution of 1830 the Louvre was stormed by the mob, and it was set on fire in 1871 by the Communards, fortunately without suffering serious damage.

The Louvre consists of two main divisions: the OLD LOUVRE, comprising the buildings round the Cour du Louvre or E. courtyard, and the NEW LOUVRE, the modern buildings N. and S. of the Place du Carrousel, together with the wings stretching W. to the pavilions of the Tuileries. On the W. side of the Cour du Louvre, to the S. of the Pavillon Sully, is the oldest existing part of the Palace (early 16th cent.), by *Lescot*, with sculptural decorations by *Jean Goujon* and *Paul Ponce*. The N. half of the W. façade, and part of the N. façade were designed by *Lemercier* in imitation of Lescot; the caryatids on the Pavillon Sully are by *Sarrazin*. The remainder of the Court was built after 1660 by *Levau*. The uppermost stories on the N., E., and S. sides, quite out of keeping with Lescot's charming attic, were added in the 17–18th cent., to bring them to the height of the great colonnade of 52 Corinthian columns and pilasters that now forms the exterior E. façade of the Old Louvre. The work of *Claude Perrault* (1667–1670), it was designed without due regard to dimensions, and a new outer façade was added on the S. side of the Old Louvre, to meet its projecting S. end. The exterior N. façade was left untouched.

The Galerie du Bord de l'Eau, the long S. façade of the Louvre, along the Seine, was the work of *Pierre Chambiges*, architect to Catherine de Médicis, and *Thibaut Métezeau*, as far as the Pavillon de Lesdiguières. Henri IV had the gallery prolonged farther W. to the Pavillon de Flore, by his architect *Baptiste du Cerceau*; but this portion was largely rebuilt in 1863–1868. The buildings of the New Louvre, flanking the Square du Carrousel, were begun by *Visconti* in 1852 and completed by *Lefuel* in 1875. The building on the N. side, the only part of the Louvre not devoted to the collections, has been occupied since 1871 by the Ministère des Finances.

The Collections in the Louvre.

ENTRANCES. The principal entrance is in the Pavillon Denon, the central pavilion on the S. side of the Square du Carrousel. Other entrances are by the Porte Barbet-de-Jouy, on the Quai du Louvre (200 yds. W. of the Pont des Arts), and in the Pavillon de La Trémoille, on the Quai des Tuileries. Sticks and umbrellas must be left at the entrances.

ADMISSION. The galleries of the Louvre are closed every Tuesday, and on New Year's Day; the day after Ascension; May 1st; the 2nd Wednesday after Easter and Whitsun; July 14th; and Nov. 11th. Also on Aug. 15th, Nov. 1st, and Christmas Day, provided that these dates do not fall on a Sunday.

Admission: 30 fr. (15 fr. for those holding a Student's Card); free on Sundays.

GUIDE-LECTURES. Visitors should consult the notice boards for times, etc., in the 'Galerie de Vente,' at the main entrance.

HISTORY OF THE COLLECTIONS. The nucleus of a royal art collection was formed by Francis I (d. 1547). At his request Leonardo da Vinci spent the last few years of his life in France, dying there in 1519. Henri II and his queen, Catherine de Médicis, carried on the tradition of their predecessor. Louis XIV made some notable additions to his collection of Old Masters, and Louis XVI acquired some important paintings of the Spanish and Dutch Schools. In 1793 the Musée de la République was opened to the public, and a large number of the most famous paintings in Europe, captured by the victorious Republican and Napoleonic armies, were exhibited here; though after 1815 the French Government was obliged by the Allies to return them to their former owners. Under Louis XVIII, the Venus de Milo and over a hundred pictures were acquired. In 1848 the Museum became the property of the State, and an annual grant was made for the purchase of works of art. The Second Empire saw the addition of the Campana, Sauvageot, and La Caze collections; and since 1870 the Museum has been enriched by many other valuable collections. A general re-organisation of the collections, begun in 1932, was naturally interrupted during the war years, 1939–45, when the collections were dispersed, for the sake of security, throughout the country. The work was re-started in 1945 but, owing to post-war difficulties, at the time of writing many of the collections (including the Paintings) have not yet been restored to their permanent place. Visitors should therefore be prepared for extensive modifications of the arrangement described below.

GROUND FLOOR.

Greek and Roman Sculpture. We enter by the Pavillon Denon, on the S. side of the Square du Carrousel. Opposite is the Vestibule Denon, with the Galerie de Vente and the cloakrooms beyond.

GALERIE MOLLIEN (to the right of the Vestibule). On the floor and end walls are Byzantine mosaics from Kabr-Hiram (Phœnicia); at the end are fine Græco-Phœnician sarcophagi from Carthage.

The adjacent staircase (Escalier Mollien) and lift ascend to the galleries of paintings. On the first landing is a bronze copy of the Laocoön (in the Vatican), cast at Fontainebleau under Francis I, from a mould brought from Italy by Primaticcio.

From the GALERIE DENON (to the left of the Vestibule), with more sarcophagi and bronzes from the antique, we reach the foot of the Escalier Daru, which ascends to the Picture Galleries (p. 134). On the top landing is the **Nike of Samothrace, or 'Winged Victory.'

This magnificent statue of Parian marble was found near the ruins of a Doric temple, on the island of Samothrace, in 1863. Further excavation in 1950 led to the discovery of the mutilated right hand, and established the probable date of the statue as c. 200 B.C. The breast and left wing are of plaster.

We pass to the left of the staircase, through the *Rotonde d'Anne d'Autriche* (Pl. 12) to the SALLE ARCHAÏQUE (Pl. 1). Greek sculpture of the 7–5th cent. B.C. 3096. Statuette of 'La Dame d'Auxerre'; 3101. Apollo of Paros; 2792. Torso of Apollo; *701. 'Exaltation of the Flower' (bas-relief);

**686. Hera of Samos, one of the oldest and best authenticated works of Ionic sculpture (c. 520 B.C.). The name Cheramues is inscribed on the mantle.

The SALLE DU PARTHENON (Pl. 2) is devoted to sculpture of the 5th cent. B.C., the apogee of Greek art. Among the outstanding exhibits are: *738. Fragment of the East Frieze of the Parthenon at Athens (the greater part of the frieze, which represents the Panathenaic procession, is in the British Museum); 696. Frieze with Apollo and Hermes and nymphs and graces; 716, 717. Metopes from the temple of Zeus at Olympia, with Herakles overcoming the Cretan bull, and presenting to Athene one of the Stymphalian birds. In the passage leading to the following room, *740. The 'Laborde Head,' a fine head of a goddess from one of the pediments on the Parthenon. The SALLES DE PHIDIAS and DE POLYCLÈTE (Pl. 3, 4) contain replicas of 5th and 4th cent. sculpture, including works by Pheidias and Polykleitus and their respective schools. *3070. Torso of Athene, known as the 'Medici Torso,' a Roman replica of an original work of the Pheidian school. The statue was found in Rome by Ingres. 525. Venus Genetrix, 'Great Mother of Æneas' race.' The apple is an idea of the restorer; the original is attributed to Callimachus. —SALLES DE PRAXITÉLÈS (Pl. 5, 6). Replicas of works by Praxiteles and his school (6th cent. B.C.), including *439. Venus of Arles; *441. Apollo Sauroktonos; *2184. Aphrodite of Cnidos, the most celebrated of Praxiteles's works.

SALLE DE LA VÉNUS DE MILO (Pl. 7). In the centre, **399. Vénus de Milo, one of the most beautiful and one of the most celebrated antiques that have come down to us. This famous statue, unrecorded by any ancient writer, was found in 1820 by a peasant in the island of Melos (Milo) in the Greek Archipelago. Purchased for 6000 francs by the French Ambassador in Turkey, it was presented to Louis XVIII, and restored in the Louvre. It was found in five fragments and is 6 ft. 8½ in. in height. The goddess is nude to the waist; the drapery at the back is rough-hewn. The statue was once held to date from the 4th cent. B.C., and much controversy revolved round the base and the disputed inscription to 'Agesandros, son of Menides, of Antioch on the Mæander.' It is now generally regarded as a copy by an unknown master of the 2nd or 1st cent. B.C., after a 4th cent. original.

SALLE DE LYSIPPE (Pl. 8). Works after Lysippus, the great master of the Alexandrine period (4th cent. B.C.). Note especially 83. Hermes fastening his sandal, antique copy of the original; and 448. Eros stringing his bow.—SALLE DES POÈTES GRECS (Pl. 9). *440. Bust or term of Homer, Hellenistic period (4th–1st cent. B.C.).—SALLE D'ALEXANDRE

(Pl. 10). 436, 855. Two busts of Alexander the Great (336–323 B.C.); *1204. Head of Antiochus the Great (ruler of Syria, 223–183 B.C.).

We pass through the CORRIDOR DE PAN (in the two cases on the right wall are female heads, fragment of a funerary stele, etc., of the 4th cent. B.C.). On the right is the SALLE DES CARIÁTIDES (Pl. 11), so called from the *Caryatids by *Jean Goujon*, which support the gallery at the far end. The other decorations and the *Chimneypiece at the nearer end are by *Percier* and *Fontaine* (c. 1806).—The gallery contains sculpture of the Hellenistic period. In the centre, opposite the first window: 2240. Crouching Venus, known as the 'Vénus de Vienne.' On her back are traces of the left hand of a Cupid. On the right, by the second window, 324. Wounded Gaul. In the centre, *589. Huntress Artemis, known as 'Diana of Versailles' (c. 100 A.D.), acquired by Francis I from Rome. By the third window (l.), *542. Marsyas suspended by the wrists to a trunk of a pine tree. Centre, far end, *40. Boy with a goose, marble replica of a bronze attributed to Boethos (found at Rome in 1789). In a recess (l.), *Sleeping Hermaphrodite (the mattress added by Bernini).

We turn right through the Salle Archaïque, into the ROTONDE D'ANNE D'AUTRICHE (Pl. 12), with ceiling paintings by *Mauzaisse* and decorations in stucco by *Michel Anguier* (1653). To the right, *86. Borghese Vase, an antique replica of an original of the 1st cent. B.C., decorated in relief with a Bacchic orgy. Busts or terms of philosophers.—To the left of the Rotonde is the SALLE DU GLADIATEUR BORGHÈSE (Pl. 13), with walls and ceiling by *Meynier*. In the centre, 527. Fighting Gladiator, or 'Borghese Warrior', signed on the tree trunk by Agasias, an otherwise unknown sculptor of the late Hellenistic period (found at Anzio in the 17th cent.). On the walls, copies and originals of Greek bas-reliefs. The SALLES DES RELIEFS FUNÉRAIRES ET VOTIFS (Pl. 14, 15) are devoted to Greek steles, mostly of the 5th–4th cent. B.C.

COUR DU SPHINX. Antique monumental sculpture. N. Wall, *2829. Metopes and bas-reliefs from the architrave of the Temple of Assos (near Troy) in Asia Minor. The scenes represent Hercules battling against Triton, a banquet, processions of animals and centaurs, etc. W. Wall, 2881. Frieze from the Temple of Artemis at Magnesia on the Mæander, illustrating a battle between Greeks and Amazons (2nd cent. B.C.); *593. God of the Tiber, a colossal group, found, along with the Nile (now in the Vatican), in the 16th cent. In the centre, 3444. The Four Seasons, a huge mosaic from near Antioch (4th cent.).—SALLE DES RELIEFS ROMAINS (Pl. 16). 1096. Sacrifice to Mars, from the Temple of Neptune in the Campus Martius at Rome. 978, 1089. Augur consulting the entrails

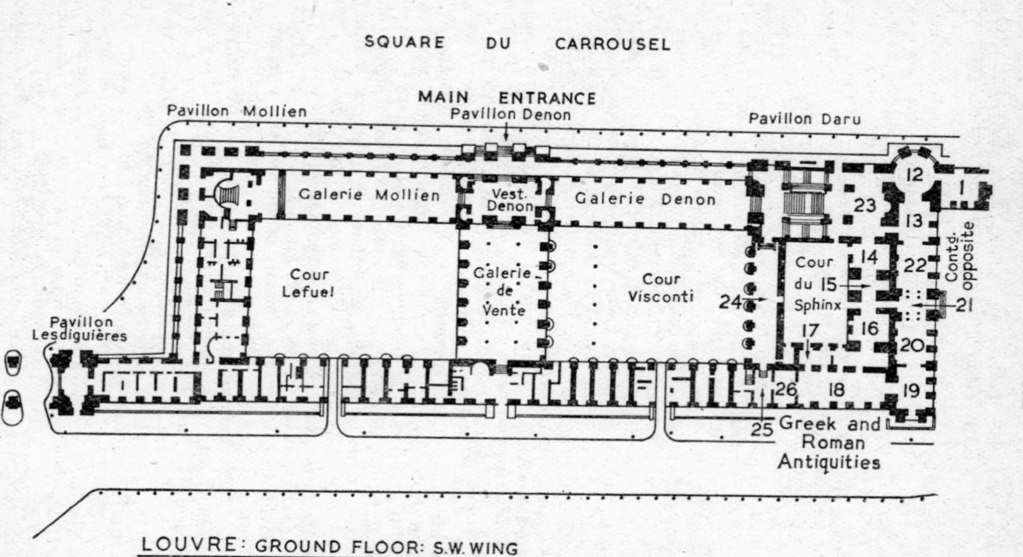

LOUVRE: GROUND FLOOR: S.W. WING

of a bull before the Temple of Jupiter in the Forum of Trajan, Rome (2nd cent. A.D.).—SALLE DES MUSES (Pl. 17). Roman busts of the Republican and Augustan periods. First bay on the right, *3445. Head of an unknown Roman woman (1st cent. B.C.).—SALLE D'AUGUSTE (Pl. 18), with ceiling

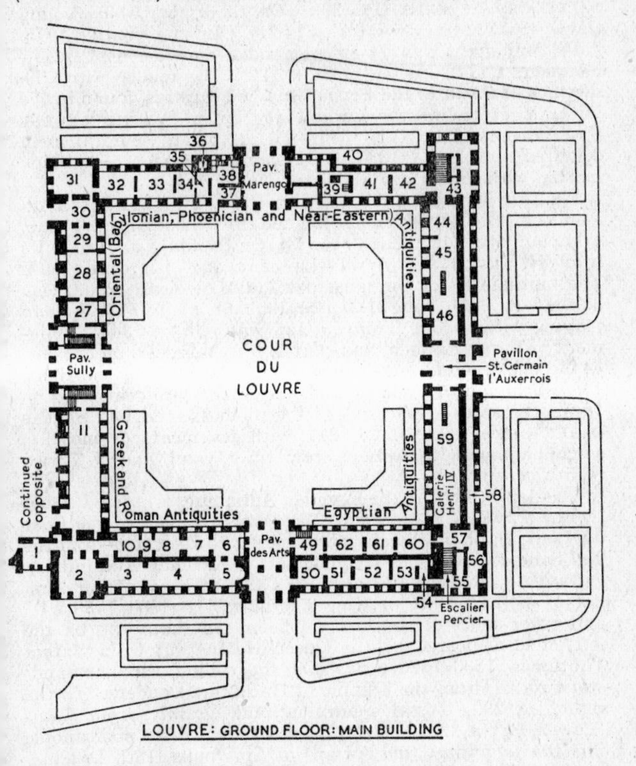

LOUVRE: GROUND FLOOR: MAIN BUILDING

painting by *Matout*. Roman busts of the 1st cent. B.C. to the 1st cent. A.D. At the far end, *1212. Statue of Augustus; on each side of it, 1210–11. Youths wearing the golden 'bulla.' On the left, *1207. Roman orator as Mercury (probably Julius Cæsar), an almost intact statue of Parian marble, found at Rome, and signed 'Cleomenes of Athens, son of Cleomenes,' on the tortoise at the foot. Busts of

Claudius, Caligula, and others.—SALLE DES ANTONINS (Pl. 19). This, and the three following rooms, with ceiling-paintings by *Romanelle*, contain busts and effigies of Emperors and others (1st–3rd cent.), including (l.) 1205. Antinous as Osiris, the eyes of which were represented by semi-precious stones.—SALLE DES SÉVÈRES (Pl. 20). On the right, 3440. Young Gaul.—SALLE DE LA PAIX (Pl. 21). In the centre, 1075. Julia Mammæa, mother of Alexander Severus, as Ceres.—SALLE DES SAISONS (Pl. 22). 3441. Bas-reliefs with the sacrifice of a bull to the Persian sun-god Mithras, found in the Mithraic grotto of the Capitol at Rome.—VESTIBULE DES PRISONNIERS BARBARES (Pl. 23). Roman sculptures in coloured marbles: *1354. Old fisherman, a statue in black marble with drapery in alabaster.

We turn left, past the Escalier Daru, into the SALLE DU PHŒNIX (Pl. 24), which is devoted to frescoes from Rome, Pompeii, etc. (1st cent. B.C.–1st cent. A.D.), and mosaics from N. Africa and Syria (1st cent. B.C.–4th cent. A.D.). The motifs are, for the most part, mythological. Paintings: on the left, P 23. Winged Genius (1st cent. B.C.); P 1. Woman playing with a goat (Pompeii, 1st cent. A.D.); *3443. Judgment of Paris (Antioch, 2nd cent. A.D.). Mosaics: on the left, 3442. The Phœnix (Antioch, 5th cent. A.D.); on the right, 1880. Triumph of Neptune and Amphitrite (3rd cent. A.D.).—Down the steps at the end of the room are the two SALLES D'ART CHRÉTIEN (Pl. 25, 26), with fragments of mosaics, sarcophagi, and inscriptions from Italy, Gaul, and N. Africa (4–5th cent.).

The department of the **Egyptian Antiquities** is entered either by the Pavillon St-Germain-l'Auxerrois (E. side of the Cour du Louvre), or by the staircase leading to the crypt from the 2nd Salle de Praxitélès (Pl. 6, Greek and Roman Antiquities).

CRYPT. On the staircase (l.), C 26. Stele of Antef, first herald in the service of King Thothmes III (1504–1450 B.C.) and other steles of the 12th Dynasty. In the crypt, on the left, stele dedicated by the Queen Hatshepsut to her father Thothmes (1530–1520 B.C.). On the ceiling, circular sandstone zodiac from the Temple of Hathor at Dendera. To the right, A 23. Colossal sphinx in pink granite, from Tanis (Lower Egypt, 22nd Dyn.). On the staircase, six canopic jars that contained the entrails of Apis bulls (18th Dyn.).—ROOM 1 (Pl. 49). A 24. Colossal statue of Seti II (19th Dyn.) in red sandstone.

ROOM 2 (Pl. 50). SALLE DU MASTABA. To the right, *Sacrificial chamber of the 'mastaba' or tomb of Akhout-Hetep, a high Egyptian dignitary (c. 2500 B.C., 5th Dyn.). The offerings of food and drink were placed on the table of pink granite, now in the recess immediately opposite the entrance. The sculptures in bas-relief, which are among the finest extant examples of the Ancient Empire, depict funeral scenes. Inscribed on the cylinder above the door are the occupant's names and titles.

Room 3 (Pl. 51). On each side of the entrance, two huge vases of the 3rd millennium B.C. A 39. Diorite statue of an official of the 3rd Dyn. (c. 2750 B.C.), seated on a large block. *Stele of King Djet, known as the Serpent King, as his name is represented here by a serpent. The sculpture was found in the king's tomb at Abydos (c. 3000 B.C.). In the recesses, bas-reliefs, and statues of the 4th and 3rd Dynasties.

Room 4 (Pl. 52). Old Empire (2723–2242 B.C.). Wall case in the S. passage, A 42. Stele of Nefertiabet, in painted stone (4th Dyn.). He is seated before a table of offerings, dressed in a leopard's skin. *Three fine columns in pink granite with palm-leaf capitals; the column on the left is marked with the name of King Uni (5th Dyn.); the other two, which were taken by Rameses II, are undoubtedly of the same period. In the centre, Sarcophagus in the 'palace façade' style, found at Abu Roash (5th Dyn.). Statues, steles, etc., of the 5th Dynasty.
Room 5 (Pl. 53). In the centre, small limestone **Figure of a scribe seated cross-legged, known as the 'Scribe Accroupi.'

This statue, one of the masterpieces of the Old Empire, is remarkable for its lifelike appearance. The eyes are of white quartz, rock crystal, and ebony.

In the wall-cases, alabaster and stone vessels dating from pre-dynastic times to the 6th Dyn. (c. 3400–2300 B.C.). In the passage, limestone group of the official Raherka, and his wife Merseankh (5th Dyn.).—Room 6 (Pl. 54). Middle Empire (2242–1580 B.C.). On the left (W. wall), fine limestone lintel of Sesostris III (1887–1850 B.C.); the king is shown making an offering of bread. In the recess (N. wall), A 20. Colossal royal statue in diorite. In a recess (E. wall), A 24. Sandstone statue of the scribe Mentuhotep. The reliefs on the E. wall should also be noted.—Room 7 (Pl. 55). On the right, in the cases: Statuette of Sesostris III, in green schist, and a fine head of the same king in grey granite (r. case); limestone dog's head; statue of a functionary of the 12–13th Dyn.; statue in black granite of Sesostris III, as an old man; wooden statue of the Chancellor Nakhti, from Assiut, one of the largest wooden funerary effigies known (c. 2100 B.C.); Sesostris III, as a young man. In the case (r.) of the third recess, **Statue of stucco and painted wood known as the 'Porteuse d'Auge.'

A young girl, clothed in a tunic of netted pearls, carries on her head a little trough containing one of the rear hooves of an ox—an essential offering in Egyptian ceremony.

A 47. Red sandstone group of two high priests of Ptah, from Memphis (12th Dyn.). Wall-cases: on the right,

Statuette of a royal concubine, the thumbs of which have been intentionally cut off; on the left, five amusing little wooden figures of girls carrying offerings.—ROOM 8 (Pl. 56). On the right, two sarcophagi in wood; note the two mystical eyes painted on the left hand, exterior side. Models of funerary ships for transporting the dead down the Nile. Opposite is a case containing a treasure of gold, silver, jewellery, etc., discovered in four bronze coffers in the foundations of the temple at Tod. It was marked in the name of King Amenemhat II (1938–1904 B.C.).

ROOM 9 (Pl. 57). To the left, limestone statue of an Apis bull (30th Dyn.; 378–341 B.C.). A 10. Statue of the scribe Sethi, kneeling, and holding a naos containing a figure of Osiris (9th Dyn.). N. wall, huge basalt statue of Isis (Roman period). Around the room, canopic jars, steles, statues, etc.—The Galerie Epigraphique (ROOM 10) is temporarily closed.

GALERIE HENRI IV (Pl. 59). The end walls are divided into bays, containing sculpture, sarcophagi, naos, etc. Outstanding among these are: E. wall (r.), 3rd Bay, D 1. Sarcophagus of Rameses III, 'the last of the heroes' (20th Dyn.), the lid of which is at Cambridge; 5th Bay, Painted bas-relief of Seti I and the goddess Hathor, from the tomb of the former (19th Dyn.); 7th Bay, D 31. Red granite fragment from the base of the obelisk of Luxor, with four cynocephali adoring the rising sun and cartouches of Rameses II. W. wall, 2nd Bay, A 18. Base and feet of a huge pink granite statue of Amenophis III (18th Dyn.). A list of the peoples he subdued is inscribed on the base; 3rd Bay, A 19. Colossal head of Amenophis III, the right half of the face considerably eroded by sand and wind.—The crypt (centre), which leads to the Department of Asiatic Antiquities, contains (l.) the *Sarcophagus of the Priest T'aho, with a frieze of jackals round the top, outside, and figures of Nephthys and Isis at the head and foot within (26th Dyn.). On the right, in the recess, Wooden statue of Osiris with the diadem of Alef; in all probability this statue was actually worshipped as an idol.

We retrace our steps to R. 9 (at the foot of the Escalier Percier which leads to the Egyptian rooms on the first floor), and turn right into ROOM 11 (Pl. 60), which contains objects discovered by Mariette in 1851, in the Serapeum at Memphis. In the centre, six of the limestone sphinxes which border the approach to the Serapeum for more than 250 yards. The big sphinx at the back (Ptolemaic period) comes from Medamoud. Around the room, steles of Apis bulls, supposedly the incarnation of Ptah, the great god of Memphis; also sculptures, including the limestone statue of the god Bes (r.), from the temple of Nectanebo. The four canopic jars contained the entrails of the two Apis bulls of the 18th Dynasty.

Rooms 13, 14 (Pl. 61, 62) are devoted to objects of the Græco-Roman and Copto-Byzantine periods, following the last indigenous dynasty.

Oriental Antiquities. The visitor may enter either through the Pavillon St-Germain-l'Auxerrois (Egyptian Antiquities) or through the Salle des Caryatides (Greek and Roman Antiquities) to reach the Crypte Sully, which is situated underneath the Pavillon de l'Horloge or de Sully.

Crypte Sully. Sculptural and architectural fragments from Palestine, Carthage, Arabia, and Syria. 2nd Bay (r.), **Moabite Stone, or stele of Mesha, King of Moab (896 B.C.), found in 1868 in a remote village E. of the Dead Sea.

The 34-line inscriptions, recording victories over the Israelites, in the reigns of Omri, Ahab, and Ahaziah, is one of the most important, if not the earliest example of the alphabetic writing which has come down to us from the Phœnicians through Greek and Latin.

Room 1 (Pl. 27). Sumerian antiquities discovered by the Sarzac, Cros, and Parrot expeditions at Lagash (Mesopotamia), and Semitic reliefs and sculptures of the Akkadian dynasty (3000 B.C.) recovered by the J. de Morgan expedition at Susa. Wall-case 1. Sumerian objects of the 4th–3rd millennium; note the small limestone plumed figure from Tello (Chaldæa). 2nd shelf. On the right, **Stele of the Vultures, commemorating the victory of Eannadu, a Sumerian prince, over his rival city, Umma. In the centre, *Vase of beaten silver with a decoration of animals in relief, known as the 'Vase d'Entemena' (Case 8).—Room 2, Sumer (Pl. 28). Sumerian antiquities of c. 2400 B.C. E. and W. walls, diorite statues of Gudea, ruler of Lagash. On the left, two large clay cylinders covered with a cuneiform inscription relating to Gudea's skill as an architect (Case 13). Case 14. *Drinking goblet belonging to Gudea, decorated with two intertwined serpents and two winged dragons with scorpions' tails (dedicated to Ningizzida, patron-god of Gudea). Case 16. *Alabaster statuette of Ur-Ningirsu, son of Gudea.

Room 3, Marib and Larsa (Pl. 29). Objects from the Temple of the goddess Ishtar (c. 3000 B.C.) at Marib, including an alabaster *Statue of the intendant of Marib, Ebih-Il (Case 9); head of Ishtar (Case 8); on the wall, two mural *Paintings from the Palace, representing Ishtar investing King Zimrili with the regal powers, and a sacrificial scene. Two bronzes, one representing a man on one knee, his face and hands covered in gold leaf, the other a group of three rampant ibex, with horns interlaced, from Larsa (Case 13). *Ceremonial Vase from Larsa, with Ishtar, and figures of animals (Case 5).

ROOM 4, Babylon (Pl. 30). In the centre, **Code of Hammurabi, a cone of black basalt, covered with the closely written text of the 282 laws embracing practically every aspect of Babylonian life of c. 2000 B.C. At the top of the cone is a bas-relief representing the god Shamash dictating the law to King Hammurabi. Along the E. wall, Statues of the Princes of Ashnunnak, a rival state near Babylon. The statues were captured by Shutruk-Nakhuntè, a Babylonian prince, who erased the original inscriptions and substituted his own (c. 1100 B.C.). In the window recess, Babylonian 'kudurrus,' or boundary-stones, with inscriptions.

ROOMS 5–13 contain mainly the results of excavations made at Susa (Mesopotamia). R. 5, Iran (Pl. 31). Bronzes and ceramics of 4th–2nd millennium B.C. (Case 1); *Ceramics from Susa, known as 'Style I,' of the 4th millennium B.C. (Cases 2 and 3). Case 5. Jewellery, goldsmiths' work, silverware, etc., from all periods and regions of the Near East. The ornamental *Vase-handle of silver inlaid with gold, representing a little ibex, is particularly beautiful.—ROOM 6, Susa (Pl. 32). Exhibits exclusively from Susa. In the centre, bronze *Statue of Queen Napir-Asu, wife of King Untash-Gas of Susa (1500 B.C.). On the left (Case 5), *Ritual scene in bronze, known as the Sit Shamshi, a ceremony celebrating the rising of the Sun. Opposite (Case 4), Alabaster *Vase, known as the 'Vase à la Cachette,' the other objects displayed in the case were hidden inside it.—SALLE DU CHAPITEAU (Pl. 33). *Capital in grey marble from the Palace of Artaxerxes II at Susa (405–362 B.C.). In the centre (Case 1), lion in enamelled terra-cotta (1100 B.C.); on the walls, reliefs of winged bulls, lions, etc., in enamelled tiles. On the right (Case 6), two drinking horns, one in silver, the other in bronze. —ROOMS 8–11 (Pl. 34–37). Friezes of enamelled tiles (*Archers, griffins, and winged sphinxes) from the Palace of Darius I at Susa (6–4th cent. B.C.). In R. 10, Bronze utensils, weapons, and ceramics from Luristan.—ROOM 12, Sassanid and Mussulman antiquities (3rd–4th cent. A.D.).—We descend to the Crypte Marengo; on the right (R. 13) of the staircase are four large earthenware pots from Susa (3rd–1st cent. B.C.).

CRYPTE MARENGO. Phœnician sarcophagi, including (l.) the *Sarcophagus of Eshmunazar, king of Sidon (5th cent. B.C.). Although Egyptian in style, the inscription, a long malediction against any eventual violator of the tomb, is in Phœnician.—ROOM 14. Busts and funerary reliefs from tombs found at Palmyra, in Syria (2nd–3rd cent. A.D.).— We ascend to ROOM 16 (Pl. 39), which is devoted to Cypriot ceramics, and ROOM 17, containing objects excavated at Dura-Europos, including (l.) a small headless statue of

Aphrodite. On the right of the staircase (R. 15) are Phœnician sculptures from Um-el-Awamid and Sidon.

Room 18 (Pl. 41). Collections from the great Phœnician cities of Baalbek, Sidon, Tyre, Byblos, and Ras-Shamra. Case 1, Glassware, terra-cotta figures, etc.; Case 2, Bronzes, including statuettes of gods, warriors, etc. Two earthenware Mycenean jars (15–16th cent. B.C.), and a sphinx dedicated by Ita, daughter of the Pharaoh Amenemhat II (1938–1904 B.C.). The sphinx was originally in 522 pieces. Case 4. In the centre, statuette of Jupiter of Heliopolis, flanked by two bulls; Votive hand and other examples of the same cult. Case 8. Tools and weapons from Ras-Shamra (15–14th cent. B.C.). In the centre of the room, bust of the Pharaoh Osorkoni (924–895 B.C.). On the walls are steles, reliefs, and architectural fragments.—Room 19 (Pl. 42). In the centre, huge monolithic ritual vat, known as the *Vase of Amathus, from a sanctuary in Cyprus (6–4th cent. B.C.). A bull is represented on each of the four handles; around the room and on the walls, funerary statues, heads, and reliefs from Cyprus; in the cases (1–8), terra-cotta figurines, and ceramics.—Room 20 (Pl. 43). Hittite and Cappadocian antiquities. On each side of the door, three little bas-reliefs from Tell Halaf. Winged genius (l.); hunter drawing his bow (r.); and a lion rampant (r.). To the left, statues of the divinities Hada and Ishtar standing on a bull and a lion. To the right, head of a divinity, from Djabboul; steles, etc. Wall cases with ceramics, bronze animals, small stele of the god Teshub (Tell Ahmar); to the right, Hittite votive shoe; head of a bull, in terra-cotta, from Boghaz-Keui; rein-guides in bronze (Case 2).—In the passage to R. 21, bronze covering of a column from Khorsabad; statuette of the demon Pazuzu, from Assurdan; jewellery, etc. (Case 1); stele of Sargon II, King of Assyria, recording his campaign of 714 B.C.; heads of demons, etc. (Case 2).—Rooms 21–23 (Pl. 44–46) are mainly devoted to reliefs (7–9th cent. B.C.) from the great Assyrian palaces at Nimrud (Nos. 1–11), Khorsabad (Nos. 12–58), and Nineveh (Nos. 59–74). In the cases (r.) in R. 21, carved *Ivories from Arslan-Tash. In the four corners of R. 22, Winged *Bulls (7th cent. B.C.) from Khorsabad, each with an extra leg, for the sake of symmetry. Note especially the reliefs of King Assurnasirpal (No. 7) and King Tiglath-pileser III (No. 9); also a fine bronze lion from Khorsabad. The desk cases (r.) contain fragments of wall paintings from Tell Ahmar.

The staircase in the centre of the room leads to the department of Egyptian Antiquities. The first half of the Crypt (which contains the famous 'idol' of Osiris, see p. 130) is decorated with reliefs from the Palace of Assurbanipal at Nineveh. The two bulls at the head of the stairs come from the temple at Arslan-Tash (8th cent. B.C.).

First Floor

To reach the **Picture Galleries** we pass through the Galerie Denon and ascend the Escalier Daru at the far end. On the top landing is the magnificent 'Winged Victory' (p. 123).

From the landing we turn right into the Salles des Fresques. 1st Bay: *Botticelli*, Frescoes from the Villa Lemmi, near Florence. 2nd Bay: *Luini*, Nativity, Adoration of the Magi, two frescoes from an oratory near Milan. Between them, *Fra Angelico*, Christ on the Cross. On the right, *Ant. Rizzo* (d. 1499), Two statues of pages, from a tomb in Venice.—At the farther end is the Salon Carré, which is devoted to paintings of the Spanish School, including *Pedro Diaz of Oviedo*, Robing of St. Ildefonso by the Virgin; *El Greco*, St. Louis, King of France; *Murillo*, '*Angels' Kitchen' (the Legend of San Diego), *Beggar Boy.

We turn right into the Grande Galerie, which is divided into bays, and contains a large proportion of the paintings by Old Masters, arranged in schools. At certain points grey granite columns and porphyry vases separate the schools.

In the first two bays, the S. wall (l.) is devoted to the Florentine, Umbrian, and Lombard Schools, the N. wall to the Venetian and other N. Italian Schools. Section A. S. wall: *Botticini*, *Virgin in Glory; *School of Botticelli*, Virgin and Child with St. John the Baptist. N. wall: *Genoese School*, Triptych of the Annunciation (15th cent.).—Section B. S. wall: *Mantegna*, *Wisdom and Virtue triumphant over the Vices, and *Parnassus, with Mars and Venus and the Muses. N. wall: *Mantegna*, **Virgin of Victory, painted by him as court painter at Mantua to commemorate the victory at Fornovo (1495) over Charles VIII of France.—Section C. S. wall: *Lorenzo Costa*, Triumph of Peace, represented by the Court of Isabella d'Este in the Garden of the Muses, Combat of Love and Chastity.—N. wall: *Bartolomeo Veneto*, Circumcision.—Section D. S. wall: *Perugino*, Virgin and two Saints; Works by *Luca* and *Francesco Signorelli*. N. wall: Paintings by *Gentile Bellini* (the elder brother of Giovanni) and his school.—Section E. S. wall: Works of the Umbrian and Lombard Schools including, *Francia*, The Crucifixion. N. wall: ***Giorgione*, 'Fête Champêtre,' an idyllic group, one of the masterpieces of this short-lived Venetian; ***Titian*, Man with a Glove, a fine portrait of 1518.—Section F. S. wall: Works by *Leonardo da Vinci* and his pupils: Annunciation, Madonna and Child, Jesus and St. Anne, *Virgin of the Rocks, probably earlier (1482) than the similar composition in London.—N. wall: *Titian*, Virgin and Saints, St. Jerome; works by *Moretto da Brescia*, *Lorenzo Lotto*, and others.—Section G. S. wall: Works by

Andrea Solario, Marco d'Oggiono, and others, of the School of Leonardo da Vinci.—N. wall: *Titian,* Virgin with the Rabbit (c. 1518); *Tintoretto,* Paradise, a cartoon for the colossal painting in the Doge's Palace in Venice, Portrait of a Man, Self-portrait (1590); works by *Paolo Veronese* and *Palma Giovane.*

Central Tribune. S. wall: *Leonardo da Vinci,* **Monna Lisa, known as the 'La Gioconda,' a portrait of the third wife of Francesco del Giocondo.

Leonardo worked intermittently on this portrait for four years from 1500. In spite of drastic restoration at different periods, this remains one of the outstanding achievements of the Italian Renaissance. In August 1911 it was stolen from the Salon Carré by a thief disguised as a workman, but was recovered in Florence in December 1913.

Titian, Young woman at her toilet, *Allegory in honour of Alfonso of Avalos (c. 1533). N. wall: *Titian,* *Portrait of Francis I of France; *Raphael,* **Portrait of Baldassare Castiglione, a fine work of his latest years, Portrait of Joan of Aragon.

4th Bay. Section A. S. wall: *Raphael,* St. George and the Dragon, **Madonna, known as the 'Belle Jardinière,' an early work (1507) of delicate and poetic charm, St. Michael overcoming Satan, Two portraits of the school of Raphael. N. wall: *Correggio,* *Mystic marriage of St. Catherine, *Jupiter and Antiope, Allegories of Virtue and Vice.—Section B. S. wall: *Nicolo dell' Abate,* The Abduction of Proserpine; *Bronzino,* Portrait of a Sculptor; *Pontormo,* Holy Family. N. wall: *Andrea del Sarto,* Holy Family; *Sebastiano del Piombo,* Visitation; *G. C. Procaccini,* Holy Family; *Paolo Zaccia,* Viol Player.—The remainder of this bay and the next two bays are occupied by works of the Bolognese Schools and other 'Eclectic' Schools of the 17th cent., with good examples of *Caravaggio, Domenichino, Guido Reni, Luca Giordano,* the *Carracci, Salvator Rosa, Guercino,* and others. In the 7th and 8th Bays are some charming paintings by *Guardi* for festive occasions at Venice, a good portrait by *Maratta,* and a typical *Magnasco* (Feast of the Gypsies); also two fine works by *Canaletto,* typical examples of *G. B. Tiepolo,* and views of Rome by *Panini.*

The Salle des Etats, reopened June 1950, contains paintings of the Venetian School. *Carpaccio,* St. Stephen preaching; *Iacopo Bellini,* Madonna and donor (probably Sigismondo Malatesta); *Giov. Bellini,* Christ blessing, an early work; *Mantegna,* St. Sebastian; *Lor. Lotto,* St. Jerome (a very early panel of 1500); *Cima,* Madonna and saints, large and finely coloured; *Palma Vecchio,* Annunciation to the Shepherds (with forged signature of Titian); *Titian,* Holy Family, Man with a belt (a little later than the better-known Man with a glove); *Tintoretto* (or *Iac. Bassano*), Man holding a handkerchief; *Seb. del Piombo*, Visitation (1521).

Some of the finest Italian paintings are not yet on view but will be exhibited in the rooms adjoining the Salle des Etats. The following is a summary of some of the most notable works: *Perugino*, Holy Family with St. Catherine, Combat of Love and Chastity, St. Sebastian; *Raphael*, St. George and the dragon, St. Michael (an early work painted on the back of a chessboard for the Duke of Urbino); *Raphael* (or *Perugino*), Apollo and Marsyas; *Giulio Romano*, Madonna with the Blue Diadem; *Mainardi*, Young man and woman; *Leonardo da Vinci*, Annunciation, St. John the Baptist, Lucrezia Crivelli; *Boltraffio*, Madonna of the Casio Family; *Ambr. de Predis*, Bianca Maria Sforza (1492); *Bianchi-Ferrari* (master of Correggio), Madonna with St. Benedict; *Andrea del Sarto*, Charity; *Fra Bartolomeo*, Holy Family and saints (1511).

We retrace our steps from the W. end of the Grande Galerie and turn left into the PETITES SALLES, which are at present devoted to a temporary exhibition of the Flemish and Dutch Schools. The small staircase (l.) leads to four other rooms on the second floor, containing a temporary exhibition of paintings of the British and German Schools.

The following is a summary of the chief paintings of these schools, which will be on view when the arrangement of the picture galleries is complete.

FLEMISH SCHOOL: *Jan van Eyck*, Madonna, with the Chancellor Nicolas Rolin, a magnificent work (before 1430) taken by Napoleon I from Autun cathedral; *Memling*, Portrait of an old lady, Mystic marriage of St. Catherine, John du Celier presented by St. John (c. 1475); *Van der Weyden*, Salvator Mundi, with saints, a remarkably fine triptych; *Quentin Matsys*, Banker and his wife, the original of a well-known type; *Mabuse*, Jean Carondelet, Chancellor of Flanders (1517), Madonna; *Hieronymus Bosch*, Ship of Fools; *Antony Mor*, Dwarf of Charles V. *Rubens* is represented by many fine examples including 21 large allegorical paintings of the life of Marie de Médicis, designed in 1621–25 for the Luxembourg Palace, and two sketches for this series (the Fates spinning the web of life, and the Triumph of Truth); also Thomyris with the head of Cyrus, Ixion deceived by Juno; many religious subjects, including the Flight of Lot from Sodom, Abraham's Sacrifice, and the Adoration of the Magi; and several fine portraits, including the ambassador Henri de Vicq, and Helena Fourment, the artist's second wife. *Van Dyck* is equally well, if not so copiously, represented, with a Madonna and portraits of Charles I, a magnificent work of 1625, of the Elector Palatine and Prince Rupert, of the Duke of Lennox as Paris, and of Francisco de Moncada, commander of Spanish troops in the Netherlands. Here also are several good examples of *Jordaens* and *Teniers*.

DUTCH SCHOOL. *Rembrandt*, Hendrikje Stoffels and her child as Venus and Cupid (1662), and an even more striking portrait of Hendrikje herself (1652), The artist at his easel, The artist's brother Adrian, Carcase of an ox (repellent but masterly), Christ at Emmaus (1648), the most poignant and effective of his religious works, The Good Samaritan, Holy Family in the carpenter's shop (1640) ; *J. van Ruysdael*, Sunny landscape ; *Frans Hals*, Lady in a black dress, The Beresteyn family, Portrait of Descartes, Gipsy girl, vivacious and popular, Itinerant painter ; *B. van der Helst*, The Reepmaker family ; *Cuyp*, Starting for the ride, Herdsman with cattle ; *A. Brouwer*, The smoker, The operation ; *N. Maes*, Grace before meat ; *J. Steen*, Family meal, 'Bad company' ; *P. de Hooch*, Interior, Lady playing cards ; *Jan Vermeer*, Lacemaker ; *Paul Potter*, Cows and sheep in a field, Horses at a cottage door ; *G. Dou*, Grocer's shop, Dropsical woman, Dentist ; *Terborch*, The gallant soldier, Concert ; *Metsu*, Music lesson, and other good examples.

BRITISH SCHOOL. *Romney*, Sir J. Stanley ; *Bonington*, Francis I and the Duchesse d'Etampes, Coast of Normandy ; *Lawrence*, J. J. Angerstein and his wife, Mary Palmer ; *Raeburn*, Capt. Hay of Spott ; *Constable*, Hampstead Heath ; *Whistler*, Portrait of his mother, "an arrangement in black and gray."

GERMAN SCHOOL. *Hans Holbein the Younger*, Erasmus, an outstanding portrait painted for Sir Thomas More, Nicholas Kratzer, The astronomer (1528), Anne of Cleves (1539) ; *Dürer*, An old man (1520) ; and a small but interesting selection of primitives.

Among the SPANISH PAINTINGS not yet arranged are : *El Greco*, Christ on the Cross ; *Ribera*, Club-footed beggar-boy ; *Murillo*, Immaculate Conception, the best of the innumerable versions of this subject, brought from Spain by Soult ; *Velazquez*, Infanta Margarita (c. 1655), Mariana of Austria (c. 1651) ; *Zurbaran*, Funeral of a bishop.

Beyond the landing of the Escalier Mollien, the GALERIE MOLLIEN is devoted to the French Romantic School of the 19th cent. with many large works of greater historical than artistic significance. *Courbet*, Burial at Ornans (1851), The Studio ; *Géricault*, *Raft of the 'Medusa' ; *Delacroix*, Capture of Constantinople by the Crusaders, Algerian women ; *Chassériau*, The two sisters (1845) ; *Devéria*, Birth of Henry IV at the Château de Pau ; *Delacroix*, Liberty guiding the people (July 28th, 1830) ; *Gros*, Napoleon at the battle of Eylau

(1807), with portraits of his marshals; *Géricault*, Officer of the Chasseurs de la Garde; *Courbet*, Battle of the stags; *Géricault*, Wounded cuirassier; *Decamps*, Defeat of the Cimbri (1833).—This collection is continued in the SALLE DENON. *Thomas Couture*, Romans of the Decadence, well known but tiresome; *Chassériau*, The chaste Susanna; *Courbet*, Roe-deer's haunt; *Troyon*, Oxen returning to the farm (1859); *Ziem*, Venice.—The GALERIE DARU contains French paintings of the classical school. *Prud'hon*, Christ on the Cross, Empress Josephine; *David*, Rape of the Sabines, characteristically lifeless, Coronation of Napoleon I in Notre-Dame (1804); *Girodet-Trioson*, Atala (from Chateaubriand's romance); *Gros*, Christine Boyer; *Gérard*, Marquise Visconti; *David*, Madame Récamier, in a familiar pose; *Gros*, Napoleon visiting the plague-stricken at Jaffa; *Guérin*, Return of Marcus Sextus (1799); *Ingres*, Apotheosis of Homer, designed for a ceiling (1827); *Prud'hon*, Justice and Divine Vengeance pursuing Crime, painted in 1808 for the Palais de Justice.

Many of the French paintings are not yet on view in the Louvre, and the following is a summary of those which have yet to be arranged, up to the mid-19th century. A selection of these earlier paintings (changed at intervals) is to be seen at the Petit-Palais in the Champs-Elysées (Rte. 2), others are temporarily on the 2nd floor of the Louvre (see below), while the splendid collection of paintings of the late 19th cent. Impressionist School (including the Camondo Collection) is on view at the Jeu de Paume (Rte. 28).

FRENCH PRIMITIVES AND 16TH CENT. SCHOOL. *Malouel* and *Bellechose*, Last Communion and Martyrdom of St. Denis, from Dijon (15th cent.); *Master of Moulins*, St. Mary Magdalen and donor, Pierre Duke of Bourbon; *Jehan Fouquet*, Two miniatures taken from the Book of Hours now at Chantilly; *Nic. Froment* (?), King René and Jeanne de Laval; *Fr. Clouet*, Pierre Quthe (1562), one of the few works certainly by this artist; *16th cent. French School*, Portrait of Francis I, and many other remarkable early works.

FRENCH 17TH CENT. SCHOOL. Several good works by the *Brothers Le Nain* (Family group, 1642, etc.); *Philippe de Champaigne*, Richelieu, Arnauld d'Andilly, Sister Angélique of Port Royal; *N. Poussin*, Diogenes, Portrait of the artist, and many other characteristic works; *Claude*, Seaport, Ford, and several other typical landscapes; *Rigaud*, Louis XIV, and other portraits; *Mignard*, Mme de Maintenon, Portrait of the artist, etc.; portraits by *Largillière*, *Nanteuil*, and others.

FRENCH 18TH CENT. SCHOOLS. *Watteau*, L'Embarquement pour Cythère, Le Faux Pas, L'Indifférent, Jupiter and Antiope, Pastoral scene, Gay company in a park, and the famous

'Gilles'; *Boucher*, The Graces, a brilliant sketch, Toilet of Venus, and other characteristic works; *Fragonard*, Coresus and Callirrhoë, La chemise enlevée, Sleeping Bacchante, Music lesson; *Pater*, La toilette; *Chardin*, The castle of cards; also works by *Nattier*, *Lancret*, *Boilly*, *Greuze*, and others. Pastels by *Quentin de la Tour*, *Perronneau*, *Chardin*, and *Rosalba Carriera*.

French Schools of the mid-19th Cent. *Corot*, Dance of shepherdesses, The road, and many other fine landscapes, Lady in blue, Peasants' house near Paris; *Millet*, 'La Tricoteuse,' Girl churning; *Daubigny*, Spring; *Meissonier*, "Les Amateurs de Peinture" (1860), Campaign of 1814, with portraits of generals (1864); also works by *Fromentin*, *Decamps*, *Isabey*, *Courbet*, *Géricault*, *Th. Rousseau*, *Troyon*, *Delacroix*, and *Dupré*; and drawings of *Ingres* and *Delacroix*.

We leave the Galerie Daru by the E. door; on the left of the doorway is the *Virgin with Angels, by *Cimabue* (Florentine School, c. 1272–1302). To the right is the Salle des Sept Mètres, which is devoted to the Sienese and Florentine Schools of Italian painting (late 13th–late 15th cent.), arranged in five bays.

1st Bay: *Taddeo di Bartolo*, Crucifixion; *Bartolo di Maestro Fredi*, Presentation in the Temple; *Simone Martini*, *Bearing of the Cross; *Bernardo Daddi*, Madonna with angels, the Annunciation, and the Crucifixion; *Lorenzo Monaco*, Jesus on the Mount of Olives, and the Holy Women at the Tomb, a diptych.—*Giotto*, *St. Francis of Assisi; *Fra Angelico*, **Coronation of the Virgin, an early and fascinating work, with many saints and their emblems, and (in the predella) the Legend of St. Dominic.—*School of Verrocchio*, Madonna; *Filippo Lippi*, Madonna with St. Frediano and St. Augustine; *Girolamo di Benvenuto*, Judgment of Paris; *Fra Angelico*, Martyrdom of SS. Cosmas and Damian; *Paolo Uccello*, Battle of San Romano; *Pisanello*, *Ginevra d'Este; *Lorenzo di Credi*, Madonna and Child; *Domenico Ghirlandajo*, The Visitation.—*Botticelli* (?), Madonna with five angels; *Benozzo Gozzoli* (Fra Angelico's favourite pupil), Triumph of St. Thomas Aquinas; *Piero di Cosimo*, Madonna with a dove; *Botticelli*, Madonna of the Guidi, Portrait of a young man (two works ascribed to the master's youth); *Francesco Botticini*, Madonna; *Francesco di Giorgio*, Rape of Europa.

Part of the French School (16–18th cent.) is on temporary exhibition in four rooms on the second floor reached by the staircase in Salle A (opposite the landing of the Escalier Percier) of the Egyptian Antiquities on the first floor.

From the Salle des Sept Mètres, bear right across the landing of the Escalier Daru, mount the steps (l.), and pass along the corridor into the Rotonde d'Apollon (mosaic floor by

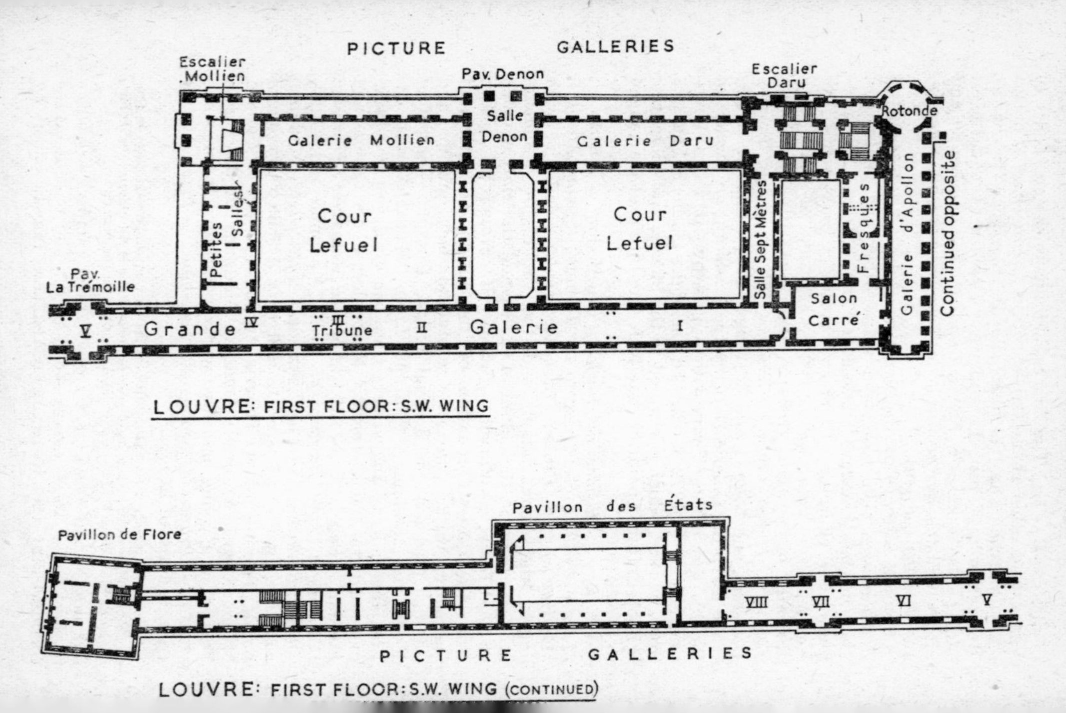

LOUVRE: FIRST FLOOR: S.W. WING

LOUVRE: FIRST FLOOR: S.W. WING (CONTINUED)

Belloni, in the centre, 'Apollon de Lillebonne,' a Roman statue in gilded bronze). On our right is the entrance to the GALERIE D'APOLLON, with a 17th cent. grille from the Château of Maisons-sur-Seine. Built under Henri IV, burned down in 1661, but rebuilt under Louis XIV by Charles Lebrun, this magnificent gallery is finely proportioned and well lighted,

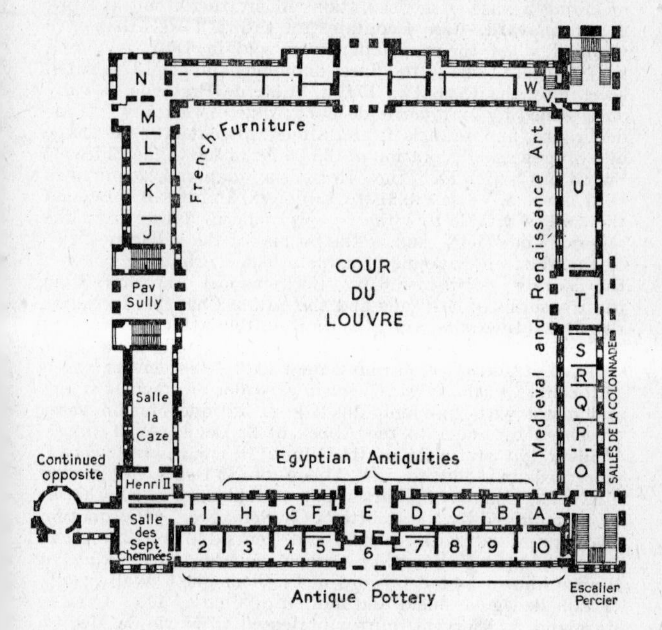

LOUVRE: FIRST FLOOR: MAIN BUILDING

and the decorations, including the ceiling-paintings (notably the central subject, Apollo's Victory over the Python, by *Delacroix*), are admirable.

The glass cases contain a magnificent collection, of the highest historical and artistic worth, of **Medieval and Renaissance Goldsmiths' Work,** gems, objects in rock crystal, etc. In front of the entrance is a large Florentine mosaic table. In the centre, Cases 1, 3, and 5 contain what is left of the remarkable collection of gems belonging to Louis XIV. Case 1.

Semi-precious vessels of lapis-lazuli, jade, amethyst, amber, and red and green jasper. Case 2. Bronze statuette of Charlemagne (9th cent.); *Crown of St. Louis (c. 1255), presented to St. Louis by the Dominicans of Liége; 'Ring of St. Louis' (15th cent. gold ring); Crown of Napoleon 1. Case 3. French rock crystals from the royal collection, including a vase with decorations illustrating Noah at work in his vineyard. Case 4 contains the Crown Jewels that were retained when the remainder were sold in 1887, including the '*Regent,' one of the finest diamonds known (137 carats), bought by the Regent in 1717; 'Côte de Bretagne,' a ruby once owned by Marguerite de Foix, Anne of Brittany, Claude de France, and Francis I, and afterwards cut into the shape of a dragon as a decoration of the Order of the Golden Fleece; Sword of Charles IX; the 'Hortensia' diamond, acquired in 1691. Case 5. Vessels in agate, sardonyx, and basalt. Beyond the case is a table-top (the base is modern) dating from the reign of Louis XIV, and at the far end of the gallery are two of the thirteen Savonnerie carpets which originally covered the flooring. Wall-case 6 (r.). Ecclesiastical ornaments from the treasuries of St-Denis and the Sainte Chapelle, including two Byzantine reliquary plaques from the latter; **Antique (? Egyptian) porphyry vase mounted in silver gilt as an eagle, with a Latin inscription round the neck; **Serpentine paten (9th cent.; Carlovingian ?) set in a border of precious stones and inlaid with gold dolphins; Four antique Muslim vases presented by Suger to the Abbey of St-Denis. Wall-case 7. **Silver gilt statuette of the Virgin (French; 14th cent.), presented in 1339 to the Abbey of St-Denis by Jeanne d'Evreux, widow of Charles IV; *Gold sceptre of Charles IV surmounted by a statuette of Charlemagne; **Coronation gold spurs, set with garnets and fleurs-de-lys (12th cent., restored in the 19th cent.); Coronation sword of the kings of France known as the 'Sword of Charlemagne.' Wall-case 8. *Enamelled gold shield and morion of Charles IX; Candlestick and rock crystal mirror presented to Marie de Médicis on her marriage to Henri IV (1600). Wall-cases 9 and 10. Reliquaries and church plate from the Chapel of the Order of the Saint-Esprit, founded by Henri III in 1578.

From the Rotonde d'Apollon we turn right into the SALLE DES BIJOUX. In the cases are exhibits from the *Treasure of Boscoreale (near Pompeii), a collection of silver objects discovered in 1895 in a fine state of preservation on the site of a villa overwhelmed by an eruption of Vesuvius (79 A.D.). Beyond is the SALLE DES SEPT-CHEMINÉES, which contains the two huge but unemotional paintings by *Paolo Veronese*: Christ in the House of Simon (presented to Louis XIV by the Venetian Republic in 1665), and the Marriage at Cana (painted

—SALLE H. Ptolemaic and Coptic Periods. Case 1. Ptolemaic pottery, and terra-cotta figures; Coptic liturgical bronzes, pottery, glass, ivory, and ornamental woodwork; Jewellery and other precious objects, including a priest's ceremonial breast-plate decorated with a winged scarab.

Returning through the Salle Clarac again, we turn right into the SALLE HENRI II which is devoted to **Etruscan Pottery,** so called because vases of this type were first found in greater quantities in Etruria than in Greece. In the cases are examples of Etruscan ware in black and red, decorated with reliefs and paintings. On the right, Terra-cotta sarcophagus from a tomb at Cervetri (Campana collection; 6th cent. B.C.); six Etruscan terra-cotta **Panels from Cervetri, apparently from a burial chamber (600 B.C.), and representing scenes of death and sepulchral ceremonies.—The SALLE LA CAZE contains **Greek, Roman, and Etruscan Bronzes,** jewellery, arms, utensils, etc. On the right of the doorway, Roman cockerel, found at Lyons; Case 25. Apollo, the 'messenger.' In the centre, Hermes (Roman); on the left, '*Apollo of Piombino,' an antique Greek statue retrieved from the sea near Piombino, probably a replica of a work by Kanakhos (c. 500 B.C.); Case 21. Mirrors (Greek; 4th cent. B.C.); Cases, 15, 16. Bronze figurines (Roman); Case 1. Archaic Greek statuettes, including the '*Javelin Thrower'; Cases 12, 13. Statuettes and busts from Roman Gaul. The central case contains a magnificent collection of *Jewellery and goldsmiths' work, from all the periods and regions covered by the other exhibits. Cases 19–20. Syrian, Egyptian, and Græco-Roman art; Case 3. Hellenistic art, including two statuettes of Aphrodite; Case 26. Dionysos, a satyr, a flute-player, and Mænads dancing (Alexandrian style); Case 23. Engraved Etruscan mirrors (3–2nd cent. B.C.). Near the far end, '*Apollon de Lillebonne,' a bronze statue found near the Roman theatre at Lillebonne, in 1823. Cases 4, 2. Statuettes, including a winged Athene (Etruscan) and a Hercules resting (Greek; 5th cent.); Case 28. Greek bronzes, including the '*Triumphant Athlete,' an example of the best period.

In the PAVILLON SULLY is the collection of **Muslim Art,** which comprises exhibits from Syria, Mesopotamia, Persia, Turkey, Egypt, N. Africa, and Spain (6–14th cent.). The wall-cases contain faience and ceramics from Persia, Syria, Egypt, and Asia Minor. S. wall (l.), Fragment of a Persian silk winding-sheet embroidered in silver and gold, called the 'Suaire de St. Josse,' and said to have served as a covering for a relic of this saint.—By the windows, Weapons from Persia and Afghanistan (6–7th cent.); carved ivories from Spain, etc. In the centre, Case containing enamelled glass mosque lamps from Egypt (14th cent.). N. wall (r.), Magnificent Persian carpet from the Cathedral at Mantes (16th cent.). Below, The '*Baptistery of St. Louis,' a large copper basin inlaid with silver, which, according to tradition, was brought to the Château de Vincennes by Louis IX from the Crusades, and used for royal christenings.

Beyond the Escalier Henri IV we reach the department of ***French Furniture.**—Room 1 (Pl. J). Louis XIV Period. Furniture by *Charles Boulle* (1642–1752), and his workshops; bronzes by *Giov. da Bologna* and *Girardon;* Rouen faience. On the walls, Savonnerie tapestries.—Room 2 (Pl. K). Louis XV Period. Furniture by *Cressent, Migeon* and *Dubois, Séverin,* and *Oeben*; bronzes after Duplessis, by *Hervieux*; *Tapestries by *Nielson,* after Boucher. In the centre is a *Desk which belonged to Louis XV (1760–1769).—Room 3 (Pl. L) illustrates the evolution of the armchair from the 15th to the 18th cent.—Room 4 (Pl. M). Furniture by *Weisweiler, Benemann, Joubert,* and others, from Marie Antoinette's personal suites at Fontainebleau, St-Cloud, Marly, and the Tuileries.—Room 5 (Pl. N). Furniture of the late 18th cent. (c. 1785), mainly from the Châteaux of Bellevue, Fontainebleau, and Compiègne. Works by *Haure, Thomire,* and *Forestier.*—The rooms on the first floor of the N. side of the Cour du Louvre continue the collection of French Furniture, but are not yet open.

Medieval and Renaissance Art. We may enter this department either from the ground floor by the Escalier Percier or through the Department of Egyptian Antiquities on the first floor. We begin the visit by the Vestibule (Pl. O) of the Salles de la Colonnade, which is decorated with fine 17th cent. woodwork from the Château de Vincennes. In the cases are four ceremonial mantles of the Order of the Saint-Esprit (comp. the Galerie d'Apollon). The woodwork in the second room, the Chambre à Alcôve (Pl. P), also dates from the 17th cent., while that of the third room, the Chambre de Parade (Pl. Q), was ordered by Henri II (c. 1588) for the Pavillon du Roi du Louvre, and remounted in this room under the Restoration.

Room 1 (Early Middle Ages; Pl. R). Byzantine and Latin ivories, goldsmiths' work, and enamels of the Mosan, Rhine, and German Schools. In the centre, Copper gilt reliquary of St. Potentin, from Steinfeld near Trèves (13th cent.). On the right wall, two porphyry columns from the Basilica of St. Peter, Rome (4th cent.). Case 2. Leaf of an ivory diptych, with the name of Areobindus, one of the last Roman consuls (6th cent.); two Byzantine lions' heads in rock crystal (4–5th cent.). On the walls, Three hangings illustrating scenes in the life of St. Anatole de Salins (Bruges; early 16th cent.), and a tapestry of the Adoration of the Magi (Flemish; 15th cent.).

To the left, by the exit, Limoges enamels of the 12–13th cent., including a Eucharistic dove for the safe-keeping of the consecrated Hosts.—R. 2 (Pl. S). By the windows, Altar-piece in ivory, with the lives of Christ, St. John the Baptist, and St. John the Evangelist (N. Italy, c. 1400). In the centre, 13–14th cent. ivories from the Paris workshops, notably: *Descent from the Cross (Case 2A); **Coronation of the Virgin; the Annunciation (Case 2C); small enamelled casket, called the 'Cassette de St. Louis' (Limoges, 13th cent., Case 2B); enamel ciborium, signed and dated, 'G. Alpais, 1225' (Limoges). On the walls, Flemish and Brussels tapestries, including St. Luke painting the Virgin (Brussels, 16th cent.), and (r.) Madonna in Glory (Flanders, 1485). Between the rooms, fragments of 13th cent. stained glass from Reims, depicting the legend of St. Nicaise.

SALLES DE LA RENAISSANCE. 1st ROOM (Pl. T). By the windows, 15–16th cent. Florentine bronzes, including the Flagellation, attributed to *Donatello*; Gnome with a Snail (Paduan School, 15th cent.); *Eight bronze plaques in the classical style, by *Andrea Riccio* (1470–1532), from the tomb of Marcantonio della Torre, at Verona. Cases contain 16th cent. engraved Italian crystals (including works by *Valerio Belli*), twelve small busts of Cæsars (Italy, 16th cent.), vessels in jasper (Italy, 15–16th cent.), French and Italian medals, etc. In the centre, the '*Spinario,' a Renaissance cast of the antique original (c. 1541); 16th cent. Florentine table with a fountain in bronze (Spain). In the central cases, *Bronzes of the Florentine and Paduan Schools (15–16th cent.), including works by *Riccio, Donatello, Verrocchio*, and *Bellanno*; medals and plaquettes from various sources. The Renaissance furniture includes (by the exit) the throne of the archbishops of Vienne (France, 16th cent.). Between the rooms are fragments of Swiss stained glass (16–17th cent.; note the little enamel fly on one of the panels). 2ND ROOM (Pl. U). The cases in the centre contain a superb collection of Italian and Limoges **Enamels, mainly of the 15–16th cent., but still virile, though more elaborate, in the 17th. Case 2. Medallion with a self-portrait by *Jean Fouquet*. Cases 3, 4, 5. Limoges enamels from the workshops of the '*Maître de l'Enéide*,' *Poillevé, Jean* and *Pierre Pénicaud, Nouailher*, and others (16th cent.), and by *Léonard Limousin* and his school (16th cent.); in Case 5. **Portrait of the Constable Anne de Montmorency, in a frame set with plaques, signed and dated by *Léonard Limousin*, 1556. Cases 6, 7. Enamels by *Pierre Reymond* and his school.

Cases 8, 9, 10. Enamels by *Suzanne Court, Pierre Courteys, Jacques I* and *Jacques II Laudin, Pape, Jean Limousin,* and *Jacques* and *Pierre Nouailher.* The eight wall-cases and one central case (17), contain a magnificent collection of Hispano-Moresque, French, and Italian *Ceramics of the 15–17th cent.; note especially four panels of inlay work, attributed to *Fra Vicenzo da Verona* (c. 1500), and four ceramic medallions attributed to *Girolamo della Robbia,* from the Château of St-Germain-en-Laye (16th cent.). Below, in the centre, is a large 16th cent. French medal chest; and on the two steps are decorated paving tiles from Isabelle d'Este's palace at Mantua and the Petrucci Palace at Siena. At the opposite end is a similar chest flanked by two fine oak cabinets of the 16th cent., on top of which are a faience bust of a woman, from Urbino, and a Christ attributed to *Giovanni della Robbia* (Florentine, 16th cent.). Around the walls is a series of twelve tapestries, 'Les Chasses de Maximilien,' illustrating hunting scenes (Brussels, c. 1530).—The small antechamber (Pl. V; l.) contains a case of 16th cent. 'dinanderie' and goldsmiths' work, the armour of Henri II, and an ivory statue of the Madonna and Child (Flanders, 16th cent.).

The Salle Adolphe de Rothschild (Pl. W), with a remarkable collection of Renaissance goldsmiths' work, etc., bequeathed to the Louvre in 1900, is not yet open to the public. The room has a Venetian ceiling of carved and gilded wood (late 15th cent.), and among the special treasures of the collection are a bas-relief of the Madonna, by *Agostino di Duccio*; a 13th cent. reliquary, from Belgium; a Venetian incense-vase (15th cent.); a carved wood statuette of St. Catherine (German, 16th cent.); and a fine Flemish tapestry of the Miracle of the Loaves (15th cent.).

Sculpture of the Middle Ages, Renaissance, and 17th Century. We enter this department (ground floor) either through the Porte La Trémoille (Pavillon La Trémoille), or by the staircase descending from the W. end of the Grande Galerie.

Salle Romane (Pl. 63). Sculpture of the 11–12th cent. Right to left. Fragment of the arcade of the cloister at St-Genis-les-Fontaines; two carved capitals from Moutiers-St-Jean; Christ on the Cross, in painted wood (French); 12th cent. Door from the priory of Estagel (Gard), flanked by statues of Solomon and the Queen of Sheba, from the portal of Notre-Dame de Corbeil. By the windows: Head of Christ; Madonna (Ile de France School); Merovingian capital, re-carved in the 11th cent., from the Abbey of Ste-Geneviève in Paris.

SALLE GOTHIQUE (Pl. 64). Sculpture of the 13–14th cent., including (above) bas-reliefs depicting the Passion of Christ (Bourges), and St. Matthew writing at the dictation of an angel (Chartres). To the right, Two angels in carved stone from the Abbey of Poissy; *Statue of Childebert I (13th cent.) from St-Germain-des-Prés; statue of St. Geneviève (13th cent.) from her church in Paris; *Madonnas (14th cent.); effigies from the tombs of Jeanne d'Evreux, Charles IV (from Maubuisson), and Blanche de Champagne; statues of St. Louis and of Margaret of Provence.

SALLE PHILIPPE POT (Pl. 65). Sculpture of the 15th–early 16th cent. In the centre, *Tomb of Philippe Pot, Grand Seneschal of Burgundy (15th cent.), one of the finest examples of the Burgundian School; Madonnas of the same school; Statue (l.) of Thomas de Plaine, President of the Parlement

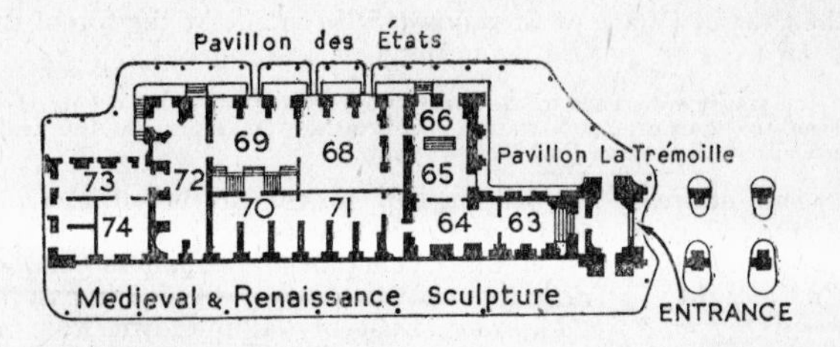

of Burgundy; tomb statues and others of the Loire and Parisian schools (15th cent.).

We descend the steps to the SALLE PAUVITRY (Pl. 66), which contains sculptures of the Schools of Philippe de Champagne, the Loire, and other 'ateliers' of the 15–16th cent. On the right, *Relief by *Michel Colombe* of St. George and the Dragon, from the Château de Gaillon (1508). In the centre, two Madonnas of the Loire School (early 16th cent.).—GALERIE FRANCO-ITALIENNE (Pl. 67). French and Franco-Italian works of the 16th cent. Tomb of Robert Legendre and Louis de Poncher, by *Guillaume Regnault* and *Guillaume Chaleveau* (Loire School, c. 1533). In the cases, head of Christ (wood), and the Infant Jesus (stone) by *Ligier Richier*; decorations from the Château de Gaillon, etc.

SALLE JEAN GOUJON (Pl. 68). In the centre: *Germain Pilon*, *Diana with the hind, from the Château d'Anet; r. to l.: *Pierre Bontemps*, Tomb of Charles de Maigny, captain of the guardians of the King's door; *G. Pilon*, *Group of the three Christian Virtues supporting an urn designed to contain the heart of Henri II, formerly in the church of the Celestines; *B. Prieur*, Funeral monument from the tomb of the Constable Anne de Montmorency; *Jean Goujon* (1515 – c. 1567), *Deposition from the Cross, from the rood screen in St-Germain-l'Auxerrois; *G. Pilon*, Painted terra-cotta model for the marble statue of the Mater Dolorosa in the Sainte Chapelle; *Jean Goujon*, *Relief of tritons and naiads, from the Fontaine des Innocents; *G. Pilon*, Kneeling bronze figure of René de Birague.

SALLE MICHEL ANGE (Pl. 69). On either side of the door, *Michelangelo* (1475–1564), *Fettered Slaves, representing the Virtues overcome by the death of Pope Julius II, for whose tomb they were designed. Above, *Benvenuto Cellini*, Bronze relief of the Nymph of Fontainebleau, from the Château d'Anet. Right to left, Bronze bust of Michelangelo (17th cent.); Italian bas-reliefs of the 15–16th cent.; Portal from the Stanga Palace at Cremona (15th cent.). At the top of the staircase, *Giov. da Bologna*, Mercury, in bronze.

The staircase descends to the SALLES COMPLÉMENTAIRES, devoted to reliefs, decorative fragments, tomb-statues, etc., from Italy and France (14–16th cent.), including works by the *Della Robbia* family.

The staircase (l.) leading up to the statue of Mercury gives access (r.) to three small ROOMS OF ITALIAN SCULPTURE (Pl. 70). First Room. Venetian and Milanese Schools. On the right: *Iac. della Quercia*, Madonna and Child, in painted wood; *Francesco Laurana*, Bust of an unknown woman; Bas-reliefs by *Mantegazza* and *Amadeo*, Madonnas, etc. Second Room. Florentine Schools. *Donatello*, Painted terra-cotta statue of a Madonna and Child; Works by *Agostino di Duccio*, *Benedetto da Maiano*, and of the Donatello and Della Robbia Schools. Third Room. Pisan School. School of *Nino Pisano*, Virgin of the Annunciation, in painted wood. In the corridor (l.) are works from the Della Robbia workshops, and two statues of Apostles (14th cent.) from Florence Cathedral.—We pass through into three other rooms devoted to GERMAN, FLEMISH AND FRENCH SCULPTURE (Pl. 71).—Room 1. *Rhenish School*. Madonna; *Hans Daucher*, Holy Family, a relief after an engraving by Dürer.—Room 2. *Rhenish School*, Wooden statue of the Madonna. In the case, wooden statuettes of the Antwerp and Malines Schools; The Passion, a retable from the church at Caligny; English alabaster bas-reliefs, etc.—Room 3. *French School*. Wooden Madonnas of the 14th cent. In the cases, sculptures of the 14–16th cent.; statuette of St. Stephen in painted wood (Burgundian School, 15th cent.); *School of G. Pilon*, Bronze bas-relief of Charles IX.

SALLE PUGET (Pl. 72). Sculpture of the 17th cent. *Tremblay* and *Gissy*, Statue of Henri IV, flanked by two slaves, by *Franqueville* and *Bordoni*, from the pedestal of the original monument of Henri IV on the Pont Neuf.—The Rotonde (r.) contains sculptures of Henri IV, including a statuette in gilded wax attributed to *Giov. da Bologna*. Above the door, *Jacques Sarrazin*, Bas-reliefs from the tomb of the heart of Louis XIII ; *Puget*, Perseus and Andromeda ; in the Rotonde (l.), *Fr. Anguier*, Monument of the Dukes of Longueville ; *Bernini*, Busts of Cardinal de Médicis (marble) and Urban VIII (bronze) ; *Mocchi*, Bust of Richelieu ; *Guillain*, Bronze statues of Louis XIII, Louis XIV, and Anne of Austria, from the Pont-au-Change (1647) ; *Coysevox*, *Tomb of Cardinal Mazarin ; in the centre, *Puget*, Milo of Crotona (1682), and Hercules at rest.

SALLE GIRARDON (Pl. 73). On each side of the door, *Girardon*, Two vases from the gardens of Versailles. In the centre, *Girardon*, Model for the equestrian statue of Louis XIV, in the Place Louis-le-Grand (Place des Victoires), destroyed in 1792 ; *Coysevox*, Crouching Venus, from the gardens at Versailles ; *Barrois*, Venus Callipyge ; *Coysevox*, *Bust of the Grand Condé. In the cases by the window, sketches by *Bernini*, and terra-cottas by *Rusconi* and *Bernini*. To the left, *Michel Anguier*, Amphitrite, from the gardens at Versailles.

SALLE COYSEVOX (Pl. 74). In the centre, *Coysevox*, *Duchess of Burgundy as Diana. On the right, *Puget*, Diogenes and Alexander, bas-relief ; *Coysevox*, Statue of the Seine, from the gardens at Marly. On the left, *Guillaume Coustou*, terra-cotta bust of Nicolas Coustou ; *Coysevox*, Nymph with a shell, from the gardens at Versailles ; busts by *Coypel*, *G. Audran*, and *Coysevox*, including a bust of Lebrun ; bronze bas-reliefs by *Desjardins*. In the cases, sketches and terra-cottas, including works by *Hurtrelle*, *M. Anguier*, and *N. Poussin*.

The SCULPTURE OF THE 18–19TH CENT. will be on exhibition in the Pavillon de Flore, when this is no longer occupied by the Ministry of Finance. The following is a summary of some of the more important works of art · *Bouchardon*, Cupid fashioning his bow from the club of Hercules (1750) ; *Houdon*, Statue of Diana (1790), busts of Rousseau, Voltaire, Buffon, and other eminent men of the age ; *Pigalle*, Bust of the surgeon Guérin ; *Pajou*, Marie Leczinska, Psyche abandoned. The early 19th cent. is represented by *Bosio*, *Chaudet*, *Chinard*, *David d'Angers*, and others, followed by *Rude*, *Pradier*, and *Maindron*. Later masters include : *Carpeaux* (Cast of 'The Dance' for the group at the Opéra) ; *Chapu* (Joan of Arc) ; *Frémiet* (Pan and bear-cubs) ; *Dalou* ; and *Barye*, with typical sculptures of animals.

19. THE MUSÉE DE L'ARMÉE.

MÉTRO station: *Invalides* (lines 8 and 14).—MOTOR-BUS 69 to Esplanade des Invalides.

ADMISSION 10 fr. per section; open daily (except Sun. morning and Tues.) 10–12.45. 1.30–5 or 5.30.

The **Musée de L'Armée** at the Invalides comprises two departments, one devoted to arms and armour, the other to military souvenirs. The *Musée des Plans-Reliefs* has not yet been reopened. Plan, see p. 111.

The **Section des Armes et Armures** (entrance on right of Cour d'Honneur) has a particularly rich collection of offensive and defensive weapons of all periods, the 15–16th century exhibits being of great artistic interest.—VESTIBULE. Chinese, Algerian, Spanish, and Russian cannon.—SALLE DE PIERREFONDS (r.). Frescoes depicting the conquests of Louis XIV in Holland; Renaissance Arms and Armour (1440–1650), including a trooper of Charles VII's reign and a German trooper of c. 1520 (centre). Many of the helmets, pieces of armour, etc., are masterpieces of Renaissance damascening, chasing and ivory carving.—SALLE FRANÇOIS-PREMIER (l.). Suits of armour worn by Louis XIII, Henri IV, Louis XIV, Charles IX, and *Francis I. *Henri II's armour with the insignia of Diane de Poitiers; *Suit said to have belonged to the Duke of Alba.

SALLE CHARLEMAGNE (through passage opposite entrance to Museum). Military uniforms of the Greeks, Romans, Franks, Crusaders, etc.; Arms and weapons of the Old and New Stone Ages; Examples of Greek and Roman, and 13th century defensive armour; Helmets of the 12–15th centuries. —SALLE LOUIS XIII (temporarily closed).—SALLE LOUVOIS. Weapons of the 18–20th cent.; note especially ornamental weapons of the Revolution and Empire (Case 6); Examples of weapons made at the 'Manufacture de Versailles' (Case 8). —SALLE ORIENTALE. Weapons from Greece, Turkey, Circassia, and the Balkans (First Section). Military costumes and armour from Persia, India, and the Far East.

We retrace our steps through the Salle Charlemagne to the corridor, passing the Cour d'Angoulême (l.) and the Cour des Victoires (r.), and mount the staircase (r.) to the SALLE 1914–1918, containing paintings, sketches, and other souvenirs of the First World War. The SALLE JOFFRE (1870–1914) is temporarily closed.—Second Floor. SALLE DES ALLIÉS. Souvenirs of the Belgian, British and Dominion, American, Yugoslav, and Czecho-Slovak armies which fought in the 1914–1918 war.—SALLE GRIBEAUVAL. Scale models of artillery pieces dating from the reign of Henri II.

The **Section Historique** is entered from the left side of the Cour d'Honneur.—VESTIBULE: Flag standards taken from the enemy during the Revolutionary and Empire periods.—SALLE TURENNE (r.). Colours of French Regiments from the First Republic to the present day (visitors remove their hats); frescoes by *Van der Meulen* and the brothers *Martin*; German regimental colours captured in 1914–1918 (far end of room). Personal souvenirs of Napoleon, including his uniform as general of division worn at Marengo (1800), a grey frock-coat, and the sword he carried at Austerlitz.—SALLE VAUBAN (formerly Salle Detaille; l. of vestibule). French Regimental Colours of the First Republic and Restoration; paintings and souvenirs of the military painter *Edouard Detaille* (1848–1912), including Napoleon reviewing the troops after Jena (1806), and The Dream; military uniforms and headdresses used by Detaille as models; frescoes by *Van der Meulen* (mostly concealed by the Detaille Collection). We ascend to the first floor.

SALLE LAFAYETTE, with souvenirs of Gen. Lafayette (1757–1834).—VESTIBULE (l.). Portraits of Marshals of France; uniforms of the Revolution and Empire.—SALLE LOUIS XIV. 1st Section: Revolutionary, Directory, and Consulate periods; uniforms and presentation weapons awarded for distinguished service during these periods. 2nd Section: Souvenirs of the Ancienne Monarchie, including the colours of the Irish Clancarty regiment (1642); portrait of Marshal Turenne attributed to *Lebrun*; small cannon presented by the province of Franche-Comté to Louis XIV after its annexation to France in 1674; uniforms and equipment; English mortar presented to a French regiment by Washington after the fall of Yorktown in 1781. 3rd Section: Souvenirs of the Invalides.—SALLE NAPOLÉON (1804–1815). Personal souvenirs of the Emperor and his family; cast of his hand; death mask; Napoleon's bed at St. Helena; stuffed skin of his horse, 'Vizir'; six busts of Napoleon at various ages, by *Eugène Guillaume*.

Second Floor. VESTIBULE. Uniforms of the Second Empire.—SALLE MAC-MAHON (1815–1870): Souvenirs of the Restoration (1815–1830), the Spanish Expedition of 1823, the Constitutional Monarchy (1830–48), the Republic of 1848, the Crimean War, etc.; and of later campaigns up to the beginning of the Franco-Prussian war, etc.—SALLE BUGEAUD. Souvenirs of Algeria; collection of cardboard soldiers.—SALLE NEY. Flag standards of the Revolutionary and Empire periods; four stools formerly belonging to the Mamelukes, taken during the Egyptian campaign of 1798.

20. THE MUSÉE DES ARTS DÉCORATIFS.

MÉTRO station: *Tuileries* (line 1).—MOTOR-BUSES 68, 69, 72, 73 to the Place des Pyramides.

ADMISSION 30 fr. (free on Sun. afternoon); open daily (except Tues. and holidays) 10–12, 2–5.

The ***Musée des Arts Décoratifs,** at 107 Rue de Rivoli, occupies the *Pavillon de Marsan*, the N.W. wing of the Palais du Louvre. This valuable and interesting museum, especially rich in French works, illustrates decorative and ornamental art from medieval to modern times.

To follow the chronological order, the visit should start on the first floor.

Ground Floor. The Central Hall and the rooms on the left are reserved for temporary exhibitions. Room 1 (r.). Recent acquisitions.—RR. 2, 3 (Restoration period). Furniture, silver and glassware, jewellery, etc. Works by *Delacroix*, *Drolling*, and *Auguste Raffet*.—RR. 4, 5 (Louis-Philippe period). Furniture belonging to Duke Ferdinand of Orleans (c. 1840); *Ingres*, Queen Marie-Amélie, and the Duchess of Orleans; Sèvres porcelain; Creil and Choisy faience; miniatures, statuettes, and bronzes, including works by *Pradier*.—RR. 6, 7. 18th cent. woodwork from a mansion in the Rue de Grenelle, re-decorated by *Ciceri*, c. 1850 (R. 6); silverware and bronzes from the Tuileries; jewellery, enamels,

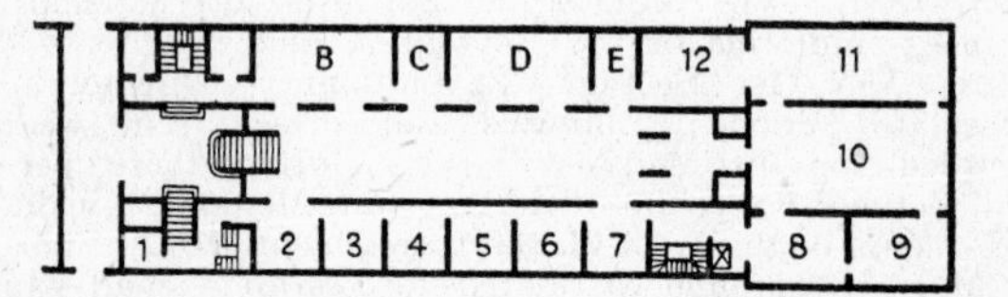

furniture, and Sèvres porcelain; drawings and frescoes by *Rossigneux* and *Mottez*, etc.—Landing of the Escalier Marsan. 18th cent. Italian toys.—RR. 8, 9 (end of the 19th cent.). Decorative paintings and water-colours by *C. Guys*, *Duez*, *R. Jourdain*, etc. Globular clock designed by *Gustave Doré*; enamels, crystals, glassware, jewellery, book-bindings, etc.—R. 10 is the Lecture Hall.—R. 11 contains examples of furniture, etc., of the 'Style Moderne' (1900–1910).—R. 12 is devoted to contemporary art.

First Floor, reached by the Escalier de Rohan, next to R. 1.—Room 13. French and Flemish decorative art of the 13–16th cent.; 15–16th cent. tapestries.—RR. 14, 15. French sculpture of the 13–16th cent.; tapestries of the 15–16th cent.; Venetian well-head; pewter, tools, mathematical instruments, etc.—R. 16 (Salle Raoul Duseigneur). French 15th cent. woodwork and stone-carving; 16th cent. German stained glass.—RR. 17–21. French tapestries, woodwork, sculptures, stained glass, and furniture, etc., of the Renaissance period. Anonymous portrait (r.) of Marie d'Angleterre (Mary Tudor, sister of Henry VIII), third wife of Louis XII; 16th cent. Limoges enamels (R. 18); late 16th cent. French tapestry (Story of Adonis; R. 19); glass cases (r.) with miniature death's-heads and skeletons, 16–19th cent.; fine 17th cent. Flemish tapestry of the Nativity (R. 21).—R. 22 (Salle Rambuteau). Book-bindings of the 16–18th cent. (on the right are bindings embossed with the arms of Madame du Barry and Madame de Pompadour). On the landing, French pottery of the 14–18th cent.—R. 23 (Louis XIII). Furniture, leather coffers, tapestries, etc.; faience from Nevers, St-Cloud, and Paris.—RR. 24–26 (Louis XIV and Regency). Tapestries after Le Brun and Audran; furniture, woodwork, etc.; in the glass case (l.) are 16–17th cent. Spanish coloured wax miniatures (R. 24); contemporary faience from Marseilles, Moustiers and Montpellier; (l.) early 18th cent. drawing-room from Avignon; (r.) drawing-room (c. 1750) painted by *Oudry* (R. 25); the carved oak door between RR. 25 and 26 is from the château of St-Germain-en-Laye; Brussels tapestry after Teniers; faience from Avignon and Apt.—RR. 27–28 (Regency and Louis XV). Panels painted by *Lancret*; doors from the Hotel de Lassay (Palais-Bourbon); balcony of an 18th cent. theatre; porcelain from St-Cloud; gilt wood bedstead with the Rohan arms; Beauvais tapestries; drawings by *Watteau, Lancret, Gillot,* and others.—R. 29. Drawings by *Nicolas Pineau* (1684–1754).—RR. 30–34. Paintings by *Boucher* and *Huet*; ceiling from the Hôtel de Flesselles in the Rue de Sévigné; faience from Aprey, Strasbourg, Paris, Sceaux, and Lorraine; 18th cent. goldsmiths' work; jewellery; busts by *Caffieri*.—R. 35. Walking sticks, swords, hunting weapons; rings (15–19th cent.); 18th cent. goldsmiths' work.—R. 36 (Salle Doisteau). Faience from Rouen and Sinceny.—R. 37 (Salle Perrin). Drawings by *Watteau, Boucher, Fragonard, Prud'hon, Ingres,* and others; 18th cent. Chinese porcelain.—R. 38 (Louis XV). Lacquer panels in the 'Chinese' style from the Hôtel du Châtelet (1770–71).—RR. 39–41. Collection Grandjean (temporarily closed).—R. 42. French glassware of the 14–18th cent.—R. 43. Chair seats and frames of 17–18th cent.—R. 44 (Salle Larcade). Woodwork and bronze furniture fittings (18th cent.).—R. 45. 17–18th cent. musical instruments.

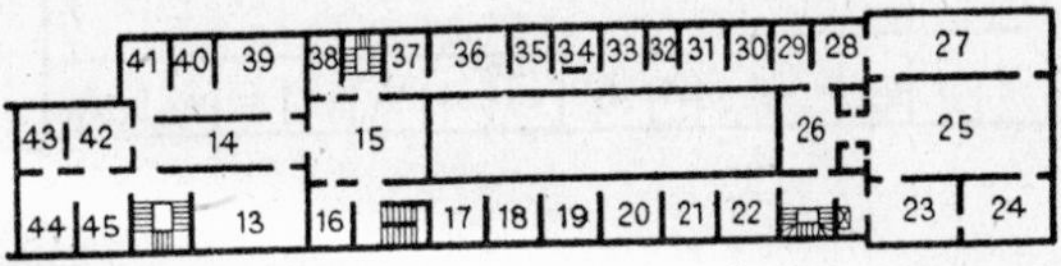

We ascend the Escalier de Rohan to the SECOND FLOOR. ROOMS 46–54. Textiles and embroideries from the 5th to the 19th cent.—On the balcony, Costumes of the 18–19th cent.—

R. 55. Lace (16–19th cent.).—RR. 56–63 (Louis XV and Louis XVI). Aubusson tapestries (rustic sports); gouaches by *Le Prince, Saint-Aubin,* and others; furniture from Marie-Antoinette's 'Turkish' boudoir at Fontainebleau and woodwork from a similar room at Versailles (R. 57); porcelain from Chantilly and Mennecy; porcelain knife-handles, etc.; painted panels in the style of *Prieur*; bust of Madame His, by *Houdon*; jewellery; Vincennes porcelain (Louis XVI); Fitzhenry collection of mustard pots; Sèvres porcelain and biscuit (Louis XVI); painted panels by *Hubert Robert*; busts of Voltaire and Rousseau, by *Houdon*; Swiss enamels, etc.—RR. 64–66 (Louis XVI). Engravings, decorative panels, etc., attributed to *Leriche*; bronze furniture

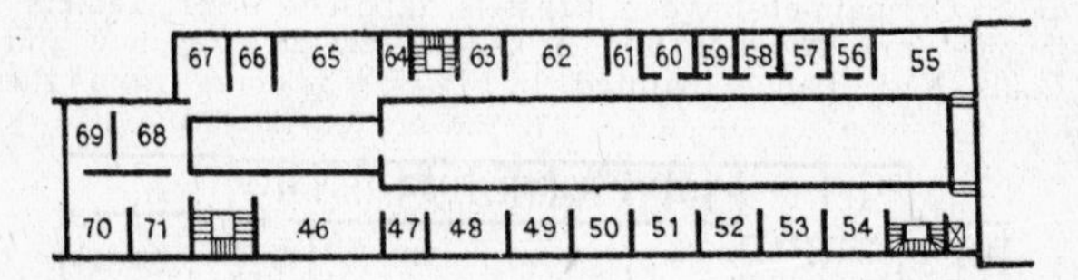

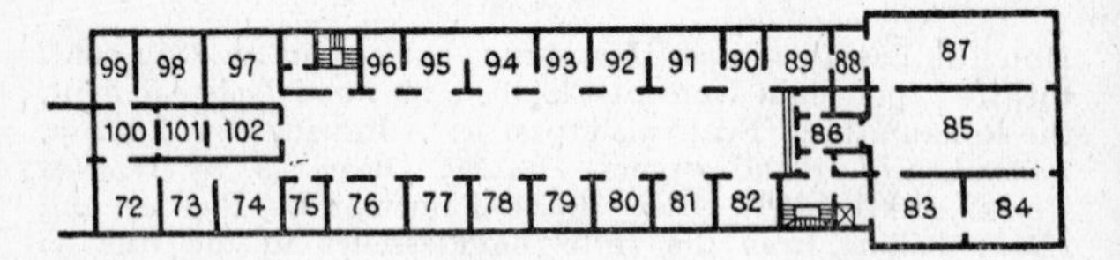

fittings; woodwork and wallpaper of c. 1780.—R. 67. Painted woodwork from a mansion in the Rue Joubert (end of the 18th cent.).—R. 68 (Salle Bariol). *Stucco-decorated woodwork from a mansion in the Place Vendôme (c. 1780–1790); furniture and Beauvais tapestries.—RR. 69–71 (First Empire). Napoleon's coronation robes and throne; *Boilly,* Houdon at work on his bust of Laplace; *Houdon,* Bust of Laplace; furniture, goldsmiths' work, jewellery, and miniatures.

The Third Floor is occupied mainly by the collections of foreign decorative art (RR. 72–74 and 97–102 were not arranged at the time of going to press). Rooms 75–80. Art of the Far East.—RR. 81, 82. Turkestan, Russia, and Poland. On the landing, Fans of all nations.—RR. 83–85 and 87. Indian and Persian art, and Muslim art in general.—R. 86 is a drawing-room of the Louis XIV period, from Lyons, with Aubusson tapestry.—R. 88. Salle Whitney.—R. 89. Art of the French Colonies.—RR. 90–92. English, Dutch, and German art.—RR. 93–96. Italian art of the 14–18th cent. Sculptures, drawings, paintings by *Magnasco,* etc.

21. THE CONSERVATOIRE DES ARTS ET MÉTIERS.

MÉTRO station: *Arts et Métiers* (lines 3 and 11).—MOTOR-BUSES 38 and 52 to 'Arts et Métiers.'

ADMISSION 16 fr. (free on Sun., and to organised student groups on weekdays); open weekdays (except Mon.) 1.30–5.30., Sun. 10–5. CATALOGUE 10 fr. LECTURES (adm. free) on applied science in the evenings between November and May.

The **Conservatoire des Arts et Métiers,** the Science Museum of Paris, is situated on the E. side of the Square des Arts et Métiers, with its principal façade in the Rue St-Martin. It occupies the church, cloisters, refectory, etc., of the ancient priory of St-Martin-des-Champs.

This wealthy priory, founded by Henri I in 1060 and presented to the abbey of Cluny by Philip I in 1078, stood outside the city until the early 14th cent. Richelieu was one of its titular priors. During the Revolution the priory was occupied by the Société des Jeunes Français, an educational institution, and later it became a small-arms factory. In 1798 it was assigned to the Conservatoire des Arts et Métiers, which had been founded by a decree of the Convention in 1794, and here were assembled the collections of Vaucanson and other scientists.

The entrance gateway (1848–1850) is flanked with statues of Science and Art, and the modern portal which leads into the Cour d'Administration (left of the Cour d'Honneur) is flanked with statues of (l.) Nicholas Leblanc and (r.) Denis Papin.

On the right of the Cour d'Honneur is the *REFECTORY, a 13th cent. masterpiece, built by Pierre de Montereau (architect of the Sainte-Chapelle). This magnificent hall, 140 ft. by 38 ft., now contains the *Library*. Note the 13th cent. reader's pulpit at the E. end, on the left, and the painting of St. Martin by Steinheil, inside the S. doorway; externally this fine Gothic door is the only relic of the original cloisters.

On the right of the Cour d'Honneur a passage leads into the Cour des Laboratoires and the courtyard in front of the church. The 13th cent. portal has been restored and the turret on the right is a modern addition. Outside the E. end of the church are the gardens of the Square du Général-Morin, on the N. side of which is Dalou's monument to Boussingault. Between the church and the library is the Great Lecture Hall.

Ground Floor. We enter the Museum by the central staircase in the Cour d'Honneur. On the first landing, above the door, between two statues, is a memorial tablet to Vaudoyer, the architect of the restorations. On the left, meteorological recording apparatus. We descend the central flight of the double staircase (designed by Antoine) to ROOM 1, and thence to ROOM 2, known as the SALLE DE L'ECHO because a whisper in one corner is distinctly audible in the diagonally opposite corner. The room contains a model of Lavoisier's laboratory, and apparatus which belonged to Gay-Lussac, as well as busts of scientists.—ROOMS 4–9 (r.). *Metallurgy*. Note the model of the balloon gondola used by Prof. Piccard in his stratospheric attempts (R. 4); models of machinery used for the production of steel, iron, copper, etc. (R. 5); models of

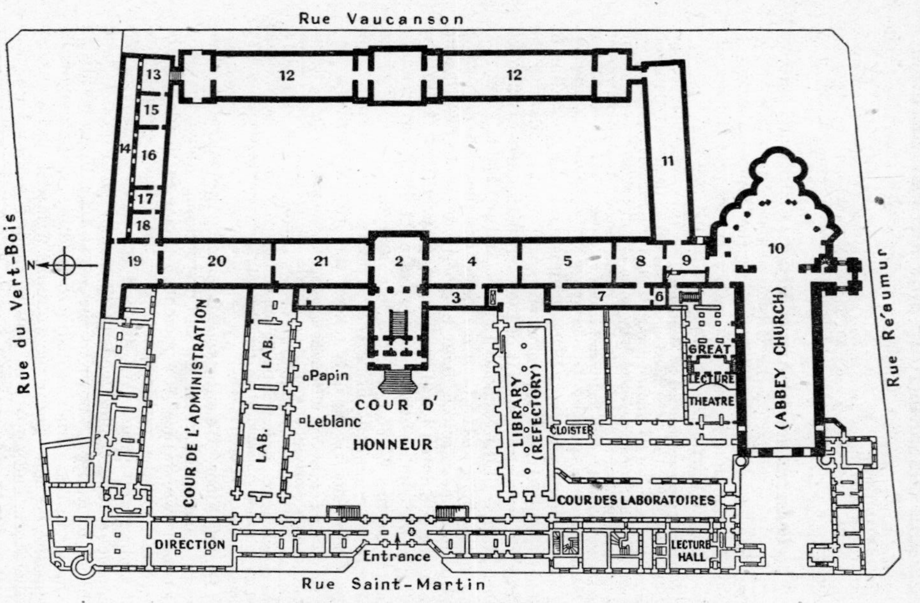

CONSERVATOIRE DES ARTS ET MÉTIERS: GROUND FLOOR

rolling-mills and samples of various metals, etc. (R. 8); power hammers, drop-forging presses, etc. (R. 9).—ROOM 10, not yet reopened, is the former *Abbey Church*, and normally contains historic machines and other apparatus. The aisleless nave dates from the end of the 13th cent.; the choir, with its 'chevet' of chapels, has perhaps the earliest Gothic vault in Paris (late 12th cent.).—ROOM 11. *Agricultural Machinery*.—ROOM 12. *Prevention of Accidents* and *Industrial Hygiene* (temporarily closed).—ROOMS 13–15. *Building Materials* (closed).

Returning to the Salle de l'Echo, we enter ROOM 21, which contains models of *Locomotives* and rolling-stock of various periods, including a model of Stephenson's "Rocket" (case on right of entrance).—ROOMS 20–16. *Astronomy, Surveying, Mathematical Instruments, Clocks*. Telescopes, field-glasses, seismograph, theodolites, etc. Clocks by Berthaud de Lepaute, de Janvier, and other celebrated 18th cent. clock makers.

First Floor. We return to the Salle de l'Echo and ascend the staircase to ROOM 23, the Salle d'Honneur.—ROOM 46 (l.) *Industrial Chemistry*. Models of apparatus used in the production of gas, etc.; materials and instruments for printing, engraving, lithography, etc.—ROOMS 47–49. *Spinning* and *Weaving*.—ROOM 37. *Photography*. Apparatus used by Daguerre and Niepce.—ROOMS 38–41. *Cinematography*. Apparatus used by Reynaud, de Marey, Lumière, and other pioneers.—ROOM 42. Scientific utilisation of photographic processes.

We retrace our steps through R. 37 to ROOMS 36 and 35. *Ceramics*. Apparatus and ovens for the manufacture of pottery, faience, enamels, etc.; in the cases are Japanese, Chinese, and English porcelain, Sèvres porcelain and faience, including a head of Balzac in Sèvres 'grès,' by Rodin.—ROOMS 34–32. *Glassware, Enamels,* and *Terra-cottas*. Terra-cottas found in a Roman tomb at Vaison. Glassware from Baccarat and Saint-Louis; glass designs by Lalique, etc.—ROOMS 31 and 32. *Mechanics*. Machine-tools, gearing, etc.—ROOM 30. *Acoustics, Optics,* and *Electricity*. Harps, harpsichords and other stringed instruments; piano belonging to Mme de Maintenon; 18th cent. harpsichord; Edison's first gramophone; optical instruments; microscope belonging to the Duc de Chaulnes (18th cent.); radio set formerly installed in the Eiffel Tower (1910); valves and electrodes, etc.—ROOMS 29, 28. *Electricity*.—ROOM 27. *Electricity* (*Heat*). Static electricity apparatus; note the machines belonging to Van Marum and de Nairve (18th cent.); original apparatus used by Coulomb in his experiments with electrostatics and magnetism; physics apparatus belonging to Charles and the Abbé Nollet; hydrostatics, compression of liquids and gases, capillary attraction, etc.—Room 26. *Mechanics and Physics.*—Room 24. *Machines.* Models of boilers; steam engines; model of Watt's steam engine; diesel engines; turbines, etc.

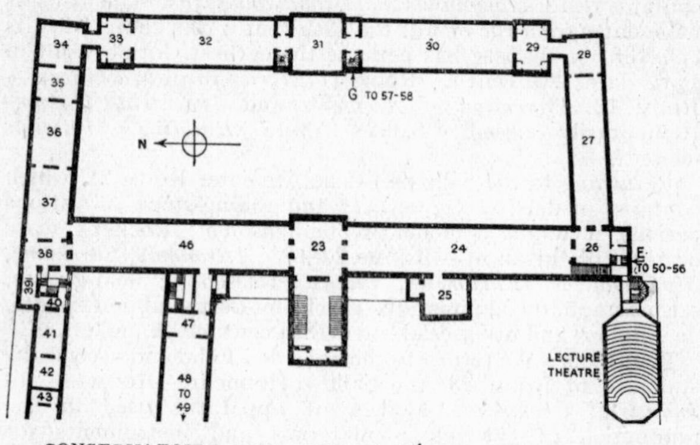

CONSERVATOIRE DES ARTS ET MÉTIERS: FIRST FLOOR

Second Floor. For RR. 50–56, we ascend staircase E, in R. 26. Room 50. *Heating and Lighting.*—Room 51. *Weights and Measures.* Collection of instruments for mechanical observations; dynamometers, manometers, revolution counters, etc.—Room 52. Drawings relating to the history of scientific apparatus.—Rooms 53–56. *Telegraphic and Telephonic Instruments* (temporarily closed).—For RR. 57, 58, we ascend Staircase G, in R. 31.—Room 57. *Geometrical Instruments.* Mathematical models, conoids, etc.—Room 58. *Calculating Machines*, including Pascal's multiplying and adding machines.

22. THE BIBLIOTHÈQUE NATIONALE.

Métro station: *Bourse* (line 3).—Motor-buses 48, 67, 74, 85 to Rue des Petits-Champs.

Admission. The *Reading Room* (Salle de Travail des Imprimés) and *Periodicals Room* (Salle Ovale) are open for readers from 9 to 6, except on Sun., holidays, and during the fortnight following the Sun. after Easter. Foreigners wishing to use the Library should apply to the Secretary's office. A letter of recommendation from their ambassador or consul (students should apply to their director of studies), and two identity photographs are necessary before an entry card is issued. The *Print Rooms* are open every weekday 10–5 (adm. free to card-holders). The *Musée des Médailles* is open 9.30–12, 2–4.45; adm. 10 fr. The *Manuscript Rooms* are open 9–5, and the *Photographic Service* 9–12, 2–5.

The **Bibliothèque Nationale** ranks with the British Museum in London as one of the two largest libraries in the world.

Besides the printed books (over five million), the library has seven other departments. The catalogue of printed books, which already fills 173 vols., has been compiled only as far as the letter S. The extensive buildings, for the most part modern, were erected at various times on the site of the 17th cent. *Hôtel Mazarin*, and occupy an area of 4¼ acres, bounded by the Rue de Richelieu, Rue des Petits-Champs, Rue Vivienne, and the Rue Colbert.

The Bibliothèque Nationale, formerly known as the *Bibliothèque Royale* and the *Bibliothèque Impériale*, is in the line of direct descent from the private libraries of the French kings. Dispersed, for the most part, at the end of the Hundred Years War, the Library was re-founded by Louis XII and moved to Blois. During the following two centuries the collection was removed to Fontainebleau and then to Paris, and in 1721, found its present home in the Rue de Richelieu. The reigns of Henri IV, Louis XIV, and Louis XV saw the addition, by purchase or gift, of many famous libraries and collections (including Colbert's library). At the Revolution the Library was greatly enlarged by the collections of the suppressed religious establishments, and in 1793 it was enacted that a copy of every book, newspaper, etc., printed in France, should be deposited by the publishers in the Bibliothèque Nationale. The yearly intake of books is now between fifteen and twenty thousand.

The gateway at No. 58 Rue de Richelieu, facing the Square Louvois, leads to the Cour d'Honneur. Under the gateway are four allegorical statues of Printing, and the allied arts. On the left is the *Dépôt Légal*, and the *Administration* and *Secretary's Offices* are opposite. To the right of the courtyard are the steps leading up to the Vestibule, with the '*Salle de Vente*' and *Refreshment Room* on the right. On the left is the cloakroom (obligatory but no charge). Opposite the entrance is the Reading Room (*Salle de Travail des Imprimés*), into which visitors may look through the glass door. This hall, which is roofed by nine faience domes, seats 344 readers who have access to nearly 10,000 books of reference. The upper galleries and the *Magasin Central*, which lies beyond the hemicycle accommodating the librarians, contain little more than a fifth (c. 1,000,000 vols.) of the total book-store (visit only by permission of the director).

At the end of the Vestibule is a staircase leading to the first floor. To the left of the staircase is a passage leading to the Periodicals Room (*Salle Ovale*). Underneath (r.) the staircase are the *Photographic Departments*. Beyond the staircase, and to the right, are the temporary consulting rooms of the *Maps and Plans Department*, and also the library of the *Société de Géographie*.

Opposite the Secretary's office is the Prints Department (*Cabinet des Estampes*), which was reopened in 1946 after a complete renovation. We first enter the Galerie Mansart, formerly Mazarin's sculpture gallery ; note his arms above the door and the carved foliage and paintings by Grimaldi. At the end of the gallery is the *Vestibule du Cabinet des Estampes*, from which a staircase and a lift both ascend to the *Students' Rooms* (1946) on the second floor (over 4,000,000 prints).

FIRST FLOOR. At the top of the staircase is the entrance to the **Musée des Médailles.** The collection, founded in the 16th cent., contains c. 400,000 medals and coins, and many cameos, intaglios, and other antiques.—ROOM 1. In the centre, Torso of Aphrodite, in Parian marble (Hellenistic). In the table-cases, French and foreign coins, medals, engraved gems, jewels, etc. The wall-cases contain Egyptian terra-cottas, small bronzes, etc.—ROOM 2. The central case contains the most precious objects in the museum. Note especially: *Ivory chessman representing a Hindu king on an Elephant, reputed to have belonged to Charlemagne; Agate bust of Constantine the Great; 'Patère de Rennes,' a Roman gold cup found in 1774; Merovingian chalice and paten (6th cent.); '**Grand Camée' from the Sainte-Chapelle, representing the Apotheosis of Germanicus, with Tiberius and Livia; it is the largest antique cameo known; Sardonyx nef from St-Denis; *Cup of Chosroes I or II, king of Persia c. A.D. 600. Case 2. *Silver hoard from the temple of Mercurius Canetonensis, found near Berthouville (Eure), including silver figurines and vessels of the 2nd cent. B.C. and others of the best Greek period. In front of the window, *Throne of Dagobert, on which the kings of France were crowned, a Roman curule chair of bronze, with arms and back added in the 12th cent. by Abbot Suger of St-Denis. In the other cases are antique terra-cotta enamels, and jewellery.—ROOM 3 (*Salle de Luynes*). Ancient arms and armour, including (1st wall-case on l.) a sword, said to have belonged to Boabdil, last Moorish king of Granada (late 15th cent.). In the cases, Greek and Etruscan vases, bronze statuettes, domestic utensils, talismans, etc.

Retracing our steps to the first landing, we mount the stairs to the Vestibule opposite. On the right is the MANUSCRIPT ROOM (more than 121,000 manuscripts, of which some 10,000 are illuminated), and on the left is the GALERIE MAZARINE. Built in 1645 by Mansart, this delicately proportioned room is now devoted to temporary exhibitions of bookbinding, book-printing, etc. The *Geographical Rooms* at the far end of the gallery are not open to the public.

23. THE MUSÉE CARNAVALET.

MÉTRO station: *St. Paul* (line 1).—MOTOR-BUS 66 to Rue Payenne.
ADMISSION 30 fr. (free on Sun.); open daily (except Tues. and holidays) 10–12 and 2–5 or 6. Umbrellas and sticks must be given up in the cloak-room (no charge) on the right of the gateway.

The ***Musée Carnavalet,** or *Musée Historique de la Ville de Paris,* at the corner of the Rue des Francs-Bourgeois and the

Rue de Sévigné, is a highly important collection illustrating the history of Paris from the 16th to the middle of the 19th century. The section on the Revolution deserves special notice.

The museum is housed in the Hôtel Carnavalet, a fine mansion begun in 1544 for Jacques des Ligneris, President of the Parlement, and adorned with charming sculptures by *Jean Goujon*. It was altered in 1660 by Mansart (comp. the Bibliothèque Nationale), who built the present façade, but retained the 16th cent. gateway with its Goujon sculptures (on the keystone, a winged figure of Abundance standing on a globe which was later carved into a carnival mask, in punning allusion to Carnavalet). Further alterations and enlargements were made in 1905–1914, and again in 1923–25. The name Carnavalet was derived from the Breton family of Kernevenoy, the second owners of the mansion. Madame de Sévigné lived here from 1677 till her death in 1696; her apartments, which were shared by her daughter, Madame de Grignan, and her uncle, the Abbé de Coulanges, were on the first floor (now RR. 46–51, 58–60, and 42).

The bronze statue of Louis XIV in the centre of the Courtyard is by *Coysevox*. Of the sculptures in the courtyard, the best are those by *Jean Goujon* on the entrance arch and above the door on the left side. The large reliefs of the Seasons, on the side opposite the entrance, were probably executed under Goujon's direction. On the right side, the relief above the door is a copy (1870) of the one opposite; those on the first story are by *Van Opstal* (1660).

From the cloakroom (RR. 1–3) we may either cross the courtyard or turn left through RR. 7–12, bear left again through RR. 13–16, to reach the stairs (l.) to the First Floor. Through the doors opposite are RR. 17–20, illustrating the Topography of Paris from the 16th to the beginning of the 18th century. On the left wall (R. 17) is an anonymous portrait of Mary Stuart, in a white mourning veil (1561).—RR. 21, 22. Drawings, sketches, and gouaches of the 18th century.—To the left of the passage (R. 22) is the Salon de Mazarin (R. 23) with richly painted and gilded woodwork, brought from the 17th cent. Hôtel Colbert de Villacerf at 23 Rue de Turenne.—Room 24 is the former bedroom of Dangeau, Louis XIV's historian, from his mansion in the Place Royale (Place des Vosges). The ceiling-painting, representing Sunrise, is by *Lebrun*. On the far wall is a portrait of Jean Mariette, by *Antoine Pesne*.—Room 25 is the dining-room from the Hôtel Dangeau. The ceiling by *Lebrun* (restored) represents Olympus, Mercury presenting Hebe to Jupiter, and the Muses (1651). On the walls are general views of Paris and its environs c. 1700–20.

Leaving R. 25, we turn right into RR. 61–63, which are devoted to the Revolution.—R. 61. Portraits of Desaix, Kléber, Robespierre as a young man, etc.; objects and documents relating to the activities of the Convention; military equipment, etc.—R. 62 is decorated with fine Louis XV panelling. On the sides of each doorway and the left window are prints illustrating the Spirit of each Revolutionary Month; 'Garden of the Musée des Monuments Français,' by *Hubert Robert*, etc.—R. 63. Examples of popular art during the Revolution. In the cases are fans, curios, miniatures, medals, faience, etc. Note the 'Iconographie des Martyrs de la Liberté,' in the second table case on the left.

We retrace our steps through R. 61 and turn right into

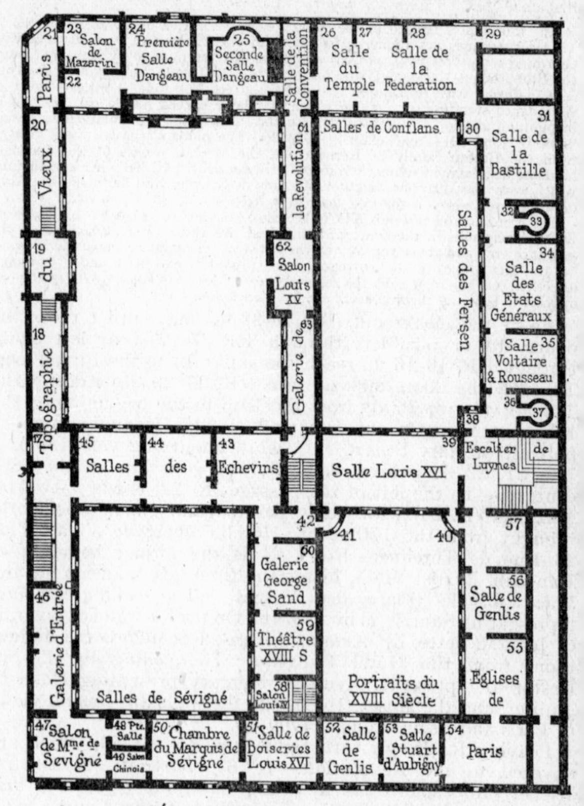

MUSÉE CARNAVALET : FIRST FLOOR

Salle de la Convention (R. 26). This room, and the three following, are decorated with woodwork from the Château de Conflans-Charenton. Souvenirs of Danton (central case); Robespierre's half-finished signature and bloodstains, following the attack on him on the 9th Thermidor (July 27th), 1794;

Couthon's mechanical chair; portraits of Marat, Robespierre, and Danton. In the case to the right of the window, works executed by *Hubert Robert* during his imprisonment; caricatures, by *Gabriel*, of notables of the Revolution. Above the fireplace, 'Festival of the Supreme Being, June 8th, 1794,' by *Naudet*. On the mantelpiece is a calendar clock marked with revolutionary months.—The SALLE DU TEMPLE (R. 27) contains personal souvenirs, letters, furniture, etc., of Louis XVI and his family during their imprisonment in the Temple. —SALLE DE LA FÉDÉRATION (R. 28). Festival of the Federation, by *Swebach-Desfontaines*; paintings by *Hubert Robert*, *Boilly*, and *Le Guay*; furniture with republican emblems; plaster *Bust of Barnave, by *Houdon*, etc.—R. 29 is devoted to Parisian life during the Revolution.—R. 30. Strong-box from the Bastille; sketch for a monument to Mirabeau; paintings by *Doncre*, *Senave*, and *Watteau*.—SALLE DE LA BASTILLE (R. 31). Model of the Bastille cut out of one of its stones by *Palloy*, who was responsible for the demolition operations; (above) Taking of the Bastille, by *Thévenin* and by *Singleton*; Demolition of the Bastille, by *Hubert Robert*. On the left, card table and slate taken from the Bastille; in the cases, souvenirs of the Bastille, including 'Lettres de Cachet' signed by Louis XV, etc.—RR. 32–37 are decorated with woodwork from the Hôtel de Breteuil at 17 Rue de Matignon, once the home of Count Axel de Fersen, the Swedish nobleman who aided Louis XVI and his family in their abortive attempt to escape from Paris in 1791.—RR. 32–33. Terra-cotta statuettes (revolutionary allegories), by *Chinard*.—R. 34 contains souvenirs of the States General, including portraits of Fauchet, Guillotin, Camille Desmoulins, and Franklin; busts of Mirabeau and Bailly; Mirabeau à la Tribune, a bronze by *Pigalle*. In the centre, Sèvres porcelain with revolutionary emblems.—R. 35. Personal souvenirs and portraits of Voltaire and Rousseau; *Portrait of Voltaire aged 24, by *Largillière*. Clock of 1791, with decorations illustrating the removal of Voltaire's ashes to the Pantheon. Death-masks of Voltaire, Rousseau, Montesquieu (central case).—R. 36. Views of Paris by *Demachy*.—R. 37 is the Rotonde from the ground floor of the Hôtel de Breteuil.—R. 38. Screens with scenes relative to the birth of the Dauphin (Oct. 22nd, 1781); paintings by *Demachy*.—The ESCALIER DE LUYNES, a reconstruction of the stairway from the Hôtel de Luynes, is decorated with fresco paintings of distinguished members of the Luynes family, by *Brunetti* (1748).

We turn right into the SALLE LOUIS XVI (R. 39). The cases on each side of the doorway contain fans, buttons, watches, etc., of the Louis XVI period. In the recess (R. 40) on the left, terra-cotta bust of an unknown lady (18th cent.); views of Paris, etc.; personal souvenirs of the royal family; *Portrait of Louis XVI, by *Duplessis*.—R. 41 (far end on left) contains faience illustrating the aeronautical efforts of the brothers Montgolfier.

We return to the landing of the Escalier de Luynes, and turn right into R. 57. Paintings by *Hubert Robert, Demachy, Maréchal*, and others.—R. 56. Woodwork from the Hôtel de Genlis; views of Paris by *J. B. Lallemand, Demachy, Génillon*, etc.—RR. 55, 54 contain woodwork of the Regency period from the Collège des Prémontrés; paintings and drawings of Paris churches, by *Hubert Robert* and *Demachy*; models of statues in St-Sulpice by *Dumont*; 18th cent. Rouen faience; paintings and drawings by *Demachy, Delarue, Jeaurat, P. D. Martin, Saint-Aubin*, and others.—R. 53. Woodwork from the Music Room of the Hôtel Stuart-d'Aubigny; terra-cotta bust of the Abbé Delille, translator of Virgil and Milton; portraits by *Tocqué* and *Vestier*, etc.—R. 52. Regency woodwork from the Hôtel de Genlis; drawings by *Cochin, Vincent, Pujos, Pajou*, etc.; paintings by *N. B. Lépicié* and *Pierre Subleyras*; faience of the 18th cent.—R. 51. Panelling from a mansion in the Rue de Grenelle. In the cases, *Drawings by *St-Aubin*. On the walls water-colours and drawings by *Carmontelle*.—R. 58 (r.) has polychrome woodwork from a mansion in the Rue de Fleurus.—R. 59 is devoted to souvenirs of personalities in the 18th cent. French theatre.—The GALERIE GEORGE-SAND (R. 60) contains the collection of souvenirs of George Sand (1804–1876) and her family, presented by Mme Lauth-Sand, granddaughter of the novelist.

We return to R. 51, and turn right into R. 50, which was the bedroom of the graceless son of the Marquise de Sévigné. In the central case, drawings by *Lancret, Pater, Watteau, St-Aubin*; 18th cent. views of Paris, etc.—RR. 47–49 comprise the apartments of Mme de Sévigné.—The SALON CHINOIS (R. 49) has lacquered panelling in a Chinese design from the Hôtel Lariboisière, and a large mirror framed in foliage (Louis XV).—The SALON DE MME DE SÉVIGNÉ (R. 47), the drawing-room of the Marquise, retains its original panelling. Above the mantelpiece is a pastel portrait of Mme de Sévigné, by *Robert Nanteuil*; opposite is a portrait of her daughter, Mme de Grignan, by *Mignard*. In the central case are personal souvenirs, letters, etc. To the left of the central window, anonymous portrait of Charles II of England. The adjoining PETITE SALLE (R. 48) contains a couch from Mme de Sévigné's house at Vichy.—R. 46 still retains its 17th cent. panelling. On the right is a bust of Henri II of Montmorency, beheaded at Toulouse in 1632; portraits of the Duc de Montausier; Louis XIII at the siege of La Rochelle; view of

Paris from the Gobelins, by *Van der Meulen*; 17th cent. views of Paris and Parisian life.—The SALLES DES ECHEVINS (RR. 45–42), dedicated to the officers of public works of the city of Paris, are temporarily closed.

We return to the landing and retrace our steps to R. 7 and up the steps on the left to the SALLE DES ENSEIGNES (R. 4). This contains a fine collection of shop and tavern signs of the 14–19th cent. In the central cases are weights and measures, engravings illustrating various trades, etc.—R. 5. Costumes of the Louis XV and Louis XVI periods; Gobelins tapestries (r.) of military scenes (1763). In the courtyard is an equestrian statue of Henri IV, by *Lemaire* (1838).—R. 6, which contains Revolutionary costumes, is temporarily closed.

We cross the vestibule of the Escalier de Luynes to R. 64. Bust of Napoleon in 1798, by *Corbet*.—SALLE DU PREMIER EMPIRE (R. 65). *Gérard*, *Madame Récamier; *Boilly*, The Conscripts of 1807 leaving the Porte St-Denis; *Prud'hon*, Talleyrand in 1809. In the cases are personal souvenirs of Napoleon and his family, including (r.) Napoleon's field outfit.—SALLE DE LA RESTAURATION (R. 66). Drawings and paintings illustrating historical events of 1815–1830, by *Boilly*, *Jacob*, *Lecomte*, and *Louis Boulanger*; views of Paris (1820–1830) by *Canella*.—R. 67. Souvenirs of the July Revolution (1830) and the insurrections of 1832; incidents of the Revolution of 1848, etc.—R. 68. *Corot*, *The Seine and the Quai des Orfèvres; views of Paris by *Adam*, *Canella*, and others.—R. 69. Portraits of 19th cent. authors and scholars, including Michelet and Théophile Gautier; views of Paris by *T. S. Boys*, *Dagnan*, etc.—R. 72 is devoted to French painters of the 19th cent.; note the *Cartoons (l.) for the ceiling paintings in the Hôtel de Ville (destroyed in 1871) by *Eugène Delacroix* (1798–1863). In the case (l.) are drawings by *Corot*, *Bonington*, and *A. L. Colin*.—R. 71 contains souvenirs of the 19th cent. French theatre, including a portrait of Marie Duplessis ('La Dame aux Camélias') by *Roqueplan*; souvenirs of Talma, Rachel, and other stage personalities.—R. 73. Souvenirs of Balzac, Alexandre Dumas (père), and Béranger.—R. 74. Souvenirs of Lamartine.—R. 75. Restoration furniture; amusing collection of statuettes by *Danton* (1800–1869).—RR. 76–79, at present closed, are normally devoted to the more recent history of Paris.

We retrace our steps to R. 7. Wrought-iron sign, 'A l'Enfant Jésus'; costumes, 1890–1900.—R. 8. Costumes c. 1880. Souvenirs of Victorien Sardou, including letters from Victor Hugo and Sarah Bernhardt.—R. 9. Costumes 1875; souvenirs of Alphonse Daudet.—RR. 10–11. Costumes c. 1830 and Second Empire, including dolls' clothes.—R. 12. Models of

19th cent. horse-buses, etc. We bear left into RR. 13–16, which are devoted to the Topography of Paris, and contain

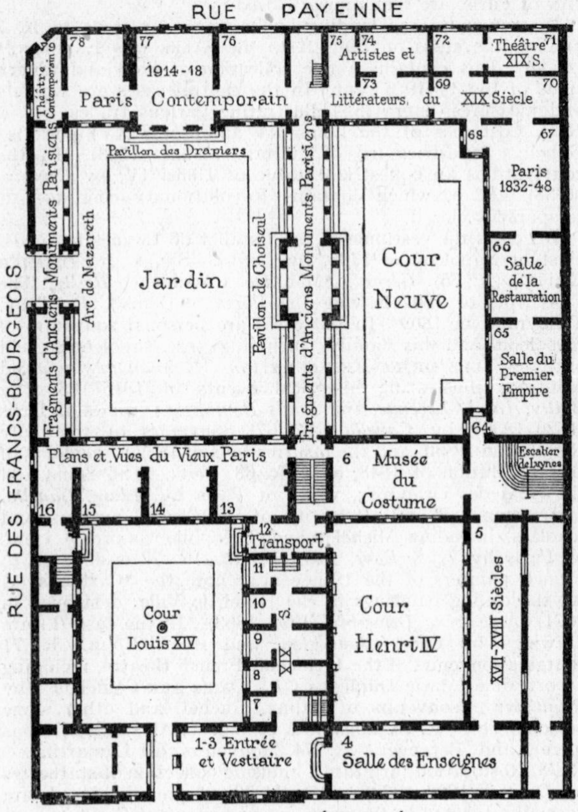

MUSÉE CARNAVALET: GROUND FLOOR

many models and plan-reliefs of the old quarters of the City, etc. Note also the chimneypiece from a provincial château (16th cent.) with the arms of Des Ligneris (R. 13).

24. THE PALAIS DE CHAILLOT.

MÉTRO station : *Trocadéro* (lines 6 and 9).—MOTOR-BUSES 30, 32, 63 to Place du Trocadéro.

ADMISSION. The three museums in the Palais de Chaillot are open daily, except Tues., from 10 a.m. ; adm. to each, 30 fr. The Musée de la Marine closes at 6 p.m. ; the Musée des Monuments Français (reproductions of works of art) closes at 5 ; the Musée de l'Homme (ethnography) closes at 4. In the Musée de l'Homme the library is open every weekday 10–12, 2–6, and cinema shows (' Le Tour du Monde ') are given on Sun. and Thurs., at 4.30 in the lecture hall.

The **Palais de Chaillot,** in the Place du Trocadéro (p. 54), erected for the Paris Exhibition of 1937, replaces the *Palais du Trocadéro,* which was designed for the Exhibition of 1878. The central block of the original structure was taken down, and the two wings completely encased in a new building by Carlus and Boileau. The present huge building consists of two curved wings, separated in the middle by a large square, and terminating in four pavilions. On the walls of the two central pavilions are gold-lettered inscriptions by Paul Valéry. The principal entrances from the Place du Trocadéro are adorned with sculptures by Delamarre and Sarrabezolles, and the two N. walls, flanking the Rue Franklin and the Av. du Président Wilson, are decorated with bas-reliefs by Debarre, Costa, Saupique, and others.

The ***Musée des Monuments Français,** founded in 1879 as the Musée de Sculpture Comparée by the architect Viollet-le-Duc, occupied the whole of the Palais du Trocadéro until 1937. It is now housed in the E. wing, or Aile de Paris, of the existing building.

At present only the sections devoted to monumental sculpture and to Romanesque mural paintings are open to the public. The arrangement of the exhibits is in perfect taste, and the lighting is exceptionally good, making the collection—admittedly a collection of copies—a real revelation of the scope of French art. The sculpture collection is illustrated and explained by documents and pictures epitomising the history of each period, while the execution and setting up of the reproductions of ancient mural paintings—many of the originals of which are fast disappearing—is a marvel of ingenuity.

A purely architectural section is at present in course of arrangement, while another gallery (not yet open) is to be devoted to the smaller masterpieces of sculpture. The later mural paintings—Gothic and Renaissance periods—are being mounted on the second and third floors, above the Romanesque paintings; and faithful copies of some masterpieces of French stained glass—from the Sainte-Chapelle and the cathedrals of Bourges, Chartres, Le Mans, and Rouen—will be exhibited in the main entrance hall.

The SECTION DE SCULPTURE occupies three large galleries, subdivided into rooms, on the left of the main entrance hall.—R. 1. Early Romanesque Period. Merovingian and Carolingian works. RR. 2–6 illustrate French Romanesque Art, divided into the schools of Languedoc, Burgundy, Western France, Auvergne, and Provence,—R. 7. ' Art of the Crusades ' (12–13th cent.) ; Frankish masterpieces from the Holy Land. —R. 8. Gothic work of the 12th cent.—RR. 9–13. Gothic sculpture of the 13th cent., mainly from the great cathedrals of Northern and Central France.—RR. 14–15. Gothic work of the 14th cent.—RR. 16–18. 15th cent. and early 16th cent. art, including some very fine tomb-statues.—RR. 19–21 cover the period 1500–30.—R. 22 (*Salle Jean Goujon*) and R. 23 (*Salle Ligier Richier*) are devoted to the sculpture of the first half of the 16th cent. ; R. 24 (*Salle Germain Pilon*) to the second half.—R. 25. 17th cent. works by *Puget, Coysevox,* and *Nicolas* and *Guillaume Coustou.*—RR. 26, 27. 18th cent. sculpture : works by *Falconet, Bouchardon* and others; busts by *Houdon, Lemoyne, Pajou, Pigalle, Caffiéri,* and others, including portraits of Molière, Voltaire, Franklin, Jefferson, and Paul Jones.—RR. 27 (*Salle Rude*) and 28 (*Salle Carpeaux*) continue the series to the middle of the 19th century.

*The SECTION DE LA PEINTURE MURALE (Wall-Paintings) occupies the upstairs rooms on the right side of the entrance hall. The *First Floor* is devoted to works of the Romanesque period (9–12th cent.), mainly taken from mural and ceiling paintings in churches of Central and Southern France. The principal masterpieces include (beginning on the left of the staircase, facing the garden) : Story of St. Stephen, from the crypt of St-Germain, Auxerre (9th cent.), the oldest surviving French example ; 12th cent. paintings, in the Catalan style, from the chapel of St-Martin-de-Fenouilla, in Roussillon ; St. Maurice and the ‘ Crowned Knight ’ (12th cent.), from the baptistery of St-Jean, Poitiers ; Christ in glory and the Greek Fathers, from the apse of the church at Berzé-la-Ville, near Cluny ; series of scriptural scenes, etc., from the choir of St-Martin-de-Vicq, near Nohant (Indre) ; the great figure of St. Michael, from the cathedral of Le Puy ; biblical and allegorical paintings from the crypt of Tavant (Indre-et-Loire ; early 12th cent.) and the chapel of St-Chef (Isère ; 11th cent.) ; Annunciation and Visitation, from Rocamadour ; scenes from the life of Christ and of the Blessed Virgin, from the Chapelle du Liget, near Loches (late 12th cent.), deeply religious in feeling ; and the majestic array of scenes from Genesis and Exodus adorning the porch and nave of the church of St-Savin in Poitou (c. 1200).

The *Second* and *Third Floors* (not open in 1950) contain mural paintings of the 13–16th cent., including frescoes from Le Petit-Quévilly, near Rouen (13th cent.), from the Papal Palace at Avignon (14th cent.), and from the château of Pimpéan, near Angers (15th cent.). Here also will be exhibited the painting from the dome of Cahors cathedral (14th cent.) and the Dance of Death from the abbey of La Chaise-Dieu (15th cent.). Later work includes the choir of the Breton church of Kernascléden, the Tree of Jesse from St-Bris (Yonne ; 16th cent.), and hunting scenes (temp. Louis XII) from the château of Rochechouart.

The **Musée de l'Homme** is installed in the Aile de Passy (W. wing) of the Palais de Chaillot. Formed by the amalgamation of the old Galérie d'Anthropologie and the Musée d'Ethnographie du Trocadéro, the museum presents a comprehensive analytical and comparative study of the Science of Man. As the exhibition is more or less self-explanatory, only a generalised description is given below.

VESTIBULE. Vitrine du Mois, recent acquisitions.—FIRST FLOOR (staircase on l.). The first room (l.) is reserved for temporary exhibitions.—ANTHROPOLOGY ROOM. Maps, diagrams, and show cases relating to the analysis and comparison of the varied physical characteristics of mankind, both prehistoric and modern ; skeletons of a giant and a dwarf ; examples of funerary rites, including a mummified woman and child from Bolivia (Case 17) ; artificial deformities (Case 13) ; skull (replica) of the Piltdown man (Case 21) ; Neanderthal man (Case 22).—PREHISTORIC AFRICAN ROOM. Stone Age implements from N. Africa and the Sahara ; cliff-drawings (Case 72).—AFRICAN ROOM (Black Races). Agricultural and fishing implements from the Sudan ; objects from the Ivory Coast ; straw-covered figure of ' Nimba,' goddess of fecundity, from French Guinea ; ceremonial masks and musical instruments from the Belgian Congo ; exhibits from Madagascar ; paintings and manuscripts from the church of Antonius at Gondar, Abyssinia.—AFRICAN AND NEAR EASTERN ROOM (White Races). Costumes, pottery, etc., of the nomadic tribes in N. Africa and the Near East ; pottery from the Atlas and Morocco ; Tuareg costumes, etc. A EUROPEAN ROOM is in preparation. — SECOND FLOOR. ARCTIC ROOM. Domestic utensils of the Eskimo ; bone carvings ; funerary masks from the Aleutian Islands (Case 258).—RUSSIAN AND ASIATIC ROOM. Costumes, weapons, religious objects, and exhibits of folklore from Northern, Central, and Southern Asia, China, Indo-China, and Japan ; funerary statues from the Ukraine and Kafiristan ; silver work from Afghanistan ; model of a Chinese actor ; costumes from Tonkin ; ceremonial masks and headgear from Siam and Malaya ; bamboo toys from Japan.—PACIFIC ISLANDS ROOM. Exhibits from Indonesia, Polynesia, Melanesia, and Australia ; paintings by Australian aborigines ; jewellery from Melanesia ; jade casket and tiki from Hawaii ; carved prow of a Maori man-o'-war ; exhibits from Easter Island.—AMERICAN ROOM. Pottery, jade, sculpture, and weapons from Mexico, Peru, Argentina, Chile, and Brazil (pre-Columbian period) ; carved necklace to assist the memory in the performance of a three-day ceremonial dance, from the Amazon basin (Case 454) ; Peruvian funerary rites ; painted bison skin robe belonging to a N. American Indian chief (18th cent.), etc.

The upper floors are occupied by the photographic and phonographic collections (third floor ; adm. only on application to the director), and the library (fourth floor ; adm. see above).

The **Musée de la Marine** occupies part of the Aile de Paris (W. wing) of the Palais de Chaillot. Devoted to the history and development of the French Navy and Merchant Marine, the museum possesses numerous models and paintings of famous French ships and naval occasions. There is also an interesting collection of hydrographical and navigating instruments.

25. THE MUSÉE DE CLUNY.

MÉTRO station: *Odéon* (lines 4, 10).—MOTOR-BUSES, 27, 38, 77, 85, 86 to corner of Boulevards St-Germain and St-Michel.

ADMISSION 30 fr. (15 fr. on Sun.); open daily (except Tues.) 10–12.45, 2–5.

The *HÔTEL DE CLUNY, which houses the Musée de Cluny, is at No. 6 Place Paul-Painlevé (5 min. walk from the Boul. St-Michel viâ the Rue Du Sommerard). Built at the end of the 15th cent. on the site of a Roman mansion, it is one of the finest extant examples of medieval French domestic architecture. The ***Musée de Cluny,** which has been entirely reorganised since 1945, is devoted to French life and art in the Middle Ages. At present (1950) many of the rooms have not been reopened.

The property was bought in 1340 by Pierre de Chalus, abbot of Cluny in Burgundy, and the mansion was built c. 1490 by Abbot Jacques d'Amboise, as the town house of the abbots, but was rarely occupied by them. In 1515 it became the residence of Mary Tudor, daughter of Henry VII and widow of Louis XII, known as 'La Reine Blanche' from the white mourning worn by her as queen of France. James V of Scotland was lodged here before his wedding with Madeleine, daughter of Francis I, in 1537. Later occupants were Card. de Lorraine, Claude de Guise, Mazarin, and the papal nuncios (1600–81). In the 18th cent. the tower was used as an observatory by the astronomer Messier, who is said to have discovered twenty-one comets here. At the Revolution the mansion became national property, and in 1833 it was bought by Alexandre Du Sommerard (1779–1842) and filled with the medieval and Renaissance relics which he had spent his life in collecting. At his death the mansion and its collections were purchased by the state.

An archway, surmounted by the Amboise arms, gives access to the courtyard. The entrance to the museum is the door in the right-hand corner.

GROUND FLOOR.—ROOM 1. *Medieval Costume* (8–16th cent.), Pins, buckles, clasps, wallets (Case 1); medieval shoes, found in a tomb (Case 2); 15th cent. Arras tapestry; carved wood *Pillar with an angel bearing a heraldic shield, from St-Pierre-le-Moutier (Nièvre); examples of worked leather (Cases 3, 4); two fragments of 14th cent. 'broderie anglaise' (above Case 4).—ROOM 2. *French and Flemish Tapestries,* including the *Miracle of St. Quentin (15th cent.), the Deliverance of St. Peter, the *Vendanges (16th cent.), and the *Concert (16th cent.).—ROOM 3. *Textiles and Embroidery.* Egyptian cloth woven in the 5–7th cent. (Case 2); bishops' mitres (14–15th cent.; Case 1); Italian, Spanish, and German fabrics (Cases 4, 5, 6).—ROOM 4. Medieval interior, including a 15th cent. fireplace and furniture; *La Vie Seigneuriale, a series of wall-hangings illustrating the activities of a nobleman's household, c. 1500.—ROOMS 5, 6. Woodwork, carpentry and joinery of the Middle Ages.

FIRST FLOOR. From R. 6 we climb the spiral staircase to ROOM 19. *Medieval Treasures*. Golden altarpiece from the cathedral at Basle, given to the cathedral by the Emperor Henry II (beginning of the 11th cent.); Byzantine and Muslim caskets, chasubles, vestments, etc. (Case 1); 11th

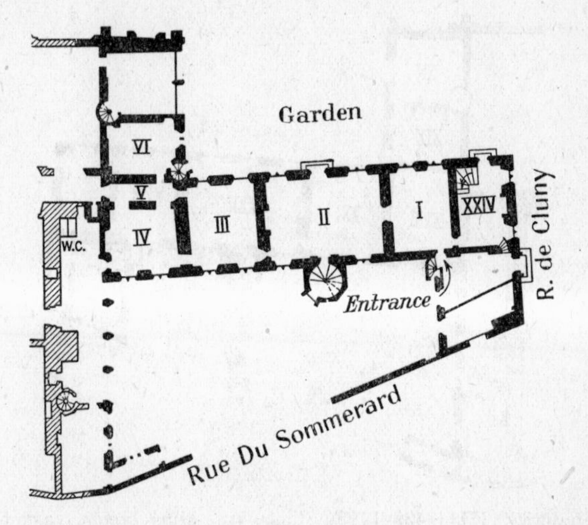

cent. crystal *Casket of Muslim work (Case 4); ivories (Cases 2, 5, 6).—The CHAPEL (R. 20), with a central pillar, is a masterpiece of sculptural decoration. In the window-vault, God the Father blessing his dying Son, and angels with instruments of the Passion. On the walls of the Chapel, and of RR. 19 and 18, twenty-three *Tapestries depicting the Legend of St. Stephen. They were woven for Jean Baillet, bishop of Auxerre (c. 1490), and for more than three centuries hung in the choir of the cathedral at Auxerre.—*ROOM 18. *Life in the Middle Ages*, a series of cases, arranged according to the ordinary activities of every-day medieval life. Case 1. The table; Case 2. The toilet; Case 3. Court life; Case 4. Military life; Case 5. Hunting; Case 6A. Riding; Case 6B. Travel; Case 6C. The Sciences; Case 7. Toys; Case 8.

Games; Case 9D. Writing; Case 9E. Books; Case 9F. Seals.—ROOM 21. *Bronze Work.* Bronze lectern, dated 1383; 15th cent. bronze ewers in the shape of lions, griffins, etc., 14th cent. cauldrons (Case 1); candlesticks and thuribles (Case 2); decorative bronzes, including a Crucifix of the 11th cent., and a crozier of the 12th cent. (Case 3); 16th cent. tapestry, the Prodigal Son.—ROOM 22. *Copper and Wrought Iron.* Wrought-iron locks and keys of the 15th cent. (Case 1); knives, helmets, spurs, and armour of the 12–15th cent. (Cases 2, 3, 5); executioner's sword, and the sword of

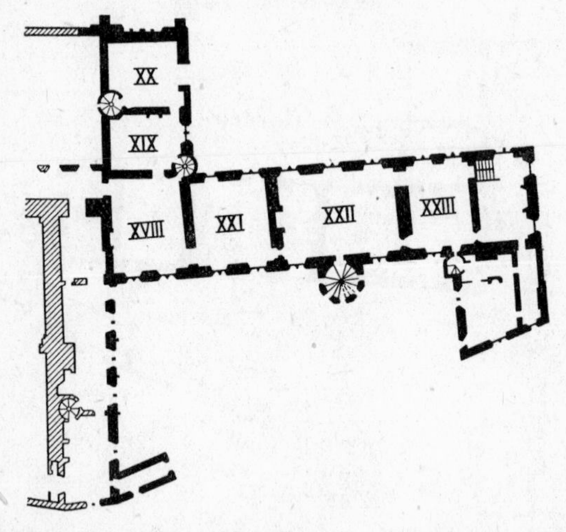

Frederick III (1439–1493; Case 4); alms boxes, caskets, etc., of the 14–15th cent. (Case 6); three medallions worked in copper, with scriptural scenes—the eyes of the figures are in enamel; 13th cent. reliquaries, etc. (Case 7). The chimney-piece (15th cent.), from Le Mans, is ornamented with a rare iron plate bearing the arms of France; in front is a cage for smoking fish or meat. On the wall opposite, Beaten copper-ware from Limoges (13th cent.).—ROOM 23. *Pewter and Lead.* Pewter ware, including a chalice of the 13th cent., and ewers of the 15–16th cent., from Eastern France or Switzerland (Case 1); objects in lead, toys, buttons, etc. (Case 2).—We descend to R. 24, or the SALLE DU SOMMERARD, with personal souvenirs of Alexandre Du Sommerard, founder of the museum (see above).

The **Palais des Thermes,** or briefly the *Thermes,* adjoining the mansion on the W., consists of the ruined baths of a Roman building (almost certainly not a ‘ palace ’), perhaps built by Constantius Chlorus during his residence in Gaul (292–306). The Thermes are at present closed to the public. They consist of a hall, 65 ft. long and 38 ft. wide, probably the *Frigidarium*, popularly believed to have been used as a throne-room by the Frankish kings, with the *Bath*, or *Piscina*, on the N. side.

26. THE MUSÉE GUIMET.

MÉTRO stations : *Iéna* (line 9), *Trocadéro* (lines 6, 9).—MOTOR-BUSES 32 or 63 to the Place d'Iéna.

ADMISSION 30 fr. (15 fr. on Sun.) ; open daily (except Tues.) 10–5. The Library, photographic and phonographic sections are open daily (except Sun. and Tues.) ; admission by written application to the Conservateurs.

The **Musée Guimet** is installed at No. 6 Place d'Iéna. Founded at Lyons in 1879 by Emile Guimet, the museum was presented by him to the state and removed to Paris in 1888. In 1945 it officially became the Département des Arts Asiatiques des Musées Nationaux. The collections illustrate the religions, history, and arts of the Far East.

GROUND FLOOR. VESTIBULE (A). *Khmer Antiquities*, from Cambodia. In the centre, head of a divinity from Angkor (12th cent.). We pass through the central hall (l.) into ROOM N. (r.), which is devoted to *Indian Sculpture* of the Amaravati (2nd–4th cent.) and Mathura schools (1st–2nd cent.). The glass case (r.) contains small terra-cotta figures of the 3rd cent.—ROOM O. *Sculptures from N.E. India* of the " post-Gupta " style (9th cent.). Under the cupola are 12–14th cent. *Bronzes from S. India ; Siva, king of the dance ; Siva, master of the arts (r.) ; etc. In the case (l.) are objects illustrating Jainism ; images of Tirthankaras and Jain divinities, etc. ; statuettes of Krishna and Vishnu, Hindu divinities.—ROOM P. *Javanese Art*. Heads of divinities (7–9th cent.) ; door lintel decorated in the Prambanan style (9th cent.) ; Javanese bronzes ; *Statuettes of Avalokitesvara, and of Kubera, god of riches—note the seven little pots of treasure at his feet. On the left is a case of leather marionettes for a shadow-theatre and a Javanese calendar on painted fabric.—ROOM I. Copies of frescoes and miniatures from India and Ceylon (6–18th cent.). CENTRAL HALL (l.). *Khmer Sculptures and Antiquities* from Cambodia. Wall-case (r.), Bronzes ; *Statue of Hari-Hara (pre-Angkorian style, 7–8th cent.), uniting the two gods Siva and Vishnu in one person ; door lintels (7–8th cent.) ; sculptures of the 9–10th cent. ; ornamental *Pediment of the temple of Bantaisrei (A.D. 967) ; three Buddhas, seated on the sacred serpent (Naga).—

ROOM M. *Antiquities from Annam.* Note especially the head of Buddha (9th cent.) and the statues of two young elephants and a dancer (10th cent.).—ROOM K. (*Salle Delaporte*). Centre : Khmer antiquities. Left : Siamese art and sculpture : Bronze statue of Buddha standing (15th cent,) ; bronze head of Buddha (15–16th cent.). On the walls, paintings and worked leather hangings (18th cent.). Right : Tibetan art. Statuettes ; religious objects ; ornaments in gilded bronze, worked silver, etc. On the walls, paintings illustrating the life

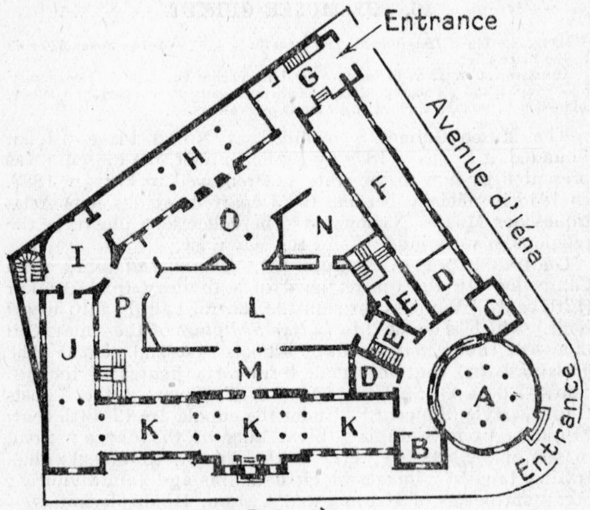

of Buddha ; Buddhist saints, etc.—ROOM F. *Khmer Sculpture* of the Bayon style (12–13th cent.) ; each statue wears the enigmatic ' Angkorian smile.'

The FIRST FLOOR contains exhibits from China, Central Asia, Afghanistan, and N.W. India. The collections of the Asiatic department of the Louvre are also exhibited here.

ROOM F. *Chinese Bronzes.* Lacquered *Cabinet decorated in gold (Ming dynasty ; 14–17th cent.). Bronze implements, ritual vases, etc., of the Chang-Yin dynasty (14–12th cent. B.C.) found at Ngan-Yang, the capital city of the dynasty. Ritual vase with a decorated base in the form of a tortoise (Case 8) ; bell of the Fighting Kingdoms dynasty, 5th–3rd cent. B.C. (Case 10); ritual *Vase (Hou style; 9th cent. B.C.; Case 16); arms, implements, ritual vases, mirrors, etc., of the Fighting Kingdoms dynasty.—ROOM G. *Chinese* **Jades*, of which the earlier ones are in the form of symbols; Pi, the sky; Tsong, the earth; Kwei, the mountain (Chou dynasty; 11–9th cent. B.C.).—ROOM H. *Chinese Sculpture.* 1st Section. Buddha from Yun-Kang (5th cent. A.D.); 2nd Section. A Buddha in meditation, Wei dynasty (6th cent. A.D.). 3rd Section. Head of a monster, Suei dynasty (6–7th cent. A.D.); funerary statuettes of the T'ang dynasty (Case 30), including a small *Stele representing Sakyamuni and Prabhutaratna (dated 518).—ROOM I. In the cases, gilded bronze figures of the Wei, Suei, and T'ang dynasties, 5–10th cent. (Case 34); on the walls: textiles from Tuen-Huang (7–10th cent. A.D.); frescoes from Qizl and Qoumtoura (Turkestan); statue of Lokapala, guardian of the four cardinal points.—ROOM J (*Salle Pelliot*). Buddhist paintings, banners, manuscripts, clay figures, etc., discovered by Paul Pelliot in Chinese Turkestan during his expedition of 1906–1908.—ROOM K (*Salle Foucher-Hackin*) is devoted to objects discovered by the French archæological mission in Afghanistan since 1922. First Section. Examples of Græco-Buddhist art from Gandara (N.W. India), 1st–8th cent. A.D. Second Section. Exhibits from Buddhist monastery of Hadda: *Genie carrying a floral offering (Case 53); *Demon wearing a fur mantle (Case 54). In the wall-case are fragments of the original frescoes from the Buddhist monastery at Kakrak (c. 5th cent. A.D.). Third Section. *Collection of Indian ivories, bronzes, Græco-Roman stuccoes, Syrian and Alexandrine glassware, and Chinese lacquer work, discovered by Joseph and Ria Hackin at Begram, Afghanistan, in 1937 and 1939–1940.

The *Grandidier Collection of *Chinese and Japanese Ceramics*, on the second floor, was transferred from the Louvre, and was opened here in May 1950. Especially notable are three statues of Lohans, or chief disciples of Buddha. Other rooms on this floor contain lacquer-work and Japanese and Annamite ceramics.

27. THE MUSÉE JACQUEMART ANDRÉ.

MÉTRO station: *Miromesnil* (line 9).—MOTOR-BUSES 43, 52, 83; nearest stop, Carrefour Friedland-Haussmann.

ADMISSION 20 fr. (10 fr. on Tues. and Sun.); open daily (except Fri.) 1–4 or 5.

The **Musée Jacquemart André,** at No. 158 Boulevard Haussmann, contains a priceless collection illustrating French art in the 18th cent. (Ground Floor), the Renaissance and Italian art (First Floor).

The house was built c. 1870 by Edouard André (d. 1894), who in 1881 married Nélie Jacquemart, a well-known portrait-painter. Mme André, who survived her husband till 1912, bequeathed their collections, home, and fortune to the Institut de France. The tasteful arrangement of the rooms and works of art as left by Mme André has been scrupulously respected.

VESTIBULE. In the centre, 1. *Pigalle,* Statue of a girl extracting a thorn from her foot, the sculptor's last work (1785).—ROOM I (Waiting Room). *12. *Mme Vigée-Lebrun,* Countess Catherine Skavronska; 28, 29. *Lancret,* Pastoral scenes; 41. *Pajou,* Bust of a girl; works by *Boucher, Drouais,* and *Pigalle.*—ROOM II (Salon Rotonde). Four panels of Gobelins tapestry (the Seasons; Louis XV period) and a Savonnerie carpet (1663). *60. *Nattier,* Marquise d'Antin; *63. *Houdon,* Bust of Caumartin; *65. *Coysevox,* Bust of Gabriel, the architect; miniatures by *Van Blarenberghe, Boucher, Petitot, Fragonard,* etc. (Cases A and B); *66. *Slodtz,* Bust of Nicholas Vleughels, the painter; *62. *Lemoyne,* Bust of the Marquis de Marigny. In the centre is a writing-table presented by Louis XV to the town of Langres.—ROOM III (Tapestry Room). 183–185. Beauvais tapestries (Russian games) after *Le Prince*; 188. *Hébert,* Mme André; 195. *Falconet,* The glory of Catherine II; 189. *Greuze,* Wille, the engraver. Works by *Lemoyne, Perronneau,* etc. Furniture of the Louis XV period.—ROOM IV (Study). 227. *Guardi,* Portico and small square; 228. *Van Goyen,* Coast-town; 231. *Reynolds,* Captain Joming; 234. *Fragonard,* The model's début. In the glass cases are MSS., books, and medals: in Case A, 255. *The Heures de Boucicaut or the Visitation, which belonged to Diane de Poitiers. Other paintings by *Greuze, Lawrence, Goya, Prud'hon,* etc.—ROOM V (Salle des Dessins). Ceiling, Peace and Justice, by *Tiepolo.* 332. *Greuze,* Girl in confusion. Drawings by *Lancret, Watteau, Pater,* and *Boucher*; 345. *Pajou,* Bust of Piron, in terra-cotta.—ROOM VI (Library). 1503. The Hunt, a Beauvais tapestry after *Boucher*; 244. *Prud'hon,* Cadet de Gassicourt; 16. *Roslin,* Self-portrait; 381. *Suzanne,* Mirabeau at the tribune, a terra-cotta statuette. Busts by *Pajou, Lemoyne,* etc.

We return through the Salon Rotonde to ROOM VII (Great Hall). *416. *J. Ruysdael,* Landscape; 418. *Fr. Clouet* (studio-piece), Catherine de Médicis; 423. *Rembrandt,* Portrait of Saskia, the painter's wife; Case with antique bronzes, gems, gold and silver, etc.; 424. *Ph. de Champaigne,* Supposed portrait of Colbert; 425. *Van Dyck,* Count Henriques de Peña; 430. *Murillo,* Franciscan Friar; *432. *Rembrandt,* Dr. Arnold Tholinx. By the windows, small 15–16th cent. bronzes; 14th cent. ivories; enamels of the 16th cent.—410–413. *Corneille de Lyon,* Four small male portraits (Case F); *409. *Rembrandt,* Supper at Emmaus (painted c. 1630); *448. *Donatello,* Martyrdom of St. Sebastian, a bronze plaquette (table A).—Room VIII (Winter Garden). *604. Wingless Victory, a Græco-Roman copy of an unknown Greek statue; Eros (2nd cent. A.D.).—Room IX (Smoking Room). Late 16th cent. Venetian ceiling. 661. *Seisenegger,* Maria Theresa, Queen of Hungary; 662. *Sir Anthony Mor,* Margaret of Parma, Regent of the Netherlands. On the mantelpiece of Istrian stone (Venetian, 16th cent.) is a bust of Charles V, after *Leone Leoni*; 657. *Pontormo* (?), Lute-player.—Staircase. Three frescoes by *Tiepolo.*—Gallery. Brussels and French tapestries (late 16th cent.).—Rooms X–XI are devoted to the Renaissance. 754. Marble doorway (Venice, late 15th cent.); terra-cottas from the *Della Robbia* workshops: *778. *Luca della Robbia,* Virgin and Child. From right to left: *849. *Venetian School* (late 15th cent.), Legend of St. Æmilianus, Bishop of Faenza (marble); 834. Marble door with the arms of the Della Rena family of Lucca (c. 1500), in a sculptured frame attributed to *Benedetto da Rovezzano*; 837. Venetian fountain of Istrian stone, from the workshop of *Pietro Lombardo*; *892. *Desiderio da Settignano,* Young hero (marble bas-relief). In the centre: 841. *Sienese School* (15th cent.), Virgin of the Nativity (painted and gilded wood); *842. *Donatello,* Bust of Lodovico Gonzaga, Marquis of Mantua; *843. *Ricciarelli,* Posthumous bust of Michelangelo (bronze).—Room XI. Stone and marble doorways of the 16th cent.; Brussels tapestry, Bearing of the Cross.—Room XII. Sculptured doors and escutcheons. ' *Encyclopædic Ceiling ' with 25 panels in grisaille, attributed to *Girolamo Moceto.* *1018. *Bruges School* (late 15th cent.), Virgin with the Child illuminating a book; *1019. *Fiorenzo di Lorenzo,* Madonna; *1029. *Carpaccio,* Embassy of Hippolyta, Queen of the Amazons, to Theseus, King of Athens. 15–16th cent. Italian bronzes and other small works of art.—Room XIII (Dining Room). Ceiling-fresco by *Tiepolo* transferred to canvas: Fame announcing the visit of Henri III. Five Brussels tapestries of the story of Achilles (1745); Sèvres, Vincennes, Meissen, and Vienna porcelain; Chinese porcelain and stoneware (Case E).

28. THE MUSÉE DU JEU DE PAUME.

MÉTRO station: *Concorde* (lines 1, 2, 12).—MOTOR-BUSES 52, 72, 73, 84, 94; nearest stop Place de la Concorde.

ADMISSION 30 fr. (15 fr. on Sun.); open daily (except Tues.) 10–12.45, 2–5.

The ***Musée du Jeu de Paume** occupies the former tennis-court at the W. end of the N. terrace of the Tuileries gardens, overlooking the Rue de Rivoli. Along with the *Orangerie*, which stands in a corresponding position on the S. terrace, it houses the national collection of works of art of the Impressionist School.

Owing to post-war repairs on the Louvre, the magnificent collection of paintings of the Impressionist School was (temporarily) removed to the Jeu de Paume in 1947. The pictures are largely derived from the bequest of Count Isaac de Camondo (d. 1911), and many of the works of art were formerly in the Musée du Luxembourg. In the present arrangement the Ground Floor is mainly devoted to the origins of Impressionism, and the First Floor to the development of and reaction to the movement.

GROUND FLOOR. VESTIBULE. Works by *Fantin-Latour* (1836–1904), and *Bazille* (1841–1870).—ROOM 2 (Salle Boudin). Precursors of the movement: *Isabey* (1804–1866), *Daubigny* (1817–1878), *Corot* (1796–1875), *Jongkind* (1819-1891), *Chintreuil* (1814–1873), *Boudin* (1824–1898), *Lépine* (1835–1892), *Camille Pissarro* (1831–1903), *Sisley* (1839–1899), *Monet* (1840–1926).—R. 3. Paintings by *Pissarro, Monet, Degas* (1834–1917), *Sisley*, and *Manet* (1832–1883), including La Femme à l'éventail, and Déjeuner sur l'herbe.—R. 4. Portraits by *Manet*, including Clemenceau, and Mme Emile Zola. Poster for the booth of 'La Goulue,' by *Toulouse-Lautrec* (1864–1901). Sculpture by *Rodin*, Bronze Age.—ROOMS A and B contain plans and diagrams explaining the history and geography, and the various techniques, of Impressionism.—R. 5 (Salle Manet). Works by *Manet*: Portrait of Stéphane Mallarmé, La Dame aux éventails, Le Balcon, La Parisienne.—R. 6 (Salle Bazille). Portrait of Bazille by *Renoir*. Paintings by *Bazille* (La Robe Rose, Réunion de famille), *Guigou* (1834–1871), *Degas, Sisley*, and *Monet*. Bust of Jules Dalou by *Rodin*.—R. 7 (Salle Degas). Paintings by *Degas* (1834–1917). Préparation à la danse, sculpture by *Degas*.—R. 8 (1st Salle Camondo). Later works of *Degas*: *L'Absinthe (portrait of M. Desboutin), *La Classe de danse, Le Pédicure; works by *Sisley*; *Toulouse-Lautrec*, La Clownesse Cha-u-Kao; *Manet*, *Lola de Valence.—R. 9 (2nd Salle Camondo). *Manet*, Le Fifre, Étude de femme nue, Femme au chapeau noir; *Degas*, Fin d'Arabesque.

FIRST FLOOR. LANDING. Paintings by *Sisley* and *Monet*, including Les Dindons, Étretat, and Femme à l'ombrelle.—R. 10 (Salle Personnaz). Works by *Sisley, Pissarro, Renoir, Lebourg, Guillaumin* (1841–1927), *Berthe Morisot*, and *Mary*

Cassatt. Sculptures by *Degas.* Paintings by *Toulouse-Lautrec*: Le Lit, Jane Avril dansant.—R. 11 (Salle Renoir). Paintings by *Auguste Renoir* (1841–1919), including many of his later works.—R. 12 (Salle Caillebotte). *Monet,* Église de Vétheuil (1878), Rochers de Belle-Isle (1886), Le Déjeuner (c. 1873), Paysage, Vétheuil (1879) ; *Renoir,* Jeune Femme à la voilette (1877), Mme Charpentier (1876), Moulin de la Galette (1876) ; *Pissarro,* Les Toits rouges (1877), La Moisson (1876) ; paintings by *Caillebotte* (1848–1894) and *Sisley.*—R. 13 (Salle Cézanne). *Paul Cézanne* (1839–1906), Les Peupliers, Dahlias, and other works ; *Van Gogh* (1853–1890), La Guinguette. Paintings by *Pissarro, Renoir,* and *Gauguin* (1848–1903).—R. 14 (Salle Gauguin). Reactions against Impressionism. *Seurat* (1859–1891), Les Poseuses ; the '*Douanier*' *Rousseau,* Charmeuse de serpents, La Guerre ; *Van Gogh,* Self-portrait, Portrait of Dr. Guchet ; *Gauguin,* La Belle Angèle. Other paintings by *Cézanne, Odilon Redon* (1840–1916), *Renoir, Berthe Morisot, Pissarro, Sisley, Mary Cassatt, Monet,* and *Toulouse-Lautrec.*—R. 15 (Salle Monet). *Monet,* Self-portrait (1917) ; Les Cathédrales, a series of paintings of the Cathedral at Rouen (explanation plan on right of doorway).

'Les Nymphéas,' a series of mural paintings of water-lilies by *Monet,* are exhibited in the **Orangerie,** 5 min. walk across the Tuileries gardens (adm. daily, except Tues, 10–12, 2–5 ; 20 fr., 10 fr. on Sun.).

29. THE MUSÉE NISSIM DE CAMONDO.

MÉTRO station : *Villiers* (lines 2 and 3).—MOTOR-BUS 84 to Av. Ruysdael.

ADMISSION 30 fr. ; open Tues., Thurs., Sat. 1–5 ; Sun. 10–12.30, 2–5. Closed on national holidays and July 14th–Sept. 15th.

The ***Musée Nissim de Camondo,** at No. 63 Rue de Monceau, was inaugurated as an annex of the Musée des Arts Décoratifs in 1936. It was bequeathed to the Union Centrale des Arts Décoratifs by Count Moïse de Camondo as a memorial to his son, Nissim, who lost his life during the First World War. The aim of the collection is to present a tastefully decorated mansion of the late 18th century.

Ground Floor. VESTIBULE. Desk by *Riesener.* Aubusson carpet 'au point de Savonnerie'—GALERIE. Fountain in red marble from the Château de St. Prix, Montmorency.—GRAND ESCALIER. Two lacquered Chinese corner cupboards (Louis XV). Official portfolio embossed with the arms of d'Argenson. Two incense burners. Two Regency armchairs upholstered in Savonnerie tapestry.

First Floor. GRAND BUREAU. Fireplace in white marble

from a mansion in Bordeaux; tables, chairs, and desks by *Charles Topino, Martin Carlin, Saunier,* and *J. B. Sené*; Aubusson tapestries; chairs by *Foliot* covered in Aubusson tapestry work; Beauvais tapestry screen representing the fables of La Fontaine, after *Oudry*.—GRAND SALON. Panelling from No. 11 Rue Royale, Paris; furniture by *Riesener, Weisweiler, Martin Carlin*; furniture cover in Aubusson tapestry by *Jacob* (formerly in the Wallace Collection); six-leaved screen of Savonnerie tapestry; 'L'Eté' (daughter of Hubert Robert), bust in marble by *Houdon*; Beauvais tapestry, 'L'Air,' after the cartoon by *Boucher*; Savonnerie carpet woven for the Grande Galerie of the Louvre (1678).—SALON DES HUET. 'Scènes pastorales,' seven door panels and three lintels painted by *J. B. Huet* (1776); table in steel and chased bronze, given to the Comte de Vergennes by Louis XVI; silver-gilt candlesticks by *Germain*, embossed with the arms of Mme de Pompadour (1762); furniture by *Oeben* and *Sené*; Savonnerie carpet (c. 1740).—SALLE À MANGER. Beauvais, Aubusson, and Savonnerie carpets and tapestries; two tables in ebony and chased bronze by *Weisweiler*; silver ware by *Auguste* and *Roettiers*, including two elegant soup-tureens by the latter ordered by the Empress Catherine II of Russia for Prince Orloff.—CABINET DES PORCELAINES. Table services in Sèvres, Chantilly, and Meissen porcelain; silver-gilt dessert service by *Dehanne* and *Cardeilhac*.—GALERIE. 'Scènes Chinoises,' Aubusson tapestry after Boucher; Savonnerie carpet (c. 1690).—PETIT BUREAU. Furniture by *Leleu, Stadler,* and *Topino*; snuff-boxes, etc., watches, and statuettes; Mme le Comte, bust by *Guillaume Coustou* (1748); medallions in terra-cotta by *J. B. Nini*; *Guardi*, four views of Venice; *Hubert Robert*, Porte St-Denis, Porte St-Martin, Monument Antique; *Duplessis*, Portrait of Necker; *Oudry*, Eight cartoons for a Gobelins tapestry, 'Les Chasses Royales' of Louis XV.

Second Floor. GALERIE. Chairs by *Nogaret*, engravings after *Chardin*.—SALON BLEU. Furniture by *Macret, Riesener,* and *Martin Carlin*: note the glass-fronted bookcase by the last; leather casket embossed with the arms of Marie-Antoinette; Family portrait, by *Gautier Dagoty*; Vues de Paris, by *Bouhot, Canella, Demachy,* and *Raguenet*.—BIBLIOTHÈQUE. Two candelabra in bronze and Sèvres biscuit by *Blondeau* after Boucher; two 'Vues de Parc,' by *Hubert Robert*; Savonnerie and Beauvais tapestries and carpets (c. 1770).—CHAMBRE À COUCHER. Panelling from a mansion in Bordeaux; furniture by *Cramer, Charles Topino,* and the brothers *Jacob*. *Danloux*, Rosalie Duthé (1792); *Lancret*, Les Rémois, painting on copper; *Lavreince*, Singing lesson (gouache); *J. A. Houdon*, Sabine Houdon, bust in plaster.—

DEUXIÈME CHAMBRE. Mahogany desk by *Riesener*; screen by *Jacob*; bed in mahogany and chased bronze (1795); 'Scènes de Chasse,' by *Demoy, de Dreux, Schayer,* and *Swabach*; Aubusson carpet (c. 1800).

30. THE MUSÉE RODIN.

MÉTRO stations: *St-François-Xavier* (line 14); *Invalides* (line 8).—MOTOR-BUS 69 to Rue de Bourgogne.
ADMISSION 30 fr. (15 fr. on Sun.); open daily (except Tues.) 1–6 (1–4 Oct.–Mar.).

The ***Musée Rodin,** in the *Hôtel Biron*, at No. 77 Rue de Varenne, contains the works and collections of *Auguste Rodin* (1840–1917), which the famous sculptor left to the State. Among the exhibits are originals of works executed in marble and bronze, and a fine selection of his drawings.

To the right of the gateway as we enter is the chapel, but we first visit the mansion, opposite the entrance.

Ground Floor. VESTIBULE. 'L'Homme qui marche'; St. John the Baptist.—ROOM 3. Early works (1863–1876): bust of J. B. Rodin, the artist's father, and his earliest known work; bust of Père Aymard; Girl with flowers in her hair; Mignon, bust of Rodin's wife; *Man with the broken nose. Drawings and water-colours (c. 1855).—ROOM 4. *The Bronze Age (replica of the original, now in the Jeu de Paume); busts of Victor Hugo, Dalou, Puvis de Chavannes; Paolo and Francesca, a marble group. Drawings after Michelangelo.—ROOM 5. Busts of Lady Warwick and Lady Sackville-West; Ugolino; Mozart.—ROOM 6. *The Kiss; *The Hand of God; Iris; 'The Cathedral,' and 'The Secret,' two studies of hands.—ROOM 7. Orpheus; Call to arms; The tempest; La source. Paintings by Rodin executed in Belgium (1871–1877).—ROOM 8. Eve; Adam and Eve; L'Eternelle Idole; Fugit Amor. Busts of Marcelin Berthelot, Malher, *Clemenceau, and Pope Benedict XV.—ROOM 9. Mère et sa fille mourante; Busts of Mme Roll, Mrs Potter-Palmer, Miss Fairfax, and Mme Rodin.

First Floor. ROOM 10. Case containing models of subjects for the Gate of Hell (see below); Meditation; Study for a statue of Balzac; Death of Adonis. Drawings and water-colours for the Gate of Hell.—ROOM 11. Temptation of St. Anthony; The athlete; The poet and the muse; Creation of Woman.—ROOM 12. The martyr; Romeo and Juliet; The good genius; Eternal Spring; Bust of Lord Howard de Walden.—ROOM 13. Crouching woman; Three studies of Psyche; Bust of G. Bernard Shaw.—ROOM 14. Christ and Mary Magdalen; Earth and Moon; Devant le mer; Shell and Pearl. Père Tanguy, Cornsheaves, Harvest, three paintings by *Van Gogh.*—Room 15. Little water fairy; Young mother; Children playing; Le Lion qui pleure; Siren. On the walls: Nude, by *Renoir*; Belle-Isle-en-Mer, by *Monet.*

Chapel. The former convent-chapel is arranged as a *Musée Monumental,* and contains plaster groups and figures for monuments. Among the most important are the following: Apollo crushing Python; Base of a monument to Sarmiento, erected in Buenos Ayres in 1895; The Burghers of Calais; The Gate of Hell, a composition Rodin was engaged upon for 20 years; The three shadows; La Défense, erected at Verdun in 1920; Genius of Eternal Repose; Balzac; Claude Lorrain.

The **Park** contains many bronzes and marbles, including: The Thinker; Victor Hugo at Guernsey, formerly in the gardens of the Palais Royal; The shadow; The Gate of Hell; Eve au rocher.

IV. EXCURSIONS FROM PARIS.

As well as being the capital of France, Paris is the centre of the ancient province of the *Ile de France*, one of the most interesting and important regions in the whole country. The number of profitable excursions is, therefore, almost unlimited, and restrictions of space allow the mention here of only a few of the most important. Abundant railway facilities and excellent roads have brought a great number of interesting points within reach of an easy day's excursion, but public road transport is less conveniently developed than in the neighbourhood of London. The excursions indicated in the following section will be found described in greater detail and supplemented in the forthcoming new edition of the *Blue Guide to Paris*.

In addition to the places mentioned below the traveller with time to spare may be reminded of the following points of interest within comfortable reach of Paris: Enghien and Montmorency; Chevreuse and Les Vaux de Cernay; Sceaux and Robinson; Meudon and Bellevue; Poissy, Pontoise, and Mantes; Rambouillet, with the President's country residence, and a lovely garden and park open to the public; and Meaux and the valley of the Marne. Farther afield, but still within a day's compass, are Chartres, Dreux, Beauvais, Compiègne and Pierrefonds, Provins, and Sens, with their famous cathedrals, churches, or castles.

Walkers will find the wooded country around St-Cloud attractive, especially the Forêt de Marly; the Forêt de St-Germain is less interesting, though also preserving some fine trees, while the Bois de Meudon is still agreeable, but apt to be over-popular at fine week-ends. Best of all, though considerably more distant, is the Forêt de Fontainebleau, the attractions of which are almost limitless.

The early Gothic architecture of the Ile de France is particularly fine, and, apart from the great churches and cathedrals of the famous towns mentioned above, the lover of medieval building may be reminded of the village churches of Gonesse, Fontenay-en-Parisis, and Louvres (on the way to Chantilly), with *St-Leu-d'Esserent a little to the W.; Lagny on the Marne; *Morienval, near Pierrefonds; and Longpont, Arpajon, and Dourdan, in the Orge valley S. of Paris.

31. VERSAILLES.

Railways (electric). From the Gare de Montparnasse to *Versailles-Chantiers* (10½ m., 17 km.), frequent trains in 20–25 min. (37 fr., 29 fr.) viâ Sèvres (R.G.) and Viroflay (R.G.). From the Gare des Invalides to *Versailles-Rive Gauche* (11 m., 18 km.), every ¼ hr. (½ hr. on Sun.) in 32 min. (fares as above) viâ Meudon and Viroflay (R.G.). From the Gare St-Lazare to *Versailles-Rive Droite* (14¼ m., 23 km.), every ½ hr. in 32 min. (44 fr., 34 fr.) viâ St-Cloud, Sèvres-Ville d'Avray and Viroflay (R.D.).—Motor-bus No. 171 from the Pont de Sèvres (terminus of Métro service 9) viâ Sèvres, Chaville, and Viroflay.

The main road from Paris to Versailles (Rte. Nat. 10) starts at the Porte de St-Cloud, crosses the Seine by the Pont de Sèvres, and traverses the town of **Sèvres,** with the woods of the Parc de St-Cloud rising on the right and the Bois de Meudon on the left. The famous *Porcelain Factory* (adm. 2–4 or 5, except Sat. and Sun.), founded in 1738 and transferred from Vincennes to Sèvres in 1758, has been a State concern since 1760. A fine historical collection of the ware produced here may be seen in the *Musée Céramique* (adm. 10–4 or 5, closed Tues.; 30 fr., Sun. free).

Another road (Rte. Nat. 185) from the Porte Maillot traverses the Bois de Boulogne by the Allée de Longchamp and crosses the Seine to *Suresnes*, beneath the fort of *Mont Valérien,* where 4500 Frenchmen were murdered during the German occupation in 1941–44. An undying flame is kept burning in memory of them, and a memorial shrine covers the bodies of 15 French men and women, killed either in battle or in the Resistance. A sharp ascent leads to (5 m.) *Montretout*, the upper part of the pleasant town of **St-Cloud** (*Rest. La Réserve*), with a race-course and two golf links near by. The royal castle of St-Cloud, where Henri III was assassinated in 1589 and Napoleon's second marriage was celebrated in 1810, was burned down during the German occupation in 1870; but its lovely park (1000 acres) is open to the public, and the fountains play on the 2nd and 4th Sun. of the summer months. About 2 m. S.W., beyond Garches, is the park of *Villeneuve-l'Etang*, with the monumental memorial (1928–30) to the Lafayette Squadron of American volunteer airmen who fought for France in the First World War. Pasteur died in the château, which is now a medical research institution.—The Versailles road crosses the park and traverses (7 m.) *Ville d'Avray* (Rest. Cabassud, Estoril, first class; des Hirondelles, less expensive, all near the Etangs, see below), a pleasant residential suburb of Sèvres, with the *Villa des Jardies* (on the left, near the station), the country retreat of Balzac, where he was visited by Victor Hugo and Théophile Gautier. Later the house belonged to Gambetta, who died here in 1882, and some relics of his sojourn are shown. The 18th cent. church, in the Rue de Sèvres, is decorated with frescoes by Corot.—Farther on the Versailles road passes the two Etangs de Ville-d'Avray (a favourite subject of Corot's brush) in the Bois des Fausses-Reposes, where a monument to the American army (statues of Lafayette and Pershing) stands at the top of the descent to Versailles.

VERSAILLES (63,114 inhab.), the chief town of the department of Seine-et-Oise and the see of a bishop, lies on a low sandy plain between two lines of wooded hills. With its regular streets and its three imposing avenues converging on the palace, it still retains the cachet of a royal city.

Railway Stations. *Rive Droite,* Rue du Maréchal-Foch, for St-Lazare; *Rive Gauche,* Av. Thiers, for the Invalides; *des Chantiers,* Rue des Chantiers, for Montparnasse.

Hotels. Trianon Palace (Pl. a), Boul. de la Reine, first class, with garden; **Royal** (Pl. b), 3 Rue Pétigny; **Vatel** (Pl. c), 38 Rue des Réservoirs; **de France** (Pl. d), 5 Rue Colbert; **de la Chasse** (Pl. e), 2 Rue de la Chancellerie; **du Cheval-Rouge** (Pl. f), 18 Rue du Maréchal-Foch; **du Sabot-d'Or** (Pl. g), 23 Rue du Maréchal-Foch; **de Noailles** (Pl. h), 18 Rue de Noailles.

Restaurants. *De Londres,* 7 Rue Colbert; *Brasserie Muller,* 23bis Av. de

St-Cloud; *Brasserie de l'Ile de France,* 45 Rue Carnot; *du Chapeau-Gris,* 7 Rue Hoche; *du Dragon,* 30 Rue des Réservoirs; *Brasserie Métropôle,* 6 Place Lyautey; *Sans Souci,* 75 Route de Rueil (continuation of Rue Maréchal-Foch); *Etoile du Sud,* 17 Rue Colbert.

Post Office, 8 Av. de Paris.—SYNDICAT D'INITIATIVE, 7 Rue des Réservoirs; kiosk at the Rive Gauche station.

Tramways from the Rive Droite and Rive Gauche stations to the Trianons (Sun. and Thurs. only).

History. Versailles emerged from obscurity in 1624, when Louis XIII built a hunting lodge here, which he subsequently developed into a small château. But the real creator of Versailles was Louis XIV, who in 1661 conceived the idea of building a lasting monument to his power and glory. Louis Levau was entrusted with the renovation and embellishment of the old château round the Cour de Marbre and at the same time Le Nôtre laid out the park. After Levau's death in 1670 the work was continued by his pupil François d'Orbay, while the interior decoration was superintended by Charles Lebrun. In 1682 Louis XIV transferred the court and the seat of government from St-Germain. Jules Hardouin-Mansart, appointed chief architect in 1676, remodelled the main body of the palace and built the two great N. and S. wings, giving the immense façade a total length of 634 yds., with 375 windows. He also built the Orangerie and the Cent-Marches in the park; the chapel, begun by him, was finished by his brother-in-law Robert de Cotte in 1710. More than 30,000 workmen were employed at one time on the building of the palace and in laying out and draining the grounds, and the cost is believed to have amounted to over 60 million livres (£10 million). In 1687 Mansart built the Grand Trianon. Under Louis XV a series of royal apartments, decorated in the current style, was incorporated in the palace; and one of the colonnaded pavilions in the entrance court, the interior of the opera-house, and the Petit-Trianon were built by J. A. Gabriel. Louis XVI redecorated a suite of apartments for Marie Antoinette and built the 'rustic village' of the Petit Trianon. At the Treaty of Versailles, signed in 1783 by England, France, and Spain, the independence of the United States was formally recognised. Versailles played an important part during the Revolution. The meeting of the Assembly of the States General was held here in 1789, and on June 20th the deputies of the Third Estate constituted themselves into the National Assembly and took the 'Oath of the Tennis Court' not to separate until they had given a constitution to France. On Oct. 6th the Paris mob, led by the women of the Halles, marched to Versailles, massacred the bodyguard, and brought the King and royal family to the Tuileries. In 1814 the palace was occupied by Tsar Alexander and the King of Prussia. Under the Restoration the second colonnaded pavilion was completed by Dufour, but the palace fell into disrepair. Its restoration as a museum (in somewhat doubtful taste) is due to Louis-Philippe. In the Franco-Prussian War Versailles became the headquarters of the German armies operating against Paris, the palace being used as a hospital and Moltke occupying No. 38 Boulevard de la Reine. On Jan. 18th, 1871, the King of Prussia was crowned German Emperor in the Galerie des Glaces; and on Jan. 26th the peace preliminaries were signed by Thiers, Jules Favre, and Bismarck at the latter's quarters, 20 Rue de Provence. In 1871–75 the National Assembly sat in the opera-house, and here the Republic was proclaimed on Feb. 25th, 1875. The two chambers still meet at Versailles for the purpose of electing the President of the Republic. During the First World War Versailles was the seat of the Allied War Council, and the Peace Treaty with Germany was signed in the Galerie des Glaces, on June 28th, 1919. An extensive restoration in 1928–32 was made possible by the munificence of John D. Rockefeller, Jr. During the Second World War Allied G.H.Q. was at Versailles from Sept. 1944 to May 1945, and many of the buildings in the town as well as those belonging to the Château (including the Grande Ecurie) were taken over by the military. Mass was said in the Chapelle Royale every Sunday for the soldiers stationed here.

Versailles was the birthplace of Louis XV (1710–74), the Abbé de l'Epée (1712–89), Houdon (1741–1828), the sculptor, Marshal Berthier (1753–1815), Louis XVI (1754–93), Louis XVIII (1755–1824), Charles X (1757–1836). Gen. Hoche (1768–97), and Ferdinand de Lesseps (1805–94; at 18 Rue des Réservoirs); the Regent Orléans died in the palace in 1723.

The Palace of Versailles.

Admission. The Galerie des Glaces, the Chapel, and the State Apartments are open daily (except Tues.)10–5. The other public rooms, including the Salles du XVIIe Siècle, the Opéra de Louis XV, the Salles du XVIIIe Siècle, the Galerie des Batailles, and the Salle du Sacre, are open daily (except Tues.) 2–5. Adm. 30 fr.

The Place d'Armes, where the great Avenues de St-Cloud, de Paris, and de Sceaux converge, is bounded on the E. by barracks, built by *Mansart* as the royal stables. Opposite are the vast buildings of the palace. Flanking the gateway are groups of sculpture: (r.) France victorious over the Empire, by *Marsy*, and over Spain, by *Girardon*; (l.) Peace, by *Tuby*, and Abundance, by *Coysevox*.

The Avant-Cour (forecourt) or Cour des Ministres is flanked by detached wings once assigned to secretaries of state. Beyond the equestrian statue of Louis XIV (1837) is the Cour Royale, between two colonnaded pavilions dating from 1772 (r.) and 1829 (l.). The visitors' entrance to the palace is in the right-hand pavilion.

Before entering the palace, visitors should inspect the charming little Cour de Marbre, a deep, marble-paved recess at the end of the Cour Royale; this was the courtyard of Louis XIII's château and the nucleus of the whole palace, but was completely transformed by *Levau* and *Mansart*.

We first enter the Vestibule Gabriel (R. 23), with the ticket office and the cloak-room (obligatory for sticks, parcels, etc.) at the far end. On the immediate right are the Salles du XVe and du XVIe Siècles, which contain a valuable collection of 15–16th cent. portraits, for the most part unsigned. Beyond the Vestibule Gabriel is the Vestibule de la Chapelle, which has handsome carved and gilded doors and contains a bas-relief of Louis XIV crossing the Rhine, by *Nicolas* and *Guillaume Coustou*. From the vestibule, we pass through the Salles du XVIIe Siècle (RR. 2–12), which contain historical portraits of the period. On the right of the parallel Galerie de Pierre (R. 16) are the five Salles des Croisades (RR. 17–21). At the far end of the gallery is the Salle de l'Opéra, the opera-house built for Louis XV by *Gabriel* in 1753–70. The National Assembly sat here from 1871 to 1875, and the Senate from 1875–1879. The foyer retains its 18th cent. decorations by *Pajou*.

Returning to the Vestibule de la Chapelle, we ascend the little staircase on the left of the chapel door to the first floor. The striking *Vestibule* (R. 83) of the chapel contains statues of Magnanimity by *Rousseau* and Glory by *Vassé* and busts of the chapel architects by *Coysevox*. We enter the royal gallery, which commands the best view of the *Chapel, begun in 1699 by *Mansart* and completed in 1710 by *Robert de Cotte*.

The high altar is of marble and gilded bronze, with sculptures by *Van Cleve* and *Guillaume Coustou*. The central ceiling-painting represents God the Father in Glory, by *Antoine Coypel*, and above the royal pew is the Descent of the Holy Ghost, by *Jouvenet*.

On the right of the vestibule is the GALERIE DE PIERRE (R. 96), and running parallel to it are ten rooms (RR. 84–93) containing paintings, and portraits and busts of famous personalities of the late 17th and early 18th cent.: *Coysevox*, Bust of John Churchill, Duke of Marlborough (R. 84); *Saint-André*, Louis XIV; *Ferdinand Elle*, Madame de Maintenon (R. 86); *Mignard*, Madame de Maintenon; *Rigaud*, Louis XIV in armour (R. 87); *P. D. Martin*, Battle of Fleurus; *Largillière*, Le Grand Dauphin (R. 89); paintings by *Van der Meulen*; busts by *Nicolas Coustou* and *Coysevox*; busts and portraits of Colbert, Molière, and Racine (RR. 92, 93). Beyond R. 93 a staircase ascends to the ATTIQUE DU NORD, with historical paintings ranging from the Restoration to the present day (RR. 151–162). Returning to the vestibule viâ the Galerie de Pierre we pass (l.) the SALLES D'AFRIQUE, DE LA RESTAURATION, etc. (RR. 98–104), of lesser general interest.

From the Vestibule (R. 83) we enter the SALON D'HERCULE (R. 105), fitted up by Louis XV in the Louis XIV style. The elaborate decorations were sculptured by *Vassé* (1729–34). In the large frame at the end, Louis XIV crossing the Rhine, after *Lebrun* and *Van der Meulen*. The portrait of Louis XIV above the chimneypiece is by *Mignard*. On the ceiling is the Apotheosis of Hercules, by *Fr. Lemoyne*, who worked for seven years (1730–37) on this masterpiece and on its completion committed suicide.

Swiss Guards used to be posted here to prevent the intrusion into the state apartments of "those freshly marked with small-pox, the shabbily dressed, petitioners, begging friars, and dogs."

The SALON DE L'ABONDANCE (R. 106) is the first of the ****King's State Apartments,** which have preserved their beautiful decorations of marble inlay, sculptured and gilded bronzes, carved doors, and painted ceilings, executed under the superintendence of *Charles Lebrun*. The ceiling-painting of the Salon de l'Abondance, which was used as a refreshment room at royal receptions, is by *Houasse* (freely restored). The battle-scenes on the walls are by *Van der Meulen*. The tapestry-covered seats here and in other rooms were made for the coronation of Charles X.

The SALON DE VÉNUS (R. 107), named after its ceiling-painting, by *Houasse*, is noteworthy for its marble decorations in the early Louis XIV style. The carved doors are by *Caffieri*; above are beautiful bronze bas-reliefs. In the central alcove is a statue of Louis XIV in Roman costume and wig, by *Warin*; and on either side of the room are ingenious perspectives by *Jacques Rousseau*.

The SALON DE DIANE (R. 108), the former billiard room, has a ceiling, by *Blanchard*. The bust of Louis XIV in the centre is by *Bernini* (1665). Over the mantelpiece, Marie-Thérèse, consort of Louis XIV, by *Beaubrun*; opposite,

Louis XIV, by *Rigaud.* Busts of Colbert, Villars, and the Grand Dauphin, by *Coysevox.*

The SALON DE MARS (R. 109), once a ballroom and concert-room, with a ceiling by *Audran,* has battle paintings by *Van der Meulen* ; Marriage of the Duke of Burgundy and Marie Adelaïde of Savoy ; Reparation made to Louis XIV by the Doge of Genoa. The paintings of Virtues above the doors, and the portrait of Louis XIV at the age of ten, over the mantelpiece, are by *Simon Vouet.* Gobelins tapestries (Louis XIV entering Dunkirk, Capture of Dôle, Siege of Tournai).

The SALON DE MERCURE (R. 110), a card-room under Louis XIV, has a ceiling by *J. B. de Champaigne,* Mercury in a chariot drawn by two cocks and preceded by the morning star. The Savonnerie carpet and the clock, by *Morand,* should be noticed.

The SALON D'APOLLON (R. 111), the former throne-room, is the last of the king's state apartments. On the ceiling, by *Lafosse,* is Louis XIV (the ' Roi Soleïl ') as Apollo in a chariot escorted by the Seasons. On the walls are Gobelins tapestries (Siege of Douai, Defeat of the Spaniards at Bruges).

The *SALON DE LA GUERRE (R. 112), together with the corresponding Salon de la Paix at the other end, forms part of the magnificent decorative ensemble of the Galerie des Glaces. The ceiling-painting represents France victorious, with a thunderbolt in one hand and a laurel-wreathed portrait of Louis XIV in the other ; in the semicircles appear Bellona in anger and figures of defeated Germany, Holland, and Spain. This is the first of the series of *Ceiling Paintings, designed by *Charles Lebrun* and executed by himself and his pupils. They are continued in the Galerie des Glaces and Salon de la Paix, forming a grandiose monument to the pride and glory of Louis XIV. The Salon de la Guerre, completed in 1678, has preserved its original decoration of coloured marble and bronze and contains six busts of Roman emperors, bequeathed by Mazarin. Over the mantelpiece is a stucco relief of Louis XIV on horseback, by *Coysevox.*

The **GALERIE DES GLACES OR GRANDE GALERIE (R. 113), 235 ft. long, 30 ft. wide, and 43 ft. high, is a masterpiece of the Louis-Quatorze style. It was begun by *Mansart* in 1679 and its decoration, designed by *Lebrun,* was completed in 1682. Among the artists employed in the decoration of the gallery were *Caffieri, Coysevox, Le Comte,* and *Tuby,* for the sculptures ; *Cucci,* for the frames of the mirrors ; and *Ladoiseau,* for the trophies on the walls. The gallery is lighted by seventeen large windows looking on to the park, and facing these are as many bevelled mirrors of equal size. The red marble pilasters have bronze capitals decorated with cocks' heads, fleurs-de-lys, and suns. The cornice of gilded stucco is adorned with crowns and the collars of the Orders of the Holy Ghost and St. Michael. The marble statues of Venus, Paris, Mercury, and Minerva in the niches are copies from the antique. The central ceiling-painting represents Louis XIV as supreme sovereign, while the numerous other paintings, large and small, depict the Victories over Holland, Germany, and Spain, the Peace imposed by Louis on his enemies, the ambassadors sent to all the people of the earth, the protection of the Arts and the People; and the great foundations established in his reign.

Opposite the windows are two doors adorned with mirrors. The second of these admits to the ŒIL-DE-BŒUF (R. 123), named after its small 'bull's eye' window. Here the courtiers used to wait for admission to the king's levée and here arose the scandals of the reign of Louis XV, somewhat monotonously recounted in the 'Chroniques de l'Œil-de-Bœuf.' The decorations are original, including the stucco frieze showing children's games on a gold background, by *Van Cleve*, *Hurtrelle*, and *Flamen*. The fine bust of Louis XIV on the mantelpiece is by *Coysevox*. A curious picture by *Nocret* represents the royal family in mythological costume.

The CHAMBRE DU ROI (R. 124), Louis XIV's bedchamber (in which he died in 1715), opens on the left of the Œil-de-Bœuf and likewise overlooks the Cour de Marbre. Here took place the ceremonious levée and 'coucher' of the king, who used to lunch daily at a little table placed before the middle window. It was from the balcony of this room that Marie Antoinette and Louis XVI, at Lafayette's desire, showed themselves to the mob on the fateful Oct. 6th, 1789. The decorations of carved wood and the balustrade separating the bed from the rest of the room are authentic. The wax bust of Louis XIV (at the age of 68), by *Antoine Benoist*, with a wig once perhaps worn by the king himself, is one of the most authentic portraits of the king in existence. The sculpture of gilded stucco above the bed is by *N. Coustou*. The two chimneypieces date from Louis XV; on one of them is a bust of the Duchess of Burgundy, mother of Louis XV, by *Coysevox*.

The CABINET DU CONSEIL (R. 125) dates in its present form from 1753. The carved *Woodwork is by *Antoine Rousseau*.

Off this room open the **Cabinets du Roi** or **Private Apartments of Louis XV** (RR. 126–129), constructed in 1738 to provide a retreat from the tedious etiquette of court life. In the first of them Louis XV died in 1744. The apartments are at present closed to the public.

We now return to the Galerie des Glaces, and at its left end enter the SALON DE LA PAIX (R. 114), which was the queen's card-room. Above the chimneypiece is a painting of Louis XV bestowing peace on Europe, by *Lemoyne* (1729);

on the ceiling, by *Lebrun*, Peace precedes France in a chariot drawn by doves.

The CHAMBRE DE LA REINE (R. 115), or queen's bedchamber, the first of the **Queen's State Apartments,** was redecorated under Louis XV and Louis XVI. In this room died Marie-Thérèse (1683) and Marie Leczinska (1768), and here the confinements of the queens of France took place. The jewel cabinet of Marie Antoinette was brought from the Château of St-Cloud. Above the doors are allegorical paintings of the children of Louis XV by *Natoire* and *De Troy*. The panels on the ceiling (Charity, Abundance, Fidelity, and Prudence) are by *Boucher*. Above the two covered doors at the end of the room are portraits of Marie Leczinska, by *Nattier*, and Marie Antoinette, by *Mme Vigée-Le Brun*. On the left is the entrance to the private apartments of Marie Antoinette (see below), but it is more convenient to visit first the Salon de la Reine and the Antichambre.

From the Chambre de la Reine we may visit the ***Cabinets de la Reine** or **Private Apartments of Marie Antoinette** (R. 122). This small and somewhat dark suite, with its superb decorations of the time of Marie Antoinette, is temporarily closed to visitors.

The SALON DE LA REINE (R. 116), or SALON DES NOBLES, was the queen's presence chamber. The Gobelins tapestries represent the Coronation of Louis XIV at Reims, Audience of the Spanish ambassador, and the Treaty between Louis XIV and the Swiss. The ceiling, Mercury protecting the Arts and Sciences, is by *Michel Corneille*.

In the ANTICHAMBRE DE LA REINE (R. 117), Marie Leczinska and Marie Antoinette (as dauphine) used to dine in public. The ceiling depicts the Family of Darius at the feet of Alexander, a copy of *Lebrun's* painting in the Louvre. The subjects of the Gobelins tapestries are the Surrender of Marsal, Capture of Lille, Louis XIV visiting the Gobelins, and Audience of the Papal nuncio. At the back, *Marie Antoinette and her children, by *Mme Vigée-Le Brun* (1787).

The SALLE DES GARDES DE LA REINE (R. 118), with coloured marble decorations of the time of Louis XIV, is now undergoing restoration. The ceiling, by the elder *Noël Coypel*, represents Jupiter with Justice and Piety. On Oct. 6th, 1789, the Paris mob burst into this room, and three of the Swiss Guards perished here in the queen's defence.

To the left of the guard-room is the landing of the ESCALIER DE MARBRE or ESCALIER DE LA REINE, built by *Levau* and *Mansart*, with beautiful marble decorations and an interesting perspective painting in the Italian style. Across the landing is a loggia (R. 119) overlooking the Cour de Marbre, in which the door on the right admits to the apartments of Mme de Maintenon (see below), while on the left open the SALLE DES

VERSAILLES

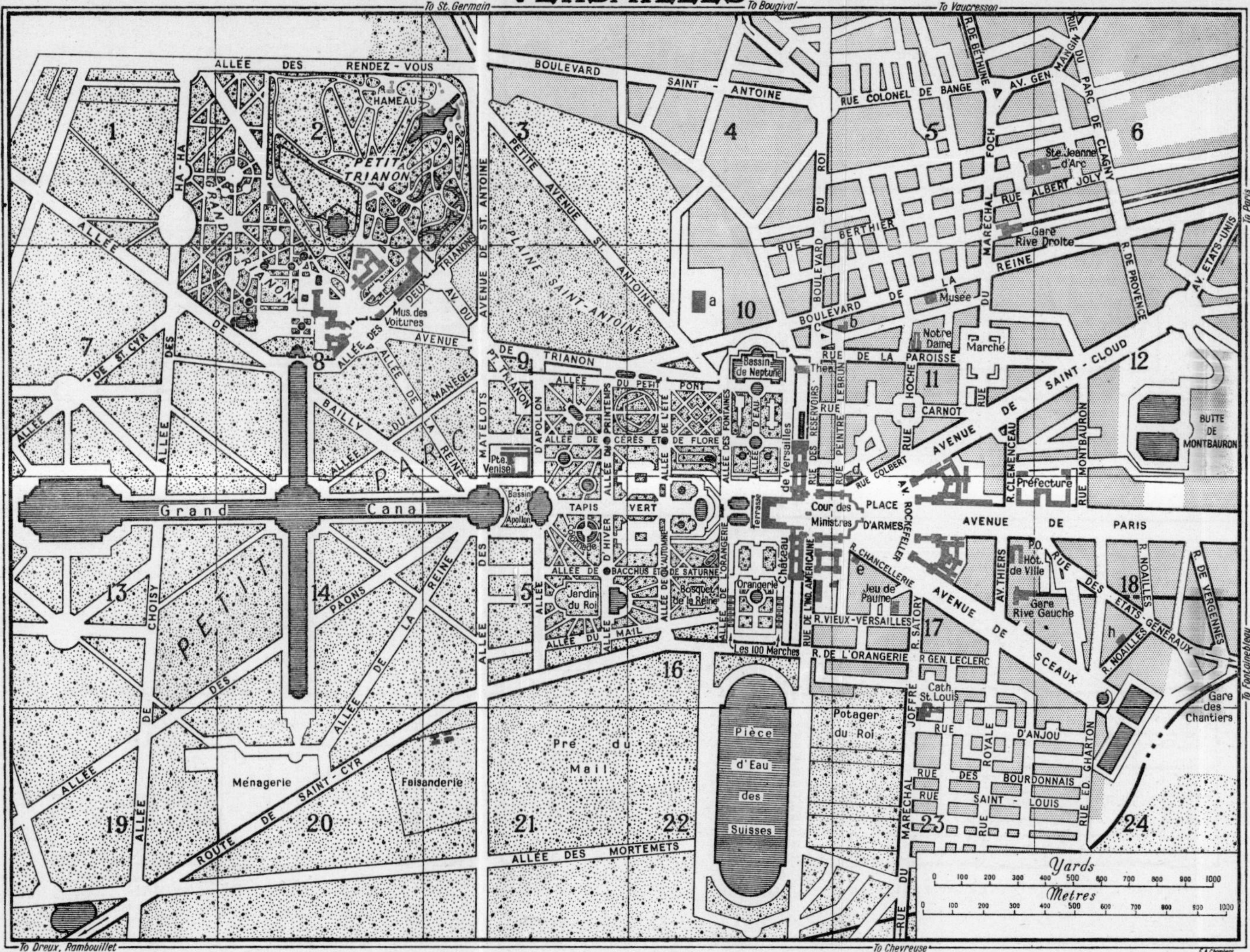

To St. Germain
To Bougival
To Vaucresson
To Paris
To Fontainebleau
To Dreux, Rambouillet
To Chevreuse
ALLÉE DES RENDEZ-VOUS
BOULEVARD SAINT-ANTOINE
RUE COLONEL DE BANGE
AV. GEN. MANGIN
RUE DU PARC DE CLAGNY
R. DE BÉTHUNE
HAMEAU
PETIT TRIANON
GRAND TRIANON
HA-HA
PETITE AVENUE ST. ANTOINE
PLAINE SAINT-ANTOINE
AVENUE DE ST ANTOINE
AV. DU DEUX TRIANONS
Mus. des Voitures
AVENUE DE TRIANON
ALLÉE DES MATELOTS
PETIT TRIANON
ALLÉE DU PETIT PONT
ALLÉE DE ST. CYR
ALLÉE DE BAILLY
ALLÉE DU MANÈGE
ALLÉE DE LA REINE
PARC
Ste Jeanne d'Arc
RUE ALBERT JOLY
MARÉCHAL FOCH
Gare Rive Droite
RUE BERTHIER
BOULEVARD DU ROI
BOULEVARD DE LA REINE
R. DE PROVENCE
AV. ÉTATS-UNIS
Musée
Notre Dame
Marché
RUE DE LA PAROISSE
RUE HOCHE
CARNOT
AVENUE DE SAINT-CLOUD
BUTTE DE MONTBAURON
RUE MONTBAURON
R. CLEMENCEAU
Préfecture
Bassin de Neptune
Théâ.
RUE DES RÉSERVOIRS
RUE PEINTRE LEBRUN
RUE COLBERT
Pte. Venise
Bassin d'Apollon
TAPIS VERT
ALLÉE DE CÉRÈS ET DE FLORE
ALLÉE D'HIVER
ALLÉE DE BACCHUS ET DE SATURNE
ALLÉE DES FONTAINES
Colonnade
Terrasse
Château
Cour des Ministres
PLACE D'ARMES
AV. ROCKEFELLER
AVENUE DE PARIS
Grand Canal
P.O.
Hôt. de Ville
AV. THIERS
RUE DES ÉTATS-GÉNÉRAUX
R. NOAILLES
R. DE VERGENNES
R. CHANCELLERIE
Jeu de Paume
AVENUE DE SCEAUX
Gare Rive Gauche
PETIT
CHOISY
PAONS
Jardin du Roi
Bosquet de la Reine
Orangerie
ALLÉE DE L'ORANGERIE
RUE DE L'IND. AMÉRICAINE
R. VIEUX-VERSAILLES
R. SATORY
ALLÉE DU MAIL
Les 100 Marches
R. DE L'ORANGERIE
R. GEN. LECLERC
Cath. St. Louis
Gare des Chantiers
Potager du Roi
RUE D'ANJOU
RUE ROYALE
RUE DES BOURDONNAIS
RUE SAINT-LOUIS
RUE ED. CHARTON
RUE DU MARÉCHAL JOFFRE
Ménagerie
Faisanderie
Pré du Mail
Pièce d'Eau des Suisses
ROUTE DE SAINT-CYR
ALLÉE DES MORTEMETS
Yards
Metres
0 100 200 300 400 500 600 700 800 900 1000
1 2 3 4 5 6 7 8 9 10 11 12 13 14 15 16 17 18 19 20 21 22 23 24
a b c d e h

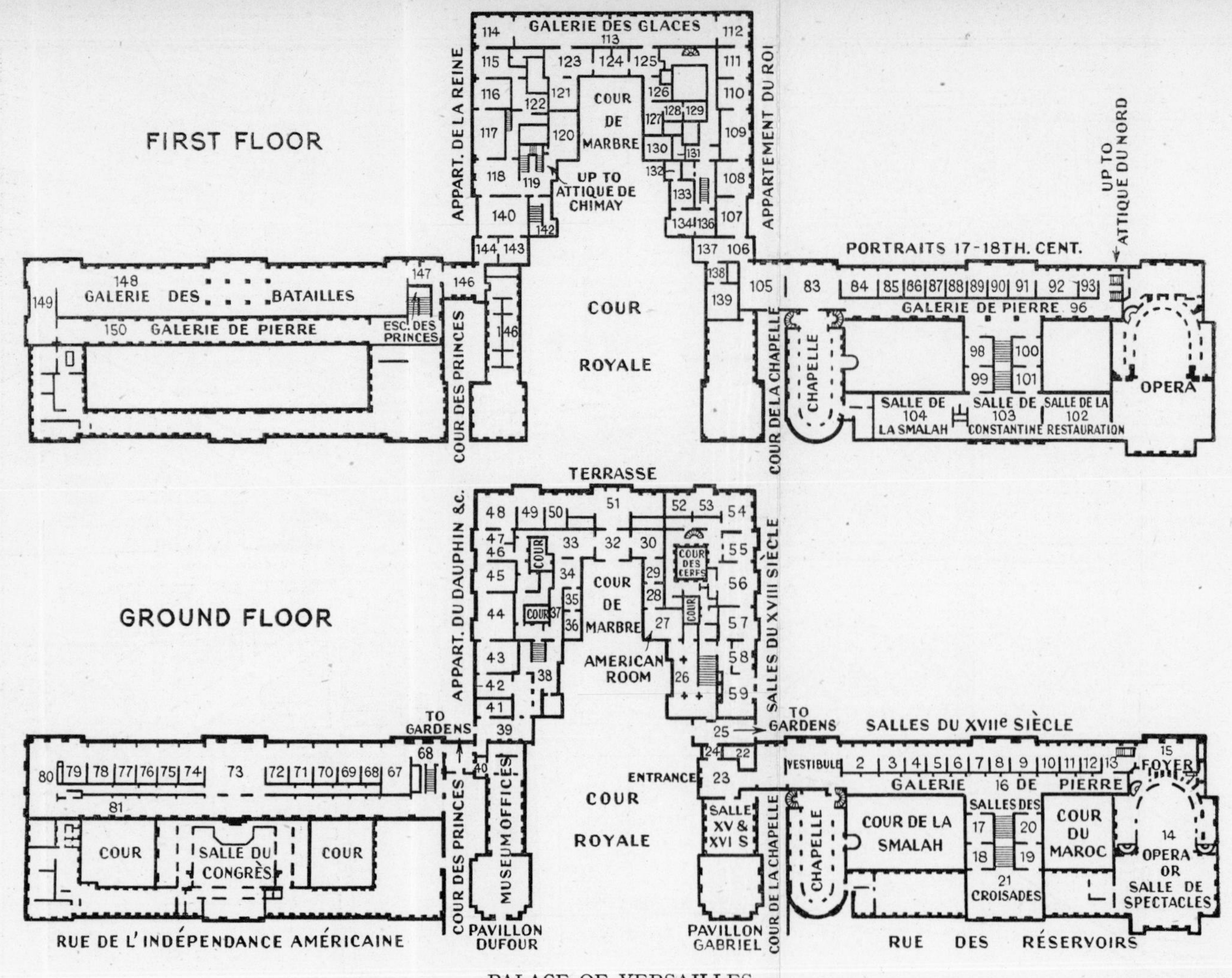

PALACE OF VERSAILLES

GARDES DU ROI (R. 120) and the ANTICHAMBRE DU ROI (R. 121), where Louis XIV dined in public and received petitions every Monday.

We may descend the Escalier de Marbre to quit the palace by the Cour de Marbre, or we may ascend the Escalier de Stuc, built under Louis Philippe, to the second floor, on which are the ATTIQUE DE CHIMAY (r.) and the ATTIQUE DU MIDI (l.), which contain historical paintings of the period 1793–1815.

The **Apartments of Mme de Maintenon** (RR. 141–143 ; shown on request), entered from the loggia (R. 119), were furnished by Louis XIV in 1682 for his mistress, who became his second wife in 1685.

In the SALLE DU SACRE (R. 140), it was the custom for the king to wash the feet of thirteen poor children on Maundy Thursday. The room was completely spoiled under Louis-Philippe, but was restored in 1948. The ceiling-painting, by *Callet*, is an allegory of the 18th Brumaire (Fall of the Directory, 1799). The sopraporte are by *Gérard*. On the walls are three huge paintings: *J. L. David*, Napoleon presenting eagles in the Champ-de-Mars (1804) ; *Gros*, Murat at the Battle of Aboukir (1799) ; *Roll*, Centenary of the States General (1889).

ROOM 144 contains portraits of artists of the Louis XIV period: *H. Rigaud*, Mignard ; *De Troy*, Mansart ; *Largillière*, Self-portrait.

The SALLE DE 1792 (R. 145) was originally the 'Salon des Marchands,' to which vendors of goods were admitted for the convenience of the inmates of the palace. It now contains military pictures. The pillar of Sèvres porcelain was given to Napoleon by the city of Paris.

We cross the landing of the ESCALIER DES PRINCES (R. 147), a notable work by *Mansart*, which gives access to the S. wing of the palace, once reserved for the princes of the blood.

The GALERIE DES BATAILLES (R. 148), nearly 400 ft. long and 40 ft. wide, was constructed under Louis Philippe by throwing into one most of the rooms on the first floor of this wing. It contains busts of famous soldiers killed in battle, and the wall-paintings form a pictorial record of French military history from Tolbiac (496) to Wagram (1809). The chronological order begins on the left. Note especially, *Delacroix*, Taillebourg (1242; defeat of Henry III of England by St. Louis).

Descending the Escalier des Princes, we may either pass out from the vestibule into the Cour des Princes and thence enter the gardens, or we may visit (l.) the SALLES DE LA RÉPUBLIQUE ET DE L'EMPIRE (RR. 67–80), on the ground floor of the S. wing, with paintings illustrating French history from 1796 to 1810.

A passage on the S. side of the Cour des Princes leads to the SALLE DU CONGRÈS (no adm.), built in 1875 to accommodate the Chamber of Deputies which sat here till 1879. The Congrès, or united sitting of the two French chambers, for the purpose of electing the President of the Republic, took place here until 1940.

Since 1947 the hall has been the meeting-place of the Union Française, a legislative body representing French territories both in Europe and overseas.

Entering the door on the right of the vestibule of the Escalier des Princes, we pass through Room 66 and the Arcade du Midi (RR. 40 and 39) to reach the vestibule of the Escalier de Marbre, in which are busts of *Louis XIV by *Warin*, Mansart by *J. L. Lemoyne*, Mignard by *Desjardins*, and Le Brun by *Coysevox*.

The **Salles du Dix-huitième Siècle,** which we enter from this vestibule, on the ground floor of the central block, looking out on the gardens, were occupied at various times by the Regent Orléans, and the sons and daughters of Louis XV, and are also known as the Apartements du Dauphin et de la Dauphine, et des Mesdames. They have been repeatedly altered, and most of the original decorations were swept away by Louis Philippe. They now contain an admirable *Collection of 18th cent. portraits. Room 42. *Rigaud*, Louis XV; *Santerre*, The Regent Orléans. Room 43. *J. B. Vanloo* and *Parrocel*, *Louis XV on horseback. Room 44. *J. B. Vanloo*, Louis XV. Room 45. Louis XVI, Louis XVIII, and Charles X were born in this room, which was also the bedroom of Marie Antoinette on her arrival in France; *Nattier*, Mme de Pompadour; *Tocqué*, *Marquis de Marigny, Tournehem, director of the royal buildings. Room 46. *Nattier*, Marie-Josèphe de Saxe (mother of Louis XVI). Room 47, the music-room of the Grand Dauphin, son of Louis XV, has retained part of its charming Louis XV decoration. Room 48. *Nattier*, Portraits of the daughters of Louis XV. The fine Louis XIV balcony of wrought and gilded iron commands a splendid view of the gardens. Room 49 was the Regent's study, where he died in 1723, and later the bedroom of the Dauphin, son of Louis XV. It preserves many decorative details, including a mirror-frame by *Verberckt*, and a red marble chimneypiece, with figures of Flora and Zephyrus by *Caffieri*. Paintings: *Nattier*, The Infanta Maria Isabella, *Marie Leczinska; *N. Coustou*, bust of Marie Leczinska. Room 50 retains some of its Louis XIV decorations.

The Galerie Basse (R. 51), below the Galerie des Glaces, has been completely altered since the reign of Louis XIV, when Molière gave several of his plays in it, including the first performance of 'Tartuffe' (1664). It contains an interesting series of paintings, by *Martin* and *Lenfant*, of the battles of Louis XV, in fine frames; statues of generals, and busts of Louis XV and XVI. Room 52 is the first of the 'Appartements des Bains,' originally fitted up as bath-rooms under Louis XIV and later occupied by Mme de Montespan, Mme de Pompadour, and the daughters of Louis XV. *Nattier*, *Mme Adélaïde as Diana, *Mme Henriette as Flora. Room 53.

Nattier, The Duke of Burgundy as an infant, Isabella, daughter of the Infanta Maria Isabella and grand-daughter of Louis XV, Marie Leczinska. Room 54. Gobelins tapestry portrait of Louis XV, after *Carle Vanloo. Roslin,* portrait of the Dauphin, son of Louis XV. Room 55. *Noël Hallé,* Allegory in honour of the Peace of 1763; *L. M. Vanloo,* Choiseul (1763); *Rigaud,* Chancellor Maupéou, Comte d'Argenson; *Carle Vanloo,* Soufflot; *Drouais,* Louis XV. Room 56. *Vassé,* Venus. Rooms 57–59 contain paintings of personalities and historical scenes of the Louis XVI period. The two views of Versailles by *Hubert Robert* (R. 58) are especially noteworthy.

We turn right (through R. 26) into Room 27, the **Room of American Independence.** Portrait of Washington, after *C. W. Peale*; *Van Blarenberghe,* Capture and Siege of Yorktown; *G. P. A. Healy,* Series of portraits of American personalities painted for Louis-Philippe. Room 28. *Vigée-Lebrun,* *Marie Antoinette; *Duplessis,* Louis XVI. Room 29. *Vigée-Lebrun,* The Dauphin and Madame Royale. Room 30. Two cartoons for the Serment du Jeu du Paume, by *David*; *Duplessis,* portraits of Mme and M. Necker; *Houdon,* bust of La Fayette. We pass through R. 32 into Room 33, which is devoted to scenes from the Revolution. Note the little bust of the Dauphin (Louis XVII) as a child, by *Deseine.* Rooms 34, 35 are devoted to the Convention and the Directory.

The ***Gardens** of Versailles (entered either from the cloak-room or the Cour des Princes) were designed for Louis XIV by *André Le Nôtre* (1613–1708), the celebrated landscape-gardener, to whom London owes Greenwich Park and Rome the Quirinal and Vatican gardens. The fountains and hydraulic machinery were the work of *J. H. Mansart* and the engineer *François de Francine,* while the sculptural decoration was executed under the supervision of *Lebrun* and *Mignard.*

The gardens were first laid out in 1661–68. The preliminary work of levelling and draining the site was prodigious, and thousands of trees were brought hither from all parts. Inspired by Italian originals which were interpreted with an amplitude and harmony hitherto unknown, Versailles is the masterpiece of French gardening. The gardens are essentially formal, with their carefully planned vistas and straight walks under the shade of melancholy boughs, their artificial lakes and ponds, arranged with geometrical precision, their groves and clumps of trees, lawns and terraces, all interspersed with innumerable statues and vases of marble and bronze, and enlivened with fountains of infinitely varied form. In their general lines and their sculptural decoration, with the characteristic stressing of the 'classical' note, the gardens remain as they were laid out under Louis XIV; but it was not until the 18th cent. that the planting of the trees was developed to its present extent, so that on the whole we have before us to-day the gardens of Louis XV and Louis XVI.

Admission. Gardens and park are open free all day to pedestrians; cars are admitted to the park on payment of 50 fr. The fountains play on the first Sun. in each month from May to Oct., and usually on the third or fourth Sun. of June, July and August. The Fêtes de Nuit usually take place on the first Sun. in June–September.

A complete exploration of the gardens would occupy well over an hour; in the brief itinerary below only the most outstanding features are singled out.

The TERRACE behind the central block of the palace is adorned with bronze statues after the antique and with marble vases typifying War (by *Coysevox*) and Peace (by *Tuby*). Straight in front, beyond the two large fountain-basins of the PARTERRES D'EAU, are the steps called the MARCHES DE LATONE, which command the best view of the palace, as well as a marvellous vista of the gardens in the other direction, especially fine at sunset. On the right of the Terrace extend the PARTERRES DU NORD, where the original design of Le Nôtre has been largely respected. Just beyond is the charming FONTAINE DU PYRAMIDE, in lead, by *Girardon*, and among the sculptures in the cross-walk (l.) is Winter, also by *Girardon*. The ALLÉE D'EAU, designed by *Perrault* and *Lebrun* (1676–88), with its charming groups of children, leads straight on to the BASSIN DE NEPTUNE (1740), the largest fountain-basin in the gardens, and one of the most attractive. Retracing our steps to the Pyramide, we turn right to reach the BAINS D'APOLLON, a grove laid out by *Hubert Robert* under Louis XVI, in a 'romantic' spirit very different from the formal symmetry of Le Nôtre. The ALLÉE DE L'ETÉ leads to the ALLÉE ROYALE or TAPIS VERT, the central lawn, 360 yds. long and 40 yds. wide, which is lined with marble vases and statues, many of them being copies of the antique. Note, on the left, Venus, by *Le Gros*, incorporating an antique torso, and Achilles at Scyros, by *Vigier*. Towards the end (r.) is the entrance to the BOSQUET DES DÔMES, with many fine statues, including Acis and Galatea, by *Tuby*, while almost opposite is the BOSQUET DE LA COLONNADE, with a circle of graceful arches by *Mansart* (1685–88) and a central group of the Rape of Proserpine, a masterpiece of *Girardon*. At the end of the Tapis Vert is the large BASSIN D'APOLLON, with a fine group of Apollo's Chariot, by *Tuby*. Behind it, and separated from the gardens by railings, is the PETIT PARC, divided by the GRAND CANAL, just over 1 m. long and 60 yds. wide, the scene of Louis XIV's boating parties. A transverse canal, nearly 1200 yds. long, leads from the Trianons to the former royal menagerie. Venetian gondoliers were originally housed in PETITE VENISE, on the right; now boats may be hired from the little boating-station in front of it, and in summer motor-launches run thence to the Trianons.

To regain the palace we may traverse the shady chestnut grove of the SALLE DES MARRONNIERS, behind the Colonnade, and, passing the BASSIN DE SATURNE and BASSIN DE BACCHUS, with charming sculptures by *Girardon* and *Marsy*, reach the BOSQUET DE LA REINE. This grove became notorious as the principal scene of the court scandal known as the 'Affair of the Necklace' (1784–85), in which Cardinal de Rohan (seeking the favour of Marie Antoinette by means of a costly gift) was cheated and robbed by the Comtesse de la Motte. Thence the PARTERRES DU MIDI lead back to the palace. To the right, flights of steps called the CENT MARCHES descend alongside the Orangery (closed) to the PIÈCE D'EAU DES SUISSES (800 yds. long and 150 yds. wide), excavated in 1678–82 by the Swiss Guards, many of whom are said to have died of malaria during the operation.

The Trianons.

The Trianons are reached from the town by tramway viâ the Boulevard de la Reine and Avenue de Trianon. From the palace they are about 20 min. walk across the park. In summer motor-boats run to the Trianons from the boating station mentioned above.

ADMISSION. Both Grand and Petit Trianon are open daily, except Tues., 2–5 or 6 (30 fr.). The *Musée des Voitures* is open daily from 2–5 or 6. The fountains of the Grand Trianon play on the third Sun. of each month from May to Sept.

The ***Grand Trianon,** a beautiful miniature palace, designed by *J. H. Mansart* and *Robert de Cotte*, with sumptuous marble decorations, was built for Louis XIV in 1687 as a retreat from the ceremonious life at the court of Versailles.

The palace was occupied for a time by Mme de Maintenon. It was redecorated for Napoleon, who frequently occupied it, and the Empire furniture which he installed still remains. In 1818 the Duke of Wellington dined here with Louis XVIII. Louis-Philippe did his best to spoil the interior decoration in 1837. In 1873 Marshal Bazaine was tried for his surrender of Metz and sentenced to death in the péristyle, then a windowed gallery. The Treaty of Trianon (1920), between the Western Allies and Hungary, was signed in the Grande Galerie. A thorough restoration of both Trianons was carried out in 1925–27.

The entrance from the courtyard is on the left, in front of the splendid open colonnade or PÉRISTYLE. In the left wing, the rooms visited are: the SALON DES GLACES, with mirrors in the Louis XIV style; the ANTICHAMBRE and CHAMBRE DE MONSIEUR (i.e. the Dauphin, son of Louis XIV), with the bedstead of Napoleon's mother, later used by Louis-Philippe; the former CHAPEL; and the SALLE DES PRINCES.

Beyond the Péristyle, in the right wing, the handsome SALON DES COLONNES OF SALON ROND has preserved most of its Louis XIV decoration. The large oak table, 8½ ft. in diameter, in one piece, was used by the ministers of Louis Philippe. Beyond the GRAND SALON (which contains a *Bowl and vases of malachite mosaic given to Napoleon by Alexander I of Russia, after the Treaty of Tilsit, in 1807), and the CABINET DU COUCHANT, which faces the setting sun, is the SALON FRAIS.

To the left (not usually open) is the GRANDE GALERIE, decorated by *Mansart*.—Beyond the SALON DES JARDINS is the wing known as TRIANON-SOUS-BOIS.

From the Salon Frais we enter the SALON DES SOURCES, which contains paintings by *J. B. Martin.* The five rooms forming the APARTMENTS OF MME DE MAINTENON were subsequently occupied by Stanislas Leczinski, King of Poland (1741), Mme de Pompadour, and Napoleon and Marie Louise; note the Empire bed from the Château de Meudon. Then follows the ANTICHAMBRE DU ROI, with a Louis XV chimney-piece. The CHAMBRE DU ROI was furnished (in poor taste) for Queen Victoria, who, however, never occupied it.

The charming **Gardens** of the Grand Trianon were laid out by *Mansart* and *Le Nôtre.* The terrace overlooking the Grand Canal, where the motor-boats land their passengers, commands a fine view. The BUFFET, designed by *Mansart*, with bas-reliefs and figures of Neptune and Amphitrite, is the chief fountain in the gardens. From the JARDIN DU ROI, behind the palace, a bridge leads to the gardens of the Petit Trianon.

Between the Grand and the Petit Trianon, to the left of the exit from the Jardin du Roi, is the **Musée des Voitures,** an interesting little collection of state carriages, mainly of the early 19th cent., notably the carriage ('La Topage') of Napoleon I, used at his marriage with Marie Louise (1810); sedan chairs of Marie Leczinska and Marie Antoinette.

The **Petit Trianon** was built by *Gabriel* in 1763–68 for Louis XV and was occupied by Mme de Pompadour and Mme du Barry. But its special interest lies in its associations with Marie Antoinette, who chose it as her favourite residence. The palace was subsequently occupied by Pauline Borghese, Napoleon's sister. The furniture was sold at the Revolution, but has been replaced by pieces belonging to Marie Antoinette or of her period.

On the left of the courtyard is the CHAPEL (not shown), and at the end is the palace, in the style of a simple but elegant private mansion. Visitors are escorted by a guide (small gratuity). We ascend the splendid staircase to the first floor. The ANTECHAMBER has sopraporte by *Natoire* and *Caresme.* The DINING ROOM has fine sculpture by *Guibert,* with a painting of a ballet danced by Marie Antoinette and her brothers at Schönbrunn. Traces of the trap-door, through which, under Louis XV, the tables used to appear ready-laid, are still visible in the floor. The PETIT SALON was Marie Antoinette's billiard-room, while the GRAND SALON was used as a concert-room. It has beautiful Louis XV woodwork; the superb furniture was designed by *Riesener, Leleu, Demay,* and others. The two vases of petrified wood are supposed to have been given to Marie Antoinette by Joseph II of Austria (her brother). The BOUDOIR was remodelled for Marie Antoinette by *Mique.* The queen's BEDROOM has a fine clock with the Austrian eagles, a marquetry table, a chest of drawers by *Gouthière,* and chairs with the queen's monogram. The bed and bedspread are of the period of Marie Antoinette.

The ***Gardens** of the Petit Trianon were originally a menagerie and a botanical garden laid out by Bernard de Jussieu but were altered for Marie Antoinette in the English style (1774–86). The HAMLET is a sort of theatrical village built by Marie Antoinette to gratify her taste for 'nature,' as popularised by Rousseau. The work of the farm, however, was done by real peasants. It comprises a mill on the edge of a lake, the queen's cottage (with dining-room, card-room, billiard-room, kitchen, etc.), the 'Maison du Colombier,' with pigeon-cote and fowl-run, a dairy where the queen used to make butter, the 'Tour de Marlborough,' and farm-buildings. Near the smaller lake is an octagonal belvedere, to the right of which is the grotto in which Marie Antoinette was resting on Oct. 5th, 1789, when she was told that the mob had broken into Versailles. We return towards the palace, passing the THÉÂTRE, where Marie Antoinette made her début in court-theatricals (1780, restored 1936; adm. occasionally on application to the Head Guardian at the Grand Trianon). We next visit the JARDIN FRANÇAIS, commanding a view of the main façade of the palace. The PAVILLON FRANÇAIS (r.) was built by *Gabriel* in 1751 for Louis XV and Mme de Pompadour.

The town of Versailles, though naturally overshadowed in interest by the palace, nevertheless contains several buildings of note. In the Rue de l'Indépendance-Américaine, facing the S. wing of the palace, is the *Grand-Commun*, built by Mansart in 1684, with a fine gate and courtyard. It formerly housed a crowd of minor court officials and is now a military hospital. No. 3 is the former *Hôtel de la Guerre* (1759). No. 5, the old Hôtel de la Marine et des Affaires Etrangères (1761), is now the *Bibliothèque de la Ville* (weekdays 2–6 or dusk; closed from Aug. 15th to Oct. 15th), with a small museum and fine Louis XV decorations. Louvois died in 1691 at No. 6, once the *Hôtel de la Surintendance*.

In the Rue du Maréchal-Joffre is the **Cathedral of St-Louis,** built by *Jacques Hardouin-Mansart* in 1743–54, a rare example of a Louis XV church. In the interior are the monument, by Pradier, of the Duc de Berri, assassinated by Louvel in 1820 (S. aisle), and paintings by *Boucher* and *Jouvenet*.

The Rue d'Anjou leads from the cathedral to the *Place du Marché-St-Louis*, with its quaint 18th cent. houses. No. 4 in the Rue St-Médéric, to the right farther on, was the *Parc-aux-Cerfs* (a house named after an old quarter of the town), purchased in 1755 by Louis XV for the indulgence of his shameless and oppressive amours.

Behind the Rue du Maréchal-Joffre, off the Rue du Vieux-Versailles is the **Jeu de Paume** (closed at present; normally open 2–5, except Tues.), the royal tennis court, built in 1686. In 1789 the deputies of the Tiers-Etat, finding themselves locked out of the States General, adjourned hither and, with Bailly as their president, took the famous oath not to separate until they had given to France a proper constitution. In 1873 it was converted into a *Museum of the Revolution*.—In the N. part of the town is the church of *Notre-Dame*, built by J. H. Mansart in 1684, the parish church of the palace (interesting registers). The pulpit (1686) is a fine example of Caffieri's work.—The *Musée Lambinet*, 54 Boul. de la Reine (open Thurs., Sat., Sun. in summer, 2–6) contains works of sculpture by Houdon, and good examples of 14–18th cent. religious art.

32. VINCENNES.

MÉTRO stations: *Château de Vincennes* (line 1), for the Château itself; *Porte Dorée* and *Porte de Charenton* (line 8) are more convenient for the Zoo and the Colonial Museum.—RAILWAY from *Paris–Bastille* (Gare de Vincennes) to *Vincennes* in c. 10 min. (c. every 20 min. on weekdays, hourly on Sun.). The trains go on to Boissy-St-Léger.—MOTOR-BUSES: Route 125 from Porte d'Orléans, 115 from Porte des Lilas.

Vincennes (*Restaurant du Cygne*, 22 Av. de Paris), a town of 49,226 inhab., c. 5 m. E. of the Louvre, has much of interest to offer the visitor. Apart from the magnificent château, the Jardin Colonial, the Musée de la France d'Outre Mer, and the Zoological gardens are well worth a visit.

The **Château de Vincennes** is rectangular in plan and is flanked by nine square towers, reduced to the level of the walls in the 19th cent., with the exception of the entrance tower, the largest and finest of all, which has lost only its statues. This is situated in the middle of the N. front, in the Avenue de Paris, just short of the Cours Marigny.

Admission, daily except Fri., 20 fr. Visitors are conducted in parties at 10, 11, 1.30, 2.30, 3.30, 4.30 (and 5.30 in summer).

History. The present castle, succeeding an earlier royal hunting-lodge fortified by St. Louis, was begun by Philip VI in 1337, and its fortification was completed by his grandson Charles V (1364–73). The chapel, however, begun by Charles, was not finished until 1552. The foundations of the Pavillons du Roi and de la Reine were laid in the 16th cent., but these buildings were not completed for nearly a century, when the château, then in Mazarin's possession, was altered and decorated by Levau. With the completion of the Palace of Versailles (c. 1680) Vincennes was deserted by the court. The château was occupied in 1745 by a porcelain factory (transferred to Sèvres in 1750), in 1753 by a cadet school, and in 1757 by a small-arms factory. It was offered for sale in 1788, like the other royal palaces, but found no purchaser, and in 1791 Lafayette rescued it from destruction by the mob. Napoleon converted the château into an arsenal in 1808, when the surviving 13th cent. buildings were demolished. In 1840 it was made into a fortress, and much of Levau's decoration was destroyed or masked by casemates; but in 1930 a scheme was set on foot to restore the castle to its earlier appearance by removing the 19th cent. accretions. During the Second World War the castle was again militarised, and the German occupying forces had a supply depôt here. In 1944, when they were endeavouring to evacuate the building, the Pavillon de la Reine was partially destroyed by an explosion.

The historical associations of Vincennes are endless. St. Louis used to administer justice beneath an oak tree in the forest. It witnessed the death of Louis X in 1316, of Philip V in 1322, of Charles IV in 1328, of Charles IX in 1574, and of Mazarin in 1661; and Charles V was born here in 1337. In 1422 Henry V of England died at Vincennes, seven weeks before the death of Charles VI, whom he was to succeed as king of France. During the reign of Louis XIII the keep was used as a state prison; and among its famous prisoners were the Grand Condé, Card. de Retz, Fouquet, Diderot, and Mirabeau. In 1804 the Duc d'Enghien, son of the Prince de Condé, arrested five days previously by Napoleon's orders, was tried by court-martial and shot the same night. Gen. Daumesnil was governor of the château from 1809 to 1814, during the Hundred Days, and from 1830 till his death in 1832. When summoned to surrender by the Allies in 1814, his answer was "First give me back my leg" (he had lost a leg at Wagram). In 1830, when the Paris mob broke into the fortress in search of some of the former ministers of Charles X, he dispersed them by threatening to blow up the powder-magazine. In 1944, three days before the evacuation, the Germans shot some thirty hostages against the interior of the ramparts.

We enter by the main gateway beneath the *Tour du Village,* 155 ft. high. In the great courtyard are (l.) the chapel and the *Pavillon de la Reine* (damaged), where Mazarin died, and (r.) the entrance to the keep and the *Pavillon du Roi.* These great 'pavilions' were built in 1654–60 by Levau, who connected them by a wall (destroyed) across the courtyard as well as converting the S. entrance of the enceinte into a triumphal arch. The Pavillon de la Reine normally houses the *War Museum* and *Library,* but these are temporarily closed owing to the damage done in 1944. The explosion, however, by blasting away the casemates, revealed much of Levau's decoration on the S. wall of the castle.

The well-preserved KEEP, 170 ft. in height, a square tower flanked with round turrets, is enclosed in a separate turreted enceinte and is the finest in France since the Château de Coucy was blown up by the Germans (in 1917). It now contains a small historical museum, but is specially notable for the vaulting and corbels on each floor.

The two doors on the ground floor facing the postern came from the prison of Louis XVI in the Temple. Henry V and Charles IX died on the 1st floor; the 2nd floor was the favourite residence of Charles V; and the 3rd floor was used in the 17th cent. for prisoners of state. The E. corridor on the 3rd floor contains the most ancient of their inscriptions(1587 onwards).

The CHAPEL was founded by Charles V in 1379 and completed under Henri II in 1552. The nave windows and the rose window have flamboyant tracery. The vaulting is notable for its lightness and grace.

The *Stained Glass of the last seven windows, by Beaurain (16th cent.), was completely restored after an explosion in 1870. The five apse windows represent scenes from the Apocalypse, while the other two represent the Labourers in the Vineyard (r.) and the Last Judgment (l.). The Duc d'Enghien (see above) is commemorated by a monument (four marble statues by Deseine; 1816), removed from the choir by Napoleon III to the oratory on the left. A pretty 14th cent. door leads into the treasury, the ground floor of which was the original chapel.

The **Bois de Vincennes,** first enclosed in the 12th cent., was replanted in 1731 by Louis XV and converted into a park for the use of the citizens of Paris. In 1860 the Bois was further enlarged to the S.W. In 1934 the ground between the E. side of the château and the Nouveau Fort (1839) was cleared and relaid to form the handsome *Cours des Maréchaux,* and it is hoped that in the near future the dreary expanse of manœuvre-ground S. of the Château will also be replanted. To the S.W. of the Château, bordering the Av. Daumesnil, is the **Parc Zoölogique de Vincennes* (open daily 9–4; adm. 30 fr.; café-restaurant), one of the finest zoos in Europe (35 acres), containing some 600 mammals and over 1200 birds. A splendid view of the Bois is obtained from the summit of the Grand Rocher at the N. end of the park. Farther W. along the Av. Daumesnil (r.) is the **Musée de la**

France d'Outre Mer (open daily, except Tues., 2–5.30 ; adm. 20 fr.), housed in a magnificent building constructed for the Colonial Exhibition of 1931. The museum is devoted to the history and development of the French colonies. Below the ground floor (entrance to the left of the vestibule) is a fine aquarium, with a collection of giant tortoises as its most noteworthy feature.

To the E. of the château the Av. des Minimes leads S.E. to the charming *Lac des Minimes* (the prettiest of the three lakes in the Bois). At the N. end of the lake a bridge crosses to the *Ile de la Porte-Jaune* (café–restaurant, boats for hire, etc.). In the Av. de la Belle-Gabrielle, to the E. of the lake, is the *Jardin Colonial* (open Thurs., 2–4), with the buildings of the Institut Nationale d'Agronomie Coloniale, and a charming little Indo-Chinese pagoda.

33. LA MALMAISON.

Motor-bus No. 258 from the Pont de Neuilly (terminus of Métro service No. 1), in c. ½ hr. viâ Puteaux, Nanterre, and Rueil, going on to St-Germain. No. 158 goes as far as Rueil only.

Rueil (8¾ m.) and *St-Germain* (12½ m. in ½ hr.) are reached from Paris (Gare St-Lazare) also by Electric Railway (frequent trains), following the oldest railway line from Paris (1837). *Maisons-Laffitte* (10½ m.) is served by motor-bus No. 262 from the Pont de Neuilly (40 min.) and by steam trains from the Gare St-Lazare (hourly in 20 min.).

In the church of *Rueil* (5½ m.), on the left of the uninteresting road from Paris, is the tomb of the Empress Josephine, erected in 1825 by her children, Eugène and Hortense de Beauharnais. The 15th cent. Italian organ-case was a gift from Napoleon III.—The station of Rueil, to the right of the road, is c. 1½ m. from Malmaison.

The famous château of **La Malmaison,** 6¾ m. from Paris, was built for Josephine Bonaparte after 1798. It is a low featureless building, but of great historical interest (open daily except Tues., 10–12 and 1.30–5 in summer, 11–12 and 1–4 in winter ; adm. 30 fr., Sun. 15 fr. ; gratuity to guide).

At the height of her power the empress held a literary and artistic salon at Malmaison, and after her divorce in 1809 she retired hither and devoted herself to gardening. She died here in 1814 of a chill caught while doing the honours of the grounds to the allied sovereigns. Napoleon spent five days here in 1815, between Waterloo and his departure for St. Helena. Malmaison was bought in 1814 by Maria Christina, Queen of Spain, and in 1861 by Napoleon III. In 1896 it was bought and presented to the state by M. Osiris.

Visitors enter by the door on the right and ascend at once to the Second Floor, which is devoted to permanent and loan exhibitions.—In R. 2 are letters and souvenirs of the King of Rome.—R. 3 reproduces the bedroom of Queen Hortense, mother of Napoleon III.—R. 4 contains souvenirs of the Second Empire.—We descend to the first floor, where visitors are divided into parties conducted by a guardian.

First Floor. The first room contains wall-papers of the Revolution and Empire. The *First Consul's Room* is a reconstitution of Napoleon's bedroom at the Tuileries, with the original furniture and hangings. Here also are Napoleon's coronation robes, and portraits of Napoleon and Josephine in coronation robes, by Lefèvre. The magnificent 'Table d'Austerlitz' is decorated with portraits of Napoleon's marshals in gold and Sèvres ware. The next room contains Napoleon's camp furniture, his mapping-instruments, and his notebook with private dossiers of his principal subordinates. The *Salle Raba Deutsch de la Meurthe* contains a suite of furniture given to the Emperor by his brother, Joseph, on the latter's elevation to the throne of Spain. The clock was presented by Louis Bonaparte (king of Holland). The *Antechamber* contains furniture from Elba and souvenirs of Josephine and Hortense. In the *Empress's Bedroom* are a screen embroidered by her, a fine Sèvres clock, and the bed in which she died in 1814. To the right of the bed is her portrait by Baron Gérard (1814). The *Emperor's Bedroom* contains Napoleon's camp-bed from St. Helena, his death mask moulded by Antommarchi, his Corsican doctor, etc. *Josephine's Boudoir* is at present closed.

GROUND FLOOR. In the *Salon* are Josephine's embroidery frame, etc., a screen embroidered by her, her bust by Chinard, and a chimneypiece given to Napoleon by Pope Pius VII. The *Music Room* is at present closed. The *Billiard Room* contains Napoleon's throne from Fontainebleau, his portrait in Gobelins tapestry, and a Savonnerie carpet with Napoleon's insignia. Beyond the *Vestibule d'Honneur* is the *Dining Room*, in which are two 'surtouts,' or sets of table-decorations, presented to Napoleon, and frescoes of Pompeian dancers by Lafitte. The gold table service was presented to Napoleon on his coronation, and was used at an official state banquet given to the King and Queen of England at the Quai d'Orsay in 1938. The *Council Chamber*, shaped like a tent, contains a writing-desk of yew-wood, the gift of the city of Bordeaux, and a clock from the Tuileries. In the *Library* are Napoleon's bureau and armchair, his field-desk, and other furniture; also busts of Josephine and Elisa Bonaparte Baciocchi, by Bosio.

The *Park*, of which but 15 acres are left out of 500, contains a rose garden planted with the varieties of roses that were grown by Josephine in 1800–15. The *Stables*, to the right of the entrance, contain the 'Opal,' the state carriage in which Josephine drove to Malmaison after her divorce, and a gala coach (temp. Louis XIV) used by Napoleon.

Travellers with time to spare may go on by motor-bus No. 258 to St-Germain past (8 m.) *Bougival* (Rest. du Coq-Hardi, not cheap), pleasantly situated on a bend of the Seine, and thence along the river viâ (8¾ m.) *Marly-la-Machine* and (9½ m.) *Port-Marly*. The original Machine de Marly was constructed for Louis XIV to raise water from the Seine to the Marly aqueduct which carried it to the gardens of Versailles. The present machine, which takes its water from underground sources, dates only from 1855–59. The little town of *Marly-le-Roi* stands at the head of a small valley, 1¼ m. above Port-Marly. Its royal château, built in 1680 by Louis XIV, was destroyed at the Revolution, but the Forêt de Marly (5000 acres), behind the town, affords pleasant walks.

10 m. **St-Germain-en-Laye** (*Hôt. du Pavillon Henri-IV*, first class; *Pavillon d'Estrées, Pavillon Franklin, Villa Dauphine*; *de l'Aigle d'Or*), splendidly placed on a hill above the Seine, is famous for its ancient royal *Castle*, built in the 12th cent. by Louis VI and completely rebuilt in 1539–48 by Francis I, except for the keep. The so-called *Château Neuf*, below the original castle, constructed by Henri II and Henri IV, was pulled down in 1776, except for the Pavillon Henri-IV. It was in this 'new' castle that Louis XIV was born in 1638, five years before the death of his father in the same building; and it remained one of the principal seats of the French Court until the completion of Versailles in 1682. Meanwhile the old château afforded refuge to the widowed Queen Henrietta Maria of England, and after 1688 it was the residence of the exiled James II, who died there in 1701. His tomb, erected by George IV in the church, opposite the castle, contains only his heart.

After many vicissitudes the château became a museum under Napoleon III, and it now houses the ***Musée d'Antiquités Nationales** (open daily, except Tues. 10–12, 1.30–5; adm. 30 fr.), a magnificent collection of prehistoric and Gallo-Roman antiquities. The Treaty of St-Germain, between the Western Allies and Austria, was signed in the château in Sept. 1919.

To the N. of the castle is the *Parterre*, a park originally laid out by Le Nôtre. At its S.E. corner is the *Pavillon Henri-IV* (see above), now a famous hotel, where Dumas wrote 'The Three Musketeers' and 'Monte Cristo,' and where Thiers died in 1877. The *Terrace of St-Germain*, extending N. from the Pavillon for 1½ m., commands a magnificent view, compared by James II to that from the Terrace at Richmond. It leads N. to the Grille Royale, at the entrance to the *Forêt de St-Germain*, a former royal hunting-ground over 9000 acres in extent, with many fine drives and walks.

Near the N. end of the forest is **Maisons-Laffitte** (*Hôt. de la Vieille-Fontaine*), a residential town on the Seine, 4 m. from St-Germain viâ Carrières-sous-Bois, 5½ m. through the forest. It possesses a well-known racecourse and training stables, and a celebrated *Château*, the masterpiece of François Mansart (1642–51) now containing a notable collection of 17–19th cent. French furniture (open 10–12, 2–4 or 5; closed all day Tues. and on Fri. morning; adm. 30 fr.). The château was bought in 1818 and the park cut up into building-lots by Jacques Laffitte, banker who had profited by the Napoleonic wars.—From Maisons motor-bus No. 262 returns to Paris in c. 40 minutes.

34. SAINT-DENIS AND CHANTILLY.

RAILWAY from the Gare du Nord to *St-Denis*, frequent service in 9 min.; to *Chantilly*, 25½ m. (41 km.) in ½–1 hr.

MOTOR-BUSES to *St-Denis*. Nos. 154, 168 from the Porte de Clignancourt (Métro service 4); 153, 156 from the Porte de la Chapelle (Métro service 12); 142 from the Porte de St-Ouen (Métro service 13).

AUTOCARS of the Renault and Citroën companies to *Chantilly* twice daily in summer from the Porte Maillot (Boul. Gouvion-St-Cyr) in 1½ hr., going on to *Senlis*.

ROAD ROUTE. The most direct route to (2½ m.) *St-Denis* (Rte. Nat. 1) is from the Porte de la Chapelle, traversing the uninteresting suburb of *La Plaine-St-Denis*. The alternative routes from the Porte de Clignancourt or Porte de St-Ouen, through *St-Ouen*, or from the Porte Maillot or Porte Champerret viâ *Clichy* and *St-Ouen*, are only a little longer.

SAINT-DENIS (*Restaurant Chotard*, 5 Rue de la République; *du Grand-Cerf*, opposite the basilica), now a rather unattractive industrial suburb of Paris, on the right bank of the Seine, was founded on the traditional site of the burial place of the missionary apostle of Paris (comp. Montmartre). It is celebrated for its basilica, containing the tombs of the royal house of France.

The ***Basilica of St-Denis,** in the centre of the town, though in itself a fine example of Gothic architecture, is overshadowed in interest by its series of royal tombs, a gallery of French funerary sculpture from the time of St. Louis (c. 1250) to the close of the 16th century.

History. The abbey of St-Denis was founded in the 5th cent. at the instance of St. Geneviève, and the saint's shrine (the exact site of his burial is uncertain) was beautified by Dagobert I (d. 638). The first substantial church on the present site was built by Abbot Fulrad in 750–775, but this was replaced by Abbot Suger, minister of Louis VI and Louis VII, and the narthex (W. porch) and apse (c. 1136–44), which survive from his building, rank among the most important examples of the earliest Gothic architecture. The crypt, of the same period, retains the Romanesque arch. The rest of the church was rebuilt in 1240–81 from the design of Pierre de Montereau (d. 1267), and the chapels on the N. side of the nave were added c. 1375.

It was not until the time of Louis XI (St. Louis; d. 1270) that St-Denis became recognised as the mausoleum of the royal house. The existing tombs of earlier kings were mostly made at the order of St. Louis, though a few were brought here from other churches after the Revolution (see below). In 1422 the body of Henry V lay in state in the church on its way from Vincennes to Westminster. Seven years later Joan of Arc dedicated her armour here, but the English captured the town soon after and held it until 1436. When Condé's Huguenots took the place in 1567 he prevented them from despoiling the basilica; in the same year he was defeated in the plain to the S., though the Catholic leader, Montmorency, was mortally wounded. In 1593 Henri IV solemnly abjured protestantism at the W. doorway.

After some injudicious alterations in the 18th cent., the abbey was suppressed at the Revolution, when the church was unroofed, the tombs rifled and dispersed, and the royal ashes desecrated. Many of the monuments were saved from complete destruction by Alexandre Lenoir, who preserved them in his Musée des Petits-Augustins (École des Beaux-Arts). Restoration was taken in hand by Debret in 1813, but was so incompetently carried out that the stability of the N. tower was endangered, and it had to be taken down in 1847. A subsequent restoration by Viollet-le-Duc and Darcy went some way to repair the harm but the explosion of a bomb-dump in 1918 caused further damage.

Exterior. The W. front, though dating from Suger's time, was disfigured at the Revolution and poorly restored thereafter; but the surviving (S) tower is of good 12th cent. design, with a low modern steeple. The N. transeptal portal (accessible on application to the Gardien Chef) also dates partly from Suger, but the rose window above it is 13th cent. work, as is also the portal of the S. transept.

Admission to the W. part of the nave is free; visitors to the royal tombs and the crypt are conducted (rapidly) in parties every ½ hr. on weekdays (except Tues.), 10–12 and 2–4 or 5, on Sun. 2–4 or 5 (30 fr.). For a more leisurely visit, apply for a student's ticket to the Administration des Beaux Arts, 3 Rue de Valois, Paris 1, which admits also to the ritual choir.

Interior (only the more important tombs are listed here). The conducted visit begins in the N. Aisle, in which are the tombs (13–14th cent.) of members of the royal family, including *Louis* (d. 1260), eldest son of St. Louis, with Henry III of England as one of the bearers.—N. Transept. Tomb of *Louis XII* (d. 1515) and *Anne of Brittany* (d. 1514), by Jean Juste (Giovanni di Giusto). The royal pair are depicted naked and recumbent on the tombstone, and kneeling on the canopy; bas-reliefs illustrate episodes in the king's career. Opposite, *Henri II* (d. 1559) and *Catherine de Médicis* (d. 1558), a tomb designed by Primaticcio in 1560–73, with recumbent and kneeling effigies of the king and queen, and supporters and reliefs by Germain Pilon and other contemporary sculptors. Here also are the tombs of *Philip V* (d. 1322), *Charles IV* (d. 1328), *Philip VI* (d. 1350), and *John II* (d. 1364 at the Savoy, London), the last two by André Beauneveu ; and, by the choir steps, *Childebert I* (d. 558), an 11th cent. statue from St-Germain-des-Prés. In the chapel to the left, at the top of the steps, statues of *Henri II* and *Catherine de Médicis*, by Germain Pilon (1583).

CHOIR and AMBULATORY. The Lady Chapel and the chapels on either side of it preserve some stained glass of the 12–13th century. In the Sanctuary is the *Altar of the Relics* (by Viollet-le-Duc), on which are placed the reliquaries of St. Denis and his fellow-martyrs.—The TREASURY, off the S. side of the ambulatory, is relatively unimportant, but a 17th cent. silver-gilt altar-frontal is noteworthy.—Outside hangs a conjectural reproduction of the *Oriflamme*, the red and gold banner adopted by Louis VI as the royal standard of France. The original disappeared at the battle of Agincourt, and it was thereafter superseded by the fleur-de-lys as the royal emblem. Near the top of the choir steps is the tomb of *Frédégonde* (d. 597), queen of Chilperic I, a remarkable slab in cloisonné mosaic (12th cent.), from St-Germain-des-Prés.

On the right of the steps is the entrance to the CRYPT, the central chamber of which (Caveau Royal ; seen through narrow openings) is opened only on Jan. 21st, the anniversary of the execution of Louis XVI, and on Nov. 2nd. It contains the sarcophagi of Louis XVI, Marie Antoinette, Louis XVIII, and other 18-19th cent. royal personages. Two of the side chapels contain 12th cent. stained glass ; the tombs are of minor importance.

The S. TRANSEPT contains (among others) the tombs of *Charles V* (d. 1380), by Beauneveu ; *Charles VI* (d. 1422) ; and of *Bertrand du Guesclin* (d. 1380), the champion of France against the English (his heart is buried at Dinan, his entrails at Le Puy). Beyond is the *Tomb of *Francis I* (d. 1547) and *Claude de France* (d. 1524), a masterpiece by Philibert Delorme, Pierre Bontemps, and others, begun in 1548. Here again the royal pair appear both recumbent and kneeling (with their children), and reliefs depict the king's military exploits.—S. AISLE. *Urn, by Bontemps, with the heart of Francis I. Tomb of *Louis d'Orléans* (d. 1407), a fine Italian work of 1502–15, commissioned by his grandson, Louis XII.

In the RITUAL CHOIR (shown to ticket holders only) the splendid High Stalls (1501–07) are from the chapel of the Château de Gaillon ; the Low Stalls are 15th cent. work from St-Lucien, near Beauvais. Most of the monuments here were erected by St. Louis in honour of the early kings of France, and of these the tomb of *Dagobert I* (d. 638) is the most interesting, with reliefs showing the torment and redemption of the king's soul, and a fine 13th cent. statue of Queen

Nanthilde. The figures of Dagobert and his son are 19th cent. restorations. At the W. end of the choir are several later tombs, including those of *Louis X* (d. 1316), *Philip IV* (le Bel; d. 1314), and *Philip III* (le Hardi; d. 1285). The last, by Pierre de Chelles and Jean d'Arras, is remarkable as being the earliest known French portrait-statue.

To the S. of the basilica, the monastic buildings, rebuilt in the 18th cent. by Robert de Cotte, have been occupied since 1809 by a *Maison d'Education de la Légion d'Honneur,* for daughters of members of the Legion (adm. Thurs. and Sun. at 12, by ticket obtained from the Grande Chancellerie de la Légion d'Honneur, 1 Rue de Solférino, Paris, 7). The imposing cloister, the refectory, the chapter house, and the dormitories may be visited. The splendid wrought-iron entrance grille should be compared with that of the *Museum* (opposite), which occupies the site of the former Hôtel-Dieu (open on weekday afternoons, except Mon.; good collection of local interest).

From St-Denis Rte. Nat. 1 goes on through (4½ m.) *Pierrefitte,* beyond which we bear r. on Rte. Nat. 16 for Chantilly through (6¾ m.) *Sarcelles.*—10 m. **Ecouen** is notable for its *Château begun c. 1535 for the Constable Anne de Montmorency. This is now a school for children of members of the Legion of Honour, and may be visited on Thurs. and Sun. at 3 p.m., by ticket obtained on application to the Grand Chancellerie de la Légion d'Honneur, 1 Rue de Solférino, Paris VII. Among the artists employed in its construction were Jean Goujon and Jean Bullant, to the former of whom are ascribed the façade of the right wing, and the chimneypiece of the great hall. The vaulting of the main staircase and of the chapel are specially noteworthy. In the parish church the late-Gothic choir contains fine 16th cent. stained glass.—*Villiers-le-Bel,* c. 1 m. S.E., has a remarkable Gothic church (13–16th cent.).—Beyond (14¼ m.) the fine 18th cent. château of *Champlâtreux* (l.) we reach the ancient little town of (16 m.) *Luzarches,* once famous for the relics of the saintly physicians, Cosmas and Damian. The interesting church of St-Damien (11–14th cent. and Renaissance) bears, within its portal, sculptured medallions of the lives of SS. Cosmas and Damian (1537); of the sister-church of St-Côme (i.e. Cosmas) little remains but a ruined gable and a few arches.—The Chantilly road traverses woodland, in a clearing in the midst of which is (18 m.) *Lamorlaye,* with several training establishments associated with Chantilly.

21 m. **CHANTILLY,** a quiet little town noted for its château and superb art-collections, is also the Newmarket of France and important race-meetings have taken place here since 1836. The numerous training stables in and near the town have attracted a large English colony.

Hotels. Du Parc, 24 Av. du Maréchal-Joffre; **d'Angleterre,** Place Omer-Vallon (centre of the town); **Modern,** at the station; **du Lion d'Or,** 44 Rue du Connétable.

Restaurants. *Tipperary,* 2 Av. du Maréchal-Joffre; *du Cygne Royal* (closed in winter), 11 Rue du Connétable; *du Théâtre, de la Poste,* 67 and 92 Rue du Connétable.

Syndicat d'Initiative (March 15th–Oct. 15th), Place de la Gare and 30 Av. du Maréchal-Joffre.

Golf Course (18 holes) at *Vineuil,* ¾ m. N. of the château, with a station on the Senlis railway.

The main road from Paris passes near the station and reaches the château viâ the Av. du Maréchal-Joffre and Rue du Connétable, turning right at the Place Omer-Vallon, at the farther end of which is the *Hospice* founded by the mother of the Grand Condé. A shorter and pleasanter way (25 min.) is viâ the Route de l'Aigle through the forest and past (l.) the grand-stands and the chapel of *Sainte-Croix* (one of the seven chapels erected in the 16th cent. by Madeleine of Savoy, wife of the Great Constable) to the Carrefour des Lions, where the road on the left leads to the château.

The ***Château de Chantilly,** standing in a lake stocked with carp, consists of two connected buildings, the *Petit Château* or *Capitainerie,* on the S.W., and the modern *Grand Château,* or château proper, on the N.

History. Chantilly came into the possession of the Montmorency family in 1484, and passed to the Condés in 1632. The present Petit Château was erected about 1560 (probably by Jean Bullant) for the Constable Anne de Montmorency. The Grand Château, erected by Mansart for the Grand Condé, was described by Lord Herbert of Cherbury as " an incomparably fine residence, admired by the greatest princes of Europe." Molière's 'Les Précieuses Ridicules' was given for the first time at Chantilly in 1659. During a visit of Louis XIV in 1671, Vatel, the famous maître d'hôtel, is said to have committed suicide because the fish was late. The Grand Château was destroyed at the Revolution, but after some repairs had been carried out by the last of the Condés (d. 1830), it was entirely rebuilt by his heir, the Duc d'Aumale (1822–97), son of Louis-Philippe, from the designs of Daumet. After the confiscation of the property of the Orléans family in 1853, the Château was bought by the English banking firm of Coutts, but the property was returned to its rightful owner by a decree of the National Assembly in 1872. In spite of his banishment from France, the Duc d'Aumale bequeathed the whole domain, together with his priceless art-collections, to the Institut de France. Chantilly marks the farthest advance of the German troops in France in Sept. 1914 ; it was later the headquarters of Marshal Joffre.

ADMISSION. The château and park are open daily 1.30–4.30 or 5.30 from c. March 5th–Nov. 1st, except on Tues. and Fri. and on race days (notably the first two Sun. in June). Adm. 50 fr. ; on Sun. and Thurs. the park is open free. The park closes at 5 or 6 according to the season.

After passing the iron gates, or Grille d'Honneur, we leave on the right the *Château d'Enghien* (1770), now the curators' residence. We cross the *Terrasse du Connétable,* with a statue of the Constable Anne de Montmorency (1492–1567), by P. Dubois, pass between two bronze groups of hounds by Cain, cross the moat, and enter the *Cour d'Honneur* through a colonnade with copies of Michelangelo's Slaves. In the corner on the left of the courtyard is the chapel, with a statue of St. Louis by Marqueste.

The ****Musée Condé,** one of the most attractive collections within easy reach of Paris, is charmingly installed on the ground floor of the Grand Château and part of the first floor of the Petit Château. Though its special glory is its unique collection of French paintings and illuminations of the 15–16th cent., it offers also a comprehensive array of works of art, including a complete collection of Chantilly ware from the factory founded by the Duc de Bourbon in 1730, and a library of rare and valuable books.

GRAND VESTIBULE. On the left is the Grand Staircase. We, however, ascend the steps on the right and enter the GALERIE DES CERFS (formerly the dining-room), on the ceiling of which are the arms of the successive owners of Chantilly. The walls are hung with 17th cent. Gobelins tapestries of hunting scenes. Above the chimneypiece, Vision of St. Hubert, above the doors, Venus and Cupid, and Diana, all by *Baudry*.

GALERIE DE PEINTURE. On the right: 54. *Moroni*, Portrait; 278. *French School*, Gabrielle d'Estrées in her bath; 531. *Rosa Bonheur*, Shepherd in the Pyrenees; *515. *Meissonier*, Cuirassiers of 1805; 545. *A. de Neuville*, Fight on a railway line; *475. *Decamps*, Souvenir of Turkey in Asia; *528. *Fromentin*, Hawking; *428. *Baron Gros*, Bonaparte among the plague-stricken at Jaffa (sketch for the picture in the Louvre); 456. *Delacroix*, Doge Francesco Foscari condemning his son to banishment; *448. *Corot*, Concert champêtre. *395. *Drouais*, Marie Antoinette as Hebe; 145. *Sir J. Reynolds*, Philippe, Duc de Chartres, later Duc d'Orléans; 332. *Largillière*, Marie de Laubespine; *De Cort*, 148, 149 (opposite), Views of Chantilly (1781); *383. *Lancret*, 'Déjeuner au jambon.' On the opposite wall: 366. *De Troy*, Oyster lunch; 9. *Italian School* (probably *Giovanni di Paolo*), Angels dancing in the sunlight; *N. Poussin*, 305. Massacre of the Innocents; 301. Numa Pompilius and Egeria, 304. Holy Family. On consoles flanking the entrance are two bronzes: Stag hunt by *Barye*, Boar hunt by *Mène*. The chairs are of Beauvais tapestry. In the centre is a marble bust of the Duc d'Aumale (1822–97), by *Paul Dubois*.

From the end of the Galerie we enter the ROTONDE (Pl. 1; in the Tour Senlis), which has a ceiling-painting by *Baudry*, and a mosaic pavement from Herculaneum. By the window is a *Statue of Joan of Arc by *Chapu* (1873). On the walls are water-colours and drawings: *Meissonier*, Picture connoisseurs; *458. *Delacroix*, St. Louis at the Bridge of Taillebourg; *Watteau*, Red chalk drawing of a warrior; ***Rembrandt*, Red chalk drawing of a young woman; 139. *J. van Ruysdael*, Landscape.—We return to the Galerie de Peinture and, turning to the left, pass through the *Vestibule du Musée* (Pl. 2).

The GALERIE DU LOGIS (Pl. 3) contains many important French portrait drawings of the 16th cent. by or attributed to the *Clouets*, *Antoine Caron*, *Lagneau*, *Dumoustier*, and others, including a fine portrait of Mary, Queen of Scots (1561), and portraits of Henri III, Catherine de Médicis,

Francis II, as a child, and Triboulet, jester to Francis I. Also Voltaire, by *Paul Grégoire*.

The Vestibule du Logis (Pl. 4) contains *Drawings by Old Masters, including studies ascribed to *Raphael* and

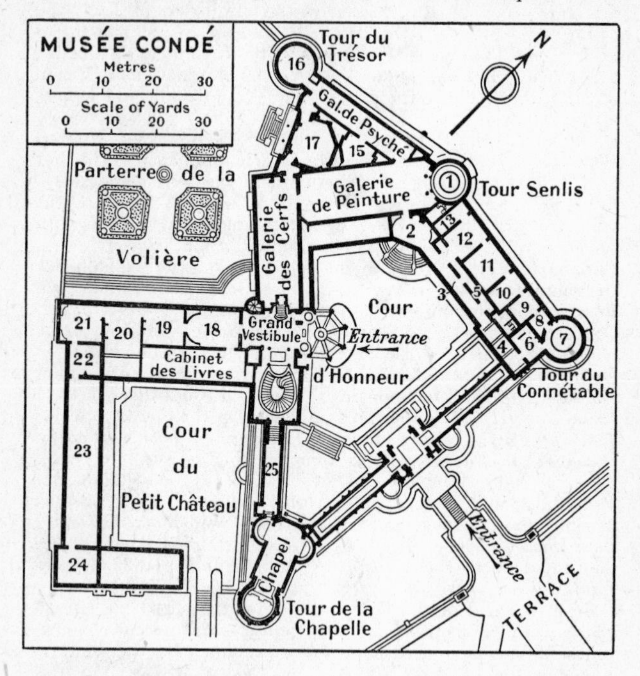

Perugino; *Leonardo da Vinci*, La Joconde (Monna Lisa), in black chalk heightened in white.

If not by Leonardo himself this drawing was at least produced in his immediate circle. The boldness it expresses rather repels, as compared with the mystery of the painting of La Joconde in the Louvre.

Petite Galerie du Logis (Pl. 5). Among the drawings on the left are those of Francis I and of Henri IV in 1610. On either side are large maps and portrait drawings. In the centre: *Greuze*, The family (a drawing of 1763), Portrait of himself. Wall-case: Sèvres and Chinese vases; *Toilet Set of the Empress Maria Theresa; distaff of the Princess de Lamballe and workbox of the Duchesse d'Aumale. We again pass through the Galerie du Logis into the—

SALLE DE LA SMALAH (Pl. 6). *553. *Bonnat,* Duc d'Aumale; 439. *Perrault* (after Horace Vernet), Louis-Philippe and his sons leaving Versailles; *Bellangé,* 464. Capture of the Smalah (1843), 464a. Capture of the Col de Mouzaïa (where the Duc d'Aumale won a decoration; 1840); 437. *Vernet,* Louis-Philippe when Duc d'Orléans (1818); *424a. *Isabey,* Marie d'Orléans, Duchess of Wurtemberg.—We now enter the—

ROTONDE DE LA MINERVE (Pl. 7) in the *Constable's Tower.* In the centre: **55. Statuette of Minerva, an exquisite Greek work of the best period, found at Besançon; vase from Nola; *Pourtalès Amphora, red figured vase of the time of Pheidias; Tanagra figures; bronze ewers from Herculaneum; Silenus, a terra-cotta from Myrina. High up on the walls are six decorative paintings of Cupids, by *Baudry.* Here also are drawings by *Poussin, Ingres, Prud'hon,* and *Claude.*

CABINET DES ANTIQUES (Pl. 8). On the left: *Sir T. Lawrence,* Francis I of Austria. Wall-case: Candelabrum and pottery from Pompeii, lamp from Tebessa; glass vases and bronze utensils, and coins minted within 10 years of the eruption of Vesuvius (79 A.D.), all found at Pompeii.

CABINET DU GIOTTO (Pl. 9). On the left: 299. *Poussin,* Leda and the swan; *111. *Enguerrand Charonton,* Virgin of Pity; 14. *C. Rosselli* (or rather Iacopo del Sellaio), Madonna. On the right wall: 1. *Giotto* (loosely so attributed and not in a good state), Death of the Virgin.

SALLE ISABELLE (Pl. 10). Left wall: 506. *Rousseau,* Landscape; 457. *Delacroix,* Corps de Garde Marocain; 140. *W. Van de Velde the Younger,* Calm Sea; 546. *J. P. Laurens,* The Duc d'Enghien; 441. *Géricault,* Race-horse leaving its stable. Middle wall: 434. *Ingres,* Francesca da Rimini; *473. *Decamps,* Turkish Landscape; 533. *Gérôme,* Duel after the ball; 424. *Boilly,* Draught-players (1817); 514. *Meissonier,* Dragoon. Right wall: 138. *J. Van Ruysdael,* Coast at Scheveningen; 479. *Decamps,* Rebecca at the well.

SALON D'ORLÉANS (Pl. 11). *552. *Bonnat,* Duc d'Aumale (1880); 521. *Jalabert,* Queen Marie-Amélie (1865); 44. *Pierino del Vaga,* Holy Family.

SALLE CAROLINE (Pl. 12). On the left wall: 330. *Largillière,* Mlle Duclos as Ariadne; *Greuze,* 393. Tender affection, *391. Girl, Study for the 'Village Marriage Contract' in the Louvre, 394. La Surprise (a very late work). Facing the window: 386. *Duplessis,* Duchesse de Chartres watching her husband's departure for Ushant (1778). On the right wall: *372. *Watteau,* L'Amante Inquiète; 319. *Mignard,* Henriette de Coligny, Comtesse de la Suze; 376. *Nattier,* Duchesse d'Orléans as Hebe ; 419. *Vernet,* Duc d'Orléans and Duc de Chartres (1788) ; 334. *Largillière,* Portrait ; *371. *Watteau,* La Sérénade. On the window wall : 315. *Mignard,* Princess Henrietta of England.

CABINET CLOUET (Pl. 13). On the left wall : *130. *D. Teniers the Younger,* Le Grand Condé (1653). Opposite the window : 335. *Rigaud,* Louis XIV (smaller original of the portrait in the Louvre) ; *Mme Vigée-Le Brun,* 404. Queen of Etruria, 403. Queen of Naples, 402. Maria Theresa. On the right wall : 241. *French School* (16th cent.), Francis I as a young man ; *François Clouet,* *258. Elizabeth of Austria, 256. Duc d'Alençon.—Returning through the Salle Caroline, we find ourselves again in the—

PETITE GALERIE DU LOGIS (Pl. 5). On the bottom shelf of the wall-case are three little Spanish ivory figures. On the wall are 24 water-colour views of Chantilly in the 18th century. We once more cross the Vestibule and the Galerie de Peinture, and enter the—

GALERIE DE PSYCHÉ. The 44 stained-glass windows (42 of which are here), representing the Loves of Cupid and Psyche (as related by Apuleius in 'The Golden Ass'), were made about 1541 for the Constable de Montmorency's château at Ecouen and were probably designed by *Michael Coxcie.* At the end is a wax portrait bust of Henri IV by *Guillaume Dubois.* On the wall are important portrait drawings of which many are ascribed to the *Clouets* and others to *Jean Perréal* : 1. Diane de Poitiers ; 5. Marshal P. Strozzi ; 9. Hercule François d'Alençon ; 13. Margaret of Valois, Queen of Navarre, sister of Francis I ; *15. Jeanne d'Albret, mother of Henri IV ; 20. Henri II ; 21. Henri, Duc de Guise ; 22. François, Duc de Guise ; 23. Jeanne, Queen of Navarre ; 24. Francis II ; *25. Margaret of France (La Reine Margot), first wife of Henri IV ; 26. Charles IX as a child ; 30. Admiral Gaspard de Coligny. Above these and near the door of the Santuario are large drawings : Children fighting, attributed to *Raphael,* Cupids dancing by *Van Dyck,* and the Last Judgment after *Michelangelo.*

The SANTUARIO (Pl. 15) contains the chief artistic treasures of the collection. **39. *Raphael,* The Madonna of the House of Orleans, an exquisite little panel painted about 1505. **38. *Raphael,* The Three Graces (or the Three Ages of Womanly Beauty), a rather earlier and smaller panel. Between these, 19. Esther and Ahasuerus, a long panel painted in tempera which, although catalogued here as being by Filippino Lippi, is probably by an unknown pupil of Botticelli ('*Amico di Sandro*').—**200–240. Forty Miniatures, plausibly ascribed to *Jean Fouquet* (1415–81), though they have not yet been proved to be the work of that early French master.

Nos. 201 and 202 (right wall) represent Etienne Chevalier and his patron saint adoring the Madonna and Child.

The highest importance is to be attached to these delicately painted illustrations, which were executed in 1453–60 for the Book of Hours ordered by Etienne Chevalier (1410–74), Treasurer of France. About 1700 they were barbarously cut out of the original book, and they remained practically unknown until 1805; they were acquired by the Duc d'Aumale in 1891 for 250,000 francs. Five other miniatures of the set are preserved, two being at the Louvre (p. 138), one in the Bibliothèque Nationale, one in the British Museum, and one in private hands; possibly some 25 more are still missing. These here shown were long ago laid down on wood, and it would not now be wise to detach them and arrange them in their correct ecclesiological order, but it is not in dispute that their condition to-day is virtually perfect after nearly 500 years.

Returning to the Galerie de Psyché, we turn to the left, to reach the—

CABINET DES GEMMES (Pl. 16) in the *Tour du Trésor* (fine views). In the table-case near the centre window are an enamel of Apollo guiding the Chariot of the Sun, attributed to *Cellini*, and the *Rose Diamond known as the 'Grand Condé' (recovered after a theft in 1926). The dagger of Abd-el-Kader, captured at the taking of the Smalah (stolen at the same time), is still missing. In the wall-cases: Large Cross from the Treasury of Basle (German, 15th cent.); Blade of the sword used by the Duc d'Aumale in the charge at the Smalah; snuff boxes, with plans and views of Chantilly (1775); *Collection of old fans, miniatures, and enamels.—We return to the Galerie de Psyché, turn sharp to the right, and pass through a small room in which is a bas-relief of the 'Departure of Phaethon' by *Jean Goujon*.

The TRIBUNE (Pl. 17) is a large octagonal room, in the middle of which is a *Vase by *Clodion*. On the panels above the cornice are represented eight houses and châteaux connected with the Duc d'Aumale, each of which gives name to the side ('façade') of the room below it: Collège Henri-IV, Aumale, Palais Royal, Palermo, Ecouen, Guise, Villers-Cotterets, and Twickenham. We begin with the 'Façade du Collège Henri-IV': *146. *Sir Joshua Reynolds*, Countess Waldegrave and her daughter (1761); 450. *Delaroche*, Murder of the Duc de Guise; 445. *A. Scheffer*, Prince Talleyrand; *370. *Watteau*, Plaisir pastoral; 125. *Van Dyck*, Gaston, Duc d'Orléans; 369. *Watteau*, Love disarmed; *Luini*, 25. Child with grapes, *24. The Saviour; *107, *108. *Memling* (?), Small Diptych with the Madonna appearing to Jeanne de Bourbon, daughter of Charles VII, and Christ on the Cross; *15. *Perugino*, Madonna with SS. Jerome and Peter; **10. *Sassetta* (not Sano di Pietro), Mystic Marriage of St. Francis to Chastity, Obedience, and Poverty (1444); **13. *Piero di Cosimo* (here ascribed to P. Pollaiuolo), Simonetta Vespucci; *11. *Pesellino* (not Lippi), Madonna with SS. Peter and Anthony; 16. *Botticelli* (?), Autumn (once loosely attributed to Mantegna); 48. *Primaticcio,* Cardinal Odet de Coligny; *105. *Flemish School,* Anthony, the 'Grand Bastard' of Burgundy; *313. *Mignard,* Molière; *Ingres,* 433. Venus Anadyomene, 431. Madame Devauçay, painted in Rome in 1807; *247. *Corneille de Lyon,* Gabrielle de Rochechouart; *F. Clouet,* *257. Jacques de Savoie, Duc de Nemours, **254. Jeanne d'Albret of Navarre; *245. *C. de Lyon,* Marguerite de France; **255. *Clouet,* Marguerite de France as a child.

We now return through the Galerie des Cerfs to the Grande Vestibule and turn to the right to visit the ***Apartments of the Grand Condé,** decorated by *J. H. Mansart* in 1684–86, and furnished with Beauvais tapestry.

ANTECHAMBER (Pl. 18). Paintings by *Oudry* and *Desportes.* Enamel of Henri IV, by *Claudius Popelin.* Chantilly, Sèvres, Chinese, and Rouen porcelain.

SALLE DES GARDES (Pl. 19). *126, *127. *Van Dyck,* Comte Henri de Bergues and Princesse Marie de Brabançon. Four *Enamel Portraits by *Léonard Limosin.* 132. *Justus van Egmont,* The Grand Condé (1658). Souvenirs of the campaigns of the Duc d'Aumale.

BEDROOM (Pl. 20). Painted panels by *J. B. Huet.* On a *Commode by *Riesener* is the despatch case of the Grand Condé.

CABINET (Pl. 21). On the mantelpiece, Louis XIV clock; on the console table, an equestrian statuette of the Grand Condé; bureau of the Duc de Choiseul; between the windows, Penthièvre candelabra of the Louis XIV period.

The SALON DES SINGES (Pl. 22) is named from the decorative panel paintings of "Singeries ou différentes actions de la vie humaine," by *Christophe Huet.* They are now in poor condition.

GALERIE DES ACTIONS DE M. LE PRINCE (Pl. 23). The panels are decorated by *Sauveur Lecomte* with scenes from the battles fought by the Grand Condé. Over the fireplace is a *Trophy, formed of his sword and pistols; above is his portrait when 22 years of age, at Rocroi, by *J. Stella*; below, a medallion by *Coysevox* of 1686, the year of the Prince's death. The flag taken at Rocroi, May 19th, 1643, is claimed to be the oldest captured colour in France. The bust of the Grand Condé in biscuit de Sèvres on the mantelpiece is by *Roland* (1785). In the *Cabinet* (Pl. 24) at the end of this gallery are a fine Boulle wardrobe and table.—We retrace our steps to the Antechamber, where we turn right to enter the—

*CABINET DES LIVRES, practically unchanged since the

death of the Duc d'Aumale. It contains a fine library of some 13,000 volumes of the 13–18th cent., many of great value and rarity. The superb bindings are worthy of study. Perhaps the greatest treasure here is the **Très Riches Heures du Duc de Berri (bought in 1855 for 18,000 francs), which is noted for its magnificently illuminated pages of the Months, executed about 1415 by *Pol de Limbourg* and his brothers, direct from nature and not treated conventionally as had previously been the universal practice.

We return to the Grand Vestibule. On the right is the GRAND ESCALIER (not open to the public), with its superb balustrade of steel and copper designed by *Daumet*, and executed by the brothers *Moreau*. The figures holding the lights on the side walls are by *Chapu*, the Gobelins tapestry on the wall is after *Boucher* and *De Troy*. In the Marble Hall at the foot of the staircase is a cast of the recumbent figure of the Duc d'Aumale on his tomb in the cathedral at Dreux.—Passing the staircase we enter the—

GALERIE DE LA CHAPELLE (Pl. 25). Drawings of the Annunciation (1526) by *Dürer*; Flight into Egypt by *Domenichino*; Head of Christ by *Seb. del Piombo*; Madonna and Child with Angels by *Raphael*.

The CHAPEL, founded by Jean Le Bouteiller early in the 14th cent., was dedicated in 1394 to SS. James and Christopher. Rebuilt in 1515 and again in 1719, it was destroyed during the Revolution, and in 1882 it was restored for the Duc d'Aumale by *Honoré Daumet*. The *Altar is by *Jean Bullant* and *Jean Goujon*. The *Woodwork (1548) and the *Stained Glass (1544; portraits of the Great Constable's children) were brought from the Château d'Ecouen. Behind the altar are the mausoleum of Henri II de Condé, with bronze figures and bas-reliefs by *J. Sarazin* (1662), and a cippus to which the hearts of the princes of Condé were transferred in 1883.

The ***Park** (adm., see p. 208) was laid out for the most part by *Le Nôtre* for the Great Condé and is adorned with sculpture and ornamental water. The principal points of interest are the Maison de Sylvie, the 'Hameau,' and the Jeu de Paume (open Thurs. and Sun. only). On the way to the MAISON DE SYLVIE we pass the chapel of ST-SÉBASTIEN (1552) and the CABOTIÈRE (Louis XIII period). 'Sylvie' was the name given to Marie Félice Orsini, Duchesse de Montmorency, by the poet Théophile de Viau, who, when he was condemned to death in 1623 for his licentious verses, was hidden by the duchess in this building. Rebuilt by the Great Condé in 1684, the Maison de Sylvie was in 1724 the scene of the romantic love-affair of Mlle de Clermont, sister of the Duc de Bourbon, and M. de Melun, who was killed in a hunting accident. It now contains Chinese curios, paintings, tapestry, woodcarvings, etc. The HAMLET, a group of cottages built in 1776 by the last Condé but one was the scene of many 'fêtes champêtres' of the period. The JEU DE PAUME (1757) or tennis-court, near an exit from the park, is now a museum and contains Abd-el-Kader's tent, tapestry, two leaden dogs from Twickenham, state carriages, etc.

On quitting the park we turn to the right, and, beyond the Porte St-Denis, enter the Rue du Connétable, the principal street of Chantilly. On the left is the

Church, built by the son of the Great Condé. Behind this are the **Grandes-Ecuries* (open Thurs. and Sun. afternoon), built by Jean Aubert in 1719–35, vast stables with room for 240 horses, beside which is a bronze equestrian statue of the *Duc d'Aumale*, by Gérôme. Thence we may strike across the racecourse to the station.

The **Forest of Chantilly** (5190 acres), stretching to the S.E. of the town, is composed mainly of oaks, limes, birches, and some splendid clumps of Scots pines. It

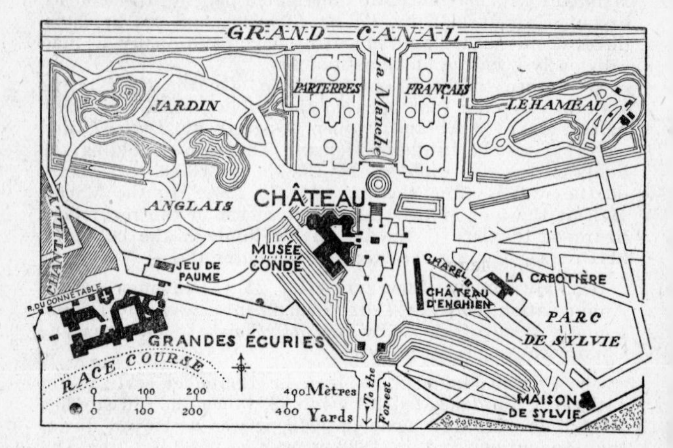

is intersected by numerous roads (signposts), many of which are covered with sand in the interests of the training-stables, while nearly all are forbidden to motors.

Travellers with time to spare should go on by road or rail to (8½ m. E.) **Senlis** (*Hôt. du Grand-Cerf*; *du Nord*), a peaceful old town with the beautiful 12th cent. church of *Notre-Dame* (formerly the cathedral), many old houses, and two concentric lines of ramparts, the inner Gallo-Roman, the outer medieval. A unique *Museum of Hunting* (Musée de Vénerie), opened in 1937, occupies the former hospital of La Charité, in the Rue de Meaux (adm. 20 fr., daily except Wed. 2–6 Sun. and holidays also 10–12).

35. FONTAINEBLEAU.

RAILWAY from the Gare de Lyon, 37 m. (59 km.) in 1–1¼ hr.

AUTOCARS, in summer, of the Renault company (starting from the Place Denfert-Rochereau; Métro services 4 and 6); of the 'Phocéens Cars' (starting from the Porte d'Italie; Métro service 7), and of the C.G.E.A. (Thurs. and Sun. morning from the Place de l'Opéra), make the journey in c. 1½ hr.

The main road from Paris to Fontainebleau (Rte. Nat. 7; 35 m., 56 km.) leaves Paris by the Porte d'Italie and, running through the suburb of *Villejuif*, passes the airport of *Orly* on the left.—8½ m. *Juvisy* stands near the confluence of the Orge with the Seine; the main road crosses the Orge on a graceful bridge of 1728.—16½ m. *Essonnes*, an industrial town with large paper-mills, is continuous with the old town of *Corbeil*, on the Seine (l.), which is also important industrially, with huge flour-mills, and printing and railway-engineering works. Near the church of St-Spire, which has a massive 12th cent. tower, is the 14th cent. gatehouse of a former abbey.—Beyond (28½ m.) *Chailly-en-Bière* (Hôt. du Lion-d'Or), where the route to Barbizon (1½ m.) bears off to the right, the main road enters the Forest of Fontainebleau, and soon passes the well-known Auberge du Grand-Veneur, a favourite tourist resort.—35 m. *Fontainebleau.*

An alternative route (Rte. Nat. 5 and 5bis; 34 m., 55 km.), leaving Paris by the Av. Daumesnil and the Porte de Picpus, traverses the Forêt de Vincennes and crosses the Marne from Charenton to Maisons-Alfort.—8 m. *Villeneuve-St-Georges*, on the Seine.—Beyond (10 m.) *Montgeron* the road runs for 5 m. through the Forêt de Sénart.—16 m. *Lieusaint.*—24½ m. **Melun** (*Hôt. du Grand-Monarque*; *de France*) is a market town of Gallo-Roman foundation, and capital of the Seine-et-Marne department. It suffered considerable damage in the fighting of 1944. As at Paris, the oldest part of the town stands on an island in the Seine. The bridges connecting this with the mainland were blown up in 1944, but are being rebuilt; there are temporary bridges farther upstream. On the island is the church of *Notre-Dame*, founded by King Robert, who died at Melun in 1031, while on the N. bank is *St-Aspais*, a 15–16th cent. church damaged in 1944.—Soon after passing the railway station of Melun, Rte. Nat. 5bis enters the forest, leaving on the left the small town of *Bois-le-Roi* (Hôt. de la Gare), a favourite resort on the edge of the forest and near the Seine.—34 m. *Fontainebleau.*

FONTAINEBLEAU, with its famous palace, second only in interest to Versailles, is finely situated in the middle of its forest and is perhaps the pleasantest and healthiest summer resort in the neighbourhood of Paris. The military headquarters of the Western Union are at present housed in part of the palace.

Railway Station (Rfmts.), N.E. of the town, c. 1½ m. from the Palace.

Hotels. De l'Aigle Noir, 27 Place Dénecourt; **Legris & du Parc,** 32 Rue du Parc; **du Cadran Bleu,** 9 Rue Grande; **du Palais,** 25 Place Dénecourt; **Moret et d'Armagnac,** 16 Rue du Château, all near the Palace; **de la Forêt,** 79 Av. du Président-Roosevelt, near the station; **des Cascades, des Chasses,** Route de Thomery, at Avon, S.E. of the park; **de Toulouse,** 183 Rue Grande; **du Cygne,** 30 Rue Grande; **des Anciens-Courriers,** 48 Rue de France; **Château du Val,** Rue des Basses-Loges, E. of the station; and many others.

Restaurants. *Le Filet de Sole*, 5 Rue du Coq-Gris, near the Palace; *du Cor-Joyeux*, 5 Rue du Parc; *Chez Arrighi*, 53 Rue de France; *Les Choupettes*, facing the Palace; *au Cerf-Noir*, 4 Rue de France; *La Potinière*, 11 Rue Dénecourt; *Brasserie de l'Union, de l'Espérance*, 142 and 117 Rue Grande.

Syndicat d'Initiative, 38 Rue Grande.

Tramway from the station to the Palace.—**Autocars** starting daily from the Place Dénecourt (c. 9.30 a.m.) and the station (in connection with the Paris train arriving c. 10 a.m.) make circuits of the forest in the forenoon (N. circuit viâ Tour Dénecourt and Gorges d'Apremont; S. circuit viâ Montigny, Marlotte, and Gorges de Franchard); afternoon circuit (Gorges de Franchard and d'Apremont, and Barbizon) from the Place Dénecourt c. 2 p.m.

Golf Course (18 holes), 1¼ m. S.W. of the Palace, on the Orléans road.

History. Fontainebleau is first mentioned as a royal fortress, where, in 1169, Thomas Becket, then a refugee in France, consecrated the chapel of St-Saturnin. Philip IV, Louis X, Philip V, and Charles IV were born at Fontainebleau, and Philip IV and V died here. But the real creator of Fontainebleau was Francis I, who here assembled a group of Italian painters and sculptors, including Serlio, Rosso, Primaticcio, Vignola, and Nicolo dell' Abate. Henri IV spent vast sums on the palace, where in 1601 his son, Louis XIII, was born. Queen Christina of Sweden retired hither in 1657, and here in 1685 Louis XIV signed the revocation of the Edict of Nantes. Louis XV received many distinguished foreign visitors here, including Peter the Great (1717) and Christian VII of Denmark (1768). Napoleon I spent twelve million francs on the restoration of the palace. Pope Pius VII was received here in 1804 on his arrival in France to crown the emperor; in 1812 he became a prisoner in the palace, and in the following year he signed an agreement renouncing temporal power. In 1814 Napoleon here signed the act of abdication, and took a touching farewell of his Old Guard in the Cour du Cheval-Blanc. Less than a year later, however, he had returned from Elba and here reviewed his old grenadiers before leading them to the Tuileries. The palace was again restored by Louis-Philippe, at enormous cost but with his usual questionable taste. In 1941–44, the Palace was the headquarters of Gen. von Brauchitsch; the town was liberated by Gen. Patton's Americans in Aug. 1944.

The roads from Corbeil (Rue de France) and from Melun (Rue Grande), the latter joined by the approach from the station, meet in the PLACE DÉNECOURT, just N. of the Palace. Thence the Rue Dénecourt leads to the Place du Général de Gaulle, with the main public entrance to the Palace. On the opposite side of this square is the doorway of the *Hôtel du Cardinal de Ferrare,* the only authentic work by Serlio (see above) surviving. Fragments of other old mansions remain in the Boul. Magenta and the Rue Royale.

The ***Palace** is composed of many distinct buildings, erected at various times and for the most part two-storied, and has been called " un rendez-vous de châteaux."

The state apartments are open daily 10–12, 2–5 in summer; 11–12, 1–4 in winter; adm. 30 fr. The chief courtyards and gardens are open all day. On Sun. and holidays in summer the Palace is overcrowded and the smaller rooms closed.—The summer schools of the American Conservatoire of Music and the American School of Fine Arts occupy the S. wing of the Cour des Adieux in June–Sept., while in the Cour des Princes and Cour Henri-IV are the military headquarters of the Western Union.

The COUR DU CHEVAL-BLANC (500 ft. by 370 ft.), which we enter first, is named after a vanished cast of the horse of the equestrian statue of Marcus Aurelius in Rome. It is known also as the COUR DES ADIEUX, from Napoleon's farewell to his Guards (see above). In front of the central pavilion is the *Escalier en Fer-à-Cheval,* a horseshoe-shaped staircase erected by Jean du Cerceau in 1634. Beneath this is the visitors' entrance.

The CHAPELLE DE LA SAINTE-TRINITÉ, built by Francis I in 1529 and decorated by Henri IV, was the scene of the marriage of Louis XV and Marie Leczinska. In the centre of the ceiling are five large religious paintings by *Fréminet.*

Above the door is the royal gallery. The elaborate altar is an Italian work dating from Louis XIII.—From the chapel we mount the Escalier François-I to the first floor.

The APARTMENTS OF NAPOLEON I, in a wing built by Louis XV, are furnished partly in the Empire style. The ANTICHAMBRE DES HUISSIERS (Pl. 4) has sopraporte by Boucher. The clock, which has ten dials, was specially made for Napoleon. Here are kept Napoleon's hat, worn on the return from Elba, and a lock of his hair. In the CABINET DES SECRÉTAIRES (Pl. 6) are a piece of the willow tree from Napoleon's grave at St. Helena and a fragment of his coffin. The CABINET DE L'ABDICATION OR SALON ROUGE (Pl. 7) still contains the little table on which Napoleon signed his abdication in 1814, and a facsimile of the actual document. In the STUDY (Pl. 8) is Napoleon's camp-bed ; in the BEDROOM (Pl. 9) with Louis XVI decorations, are the emperor's bed and the cradle of the King of Rome.

The magnificent *SALLE DU CONSEIL was built under Charles IX and decorated by *Boucher* and *Vanloo* under Louis XIV and Louis XV. The small adjacent room is the 'BRÛLE-TOUT,' where state papers were burned after the council-meetings.

The SALLE DU TRÔNE was first used as a throne-room under Napoleon. The magnificent ceiling dates from the time of Louis XIII. Above the chimneypiece is a fine portrait of Louis XIII, after an original by *Philippe de Champaigne*, which was burned in 1793. The lustre-candelabrum of rock-crystal is said to have cost 50,000 francs.

The APARTMENTS OF MARIE-ANTOINETTE occupy a wing built under Henri II. The beautiful little BOUDOIR (Pl. 13) has a ceiling-painting of Aurora by *Barthélemy*, carved sopraporte (the Muses) by *Beauvais*, window-fastenings said to have been forged by Louis XVI, and a bust of the queen in Sèvres biscuit-ware. The flooring of the room is in mahogany. The BEDROOM (Pl. 14), with its fine ceiling, was occupied successively by Marie de Médicis, Marie-Thérèse, Marie-Antoinette, Joséphine, Marie-Louise, Marie-Amélie, and the Empress Eugénie, and is sometimes known as the 'Chamber of the five Maries.' The silken hangings of the bed were given to Marie-Antoinette by the city of Lyons. The MUSIC-ROOM (Pl. 15) was Marie-Antoinette's card-room. The grisaille sopraporte and the table of Sèvres ware (1806) are noteworthy. The harp belonged to Joséphine. The SALON DES DAMES D'HONNEUR (Pl. 16) contains a fine Sèvres clock.

The GALERIE DE DIANE OR LIBRARY, over 260 ft. long, was built by Henri IV and remodelled under the Restoration, and has ceiling-paintings of that period. The *Salon* at the

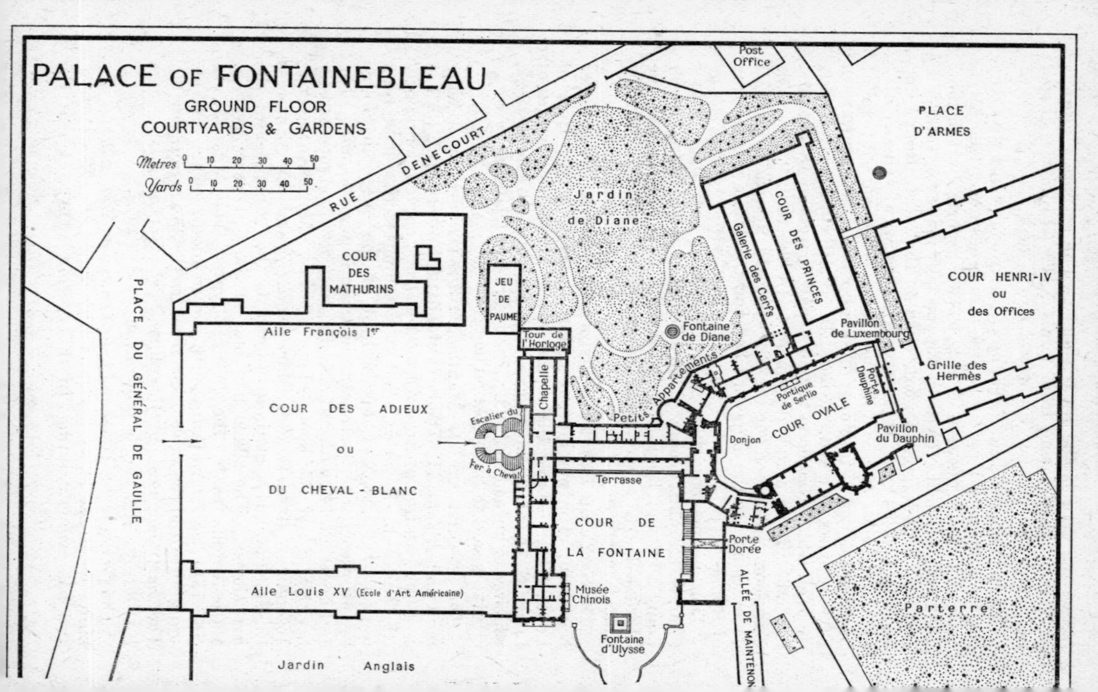

PALACE OF FONTAINEBLEAU
GROUND FLOOR
COURTYARDS & GARDENS
Metres 0 10 20 30 40 50
Yards 0 10 20 30 40 50
RUE DENECOURT
Post Office
PLACE D'ARMES
Jardin de Diane
COUR DES PRINCES
Galerie des Cerfs
COUR HENRI-IV ou des Offices
COUR DES MATHURINS
JEU DE PAUME
Aile François Ier
Tour de l'Horloge
Fontaine de Diane
Pavillon de Luxembourg
Grille des Hermès
Petits Appartements
Portique de Serlio
Porte Dauphine
Chapelle
COUR OVALE
Donjon
Pavillon du Dauphin
PLACE DU GÉNÉRAL DE GAULLE
COUR DES ADIEUX ou DU CHEVAL-BLANC
Escalier du Fer à Cheval
Terrasse
COUR DE LA FONTAINE
Porte Dorée
Aile Louis XV (Ecole d'Art Américaine)
Musée Chinois
ALLÉE DE MAINTENON
Parterre
Fontaine d'Ulysse
Jardin Anglais

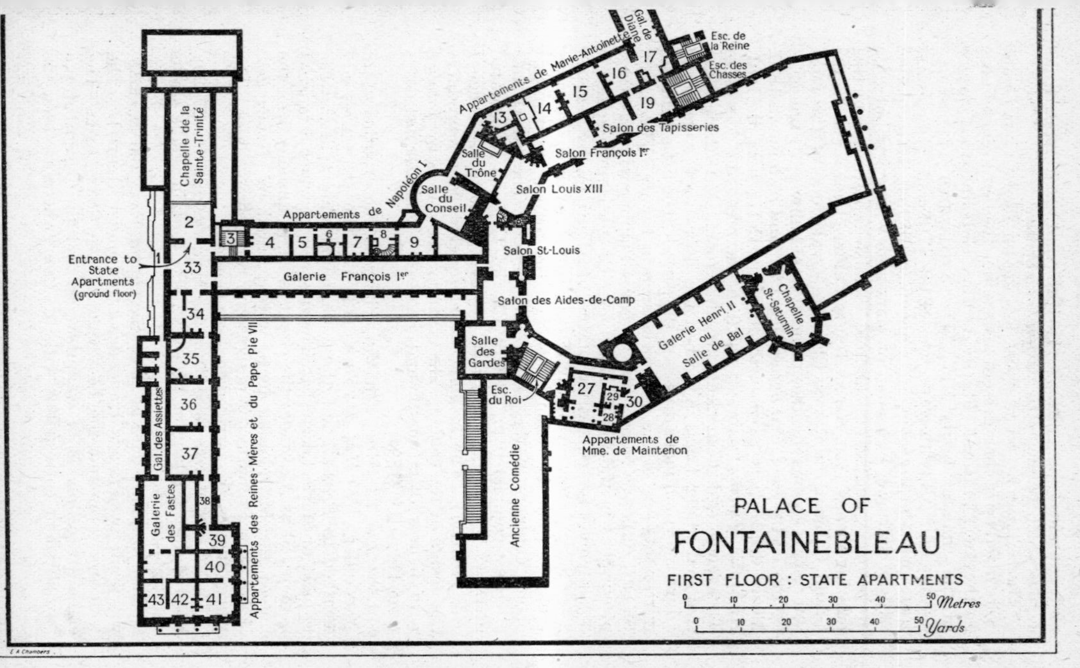
PALACE OF
FONTAINEBLEAU
FIRST FLOOR : STATE APARTMENTS
0 10 20 30 40 50 Metres
0 10 20 30 40 50 Yards
Chapelle de la Sainte-Trinité
Entrance to State Apartments (ground floor)
Appartements de Napoléon I
Salle du Conseil
Salle du Trône
Appartements de Marie-Antoinette
Gal. de Diane
Esc. de la Reine
Esc. des Chasses
Salon des Tapisseries
Salon François Ier
Salon Louis XIII
Salon St-Louis
Galerie François Ier
Salon des Aides-de-Camp
Salle des Gardes
Esc. du Roi
Galerie Henri II ou Salle de Bal
Chapelle St-Saturnin
Appartements de Mme. de Maintenon
Ancienne Comédie
Gal. des Assiettes
Galerie des Fastes
Appartements des Reines-Mères et du Pape Pie VII
1 2 3 4 5 6 7 8 9 13 14 15 16 17 19 27 28 29 30 33 34 35 36 37 38 39 40 41 42 43
E A Chambers

end contains fine editions (15–16th cent. and modern) of books which belonged to various celebrities.

The Salons de Réception, looking on to the Cour Ovale, were fitted up in their present form under the last French kings. In the Antechamber (Pl. 19) are three Gobelins (the Seasons) of the time of Louis XIV. The Salon des Tapisseries contains fine Gobelins tapestries of the 17th cent. The Salon François Premier has a chimneypiece of that king's period with a charming medallion of Mars and Venus attributed to *Primaticcio*, and several fine old Flemish tapestries depicting hunting-scenes. The Salon Louis Treize, known also as the Grand Cabinet du Roi or Chambre Ovale, one of the most interesting rooms in the palace, was built by Francis I, decorated by *Paul Bril* under Henri IV, and restored in 1837. Marie de Médicis gave birth to Louis XIII here in 1601. *Ambroise Dubois* painted thirteen pictures (the Loves of Theagenes and Chariclea) for this room, but three were removed under Louis XV when the doors were widened to admit the voluminous dresses of the period. The little Venetian mirror was one of the first to be seen in France. The Salon de St-Louis was redecorated by Louis-Philippe with paintings of episodes in the life of Henri IV. On the chimneypiece is a contemporary equestrian statue of Henri IV by *Jacquet*. The Salon des Aides-de-Camp contains three pictures removed from the Salon Louis XIII (see above) and two fine ebony cabinets of the Louis XIII period. The Salle des Gardes, completed in 1564 by Charles IX, was redecorated in 1834. The ceiling and frieze, however, date from Francis I and Henri II. The magnificent marquetry floor reproduces the design of the ceiling. The great chimneypiece, by *Jacquet*, with figures of Strength and Peace, by *Francavilla*, dates from Henri IV (1590).

Escalier du Roi. On the ceiling is the Apotheosis of Alexander, by *Abel de Pujol* (1838). The sculptures are ascribed to *Primaticcio* : the nude figures were veiled at the request of Marie Leczinska. The frescoes, in which Francis I is depicted as Alexander the Great in eight episodes from the life of the Macedonian hero, were painted by *Nicolo dell' Abate* from Primaticcio's designs and restored by Pujol. The stucco figures are ascribed to Jean Goujon.

The Apartments of Mme de Maintenon (Pl. 27–30), entered from the landing by a vestibule, contain Boulle clocks and tapestry furniture.

The *Galerie Henri-II or Salle de Bal, 100 ft. long, was built by Francis I and decorated under Henri II. The windows command the best view of the Cour Ovale. The elaborate ceiling is of walnut-wood, and the design of the parquet floor corresponds with it. Everywhere are seen the interlaced monograms of Henri II and Diane de Poitiers and the emblems of Diana (bows and arrows, and crescents). The mythological paintings were designed by *Primaticcio,* executed by *Nicolo dell' Abate* (1552), and restored under Henri IV and again in 1834.

We retrace our steps to the Salon de St-Louis and enter the *GALERIE FRANÇOIS PREMIER, 210 ft. long, which was built in 1528–44 with beautiful Renaissance decorations. The initial and salamander device of Francis I are conspicuous. The paintings, mostly by *Rosso,* are separated by bas-reliefs, trophies, etc. The frescoes represent allegorical and mythological scenes, with more or less reference to the iife of Francis I.

The VESTIBULE D'HONNEUR (Pl. 33) has six massive oaken doors. The onyx statue of a Moorish woman typifies Algeria.

The following rooms are open on weekdays (Pl. 34–43): APARTMENTS OF THE QUEEN-MOTHER (or of PIUS VII). In the ANTECHAMBER is a large tapestry by Oudry, Louis XV hunting at Compiègne. The inlaid marble table was presented to the Prince Imperial by Pius IX. The SALON DES OFFICIERS and the GRAND SALON DE RÉCEPTION both contain interesting furniture. The second room has a ceiling with the monograms of Anne of Austria and Louis XIII, and a *Gobelins tapestry, the Triumph of the Gods, said to have been designed by Raphael. The QUEEN-MOTHER'S BEDROOM has fine old Gobelins and a ceiling decorated with paintings by Cottelle de Meaux. Above the doors are portraits of Anne of Austria and Marie-Thérèse, by Desève. The *Furniture is upholstered in Beauvais tapestry, with subjects taken from La Fontaine's fables. Pius VII used to say Mass in this room during his captivity. The POPE'S STUDY contains a replica of David's portrait of Pius VII.

In the CABINET DE TOILETTE are tapestry portraits of Henri IV and Louis XIII. The POPE'S BEDROOM contains a Louis XIV bedstead. In the SALON D'ANGLE are an old Gobelins tapestry and a fine Louis XIV clock. The SALLE D'ATTENTE has sopraporte ascribed to *Mignard,* old Gobelins tapestry, and the simple bedroom furniture used by the Pope during his captivity. The ANTECHAMBER commands a view of the lake.—The GALERIE DES FASTES has superb carved foliage (Louis XV period) and ebony cabinets in the Louis XIII style.—The GALERIE DES ASSIETTES is adorned with plates painted with views of French royal palaces. On the ceiling are frescoes by *Ambroise Dubois.*

On the ground floor, between the Cour de la Fontaine and Cour Ovale and the Jardin de Diane, are the PETITS APARTEMENTS, occupied by the Dauphin and later, under Napoleon, by Louis and Joseph Bonaparte. They have preserved their Empire decoration, and contain souvenirs of the period, including Marie-Louise's tapestry-frame. Beyond is the GALERIE DES CERFS, where Christina of Sweden had her favourite, Monaldeschi, murdered in 1657. It is adorned with paintings of royal residences and contains state carriages, etc.

The **Chinese Museum** (open on request at the same hours as the rest of the palace) is entered from the Cour de la Fontaine and occupies three rooms once included in the suite of the 'grand maréchal' of the palace. It includes many beautiful examples of Chinese art and industry.

By permission of the Conservateur, visits may be paid to the *Chapelle St-Saturnin,* in the S.E. wing, rebuilt by Francis I; and to the *Theatre* and the *Musée Rosa-Bonheur,* on the S. side of the Cour des Adieux. The remainder of the palace is private.

EXTERIOR. A pleasant walk may be taken round the outside of the château, starting in the N.E. corner of the *Cour des Adieux,* where a passage between the Francis I wing (l.) and the Tennis Court (Jeu de Paume) leads to the *Jardin de Diane* (entered also from the Rue Dénecourt), with its bronze fountain-figure of Diana (1684). Turning r. we pass the outer façade of the Tour de l'Horloge, with Egyptian caryatids. Opposite is the Galerie des Cerfs. Thence we bear r. round the Cour des Princes, and, following the line of the old moat, pass between that courtyard and the *Cour Henri-IV* or *Cour des Offices* (l.; no adm.) dating from 1609, the main entrance of which faces the Place d'Armes. On our right is the *Porte Dauphine* (by Primaticcio), beneath which Louis XIII was christened; it is one of the entrances to the *Cour Ovale*, which is not open to the public. Opposite, the *Grille des Hermès*, with heads of Hermes (Mercury), separates us from the Cour des Offices. Beyond the *Pavillon du Dauphin* (r.) we reach the *Parterre*, a formal garden with ornamental waters, laid out by Henri IV. On the right is the apse of the Chapelle St-Saturnin, and farther on the *Porte Dorée*, with decorations by Primaticcio (poorly restored), admits to a passage leading to the *Cour de la Fontaine*. To the S. are the *Bassin des Carpes* and the *Jardin Anglais*, laid out for Napoleon.

The **Park** (212 acres) extends to the E. of the Parterre. Along the N. wall is the *Treille du Roi*, a vinery yielding a crop of 3–4 tons of excellent white grapes (' chasselas de Fontainebleau '; harvest festival 2nd Sun. in Oct.). On the S. side beyond a canal dug by order of Henri IV are the buildings of the *School of Artillery*, and the village of *Avon* where the 13–16th cent. church contains the tomb of Monaldeschi. In the cemetery is the tomb of Katherine Mansfield (1888–1923), the author, who died at the Prieuré des Basses-Loges.

The ***Forest of Fontainebleau,** 42,000 acres in area and 56 m. round, lies in the angle between the Seine (E.) and the Loing (S.). With its groups of ancient trees, its picturesque sandstone rocks, and its sandy heaths, it is a great attraction in spring and autumn. Oak, beech, hornbeam, birch and Scots pine are the commonest trees.

The legend of the ' Grand Veneur ' tells how Henri IV shortly before his assassination hearing the sound of a rapidly approaching hunt, suddenly found himself faced by a Black Huntsman of huge and hideous appearance who uttered a warning cry and straightway vanished.

The forest is best explored on foot; but it is traversed by several good roads, and a fair idea of its attractions may be gained from the circular tours made by motor-coaches (see above) on Thursdays and Sundays (Easter–Oct.).

The best general view of the forest and its surroundings is commanded by the *Tour Dénecourt* (3 m. N.E. of the palace), a tower erected in 1851 by C. F. Dénecourt (1788–1875), nicknamed ' Le Sylvain,' who devoted his life and fortune to the study of the forest.—The most famous of the picturesque sites in the forest (alluded to in Stevenson's short story ' The Treasure of Franchard ') are the *Gorges de Franchard* (3–5 m. W.; good restaurant), a rocky wilderness c. 3 m. in circumference, lying S. of the road to Arbonne and Milly; and the *Gorges d'Apremont* (3½–4½ m. N.W.), another remarkable rock-strewn area a little farther N., not far S. of the main road to Paris. Though skirted by roads, the actual gorges must be explored on foot. They can easily be combined in one excursion, which may be prolonged to **Barbizon** (*Hôt. les Charmettes*; *des Pléïades*; *du Bas-Bréau*; *Bellevue*), a village on the W. edge of the forest, 5½ m. N.W. of Fontainebleau. It was famous in the last century as the headquarters of the Barbizon School of painters, headed by Corot, J. F. Millet, Th. Rousseau, Diaz, and Daubigny. Rousseau (1812–67) and Millet (1814–72) are buried in the cemetery. Though more sophisticated than in their day, Barbizon is still a favourite resort of artists.

SUMMARY OF MOTOR-BUSES AND UNDERGROUND RAILWAYS OF PARIS

Explanations. The map on the following pages shows the motor-bus routes traversing central Paris. The diagram inside the back cover shows the lines of the underground railways (Métro) in central Paris. The following list indicates the bus-routes mainly within the municipal area of Paris (numbered 20 to 99), followed by a few of the more important suburban routes (three-figure numbers) outside that area. There is a special motor-bus route ' P.C.' (i.e. Paris-Ceinture) which encircles the whole of Paris by way of the Boulevards Extérieurs, except that part which is bounded by the Bois de Boulogne. It runs in two sections : Porte de Vincennes–Porte Maillot (N. half) ; Porte de Vincennes–Porte d'Auteuil (S. half).

A. MOTOR-BUSES

In the following list the ternimal points are mentioned first ; then important intermediate points in brackets.

20. Gare Saint Lazare–Gare de Lyon (Grands Boulevards).
21. Gare Saint Lazare–Place Saint Michel (Opéra, Louvre, and Cité).
26. Gare Saint Lazare–Cours de Vincennes (Gare du Nord, Buttes-Chaumont, Père-Lachaise).
27. Gare Saint Lazare–Porte de Vitry (Opéra, Louvre, Luxembourg, Gobelins).
28. Gare Saint Lazare–Porte d'Orléans (Champs-Elysées, Invalides, Montparnasse).
30. Gare de l'Est–Place du Trocadéro (Place Clichy, Parc Monceau, Etoile).
31. Gare de l'Est–Place de l'Etoile (Boul. Barbès, Av. de St-Ouen, Av. de Villiers).
32. Gare de l'Est–Passy (Gare St-Lazare, Champs-Elysées, Pl. du Trocadéro).
38. Gare de l'Est–Porte d'Orléans (Châtelet, Cité, Luxembourg).
43. Gare du Nord–Neuilly (Gare St-Lazare, Faubourg St-Honoré, Ternes).
47. Gare du Nord–Kremlin-Bicêtre (Châtelet, Cité, Gobelins).
48. Gare du Nord–Porte de Vanves (Grands Boulevards, Louvre, Beaux-Arts, Montparnasse).
49. Gare du Nord–Porte de Versailles (Gare St-Lazare, Champs-Elysées, Invalides).
52. Place de la République–Saint Cloud (Grands Boulevards, Etoile, Passy, Auteuil).
58. Place de la République–Porte de Vanves (Halles, Pont-Neuf, Luxembourg, Montparnasse).
62. Porte de Saint Cloud–Place Daumesnil (Montsouris, Av. d'Italie).
63. Gare de Lyon–Porte de la Muette (Boul. St-Germain, Quai d'Orsay, Trocadéro).
65. Gare d'Austerlitz–Aubervilliers (Gare de Lyon, Place de la République, Gares de l'Est and Nord).
66. Square des Batignolles–Place Daumesnil (Gare St-Lazare, Opéra, Place des Vosges, Bastille).
67. Place Pigalle–Place de Rungis (Bibliothèque Nationale, Louvre, Ile-St-Louis, Jardin des Plantes).
68. Place Clichy–Montrouge (Opéra, Tuileries, Boul. Raspail).
69. Père Lachaise–Place Balard (Bastille, Louvre, Tuileries, Gare des Invalides, Champ de Mars).

MOTOR-BUS ROUTES

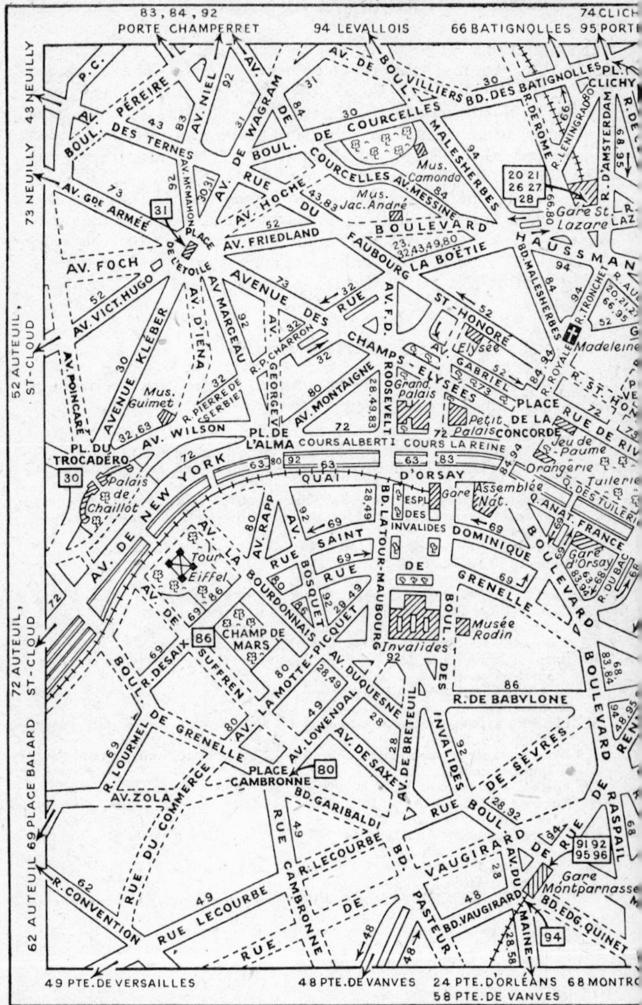

CENTRAL PARIS

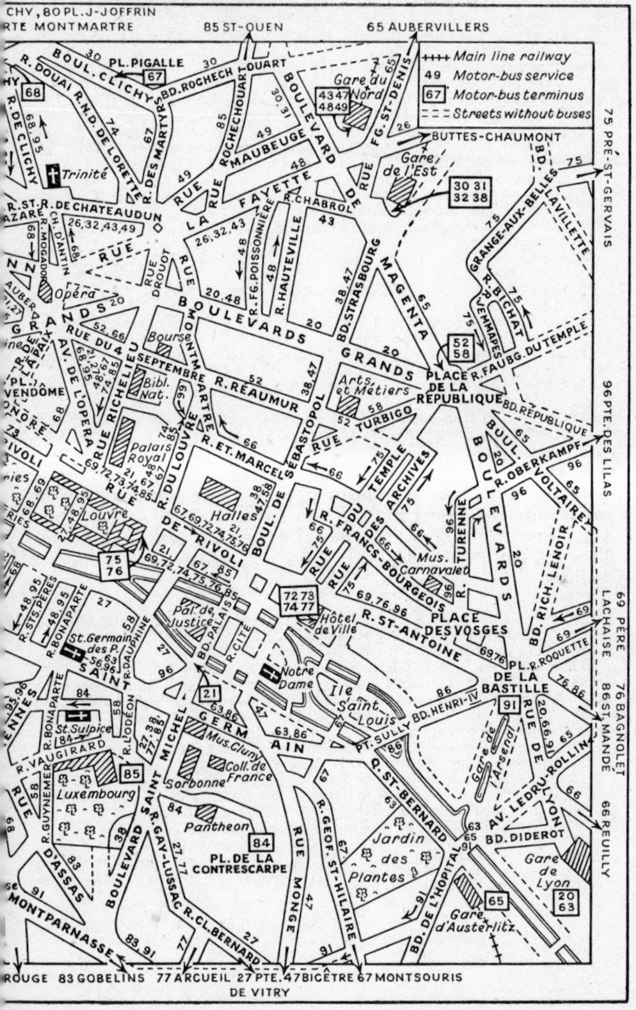

72. Hôtel de Ville–Saint Cloud (Louvre, Concorde, Cours la Reine, Av. de Versailles).
73. Hôtel de Ville–Neuilly (Louvre, Concorde, Champs-Elysées, Etoile, Porte Maillot).
74. Hôtel de Ville–Clichy (Louvre, Bibliothèque Nationale, N.D. de Lorette, Place Clichy).
75. Louvre–Porte Brunet (Hôt. de Ville, Archives, Place de la République, Buttes-Chaumont).
76. Louvre–Bagnolet (Hôt. de Ville, Bastille, Père Lachaise).
77. Hôtel de Ville–Arcueil (Cité, Luxembourg, Montsouris).
80. Place Cambronne–Mairie du XVIIIe (Champ de Mars, Champs-Elysées, Gare St-Lazare, Montmartre).
83. Gobelins–Porte de Champerret (Luxembourg, Palais-Bourbon, Champs-Elysées, Ternes).
84. Porte de Champerret–Place de la Contrescarpe (Parc Monceau, Concorde, Palais-Bourbon, Luxembourg).
85. Gare du Luxembourg–Saint Ouen (Cité, Louvre, Bibliothèque Nationale, Montmartre).
86. Champ de Mars–Saint Mandé (near Invalides, St-Germain-des-Prés, Bastille, Nation).
91. Gare Montparnasse–Bastille (Jardin des Plantes, Gares d'Austerlitz and de Lyon).
92. Gare Montparnasse–Porte de Champerret (Invalides, Place de l'Alma, Etoile).
94. Gare Montparnasse–Levallois (Boul. Raspail, Concorde, St-Augustin, Parc Monceau).
95. Gare Montparnasse–Montmartre (Beaux-Arts, Louvre, Opéra, Gare St-Lazare).
96. Gare Montparnasse–Porte des Lilas (St-Germain-des-Prés, Cité, Hôt. de Ville, Place des Vosges, Ménilmontant).

Most of the **Suburban Motor-Buses** start at the outer termini of the various Métro lines and are used mainly by suburban residents going to and from their places of work. They are crowded at the morning and evening rush-hours. The following services are those of principal interest to visitors.

126. Porte d'Orléans (Métro 4; near the Cité Universitaire) to Porte de St-Cloud (Métro 9) viâ Malakoff, Vanves, and Issy-les-Moulineaux.
142. Porte de St-Ouen (Métro 13) to St-Ouen, St-Denis, and Stains.
152. Porte de la Villette (Métro 7) to Le Bourget (Aéroport).
153, 156. Porte de la Chapelle (Métro 12) to St-Denis and Villetaneuse.
154. Porte de Clignancourt (Métro 4) to St-Denis and Enghien-les-Bains.
158, 258. Pont de Neuilly (Métro 1) to Rueil (158), La Malmaison, Bougival, and St-Germain-en-Laye.
168. Porte de Clignancourt (Métro 4) to St-Denis and Sarcelles.
170. Porte des Lilas (Métro 3, 11) to Aubervilliers and St-Denis.
171. Pont de Sèvres (Métro 9) to Sèvres, Chaville, Viroflay, and Versailles.
188. Porte d'Orléans (Métro 4) to Bourg-la-Reine, Parc de Sceaux, and Antony.
190bis. Issy-les-Moulineaux (Métro 12) to Le Plessis-Robinson.
194bis. Porte d'Orléans (Métro 4) to Le Plessis-Robinson and Malabry.
262. Pont de Neuilly (Métro 1) to Colombes, Bezons, and Maisons-Laffitte.
285. Porte d'Italie (Métro 7) to Villejuif, Orly (Aéroport), and Savigny-sur-Orge.

B. MÉTROPOLITAIN

Each line is indicated by a numeral, and is known by the names of its termini. In the list of stations, *Interchange Stations* (Correspondances) are followed by brackets with figures indicating the intersecting lines.

1. Pont de Neuilly–Château de Vincennes

Pont de Neuilly
Sablons
Porte Maillot
Argentine
Etoile (2, 6)
George V
Franklin-Roosevelt (9)
Champs-Elysées-Clemenceau
Concorde (8, 12)
Tuileries
Palais-Royal (7)
Louvre
Châtelet (4, 7, 11)
Hôtel de Ville (11)
St-Paul
Bastille (5, 8)
Gare de Lyon
Reuilly-Diderot (8)
Nation (2, 6, 9)
Porte de Vincennes
St. Mandé-Tourelle
Bérault
Château de Vincennes

2. Porte Dauphine–Nation

Porte Dauphine
Victor-Hugo
Etoile (1, 6)
Ternes
Courcelles
Monceau
Villiers (3)
Rome
Place Clichy (13)
Blanche
Pigalle (12)
Anvers
Barbès-Rochechouart (4)
La Chapelle
Stalingrad (5, 7bis)
Jean-Jaurès (5, 7)
Col. Fabien
Belleville (11)
Couronnes
Ménilmontant
Père Lachaise
Philippe-Auguste
Bagnolet
Avron
Nation (1, 6, 9)

3. Pont de Levallois–Porte des Lilas

Pont de Levallois-Bécon
Anatole-France
Louise-Michel
Porte de Champerret
Péreire
Wagram
Malesherbes
Villiers (2)
Europe
Gare St-Lazare (12, 13)
Havre-Çaumartin (9)
Opéra (7, 8)
Quatre-Septembre
Bourse
Sentier
Réaumur-Sébastopol (4)
Arts-et-Métiers (11)
Temple
République (5, 8, 9, 11)
Parmentier
St-Maur
Père Lachaise (2)
Martin-Nadaud
Gambetta
Pelleport
St-Fargeau
Porte des Lilas (11)

4. Porte de Clignancourt–Porte d'Orléans

Porte de Clignancourt
Marcadet-Poissonniers (12)
Château-Rouge
Barbès-Rochechouart (2)
Gare du Nord (5)
Gare de l'Est (5, 7)
Château-d'Eau
Strasbourg-St-Denis (8, 9)
Réaumur-Sébastopol (3)
Etienne-Marcel
Halles
Châtelet (1, 7, 11)
Cité
Odéon
St-Germain-des-Prés
St-Sulpice
St-Placide
Montparnasse (6, 12, 14)
Vavin
Raspail (6)
Denfert-Rochereau (6, S)
Mouton-Duvernet
Alésia
Porte d'Orléans

5. Pantin–Place d'Italie

Eglise de Pantin
Hoche
Porte de Pantin
Ourcq
Laumière
Jean-Jaurès (2, 7)
Stalingrad (2, 7bis)
Gare du Nord (4)
Gare de l'Est (4, 7)
Jacques-Bonsergent
République (3, 8, 9, 11)
Oberkampf (9)
Richard-Lenoir
Bréguet-Sabin
Bastille (1, 8)
Arsenal (closed)
Quai de la Rapée
Gare d'Austerlitz (10)
St-Marcel
Campo-Formio
Place d'Italie (6, 7)

6. Etoile–Nation

Etoile (1, 2)
Kléber (closed)
Boissière
Trocadéro (9)
Passy
Bir-Hakeim (Quai de Grenelle)
Dupleix
La Motte-Picquet (8, 10)
Cambronne
Sèvres-Lecourbe
Pasteur (12)
Montparnasse (4, 12, 14)
Edgar-Quinet
Raspail (4)
Denfert-Rochereau (4, S)
St-Jacques
Glacière
Corvisart
Place d'Italie (5, 7)
Nationale
Chevaleret
Quai de la Gare
Bercy
Dugommier
Daumesnil (8)
Bel-Air (closed)
Picpus
Nation (1, 2, 9)

7. 7bis. Ivry–Pré-St-Gervais or Porte de la Villette

Trains run alternately to Pré-St-Gervais and Porte de la Villette, diverging at Louis-Blanc.

Mairie d'Ivry
Pierre-Curie
Porte d'Ivry
Porte de Choisy
Porte d'Italie
Maison-Blanche
Tolbiac
Place d'Italie (5, 6)
Gobelins
Censier-Daubenton
Monge
Jussieu (10)
Sully-Morland
Pont Marie
Châtelet (1, 4, 11)
Pont Neuf
Palais-Royal (1)
Pyramides
Opéra (3, 8)
Chaussée-d'Antin (9)
Le Peletier
Cadet
Poissonnière
Gare de l'Est (4, 5)
Château-Landon
Louis-Blanc (7bis)
Jean-Jaurès (2, 5)
Bolivar
Buttes-Chaumont
Botzaris
Place des Fêtes (11)
Pré-St-Gervais

From Pré-St-Gervais the line forms a loop, returning to Botzaris viâ **Danube.**—Line 7bis runs from Louis Blanc (see above) viâ **Stalingrad** (2, 5), **Riquet, Crimée,** and **Corentin-Cariou,** to **Porte de la Villette.**

8. Place Balard–Charenton

Place Balard
Lourmel
Boucicaut
Félix-Faure (closed)
Commerce
La Motte-Picquet (6, 10)
Champ de Mars (closed)
Ecole Militaire
La Tour-Maubourg
Invalides (14)
Concorde (1, 12)
Madeleine (12)
Opéra (3, 7)
Richelieu-Drouot (9)
Montmartre
Bonne-Nouvelle
Strasbourg-St-Denis (4, 9)
St-Martin (closed)
République (3, 5, 9, 11)
Filles-du-Calvaire
St-Sébastien-Froissart
Chemin-Vert
Bastille (1, 5)
Ledru-Rollin
Faidherbe-Chaligny
Reuilly-Diderot (1)
Montgallet (closed)
Daumesnil (6)
Michel-Bizot
Porte Dorée
Porte de Charenton
Liberté
Charenton-Ecoles

9. Pont de Sèvres–Montreuil

Pont de Sèvres
Billancourt
Marcel-Sembat
Porte de St-Cloud
Exelmans
Michel-Ange-Molitor (10)
Michel-Ange-Auteuil (10)
Jasmin
Ranelagh
Muette
Pompe
Trocadéro
Iéna
Alma-Marceau
Franklin-Roosevelt (1)
St-Philippe-du-Roule
Miromesnil
St-Augustin
Havre-Caumartin (3)
Chaussée-d'Antin (7)
Richelieu-Drouot (8)
Montmartre
Bonne-Nouvelle
Strasbourg-St-Denis (8)
St-Martin (closed)
République (3, 5, 8, 11)
Oberkampf (5)
St-Ambroise
Voltaire
Charonne
Boulets-Montreuil
Nation (1, 2, 6)
Buzenval
Maraîchers
Porte de Montreuil
Robespierre
Croix de Chavaux
Mairie de Montreuil

10. Gare d'Austerlitz–Porte d'Auteuil

Gare d'Austerlitz (5)
Jussieu (7)
Cardinal-Lemoine
Maubert-Mutualité
Cluny (closed)
St-Michel
Odéon (4)
Mabillon (closed)
Croix-Rouge (closed)
Sèvres-Babylone (12)
Vaneau (closed)
Duroc (14)
Ségur
La Motte-Picquet (6, 8)
Emile-Zola
Charles-Michels
Javel
Eglise d'Auteuil
Michel-Ange-Auteuil (9)
Porte d'Auteuil

From Porte d'Auteuil the line forms a loop, returning to Javel viâ **Michel-Ange-Molitor (9)**, Chardon-Lagache (closed), and **Mirabeau.**

11. Châtelet–Les Lilas

Châtelet (1, 4, 7)
Hôtel de Ville (1)
Rambuteau
Arts-et-Métiers (3)
République (3, 5, 8, 9)
Goncourt
Belleville (2)
Pyrénées
Jourdain
Place des Fêtes (7)
Télégraphe
Porte des Lilas (3)
Mairie des Lilas

12. Issy–Porte de la Chapelle

Mairie d'Issy
Corentin-Celton
Porte de Versailles
Convention
Vaugirard
Volontaires
Pasteur (6)
Falguière (closed)
Montparnasse (4, 6, 14)
N.D. des Champs
Rennes (closed)
Sèvres-Babylone (10)
Bac
Solférino
Chambre des Députés
Concorde (1, 8)
Madeleine (8)
Gare St-Lazare (3, 13)
Trinité
N.D. de Lorette
St-Georges
Pigalle (2)
Abbesses
Lamarck-Caulaincourt
Jules-Joffrin
Marcadet-Poissonniers (4)
Marx-Dormoy
Porte de la Chapelle

13. Gare St-Lazare–St-Ouen or Porte de Clichy

Gare St-Lazare (3, 12)
Liége (closed)
Place Clichy (2)
La Fourche (see below)
Guy-Moquet
Porte de St-Ouen
Garibaldi
Mairie de St-Ouen
Carrefour Pleyel (in construction, 1951, beyond Porte de St-Ouen)

From La Fourche alternate trains run viâ **Brochant** to **Porte de Clichy.**

14. Invalides–Porte de Vanves

Invalides (8)
Varenne (closed)
St-François-Xavier
Duroc (10)
Montparnasse (4, 6, 12)
Gaîté
Pernety
Plaisance
Porte de Vanves

S. Ligne de Sceaux

This line, though connected with the Métro at Denfert-Rochereau, runs on the Métro system of fares only from the **Gare du Luxembourg** (the starting-point) to **Port-Royal, Denfert-Rochereau (4, 6),** and **Cité Universitaire.** It goes on thence as an ordinary suburban railway viâ *Gentilly, Arcueil-Cachan,* and *Bourg-la-Reine* to *Sceaux* and *Robinson,* or to *Massy-Palaiseau,* and thence continues c. hourly to *St-Rémy-lès-Chevreuse.* Not all the trains stop at all stations.

Gare St-Lazare–Auteuil-Boulogne

Electric trains c. every 20 min. from the main-line station viâ *Pont Cardinet* (where trains are always changed), *Péreire-Levallois, Neuilly-Porte Maillot, Av. Foch, Av. Henri-Martin,* and *Passy,* to *Auteuil-Boulogne.* This line is *not* connected with the Métro.

INDEX

Names of buildings, collections, etc., and topographical names are printed in black type, names of eminent persons in italics, other entries in Roman type. Names beginning with *Saint* (*St.*) or *Sainte* (*Ste*) are indexed under 'Saint.' *Avenues, Boulevards, Cafés, Châteaux, Hôpitaux, Hôtels* (mansions), *Musées, Places, Rues, Squares,* etc., are indexed in alphabetical sub-groups under these headings. An alphabetical list of *Theatres* will be found on p. xxxi of the text.

Abattoirs 59
Abbaye de Longchamp 57
,, **de Ste-Geneviève** 84
Abélard 87, 60
Acacias, Les 58
Académie Française 92
Académie de Médecine 95
,, **de Musique** 19, 1
,, **de Paris** 87
Academies of the Institut 92
Accueil de Paris 26
Adélaïde de Savoie 43
Affre, Abp. 30, 78
Aguesseau, H. F. d' 56
Air Services xv
Air Termini xix
Albert I (*of Belgium*) 51
Albertus Magnus 86
Alembert, Jean d' 33
Alexander I 3, 187
Alphand, Ad. 56
Ambassadeurs, Th. des 8, xxxi
American Churches xxxv, 51, 113
American Clubs and Societies xxxvi
American Embassy 8
American Independence 8, 195
American Memorial Cloister 52
American Volunteers' Monuments 54, 186
Ampère, Jean 108
Amusements xxx
Anne of Austria 19, 28, 116
Apremont, Gorges d' 224
Aquarium 54
Aqueduc de Marly 203
Arc de Triomphe du Carrousel 5
,, ,, ,, **de l'Etoile** 10
Archives Nationales 33
Arènes de Lutèce 83
Armagnac, Comte d' 74
Armenian Church 51
Armenonville 58
Arrival in Paris xix
Arrondissements xlii
Arsenal 29
Art Exhibitions xxxii
Arts-et-Métiers, Conservatoire des 157, 37
Arvers, Félix 79
Assemblée Nationale 102
Assumption, Church of the 3
Athletics xxxiii
Auber, D. F. 39
Aumale, Duc d' 208
Auteuil 56, xxxiv
Automobile Club 8, xxxvi
Avenue Alexandre-III 10
,, **de Breteuil** 113
,, **des Champs-Elysées** 8
,, **Daumesnil** 62
,, **Foch** 56
,, **Franklin D. Roosevelt** 51
,, **de Friedland** 48
,, **Gabriel** 8
,, **Gambetta** 61
,, **du Général-Leclerc** 120
,, **George-V** 51
,, **Georges - Mandel** 55
,, **de la Grande Armée** 48
,, **Henri-Martin** 55
,, **d'Iéna** 54
,, **Jean-Jaurès** 59
,, **Kléber** 54
,, **Marceau** 52
,, **Marigny** 10
,, **de Messine** 47
,, **Montaigne** 51
,, **de Neuilly** 50
,, **de l'Observatoire** 89, 117
,, **de l'Opéra** 1
,, **du Président-Wilson** 52
Avenue Raymond-Poincaré 55
,, **de la République** 60
,, **du Roule** 50
,, **de Tourville** 113
,, **Victor-Hugo** 55
,, **Victoria** 25
,, **de Villiers** 46
Avon 224

Bagatelle 58
Bailly, Jean Sylvain 26, 74, 34, 114
Bal Bullier 117
Balzac, Honoré de 56, 24, 30, 36, 39, 48, 55, 61, 95, 96, 101, 117, 118, 186
Banks xxxvi
Banque de France 20
Barbès, Armand 26
Barbizon 224
'Barrière de Clichy' 40
Bart, Jean 36
Barthélemy, Abbé 18
Barye, Antoine Louis 17, 28, 79, 199
Basilique de St-Denis 205
Basilique du Sacré-Cœur 43
'Basoche' 72
Bastille 17, 165
Batignolles, Les 46
Baudelaire, Ch. 80, 28, 79, 119
Baudin, J. B. A. 61
Bazaine, Marshal 198
Beardsley, Aubrey 104
Beauharnais, Vicomte A. de 97
Beauharnais, Eugène de 110, 202
Beaumarchais, Pierre Caron de 16, 32, 61, 96
Becket, Thomas 218
Bedford, Duke of 30
Belgian Monument 51
Belleville 59

Béranger, Pierre Jean de 16, 61
Bercy, 64
Bergson, Henri 55
Berlioz, Hector 18, 44
Bernard, Claude 87
Bernhardt, Sarah 3, 46, 61
Berri, Duc de 199
Berthelot, Marcelin 86
Berthier, Marshal 187
Bertrand, Gen. 110
Berwick, Duke of 115
Bibliography xl
Bibliothèque de l'Arsenal 29
„ **Historique de la Ville de Paris** 32
„ **Jacques-Doucet** 86
„ **Mazarine** 93
„ **Nationale** 160, 18
„ **Ste - Geneviève** 86
„ **Thiers** 40
Bicycles xvii
Billiards xxxiii
Biron, Duc de 28
Bismarck, Prince von 187
Bizet, Georges 61
Blanc, Louis 26
Blanche, J. E. 55
Blanche of Castille 21
Blanqui, Auguste 26
Blind Asylum 113
Boileau, Nicolas 56
Bois de Boulogne 56
Bois de Vincennes 201
Bois-le-Roi 217
Bolingbroke (Henry IV) 34
Bolivar, Simon 18
Bonaparte, Jérôme 74
„ *Joseph* 112, 223
„ *Pauline* 48, 198
Bonheur, Rosa 223
Books about Paris xl
Bossuet, Jacques-Bénigne 4, 27, 100
Botanical Galleries 90
Boucicaut, Mme 108
Bougainville, L. A. de 44
Bougival 203
Boulevard Arago 116
„ **Beaumarchais** 16
„ **de Bonne-Nouvelle** 15
„ **des Capucines** 12
„ **de la Chapelle** 58
Boulevard de Clichy 40
„ **de Courcelles** 46
„ **Diderot** 62
„ **des Filles-du-Calvaire** 16
„ **Garibaldi** 114
„ **de Grenelle** 114
„ **Haussmann** 44, 47
„ **Henri-IV** 28
„ **de l'Hôpital** 91
„ **des Invalides** 113
„ **des Italiens** 14
„ **Jules-Ferry** 60
„ **de la Madeleine** 12
„ **de Magenta** 37
„ **Malesherbes** 46
„ **de Ménilmontant** 60
„ **Montmartre** 15
„ **du Montparnasse** 118
„ **du Palais** 75
„ **Poissonnière** 15
„ **de Port-Royal** 116
„ **Raspail** 108
„ **Richard-Lenoir** 60
„ **Rochechouart** 42
„ **St-Denis** 15
„ **St-Germain** 81, 103
„ **St-Jacques** 119
„ **St-Marcel** 90
„ **St-Martin** 16
„ **St-Michel** 81, 88
„ **de Sébastopol** 24
„ **de Strasbourg** 38
„ **du Temple** 16
„ **de la Villette** 59
„ **Voltaire** 61
Boulogne 57
Bourdelle, Antoine 119, 52
Bourget, Le xix
Bourse, La 18
Bourse de Commerce 21
Boxing, xxxiii
Boylesve, René 55
Briand, Aristide 54, 103
Bridge, see **Pont**
Brinvilliers, Marquise de 26, 28
British Council xxxvi
British Embassy 48
Brosse, Salomon de 73, 97, 98
Budé, Guillaume 37, 87
Buffon, Comte de 83, 90
Butte Montmartre 42
Buttes Chaumont 59
Cabaret du Chat-Noir 40
„ **de l'Epée-de-Bois** 36
„ **de la Pomme-de-Pin** 83
Cabaret Shows xxxii
Cadoudal, Georges 74
Caen, Comtesse de 93
Café des Deux-Anges 104
„ **des Deux-Magots** 105
„ **du Dôme** 118
„ **de Flore** 105
„ **Procope** 96
„ **de la Rotonde** 118
„ **Voltaire** 96
Cafés xxv
Cagliostro, Comte de 20
Calendar of Events xxxix
Calvin, Jean 86
Carnavalet Museum 162
Carnot, Lazare 3
Carpeaux, J. B. 2, 89
Carrefour de l'Observatoire 117
Carrefour de l'Odéon 96
Carrefour Richelieu-Drouot 15
Carrefour Vavin 118
Cartier, Jacques 51
Cartouche, Louis 26
Caserne des Célestins 28
Caserne Vérines 16
Casino de Paris xxxii
Catacombs 119
Catherine de Médicis 6, 21, 30, 121, 123, 205
Cattle Market 59
Cellini, Benvenuto 92
Cemeteries (see also Cimetières) xxxvii
Chaillot, Th. de 54, xxxi
Chailly-en-Bière 217
Chambers of Commerce xxxvi
Chambiges, Pierre 122
Chambre des Députés 102, 193
Chambre des Notaires 25
Champaigne, Ph. de 27
Champ de Mai 114
Champ de Mars 113
Champlâtreux 207
Champs-Elysées 8
Champs-Elysées, Th. des 51, xxxi
Chansonniers xxxii
Chantilly 207, xxxiv
„ **Forest** 216

Chantilly Park 215
Chapelle Expiatoire 45
,, **des Otages** 59
,, **St-Ferdinand** 50
,, **St-Pierre** 104
Charcot, Dr. 91
Charenton-le-Pont 217
Charles IV 218, 200, 206
,, *V* 200, 121, 206
,, *VI* 206
,, *IX* 121, 200
,, *X* 187, 6
Charles the Bold 92
Charonne 61
Château de Chantilly 208
,, **d'Enghien** 208
,, **de Madrid** 58
,, **de Maisons** 204
,, **de la Muette** 55
,, **de St-Germain** 204
,, **de Vincennes** 200
Chateaubriand, Vicomte de 103, 104, 116
Châtelet, Mme du 19
Châtelet, Th. du 25
Chaville 186
Chénier, André 6, 15, 62, 74
'Chimères' 76
Chinese Museum 223
Chopin, F. F. 3, 15, 39, 45, 47, 61
Chouans 104, 74
Christian VII 218
Christina, Queen 28, 218, 223
Churches, American xxxv
,, English xxxv
Cimetière de Belleville 59
,, **des Innocents** 22
,, **de Montmartre** 42
,, **du Montparnasse** 119
,, **de Passy** 55
,, **du Père-Lachaise** 60
,, **de Picpus** 62
,, **Ste-Catherine** 91
Cinemas xxxii
Cirque d'Hiver 16, xxxii
,, **Médrano** 42, xxxii
Cité, The 65
Cité Universitaire 120
Clarke, Mrs. 104
Clemenceau, Georges 10, 55
Clubs xxxvi
Cluny Museum 172, 88
Colbert, J. B. 20, 23, 92, 121
Coligny, Adm. de 21
Collège des Bernardins 82
,, **des Bons-Enfants** 83
,, **de Bourgogne** 81
,, **de Clermont** 87
,, **des Ecossais** 83
,, **Fortet** 86
,, **de France** 87
,, **d'Harcourt** 88
,, **des Irlandais** 83
,, **des Lombards** 82
,, **Mazarin** 92
,, **de Montaigu** 86
,, **de Navarre** 84
,, **des Prémontrés** 81
,, **des Quatre-Nations** 92
,, **Rollin** 42
,, **Ste-Barbe** 86
Comédie-Française, 4, 96, xxx
Commune and Communards 6, 19, 25, 26, 30, 40, 42, 59, 61, 122
Comte, Auguste 32, 88
Concerts xxxiii
Conciergerie 74
Condé, Louis II de (le Grand) 61, 200, 205, 208, 214
Conseil d'Etat 19
Conseil de la République 97
Conservatoire des Arts-et-Métiers 157, 37
Conservatoire de Musique 46
Constant, Benj. 45
Constantius, Chlorus 175
Consulates xxxv
Coquelin aîné, Constant 16
Corbeil 217
Corday, Charlotte 7, 34, 45, 73, 82, 107
Cordeliers, Club des 81
Cordeliers, Couvent des 81
Corneille, Pierre 3, 122
Corot, J. B. 38, 61, 95, 101, 186, 224
Cotte, Robert de 3, 108, 198, 207
Coulanges, Abbé de 163
Couperin, François 27
Cour des Comptes 3
,, **du Commerce-St-André** 80
,, **de Rohan** 80
Courbevoie 50
Cours Albert-Ier 51
,, **des Maréchaux** 201
,, **la Reine** 51
,, **de Vincennes** 62
Courses for Foreign Students xx
Coustou, Guill. 110
Coysevox, Antoine 151
Crébillon, Prosper 27
Crédit Municipal 33
Cricket xxxiii
Crimean Monument 37
Currency xvii
Custom House xvii
Cuvier, Georges 90
Cycling xxxiii

Dagobert, King 205, 206,
Damiens, R. F. 26, 74
Dancing xxxii
Dangeau, Marq. 31
D'Annunzio, Gabriele 28
Dante 81, 82
Danton, G. J. 7, 74, 82, 97
Darboy, Abp. 60, 78
Daubigny, C. F. 61, 224
Daudet, Alphonse 31, 61, 103, 8
Daumesnil, Gen. 200
Daumier, Honoré 61
David, Louis 25, 97
David d'Angers, Pierre Jean 109, 114
Deaf and Dumb Asylum 115
Debussy, Claude 56, 55
Defence of Paris Monument 40
Deffand, Marquise du 33
Delacroix, Eug. 61, 95, 101, 103, 107
Delaroche, Paul 95
De Launay, Marq. 26
Delorme, Marion 31
Delorme, Philibert 6, 37, 95
Dénecourt, C. F. 224
Department Stores xxxvii
Déroulède, Paul 45
Descartes, René 107
Desmoulins, Camille 19, 74, 81, 87, 96, 97, 100
Diamond Necklace Affair 197, 29
'Diana of Versailles' 125
Diane de France 32
Diane de Poitiers 51
Diaz, Narcisse 224
Dickens, Chas. 40, 48
Diderot, Denis 19, 200
Directories xxxiv
Dôme des Invalides 111
Donizetti, Gaetano 18
Doré, Gustave 51, 104
Doumer, Pres. 48
Dreyfus, Capt. 114
Du Barry, Mme 38, 74, 198

Du Cerceau, Bapt. 6, 30, 122
Duguesclin, Bertrand 206
Dumas fils, Alex. 46
Dumas père, Alex. 45, 46, 204
Dumas, J. B. 104
Duplessis, Lucile 96, 100
Duplessis, Marie 12

Echevins 26
Ecole des Beaux-Arts 94
,, **de Botanique** 90
,, **Coloniale** 89
,, **de Droit** 86
,, **des Langues-Orientales** 101
,, **de Médecine** 81, 104
,, **Militaire** 113
,, **Normale Supérieure** 115
,, **de Pharmacie** 89
,, **Polytechnique** 84
,, **des Ponts-et-Chaussées** 101
,, **Pratique de la Faculté de Médecine** 101
,, **Supérieure des Arts Décoratifs** 83
,, **Supérieure des Mines** 89
,, **des Travaux Publics** 82
Ecouen 207
Edouard VII, Th. 14, xxxi
Edward VII 14
Egouts 12
Eiffel Tower 114
Elisabeth, Mme 7, 36, 74
Elysée 8
Embassies xxxv
Enghien, Duc d' 200
English Churches xxxv
Entrepôt des Vins 64
Entrepôts de Bercy 68
Epée, Abbé de l' 115, 187
Esplanade des Invalides 109
Essonnes 217
Eugénie, Empress 76, 219
Expenses xx

Fabre d'Eglantine, Ph. 97
Fantin-Latour, Ignace 95, 98
Faubourg St-Antoine 61
,, **St-Germain** 91
,, **St-Honoré** 48
,, **St-Marceau** 82
,, **St-Marcel** 91
,, **St-Martin** 37
,, **du Temple** 60
Fauré, Gabriel 55
Favart, Charles 15
Favre, Jules 45, 187
Fencing xxxiii
Fénelon, François de la Mothe 79, 100
Ferries, Car xv
Ferry, Jules 51
Fersen, Axel de 165
Fête de la Fédération 113
Feuillants, Club des 6
Fieschi, J. M. 16
'Figaro' Office 10
Fire Brigade Headquarters 75
Flandrin, Hippolyte 105
Flaubert, Gustave 16
Fléchier, Esprit 100
Foch, Marshal 108, 112, 54
Foire à la Ferraille 60
,, aux Jambons 60
,, St-Germain 107
Folies-Bergère xxxii
Fontaine Gaillon 1
,, **des Innocents** 23
,, **de Joyeuse** 31
,, **Louvois** 18
,, **Médicis** 98
,, **Molière** 19
,, **de l'Observatoire** 89
,, **des Quatre-Evêques** 100
,, **des Quatre-Saisons** 108
,, **de la Reine** 24
,, **St-Michel** 80
,, **du Vertbois** 37
Fontainebleau 217
,, **Forest** 224
,, **Palace** 218
Football xxxiii
Force, La 32
Fôret de Chantilly 216
,, **de Fontainebleau** 224
,, **de Marly** 204
,, **de St-Germain** 204
Foucault, Léon 85
Foucher, Adèle 108
Foullon, Joseph 26
Fouquet, Nicolas 30, 200
Français, Théâtre 4, xxx
France, Anatole 29, 50, 56, 94
Franchard, Gorges de 224
Franchet d'Espèrey, Gen. 110
Francis I 51, 58, 72, 80, 86, 121, 123, 125, 204, 206, 218
Francis II 76
Franck, César 89, 104, 119
Franklin, Benjamin 48, 55, 103, 115

Gaîté-Lyrique, Th. de la 37
Galerie des Glaces 190
Galigaï, Eléonore 26
Gallieni, Marshal 112
Gambetta, Léon 5, 48, 85, 96, 186
Games xxxiii
Garches 186
Garden, see **Jardin**
Gare d'Austerlitz 89, xix
,, **de la Bastille** 17, xix
,, **de l'Est** 38, xix
,, **des Invalides** 109, xix
,, **du Luxembourg** xix
,, **de Lyon** 62, xix
,, **Montparnasse** 118, xix
,, **du Nord** 38, xix
,, **d'Orléans** 89, xix
,, **d'Orsay** 102, xix
,, **St-Lazare** 45, xix
Garnier, Charles 1
Garnier, François 117
Gaskell, Mrs. 104
Gassendi, Pierre 37
Gautier, Théophile 31, 50, 79, 186
Gavarni 39
Gay-Lussac, J. L. 157
General Hints xix
General Post Office 20, xxix
Geological Galleries 90
George VI 103
George, Mlle 100
Géricault, Th. 39
Gering, Ulrich 87
German Embassy 102
Gibbon, Edward 39, 100
Gibet de Montfaucon 60
Gide, André 89, 108
'Gioconda, La' 135, 210
Giraud, Gen. 110
Giraudoux, Jean 113
Girondists 7, 73, 74
Gobelins 116
Goldoni, Carlo 78
Golf xxxiii
Goujon, Jean 23, 95, 122, 163
Gounod, Charles 47
Grand Châtelet 25
Grand Palais 10
Grand Trianon 197
Grands Boulevards 11
Greek Catholics 81
Greek Church 52

Grignan, Mme de 163
Grouchy, Marshal 110
Guénégaud, Th. de 96
Guide Lectures 123
Guillotin, Dr. 80
Guillotine 5, 7, 60, 80
Guise, Claude de 172
Guise, Duchesse de 97
Gymnase, Th. du 15, xxxi

Halle aux Vins 89
Halles Centrales 22
Hanse des Marchands 26
Hardouin-Mansart, see *Mansart*
Haussmann, Baron 44, 81
Haüy, Valentin 113
Hébert, Jacques-René 7, 97
Heine, Heinrich 10, 80
Henner, J. J. 46
Henri II 30, 121, 123, 205
,, *III* 186
,, *IV* 23, 29, 42, 70, 117, 121, 205, 218, 224
Henrietta Maria 19, 116, 122, 204
Henry IV 34
,, *V* 92, 200, 205
,, *VI* 73, 76
Hérédia, J. M. de 29
Herrick, Myron T. 48, 54
Hertford, Lord 14, 58
Hirsch, Baroness 108
Hoche, Gen. 187
Holidays xxi
Holy Trinity Church 51
Hôpital Beaujon 48
,, **Broca** 116
,, **Curie** 83
,, **des Enfants-Malades** 113
,, **Laënnec** 108
,, **Lariboisière** 38
,, **de la Maternité** 116
,, **Necker** 113
,, **Pasteur** 119
,, **de la Pitié** 91
,, **St-Antoine** 62
,, **St-Louis** 60
Horse-racing 57, xxxiii
Hortense, Queen 14, 202, 203
Hospice des Enfants-Trouvés 62
,, **La Rochefoucauld** 120
,, **Quinze-Vingts** 64
,, **de la Salpêtrière** 91
Hotels (for travellers) xxi

Hotels (mansions and public buildings):
Hôtel des Abbés-de-Fécamp 80
,, **d'Albret** 32
,, **d'Argenson** 108
,, **d'Artois** 24
,, **d'Aubray** 28
,, **d'Aumont** 28
,, **d'Avaray** 108
,, **Barbette** 32
,, **Beauharnais** 102
,, **Beauvais** 28
,, **Biron** 108, 183
,, **de Bouillon** 94
,, **de Boulogne** 104
,, **de Bourgogne** 24
,, **de Bragelonne** 32
,, **de Brancas** 33
,, **de Brégis** 33
,, **de Bretonvilliers** 79
,, **de Brienne** 104
,, **de Brissac** 108
,, **Carnavalet** 163
,, **de Chalons-Luxembourg** 28
,, **de Charny** 28
,, **du Châtelet** 108
,, **de Châtillon** 104
,, **de Chaulnes** 31
,, **Chenizot** 79
,, **de Chimay** 94
,, **de Choiseul-Praslin** 108
,, **de Choisy** 33
,, **de Clermont-Tonnerre** 104
,, **de Clisson** 34
,, **de Cluny** 172
,, **de Condé** 96
,, **de Conti** 92
,, **de Coulanges** 31
,, **Dangeau** 31
,, **-Dieu** 75, 81
,, **Drouot** 15
,, **d'Estrades** 31
,, **d'Estrées** 108
,, **Fieubet** 28, 67
,, **de Gourgues** 31
,, **du Grand-Veneur** 31
,, **de Guise** 34
,, **d'Hercule** 80
,, **Hérouët** 33
,, **de Hollande** 32
,, **des Invalides** 109
,, **de Jean-de-Fourcy** 32
,, **de Juigné** 32
,, **Lambert** 79
,, **Lamoignon** 32
,, **de Lassay** 103

Hotels (mansions and public buildings)—*continued*
Hôtel de Lauzun 79
,, **Le Charron** 79
,, **Le Peletier de St-Fargeau** 32
,, **de Massa** 118
,, **de Matignon** 108
,, **de Mayenne** 29
,, **Mazarin** 161
,, **de Mesmes** 104
,, **des Monnaies** (Mint) 93
,, **de Montmor** 34
,, **de Montmorency** 34
,, **des Mousquetaires-Noirs** 64
,, **de Nesle** 92
,, **de Nevers** 18
,, **d'Ollone** 21
,, **d'Ormesson** 29
,, **d'Orsay** 108
,, **de Persan** 95
,, **Pimodan** 79
,, **Pontalba** 48
,, **des Postes** 21
,, **de la Présidence** 108
,, **du Président-Hénault** 28
,, **de la Reynie** 37
,, **de la Roche-foucauld** 104
,, **de Rohan** 33
,, **de Roquelaure** 104
,, **de Sagan** 104
,, **de St-Aignan** 34
,, **du Sénat** 96
,, **de Sens** 28
,, **de Sillery-Genlis** 93
,, **des Sociétés Savantes** 80
,, **de Soissons** 21
,, **de Soubise** 33
,, **de Sourdéac** 98
,, **de Strasbourg** 33
,, **de Sully** 29
,, **Thiers** 40
,, **de Toulouse** 20
,, **de la Trémouille** 98
,, **des Ventes-Mobilières** 15
,, **de Vibray** 32
,, **de Villacerf** 31
,, **de Ville** 26
,, **de Vitry** 31
,, **de la Vrillière** (Banque de France) 20

Hotels (mansions and public buildings)—*continued*
Hôtel de la Vrillière (Rue St-Florentin) 3
Houdon, Jean A. 187, 151, 199
Huchette, Th. de la 80, xxxi
Hugo, Victor 31, 8, 29, 39, 55, 76, 86, 100, 107, 108, 118, 186

Identity Cards xvii
Ile de la Cité 70
,, **des Cygnes** 69
,, **de Folie** 57
,, **de France** 185
,, **de la Porte-Jaune** 202
,, **de Puteaux** 58
,, **St-Louis** 78
Illustre Théâtre 28, 96
Impressionist School 180, 46
Imprimerie Nationale 114
Information Bureaux xxx
Ingres, J. A. D. 101, 61
Institut Agronomique 83
,, **d'Art et d'Archéologie** 89
,, **de Biologie** 115
,, **Catholique** 100
,, **de Chimie Appliquée** 115
,, **de Chimie Biologique** 119
,, **de France** 91
,, **de Géographie** 115
,, **des Jeunes Aveugles** 113
,, **des Langues Modernes** 82
,, **Léonard de Vinci** 104
,, **Musulman** 90
,, **Océanographique** 115
,, **d'Optique** 113
,, **Pasteur** 118
,, **du Radium** 115
,, **des Sciences Politiques** 104
,, **Tessin** 96
Invalides, The 109
Irving, Washington 3
Isabeau de Bavière 32, 92
Isabella of France 72
Italian Embassy 108

Jacobin Club 4
James II 83, 115, 204
James V of Scotland 172
Jardies, Les 186
Jardin d'Acclimatation 58
Jardin Colonial 202
,, **Fleuriste** 56
,, **du Luxembourg** 98
,, **des Plantes** 89
,, **du Ranelagh** 55
,, **des Tuileries** 5
Jaurès, Jean 86
Javel 114
Jefferson, Thomas 10, 14
Jeu de Paume (Tuileries) 6, 180
Jeu de Paume (Versailles) 199
Joan of Arc 59, 205, 5
Joan of Burgundy 92
John II 206
Johnson, Dr. 115
Joffre, Marshal 56, 113, 208
Jones, Paul 60, 96
Joséphine, Empress 1, 76, 97, 108, 202, 219
Julian the Apostate 72
July Column 71
Juvisy 217

Kléber, Gen. 110
Kock, Paul de 16

Lac des Minimes 202
Lafayette, Gen. 45, 62, 17, 102, 153, 6
La Fontaine, Jean de 21, 60
Lamartine, Alph. de 55
Lamballe, Princesse de 20, 62
Lamennais, Félicité Robert de 34
Lamorlaye 207
La Motte, Mme de 197
Language xix
Laplace, Marquis de 104
La Rochefoucauld, Card. de 108
Larrey, Baron 116
Latin Quarter 79
Lauzun, Duc de 79
La Vallière, Louise de 116
Lavoisier, Antoine 6, 157, 12
Law, John 37, 3
Law Courts 70
Lawn Tennis xxxiv
Lazaristes, Eglise des 108
Lebon, Philippe 79
Lebrun, Charles 82, 88, 117, 187, etc.
Leclerc, Gen. (*Hautecloque*) 26, 110
Lecouvreur, Adrienne 95
Leczinski, Stanislas 198
Ledru-Rollin, Alex. 28
Legations xxxv
Lemaistre, Ant. 116
Lemaître, Frédérick 16
Lemercier, Jacques 3, 19, 21, 87, 88, 122, etc.
Lemercier, Pierre 23
L'Enclos, Ninon de 17, 30, 32
Lenoir, A. 205
Lenormand, Marie 96
Le Nôtre, André 4, 6, 187, 195, 215
Leonardo da Vinci 123
Lescot, Pierre 23, 122
Lesseps, Ferd. de 187
Levau, Louis 6, 28, 79, 91, 92, 122, 187, 200, etc.
Leverrier, Urbain 118
'Liberty' Statue 70
Libraries, see **Bibliothèques**
Lieusaint 217
Lion of Belfort 119
Liszt, Franz 38
Littré, Emile 80
Longchamp 57, xxxiv
Longfellow, H. W. 88
Lorraine, Card. de 172
Lost Property xx
Louis VI 43, 72, 204
,, *VII* 72
,, *IX* (*St. Louis*) 72, 74, 200
,, *X* 218, 200, 207
,, *XI* 72
,, *XII* 161, 187, 205
,, *XIII* 218, 204, 222, 224
,, *XIV* 204, 73, 97, 109, 117, 20, 122, 123, 187, 191, 193, 208, 218
,, *XV* 187, 7, 121, 191, 199, 218
,, *XVI* 187, 6, 7, 26, 34, 36, 45, 113, 123, 191
,, *XVII* 36, 62, 195
,, *XVIII* 187, 6, 123, 197
Louis-Philippe 6, 16, 19, 50, 187, 197, 218
Louvel, Louis 26
Louvois, Marq. de 199
Louvre, The 121, 5
Antiquities:
Babylonian 132
Egyptian 127, 144
Greek & Roman 123, 143, 145
Medieval & Renaissance 141, 146
Muslim Art 145

Louvre, The—*continued*
Antiquities:
Oriental 131
Phœnician 133
Sumerian 131
Bronzes 145, 147
Ceramics 143, 145
Enamels 147
Furniture 146
Galerie d'Apollon 141
„ Daru 138
„ Mollien 137
Goldsmiths' Work, 141, 146, 148
Grande Galerie 134
Guide Lectures 123
Ivories 146
Jewellery 142
Paintings 134
Pottery 143, 145
Rothschild Collection 148
Salle des Cariatides 125
„ Coysevox 151
„ des Etats 135
„ Girardon 151
„ Jean Goujon 149
„ du Mastaba 128
„ Michel-Ange 150
„ du Parthenon 124
„ Puget 150
„ des Sept-Mètres 139
Salon Carré 134
Sculpture:
Greek & Roman 123
Medieval & Renaissance 148
Modern French 151
Lulli, J. B. 1, 19, 20
Lumière, Louis 14
Luna Park xxxii
Lutetia 65
Luxembourg, Palais du 97
Luxembourg, Salle du 96, xxxi
Luzarches 207
Lycée Charlemagne 29
„ **Condorcet** 44
„ **Fontaine** 56
„ **Henri-IV** 84
„ **Louis-le-Grand** 86
„ **Pasteur** 50
„ **St-Louis** 88

Mabillon, Jean 105, 107
Madeleine, La 11
Maeterlinck, Maurice 55
Maginot, André 86
Maintenon, Mme de 31, 193, 197
Maison des Artistes xxxii
„ **des Aveugles** 113
„ **de la Chimie** 104
Maison François-I 51
Maisons-Alfort 217
Maisons-Laffitte 204
Malesherbes, Lamoignon de 74
Malherbe, F. de 20
Mallarmé, Stéphane 45, 96, 104
Malmaison 202
'*Man in the Iron Mask*' 17, 28, 29
Manège, The 7
Manet, Edouard 45, 46, 55, 95
Manin, Daniele 39
Mansart, François (fl. 1620–66) 20, 28, 30, 92, 116, 162, 204, etc.
Mansart, Jacques Hardouin (fl. 1750) 199
Mansart, Jules Hardouin (d. 1708) 3, 19, 20, 28, 30, 104, 109, 187, 208, etc.
Mansfield, Katherine 224
Marais, The 30
Marat, Jean Paul 80, 81, 82, 86
Marcel, Etienne 11, 25, 26
Marché aux Bestiaux 59
„ **des Carmes** 82
„ **aux Fleurs** 75
„ **St-Germain** 107
„ **St-Honoré** 4
Margaret of Burgundy 92
Margaret of Navarre 51
Margaret of Valois 84, 121
Maria Christina 202
Marie-Antoinette 7, 34, 36, 45, 73, 74, 75, 187, 191, 192, 198, 199, 219
Marie Leczinska 192, 218
Marie-Louise 198, 219
Marie de Médicis 97, 98, 219, 222
Marie-Thérèse 28, 192, 219
Marigny, Marq. de 8
Marigny, Th. 10, xxxi
Marivaux, Pierre de 36
Market, see **Marché**
Marly Horses 8
Marly-la-Machine 203
Marly-le-Roi 203
Mars, Mlle 51
Mary, Queen of Scots 76
Mary Tudor 172
Massacre of St. Bartholomew 121
Massenet, Jules 98
Massillon, J. B. 100
Maupassant, Guy de 47, 56, 119
Mayenne, Duc de 121
Mazarin, Cardinal 18, 19, 28, 51, 92, 151, 161, 172, 200
Mazarin, Duchesse de 93
Melun 217
Ménilmontant 61
Mérimée, Prosper 29, 95, 96
Messier, Charles 172
Métropolitain 229, xxvii
Meudon, Bois de 185
Meung, Jean de 115
Meyerbeer, Giacomo 18, 48
Michelet, Jules 24, 109
Mickiewicz, Adam 79, 51
Mignard, Pierre 4, 19, 116, 117
Millet, J. F. 224
Ministère des Affaires Economiques 113
„ **des Affaires Etrangers** 103
„ **de l'Air** 114
„ **du Commerce** 108
„ **de l'Education** 108
„ **des Finances** 5, 122
„ **de la Guerre** 103
„ **de l'Intérieur** 48
„ **de la Justice** 3
„ **de la Marine** 8
„ **de la Marine Marchande** 113
„ **du Travail** 108
„ **des Travaux Publics** 104, 113
Mint, The 93
Minuterie xxi
Mirabeau, Marquis de 23, 39, 86, 91, 200
'Miramiones' 82
Moabite Stone 131
Mobilier National 117
Mohl, Mme 104
Molière, J.-B. 19, 21, 22, 23, 24, 28, 56, 60, 87, 96, 194, 208
Molière, Th. 20, xxxi
Moltke, Count von 187
Monaldeschi, Marchese di 223, 224
Moncey, Marshal 40
Money xix
'Monna Lisa' 135, 210
Monnaie, La 93
Montalembert, Comte de 62
Montespan, Mme de 1, 194
Montesquieu, Baron de 33

Montfaucon 60
Montgeron 217
Montgomery, Comte de 26
Montmartre 40
Montmorency, Constable Anne de 28, 34, 205, 207, 208
Montmorency-Laval, Bp. 107
Montparnasse 118
Montpensier, Mlle de 80, 97
Mont-de-Piété 33
Montretout 186
Mont-Valérien 186
Montyon, Baron de 81
Monument aux Morts 61
Monument de la République 16
Moreau, Gustave 39
Morgue, The 68
Morisot, Berthe 55
Mosque 90
Motor-Buses 225, xxvii
Motor Cars xvi
Motor Coaches xxviii
Motor Cycles xvii
Motor Racing xxxiv
Moulin Rouge 42
Mozart, W. A. 24, 28
Muette, La 55
Mur des Fédérés 61
Murat, Prince 47, 48
Murger, Henri 39
Musée de l'Air 114
,, **Antoine-Bourdelle** 119
,, **d'Antiquités Nationales** 204
,, **de l'Armée** 152, 109
,, **d'Art Moderne** 52
,, **des Arts Décoratifs** 153
,, **Carnavalet** 162, 32
,, **Cernuschi** 47
,, **Chinois** 223
,, **du Cinéma** 47
,, **de Cluny** 172, 88
,, **Cognacq-Jay** 14
,, **Condé** 208
,, **Cynégétique** 90
,, **Delacroix** 107
,, **Documentaire** 33
,, **Dupuytren** 82
,, **d'Ennery** 56
,, **de la France d'Outre Mer** 201
,, **Galliera** 52
,, **Grévin** 15, xxxii
,, **Guimet** 175, 54
,, **Gustave-Moreau** 39
,, **Henner** 46
,, **de l'Homme** 170
Musée d'Hygiène 24
,, **Jacquemart-André** 178, 48
,, **du Jeu de Paume** 180
,, **de la Légion d'Honneur** 102
,, **de Mme de Caen** 93
,, **de la Marine** 172
,, **Marmottan** 55
,, **des Médailles** 162
,, **de Minéralogie** 89
,, **Monétaire** 93
,, **des Monuments Français** 169
,, **Nissim de Camondo** 181, 47
,, **de l'Opéra** 2
,, **Orfila** 81
,, **Postal** 108
,, **Rodin** 183, 108
,, **Rosa-Bonheur** 223
,, **du Service de Santé** 116
,, **Social** 104
,, **des Travaux Publics** 54
,, **de Vénerie** 216
,, **Victor-Hugo** 31
,, **des Voitures** 198
Music xxxiii
Music Halls xxxi
Musset, A. de 3, 56, 61, 96, 101, 108, 51
Mutualité, La 82
Napoleon I 1, 4, 6, 11, 48, 76, 80, 87, 93, 97, 100, 110, 112, 114, 153, 156, 167, 186, 197, 200, 202, 203, 218, 219
Napoleon I, Tomb of 112
Napoleon II (King of Rome) 76, 112
Napoleon III 14, 3, 6, 48, 76, 97, 202
National Assembly, 7, 188
Necker, Jacques 39
Necker, Mme 113
Neuilly 50
Ney, Marshal 61, 74, 97, 117
Nicot, Jean 28
Nightingale, Florence 104
'Nike of Samothrace' 123
Noailles, Marshal de 97
Nodier, Charles 29
Notre-Dame 75
,, **-d'Auteuil** 56
,, **-des-Blancs-Manteaux** 33
,, **-de-Bonne-Nouvelle** 15
Notre-Dame-des-Champs 118
,, **-de-Consolation** 51
,, **d'Espérance** 17
,, **du Liban** 83
,, **-de-Lorette** 39
,, **-des-Victoires** 20
Nouvel-Ambigu, Th. du 16, xxxi

Obelisk of Luxor 7
Observatoire 118
Odéon 96, xxxi
Offenbach, Jacques 14
Olympia 14, xxxii
Open-Air Theatre xxxi
Opéra, L' 1, xxxi
Opéra-Comique 14, xxxi
Orangery 6, 181
Oratoire 21
Oriflamme 206
Orleans, Ferdinand, Duke of 50
Orleans, Louis, Duke of 32
Orleans, Philippe, Duke of (Regent) 19, 84, 187, 194
Orleans, Philippe, Duke of (Egalité) 7, 19, 47
Orleans, Philippe, Duke of (d. 1926) 74, 90
Orly 217, xix
Orsini, Félix 14
Oscar I 47

Pailleron, Ed. 47
Paine, Tom 97, 120
Palais des Beaux-Arts 10
,, **-Bourbon** 102
,, **-Cardinal** 33, 19
,, **de Chaillot** 54, 169
,, **de la Découverte** 10
,, **-Egalité** 19
,, **de l'Elysée** 48, 8
,, **de Glace** 10, xxxii
,, **de l'Institut** 91
,, **de Justice** 70
,, **de la Légion d'Honneur** 102
,, **du Luxembourg** 97
,, **-Royal** 19
,, ,, **Th. du** 19, xxxi
,, **des Thermes** 174
,, **des Tournelles** 30
,, **des Tuileries** 6
,, **de Versailles** 188
Palissy, Bernard 107
Panthéon 85

Parc des Buttes-Chaumont 59
,, **-aux-Cerfs** 199
,, **Monceau** 47
,, **de Montsouris** 120
,, **de St-Cloud** 186
,, **Zoölogique** 201
Parcels xxix
Parlement 72
Parloir aux Bourgeois 25
Parmentier, Antoine 50, 109
Pascal, Blaise 25, 83, 84, 160
Passage Henri-IV 20
,, **des Panoramas** 15
Passports xvii
Passy 55
Pasteur, Louis 118, 113, 119, 186
Payne, John Howard 20
Pensions xxiii
Père-Lachaise 60
Perrault, Charles 7, 94
Perrault, Claude 118, 122
Peter the Great 218
Petit-Châtelet 66
,, **-Hôtel de Sully** 31
,, **-Luxembourg** 98
,, **-Montrouge** 120
,, **-Palais** 10
,, **-Pont** 66
,, **Trianon** 198
Pharmacie Centrale 82
Philip Augustus 72, 121
Philip III 207
Philip IV 218, 207
Philip V 218, 200, 206
Philip VI 200, 206
Philippe-Egalité 7, 19, 47
Picture Galleries xxxii
Pierrefitte 207
Pilâtre de Rozier 55
Pius VII 76, 218, 223
Place de l'Alma 51
,, **d'Anvers** 42
,, **de la Bastille** 17, 30
,, **Blanche** 42
,, **de la Bourse** 18
,, **Cambronne** 114
,, **du Carrousel** 5
,, **du Châtelet** 25
,, **de Clichy** 40
,, **de la Concorde** 7
,, **de la Contrescarpe** 83
,, **Dauphine** 70
,, **Denfert-Rochereau** 119
,, **Edmond - Rostand** 89
,, **des Etats-Unis** 54
,, **de l'Etoile** 10
,, **de l'Europe** 46
Place de Grève 26
,, **de l'Hôtel de Ville** 25
,, **d'Iéna** 54
,, **de l'Institut** 91
,, **d'Italie** 117
,, **du Louvre** 21
,, **de la Madeleine** 12
,, **Maubert** 82
,, **de la Nation** 62
,, **de l'Odéon** 96
,, **de l'Opéra** 1
,, **du Palais-Royal** 5
,, **Pereire** 46
,, **Pigalle** 40
,, **de la République** 16
,, **Royale** 30
,, **St-André-des-Arts** 80
,, **Ste-Geneviève** 84
,, **St-Georges** 39
,, **St-Michel** 80
,, **St-Sulpice** 100
,, **des Ternes** 50
,, **du Tertre** 44
,, **du Trocadéro** 54
,, **du Trône** 62
,, **Valhubert** 89
,, **de Valois** 20
,, **Vendôme** 3
,, **de Verdun** 50
,, **des Victoires** 20
,, **Victor-Hugo** 55
,, **Vintimille** 40
,, **des Vosges** 30
,, **Winston - Churchill** 50
,, **de Wagram** 46
Plaine-St-Denis, La 204
Plantagenet, Geoffrey 78
Pléïade, The 83
Poincaré, Raymond 56
Police 75, xx
Police School 48
Polish Embassy 104
Polish Library 79
Polo xxxiv
Pompadour, Mme de 19, 48, 119, 194, 198
Pont Alexandre-III 69, 109, 51
,, **de l'Alma** 69, 51
,, **de l'Archevêché** 66
,, **d'Arcole** 67
,, **des Arts** 68
,, **d'Austerlitz** 68
,, **de Bercy** 68
,, **de Bir-Hakeim** 69
,, **Cardinet** 231
,, **du Carrousel** 68
,, **-au-Change** 67
,, **de la Concorde** 69
,, **-au-Double** 66
,, **de Grenelle** 70
Pont d'Iéna 69, 52
,, **des Invalides,** 69, 51
,, **Louis-Philippe** 67
,, **Marie** 67
,, **Mirabeau** 70, 114
,, **Morland** 68
,, **National** 68
,, **Neuf** 66
,, **de Neuilly** 50
,, **Notre-Dame** 67
,, **Royal** 68
,, **St-Louis** 67
,, **St-Michel** 66
,, **de Solférino** 69
,, **Sully** 67, 28
,, **de Tolbiac** 68
,, **de la Tournelle** 67
,, **-Viaduc d'Auteuil** 70
Porte d'Auteuil 55, 56
,, **Champerret** 46
,, **de Courcelles** 48
,, **Dauphine** 56
,, **des Lilas** 61
,, **Maillot** 50, 56
,, **de la Muette** 55
,, **de Neuilly** 50
,, **de Passy** 56
,, **aux Peintres** 24
,, **St-Denis** 15, 24
,, **St-Martin** 15
,, **St-Martin, Th. de la** 16
Port-Marly 203
,, **de Paris** 65
,, **-Royal-de-Paris** 116
Positivist Chapel 32
Postal Information xxviii
Postal Museum 108
Post Office, General 21, xxix
Pradier, James 101
Pré Catelan 57
Pré-aux-Clercs 107
Préfecture de Police 75
Préfecture de la Seine 26, 25
Prévôt de Paris 26, 25
Prince Imperial 76
Prison de l'Abbaye 107
,, **du Cherche - Midi** 109
,, **de la Force** 32
,, **de la Roquette** 60
,, **St-Lazare** 38
,, **du Temple** 36
Prix de Rome 93, 94
Proust, Marcel 12, 45, 48, 54
Puteaux 50
Puvis de Chavannes, Pierre 46

Quai Anatole-France 101, 69

Quai d'Anjou 79, 67
,, **de l'Archevêché** 66
,, **de Béthune** 79, 67
,, **de Bourbon** 79, 67
,, **des Célestins** 28, 67
,, **de la Conférence** 51, 69
,, **Conti** 93, 66
,, **des Grands-Augustins** 66
,, **Henri-IV** 68
,, **de l'Horloge** 67
,, **de l'Hôtel-de-Ville** 67
,, **du Louvre** 68
,, **Malaquais** 94, 68
,, **du Marché-Neuf** 66
,, **de la Mégisserie** 67
,, **de Montebello** 66
,, **de New York** 52
,, **des Orfèvres** 66
,, **d'Orléans** 79, 67
,, **de la Rapée** 58
,, **St-Bernard** 89, 68
,, **des Théatins** 101
,, **de la Tournelle** 82, 67
,, **Voltaire** 101, 68
'Quand Même' Memorial 45
Quartier de l'Arsenal 29
,, **des Batignolles** 46
,, **de Chaillot** 52
,, **de la Chapelle** 58
,, **de l'Europe** 46
,, **Latin** 79
,, **du Marais** 30
,, **Marbeuf** 10
,, **du Temple** 34
,, **de la Villette** 59
Quinze-Vingts 64

Rabelais, François 28, 80, 83
Racecourses xxxiv
Rachel, Mme 31
Racine, Jean 84, 95
Racine, Louis 36
Railway Offices xv, xviii
Railway Termini (see also Gare) xviii
Rambouillet, Mme de 96
Rameau, Jean 23
Ravaillac, François 23, 26, 74
Récamier, Mme 19, 20
Régnier, Henri de 54, 61
Renan, Ernest 100
Resistance, The 16, 26, 75, 80, 88, 93, 102, 103, 104, 186
Restaurants xxiii
etz, Card. de 200
Richard II 72
Richelieu, Cardinal 17, 19, 29, 31, 87, 88, 92, 98, 157
Riding xxxiv
Rigaud, Hyacinthe 1
'Rights of Man' Club 19
Robert, King 217
Robespierre, Max. 3, 7, 26, 33, 34, 74, 75, 87
Rodin, Auguste 83, 108, 118, 183
Rohan, Cardinal de 33, 197
Roland, Mme 7, 70, 73, 74, 107
Rond-Point des Champs-Elysées 10
Roquette, La 60
Rossini, Gioacchino 39, 55, 61
Rousseau, Jean Jacques 21, 85, 165
Rousseau, Théodore 224
Roussel, Théophile 117
Roux, Dr. Emile 119
Rowing and Sailing xxxiv
Royale, Mme 36
Rue d'Amsterdam 45
,, **de l'Ancienne-Comédie** 96
,, **des Archives** 34
,, **Auber** 44
,, **du Bac** 104
,, **Barbette** 33
,, **Beautreillis** 28
,, **des Beaux-Arts** 95
,, **de Bellechasse** 104
,, **de Bièvre** 82
,, **Blanche** 39
,, **Bonaparte** 95
,, **des Bons-Enfants** 20
,, **de Bretagne** 36
,, **Cambon** 3
,, **du Cardinal-Lemoine** 83
,, **de Castiglione** 3
,, **Caulaincourt** 40
,, **Caumartin** 44
,, **de Charenton** 64
,, **Charlemagne** 28
,, **Charles V** 28
,, **Charlot** 33
,, **de Châteaudun** 39
,, **de la Chaussée-d'Antin** 39
,, **du Cherche-Midi** 108
,, **de Clichy** 39
,, **Clovis** 83
,, **de Condé** 96
,, **de Courcelles** 48
,, **Drouot** 15
,, **Etienne-Marcel** 20
Rue du Faubourg-St-Antoine 61
,, **du Faubourg-St-Honoré** 48
,, **du Faubourg-St-Martin** 37
,, **du Faubourg-du-Temple** 60
,, **du Figuier** 28
,, **de Flandre** 59
,, **du Fouarre** 81
,, **François-Miron** 28
,, **François-Premier** 51
,, **des Francs-Bourgeois** 32
,, **Franklin** 55
,, **Galande** 81
,, **Gay-Lussac** 115
,, **Geoffroy-l'Asnier** 28
,, **Geoffroy-Marie** 15
,, **des Grands-Augustins** 80
,, **de la Grange-aux-Belles** 60
,, **de Grenelle** 108
,, **Hautefeuille** 80
,, **de l'Hôtel-de-Ville** 28
,, **de la Huchette** 80
,, **Jacob** 95
,, **de Jouy** 28
,, **La Boétie** 48
,, **de La Fayette** 38
,, **Laffitte** 14, 39
,, **Le Peletier** 14
,, **Lhomond** 83
,, **de Lille** 102
,, **du Louvre** 21
,, **du Mail** 20
,, **Mazarine** 96
,, **Monge** 82
,, **Monsieur-le-Prince** 88
,, **Montmartre** 24
,, **du Montparnasse** 118
,, **Mouffetard** 83
,, **de la Paix** 3
,, **Pavée** 32
,, **Payenne** 32
,, **des Petits-Champs** 18
,, **Pigalle** 39
,, **de la Pompe** 55
,, **du Pont-Neuf** 22
,, **de Provence** 39
,, **des Quatre-Fils** 33
,, **du Quatre-Septembre** 18
,, **Quincampoix** 36
,, **Réaumur** 17, 36
,, **de Rennes** 107
,, **de Richelieu** 18
,, **de Rivoli** 5, 25
,, **de Rome** 45
,, **de la Roquette** 17, 61
,, **Royale** 11

Rue St-André-des-Arts 80
,, **St-Antoine** 29
,, **St-Denis** 24
,, **St-Dominique** 104
,, **St-Honoré** 3, 21
,, **St-Jacques** 86, 115
,, **St-Lazare** 45
,, **St-Louis-en-l'Ile** 79
,, **St-Martin** 36
,, **des Saints-Pères** 101
,, **de Seine** 96
,, **de Sévigné** 32
,, **de Sèvres** 108
,, **Soufflot** 86
,, **du Temple** 34
,, **Thorigny** 31
,, **des Tournelles** 30
,, **de Tournon** 96
,, **de Turbigo** 24, 34
,, **de Turenne** 31
,, **de l'Université** 103
,, **de Varenne** 108
,, **de Vaugirard** 96, 88
,, **de Venise** 36
,, **Vieille-du-Temple** 32
,, **Visconti** 95
,, **Vivienne** 18
,, **Xavier-Privas** 80
Rueil 202
Ruelle du Chat-qui-Pêche 80
Russian Church 48

Sacré-Cœur 43
St-Ambroise 61
St-Augustin 45
Ste-Beuve, C. A. de 118
Sainte-Chapelle 72
St-Christophe-de-Javel 114
Ste-Clotilde 103
St-Cloud 186
St-Denis 204
St. Denis 42, 205, 206
St-Denis-de-la-Chapelle 59
St-Denis-du-St-Sacrement 31
St. Dominic 84
St-Dominique 119
Ste-Elisabeth 36
St-Esprit 62
St-Etienne-du-Mont 84
St-Eugène 15
St-Eustache 23
St. Francis Xavier 42, 86
St-François-Xavier 113
St-Gaudens, Aug. 109
St. Geneviève 84, 85, 205
St. George's 54
St-Germain-l'Auxerrois 21
St-Germain-de-Charonne 61
St-Germain-en-Laye 204
St-Germain-des-Prés 105
St-Gervais-St-Protais 27
St. Ignatius de Loyola 42, 86
St-Jacques-la-Boucherie 25
St-Jacques-du-Haut-Pas 115
St-Jean-Baptiste 59
St-Jean-Bosco 61
St-Jean-l'Evangéliste 42
St-Jean-le-Rond 76
St-Jean-St-François 33
St-Joseph-des-Carmes 100
St-Julien-le-Pauvre 81
St-Laurent 37
St-Leu-St-Gilles 24
St. Louis see *Louis IX*
St-Louis (Invalides) 110
St-Louis-d'Antin 44
St-Louis-en-l'Ile 79
Ste-Marguerite 62
St-Martin-des-Champs 157, 37
St-Médard 83
St-Merri 36
St-Nicolas-des-Champs 37
St-Nicolas-du-Chardonnet 82
Ste-Odile 46
St-Ouen 204
St-Paul-des-Champs 28
St-Paul-St-Louis 29
St-Philippe-du-Roule 48
St-Pierre (Neuilly) 50
St-Pierre, Bernardin de 90
St-Pierre-de-Chaillot 52
St-Pierre-de-Montmartre 43
St-Pierre-de-Montrouge 120
St-Roch 3
St-Séverin 80
St-Sulpice 100
St. Thomas Aquinas 84, 86
St-Thomas-d'Aquin 104
St. Vincent de Paul 38, 83, 108
St-Vincent-de-Paul 38
Salle Gaveau 48, xxxiii
,, **du Luxembourg** 96, xxxi
,, **des Pas-Perdus** 74
,, **Pleyel** 48, xxxiii
,, **Richelieu** xxxi
'Salon' xxxii
Samaritaine, La 70
Sanctuaire du Christ-Roi 83
Sand, George 39, 40, 88, 96, 166
Sarah-Bernhardt, Th. 25, xxxi
Sardou, Victorien 28, 167
Savonnerie 117
Saxe, Marshal 95
Scarron, Paul 27, 31
Sceaux, Ligne de xxvii
Scheffer, Ary 40
Schola Cantorum 115
School, see **Ecole**
Scots College 83
Scribe, Eugène 24
Scudéry, Mlle de 37
Season xix
Seine, The 65
Séminaire des Carmes 100
Séminaire des Missions Etrangères 104
Séminaire de St-Sulpice 100
Senate, The 97, 188
Senlis 216
Sévigné, Charles de 30
Sévigné, Mme de 27, 31, 32, 163, 166
Sèvres 186
Sewers 12
Shops xxxvi
Sibour, Abp. 78, 84
Smith, Adm. Sir Sidney 61
Société des Gens de Lettres 118
Société de Géographie 105
Sorbon, Robt. de 87
Sorbonne 87
Soufflot, Jacques 85
Sports xxxiii
Square de l'Archevêché 78
,, **Boucicaut** 108
,, **Emile-Chautemps** 37
,, **du Général-Morin** 157
,, **des Innocents** 22
,, **Louvois** 18
,, **Monge** 82
,, **Montholon** 38
,, **René-Le Gall** 117
,, **René-Viviani** 81
,, **St-Lambert** 114
,, **du Temple** 36
,, **du Vert-Galant** 70
,, **Willette** 42
Stade Roland-Garros 56
Staël, Mme de 34, 11, 102
Stanley, Dean 104
States-General 187, 199
Steamers, Channel xv
Steamers, River xxviii
Stendhal (*H. Beyle*) 19
Sterne, Laurence 95
Stevenson, R. L. 224
Stock Exchange 18
Suger, Abbot 205

Sully, Duc de 29
Suresnes 186
Swedish Church 48
Swimming xxxiv
Swiss Guards 6, 26, 45, 189, 197
Syrian Church 82

Tabarin, 70
Taine, Hippolyte 100
Tallard, Marshal 34
Talleyrand-Périgord, Prince 3
Tallien, Mme 14
Taxis xxvi
Taylor, Baron 16
Tea Rooms xxvi
Telegrams xxix
Telephones xxix
Temple des Billettes 34
,, **de Pentemont** 108
,, **de Ste-Marie** 29
Tennis xxxiv
Thackeray, W. M. 18, 20
Théâtre National Populaire xxxi
Theatres xxx
Thermes, Palais des 174
Thiers, Adolphe 40, 48, 61, 187, 204
Thomas, Ambr. 47
Time Tables xviii, xix
Tobacconists xxi
Toulouse-Lautrec, Henri de 42
Tour de Bois 66
,, **Eiffel** 114
,, **de l'Horloge** 72
,, **Jean-sans-Peur** 24
,, **de Nesle** 92
,, **St-Jacques** 25
,, **du Temple** 36
Touring Club de France 48, xxxvi
Tourist Agents xxx
Tourville, Adm. de 23
Trianon, Grand 197
Trianon, Petit 198
Tribunal de Commerce 75
Trinité, La 39
Trocadéro 54
Trotsky, Léon 118
Tuileries, Palais des 6
Turenne, Marshal de 31, 61, 110, 112
Turgenev, Ivan 40

Underground Railways 229, xxvii
University 87, 80
Unknown Soldier's Tomb 10

Val-de-Grâce 116
Valéry, Paul 55
Vatel 208
Vauban, Marshal de 112, 110
Vaux, Clotilde de 32
Vélodrome du Parc des Princes 56
Vendôme Column 3
Venizelos, Eleutherios 48
'Vénus de Milo' 124
Verlaine, Paul 83, 96
Vernet, Carle 101
Vernet, Horace 101
Versailles 186
,, **Gardens** 195
,, **Palace** 188
Veuillot, Louis 43
Viardot, Mme 40
Viau, Théophile de 215
Victoria, Queen 25, 198
Vigée-Lebrun, Mme 45
Vigny, Alfred de 48
Villa des Jardies 186
Ville-d'Avray 186
Villejuif 217
Villeneuve-l'Etang 186
Villeneuve-St-Georges 217
Villette, La 59
Villiers-le-Bel 207
Villon, François 83
Vincennes 200
Vinci, Leonardo da 123
Vineuil 207
Viollet-le-Duc, Eug. 76, 78, 169
Viroflay 186
Voltaire, Fr. 17, 19, 33, 79, 85, 96, 101, 269, 4

Wagner, Richard 14, 21, 96
Wallace, Sir Richard 8, 14, 58
Walpole, Horace 33
War Museum 152, 201
Washington, George 54
Watteau, J. A. 83
Wellington, Duke of 48, 197
Wells, Dr. Horace 54
Whistler, J. McN. 98, 104, 107, 118
Wilde, Oscar 61, 95
Wilson, President 47
'Winged Victory' 123

Y.M.C.A. xxxvi
Y.W.C.A. xxxvi

Zola, Emile 24, 40, 86
Zoological Gardens, 90, 200
Zouave, The 69

J. AND J. GRAY, PRINTERS, EDINBURGH

NOTES

NOTES

NOTES

NOTES

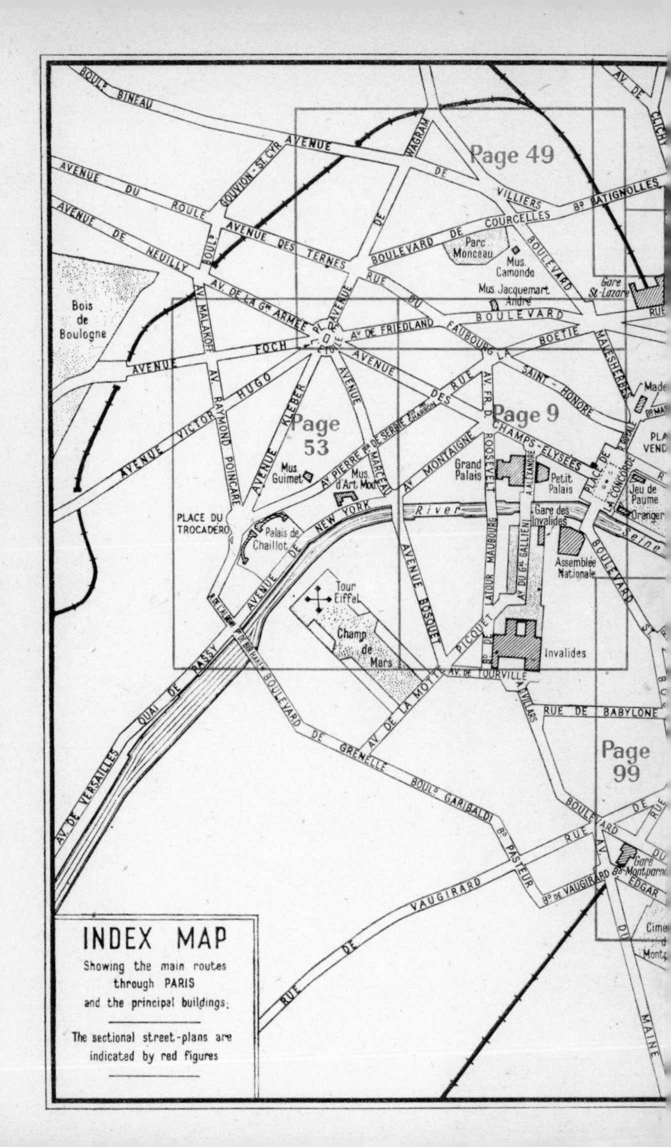
INDEX MAP
Showing the main routes through PARIS and the principal buildings.
The sectional street-plans are indicated by red figures
Page 49
Page 9
Page 53
Page 99
Bois de Boulogne
Parc Monceau
Mus. Camondo
Mus. Jacquemart André
Gare St-Lazare
Grand Palais
Petit Palais
Mus. Guimet
Mus. d'Art Mod.
PLACE DU TROCADERO
Palais de Chaillot
Tour Eiffel
Champ de Mars
Invalides
Gare des Invalides
Assemblée Nationale
Jeu de Paume
River Seine
AVENUE DE WAGRAM
BOULEVARD DE COURCELLES
AVENUE DES TERNES
AVENUE FOCH
AV. DE FRIEDLAND
AVENUE DES CHAMPS-ELYSÉES
AVENUE VICTOR HUGO
AVENUE KLEBER
AVENUE MONTAIGNE
AV. DE NEW YORK
AVENUE BOSQUET
AV. DE TOURVILLE
RUE DE BABYLONE
BOULEVARD DE GRENELLE
BOUL^D GARIBALDI
B^D PASTEUR
RUE DE VAUGIRARD
B^D DE VAUGIRARD
QUAI DE PASSY
AV. DE VERSAILLES
AV. DE LA MOTTE PICQUET
AVENUE DU MAINE